ARCTIC
OCEAN

NORTH ASIA

CENTRAL ASIA

NORTH
PACIFIC
OCEAN

SOUTHEAST ASIA

Arabian
Sea

Bay of
Bengal

INDIAN
OCEAN

AUSTRALASIA & OCEANIA

Tasman
Sea

SOUTHERN
OCEAN

ANTARCTICA

LONELY PLANET'S
BEST IN
TRAVEL
2009

850 TRENDS, DESTINATIONS, JOURNEYS & EXPERIENCES FOR THE YEAR AHEAD

MELBOURNE ✪ OAKLAND ✪ LONDON

CONTENTS

FOREWORD

The best? We've picked the brains of our authors, our staff and our travellers and come up with a collection of destinations and experiences that we rate as the stuff you really ought to consider for 2009.

It's time to plan a break from the routines of the every-day, and think of the kind of travel that will sustain you through the less exciting times of the year. We think you'll find quite a few ideas in this edition of *Best in Travel*.

Travel is two things to us: destination and experience. Well, maybe three – the journey is definitely part of the story. Flipping through this book, you'll find a mix of these. We've listed our top cities, regions and countries to explore in 2009. That's 30 great places, from the more challenging (Sierra Leone is not for the faint-hearted) to the spectacular: awesome ice anyone? Try Greenland. And there are options that include wide open spaces (try Kyrgyzstan for some nomadic wandering). For urban experiences choose from racing-to-the-future Shanghai or old-world-charm-meets-party-girl Lisbon. It's also time for Beirut, once more rising from the rubble of conflict.

You might make some plans by randomly opening a page of our Top Travel Lists and planting a finger – who knows what you might end up doing? These picks are morsels of inspiration that should get you off the beaten track and into the eclectic and bizarre. It might be cave-diving in Mexico or catching a whiff of the startling rafflesia flower in Malaysia. How about tracking yeti in the Himalaya, stealing a kiss in Casablanca, or taking a bath in a rather large champagne glass…

There's an underlying current in this edition…water. We've dedicated a special section to it. Water's the ultimate traveller, flowing around the globe, up into the atmosphere and back down again – and it started the ball rolling for the great travellers, from ancient voyages that settled Australia 40,000 years ago to later explorations. Today we swim in it, float on it, skate on its frozen surface, climb snowy peaks and throw snowballs at each other. But it's having its own way too, as it has over the aeons, shaping the land, and shaping the way we travel upon it. Importantly, it's telling us something about our effect on the planet. As climate change becomes more apparent, it is water – its abundance, its scarcity, its changing nature – that we tend to notice. Take a water trip in 2009 and ponder its role in your travels.

TONY WHEELER'S BEST IN TRAVEL

TONY WHEELER, COFOUNDER OF LONELY PLANET, LOOKS BACK ON HIS TRAVELS IN 2008 AND TELLS US HIS PLANS FOR 2009

My 2008 travels included two favourite activities – walking and weirdlands. Years ago I resolved to do at least one long walk (ie lasting at least a week) every year. In 2008 it was a town-to-town trek through Tuscany: interesting walking, Etruscan history, medieval hilltop towns, good food and wine, and comfortable hotels – could walking get any better?

I also managed shorter strolls including the coastal walk on Maria Island, off the coast of the Australian state of Tasmania.

My book *Bad Lands* tells the tale of my travels to former US president George W Bush's 'axis of evil' regimes, and an assortment of other strange places. I already have a taste for weirdlands (they are often more weird than bad) and I've been adding more of them to my list. In 2008 I went to Haiti – voodoo jazz, great naïve art and the home of Papa Doc – why has the country gone so wrong since a slave revolt threw out the French colonialists? A little further south I spent some time in Colombia, where the 'dangerous' label is past its use-by date. With tongue-in-cheek accuracy the tourist office insists 'the only risk is wanting to stay'.

I've also managed to spend a lot of time in London – is there a more international city in the world at the moment? From there I took the train to Liverpool to visit 2008's European Capital of Culture and stay in the Hard Day's Night Hotel (The Beatles are still my kind of culture). An old-fashioned and decidedly romantic train, the *Orient Express*, conveyed me from London to Venice. Then there was a circuit of Taiwan (I've been meaning to get there for years), a visit to Georgia (the back-in-the-USSR Georgia, not the southern US state), a scuba diving visit to Fiji and a week on a boat on Australia's Great Barrier Reef.

TONY'S TRAVEL PICKS 2009

#1 CHECK OUT THOSE TEMPORARY EXHIBITIONS

We always want to catch the big-name museums and galleries on our travels: the Louvre in Paris, the British Museum in London, the Smithsonian in Washington DC. But sometimes the most interesting exhibitions are the short-term ones. It is always worth checking if something really unusual will be happening when you are in town. These temporary exhibits are often moveable feasts; great exhibitions travel on from one town to another, so if you miss it in one place you might find it in another.

#2 MAKE A LONG TRIP

Chances for joining like-minded enthusiasts on crazy trips seem to be growing. Recently Maureen and I drove down the west coast of Africa in the get-there-in-an-old-banger Plymouth–Banjul Challenge. In 7000km through seven countries, our 18-year-old car's only malfunction was a puncture in Morocco, though we did get stuck in Saharan sand a few times in Mauritania. In 2009 I'll join a Lonely Planet cycling team for a stage of the Cairo to Capetown Tour d'Afrique bicycle ride.

#3 VISIT A 'STAN

In 2006 I visited Pakistan, Afghanistan and Kurdistan but I've yet to set foot in any of the old ex-Soviet Central Asian 'stans. In 2008 I missed out on an opportunity to see a space launch from the Baikonur Cosmodrome in Kazakhstan, so sampling that Silk Road route is high on my list. Countries along its way are trying to work together to promote Silk Road tourism – and perhaps 2009 will be my year to sample that historic route.

#4 SAIL SOMEWHERE

I have never hankered after one of those sailing-around-in-a-circle trips on a big cruise ship, although I have made plenty of trips on small ships: to the Antarctic, the Falkland Islands, obscure islands in the Pacific, you name it. There is one big-ship experience I would like to sample though, and that is crossing the Atlantic on a Cunard liner and passing the Statue of Liberty on the way into New York City. Perhaps in 2009 I'll get to sail out of Southampton with Manhattan as the next stop.

#5 STAY SOMEWHERE

Some of the best travel books (like Lonely Planet's *A House Somewhere*) are about staying in one place and soaking up the atmosphere there, rather than moving from place to place. In 2009 I will be doing exactly that in London, where I've established a base camp for lazy forays into Europe. Perhaps cruising into Manhattan could prompt a longer stay in that classic 'big city'.

012
ALGERIA

014
BANGLADESH

016
CANADA

018
GEORGIA

020
GREENLAND

LONELY PLANET'S
TOP 10 COUNTRIES

○ ALGERIA

'Peace. For most Algerians, the simple pleasures the rest of us take for granted…feel like being able to breathe again.'

By Anthony Ham

ALGERIA

POPULATION 33.3 MILLION ○ **CAPITAL** ALGIERS ○ **LANGUAGES** ARABIC, FRENCH ○ **UNIT OF CURRENCY** ALGERIAN DINAR (DA) ○ **COST INDEX** CUP OF TEA DA10 (US$0.15), MIDRANGE HOTEL DOUBLE ROOM DA1500-3500 (US$33-53), ONE-HOUR INTERNET ACCESS DA80-150 (US$1.10-2.25), ONE-WAY ALGIERS–TAMANRASSET AIR TICKET DA14,000 (US$210)

THE FUTURE IS NOW

How times have changed. Give or take the odd terrorist attack in the north, peace is making a big comeback and, with a quarter of Algeria's population under the age of 15, Algerians are convinced that the future is theirs. From a traveller's perspective it's hard not to agree with them. Unlike most other North African countries, Algeria has yet to sell its soul to the god of tourism. More than that, Algeria's attractions – astonishing Roman cities, landscapes and oases of Saharan legend – may even surpass those of its more famous neighbours. And the Algerians themselves – sophisticated, gregarious, eager to engage with the world – may just be North Africa's most misunderstood people.

Yes, some parts of the country are off limits. And yes, walking into your local travel agent and asking for tours to Algeria will still draw blank looks. But therein lies Algeria's charm. This is a largely safe, edgy destination that few people in the world know anything about. Now is the time to go, before that changes.

SHADOW OVER ALGERIA

Algerians do not like talking about the past, which is hardly surprising when you consider that the country tore itself apart from 1994 until 2002 in a battle for the soul of Algeria. The political violence pitted Islamic militants against everyone else. Algeria was sealed off from the outside world, civilians were killed, every Algerian who could fled into exile, and tourists stayed away in fear for their lives.

DEFINING EXPERIENCE

Waking up with the sun at Assekrem ('the end of the world'), atop the Tolkienesque Atakor plateau, being greeted by the Sahara's glory and contemplating how far you are from tourist trails and how you'll be able to tell your friends that you've been to the end of the earth and back.

RECENT FAD

Peace. For most Algerians, the simple pleasures the rest of us take for granted – a coffee in a French-style sidewalk café in Algiers, travelling around their own country without fearing for their lives – feel like being able to breathe again.

FESTIVALS & EVENTS

○ The Fête du Tapis (March/April) in Ghardaïa is a carpet festival set in one of Algeria's best markets. It draws people from all over Algeria.

TUAREG WOMEN PREPARE TO DRUM UP A HOLY CELEBRATION AT THE SPRING CULTURAL FESTIVAL OF LE TAFSIT

✪ Tamanrasset's Le Tafsit (end April) is a celebration of Tuareg culture, with camel races in Algeria's deep south.
✪ Oran's Festival National de la Chanson du Rai d'Oran, in August, showcases home-grown rai, Oran's soundtrack and one of the best sounds in world music.

LIFE-CHANGING EXPERIENCES

✪ Exploring the Hoggar Mountains by 4WD on an epic Saharan expedition.
✪ Getting up close to the millennia-old rock art in the Tassili N'Ajjer.
✪ Dune skiing in the Grand Erg Oriental, the world's largest sand sea.
✪ Searching for the spirit of Albert Camus in the Roman city of Djemila.
✪ Losing yourself in the labyrinth that is the Casbah of Algiers.

HOT TOPIC OF THE DAY

Islam and Europe. In a country where 99% of the population is Muslim and where many also have a decidedly European outlook on life, Algerians are endlessly debating the role of Islam in public life. It's all complicated by the fact that many Algerians live in France, and many more would like to join them.

RAI – ALGERIA'S STREET MUSIC

Want to know what Algerians on the street are thinking? Check out the country's most popular music genre, rai. Meaning 'state an opinion', rai, with its danceable rhythms buoyed by synthesisers and drum machines, is the perennial soundtrack to Algerian life. Rai's staples are betrayal and exile, lust and love – an earthy, bittersweet cocktail which made being a rai performer downright dangerous during the country's civil war when those rai superstars not killed by Islamic conservatives were forced into exile. With peace more or less restored, rai has travelled a long way: from 1930s Oran to the dancefloors of Paris, then back to re-colonise its own country.

RANDOM FACTS

✪ Most of Western Europe would fit within Algeria's borders.
✪ Algiers is closer to Paris than it is to Tamanrasset.
✪ Ninety per cent of Algeria is engulfed by the Sahara Desert
✪ Famous 'Frenchmen' born in Algeria include Albert Camus, Yves Saint Laurent and Zinedine Zidane.

MOST BIZARRE SIGHT

If the Unesco World Heritage–listed Tassili N'Ajjer National Park is the Louvre of Saharan rock art, then the carving known as 'La Vache qui Pleure' (The Cow that Cries) at Tagharghart is its Mona Lisa: an enigmatic masterpiece.

'…Bangladesh is a revelation that actually leaves India looking a little worse for wear.'

By Stuart Butler

BANGLADESH

POPULATION 150 MILLION ✪ **CAPITAL** DHAKA ✪ **LANGUAGE** BENGALI (BANGLA) ✪ **UNIT OF CURRENCY** TAKA (TK)
✪ **COST INDEX** CUP OF TEA TK5 (US$0.07), MIDRANGE/BUDGET DOUBLE TK700/100 (US$10/1.40), SHORT TAXI RIDE
TK100 (US$1.40), INTERNET ACCESS PER HOUR TK40 (US$0.55)

CALIFORNIA DREAMING

Let's get this straight from the start. Bangladesh is not the country of disappointment as portrayed in *Brick Lane* or by the international media, nor is it merely the poorly endowed cousin of India. Instead Bangladesh is a revelation that actually leaves India looking a little worse for wear. Any visitor who ventures here will return home with stories so improbable that claiming you have a pet unicorn is likely to be met with fewer disbelieving shakes of the head. So, what is it that makes accounts of this big-hearted nation so refreshingly unlikely? An excellent starting point is that this country, one of the poorest nations on earth has, quietly and with minimal fuss, done what California, the richest area on earth, claims is too prohibitively expensive – Bangladesh has banned all petrol and diesel vehicles from its two major conurbations and, very shortly, from the entire country. If that hasn't got the heads of the disbelievers shaking, then wait until they hear that the highest point in Bangladesh, a country famous for being frying-pan flat, is higher than the highest peak in Scotland, a country famous for being leg-achingly mountainous. With an unexpected environmental and geographical profile like this Bangladesh deserves to leave its 'basket case' stereotypes far behind and be welcomed by the wider world as the trendsetting, breathtaking and hard-working country it really is.

DEADLY HONEY

There's more than environmental enlightenment and thousand-metre peaks to make Bangladesh proud in 2009. A visitor to its green, pleasant and often waterlogged shores can relish in the joy of activities offered by no other country on earth. How does hunting for the most dangerous honey in the world grab you? Or what about going fishing with a family of fluffy otters instead of the usual rod and reel? Not enough of a lure? Then how does watching whales out at sea, or counting freshwater dolphins a hundred miles from the sea float your boat?

Away from the natural wonders you can attend the world's second-largest Muslim gathering, visit Buddhist, Hindu and Muslim temples by the bucket load, and walk through tribal villages in the mountains where your very presence is likely to be something of a revelation. And of course there is that sweaty and steamy *pièce de résistance*: the spooky world of the Sundarbans, the world's largest mangrove forest and home to tigers which kill a man every third day!

A DHAKA SHIP-LABOURER PROVES THAT BANGLADESH'S PENCHANT FOR RECYCLING DOESN'T STOP WITH PLASTIC BAGS

DEFINING EXPERIENCE

Gawping in awe at the raw, gritty side of Bangladesh while sailing, shell-shocked, down the Buriganga River, which flows through the heart of Old Dhaka presenting a shameless theatre of life and death in which nothing is tamed for tourist eyes.

FESTIVALS & EVENTS

✪ In January, join around two million others on the outskirts of Dhaka for three days of prayer, discussions and recitations at Biswa Ijtema, the second-biggest Muslim gathering after the hajj.
✪ At the Honey Hunting Festival, in Buri Goalini on 1 April, the opening of the honey-gathering season starts with religious blessings asking for protection from tiger attacks and a mad boat race into the swamps of the Sundarbans in search of liquid gold.
✪ Pohela Boisakh, the Bangladeshi New Year on 14 April, is about ornate costumes, parades and lots of noise, especially in Dhaka and Rangamati.

LIFE-CHANGING EXPERIENCES

✪ Wondering why Bangladesh can manage to ban plastic bags, replacing them with environmentally kosher jute bags, but your country can't.
✪ Straining neck muscles whilst scouring the tree-tops for the rare hoolock gibbon.
✪ Pondering the secret of five-flavoured tea – a real-life miracle of science.
✪ Squinting your eyes against the green glow emanating from zillions of rice paddies as you cruise on by like a don in the back of a tarted-up cycle rickshaw.

HOT TOPIC OF THE DAY

Originally scheduled for January 2007, but put back by 18 months, the long-awaited general elections are due to take place at the very end of 2008. When Bangladesh enters 2009 who will be in charge and how stable will this notoriously unstable country be?

RANDOM FACTS

✪ Bangladesh is the most densely populated country on earth.
✪ Bangladesh was one of the first countries to fully embrace the idea of micro-credit.
✪ The Sundarbans has the world's highest concentration of tigers.
✪ Bangladesh is home to one of the world's longest unbroken beaches, which stretches south of Cox's Bazar for some 120km.

MOST BIZARRE SIGHT

Spending an hour or more tangled up in a snaking, snarling rush-hour traffic jam consisting entirely of hundreds upon hundreds of bell-clanging bicycle rickshaws.

○ CANADA

EUROPE

NORTH AMERICA

ASIA

AFRICA

AUSTRALIA

'Winter or summer, Canada is a land of action, with an insane amount of terrain to play on…'

By Karla Zimmerman

CANADA

POPULATION 33.4 MILLION ○ **CAPITAL** OTTAWA ○ **LANGUAGES** ENGLISH, FRENCH ○ **UNIT OF CURRENCY** CANADIAN DOLLAR (C$) ○ **ANNUAL BEER CONSUMPTION PER PERSON AGED 15 & OVER** 77L ○ **CANADIANS WHO SPEAK ONLY FRENCH** 13.3% ○ **COST INDEX** B&B DOUBLE ROOM C$80-140 (US$81-142), TIM HORTONS DOUGHNUT C$0.80 (US$0.81), HOCKEY-GAME TICKET C$25-90 (US$25-91), SKIING DAY PASS C$50-80 (US$51-81)

ALL GLAMMED UP

Canada is too polite to say so, but it's ready to be feted. International chefs have stocked its tables with distinctive seafood, piquant cheeses and homegrown wines. Outfitters have harnessed its glinting glaciers, spiky mountains and spectral rainforests for epic adventures. There's always a festival rocking a street somewhere. And everyone is happy to go out and party because, baby, the economy here is booming. Thanks to Canada's oil, diamonds and natural gas, the loonie rocketed past the US dollar for the first time in 30-plus years.

It's good timing, since Canada needs to get all glammed up before the world spotlight shines on it in 2010. That's when the Winter Olympics take over the slopes and rinks of Vancouver and Whistler.

NOT SITTING AROUND

Winter or summer, Canada is a land of action, with an insane amount of terrain to play on (it's the world's second-largest country, after all). Certain areas are exceptionally well-geared for the growing number of adrenaline junkies. British Columbia's Tofino offers surfing, kayaking, whale-spotting and storm-watching. Québec's Laurentians let visitors ski, luge, rock climb, and refuel at maple-syrup shacks. Banff does it all in Alberta's Rockies: skiing, snowboarding, canoeing, horseback riding – phew!

But let's be honest, sometimes you do just want to sit around, in which case Canada's three largest cities – Toronto, Montréal and Vancouver – have your chair waiting. Cosmopolitan, cultured and foodie-filled, they're the places to kick back and crack open a cold one.

DEFINING EXPERIENCE

Zipping up the fleece to ski, hike, bike or otherwise soak up the mountains and parklands, followed by savouring fine food and drink: in the east, a Parisian-style *café au lait* and chocolate croissant; in the west, sushi or alder-smoked salmon alongside Okanagan Valley wines. Watching hockey absorbs the evenings (rink-side seats preferred).

FESTIVALS & EVENTS

✪ Hold on to your broomstick: in 2009 the World Men's Curling Championship marks its 50th birthday in Moncton, New Brunswick, from 4 to 12 April. Guys from around the globe converge to slide their final stones across the ice before the Winter Olympics.

✪ Montréal's jazz fest – or as they say in French, le Festival International de Jazz de Montréal – celebrates its 30th anniversary in 2009. From 1 to 12 July,

downtown explodes with two million people and 400 concerts, most of them outdoors and free.

☻ More than 2000 soldiers storm the Plains of Abraham from July 30 to August 2, as they re-enact the bloody battle at Québec City that determined Canada's history. It's the 250th anniversary of the French-versus-English smackdown, hence the fanfare.

☻ For nine days in early July, Canadians channel their inner cowboy at the Calgary Stampede. Men and women in tall boots and even taller hats ride bulls, wrestle steers, race chuck wagons and partake of rides and games.

LIFE-CHANGING EXPERIENCES

☻ Wheeling over the tundra to Hudson Bay's shore to watch huge, playful and sharp-clawed polar bears hunt seals in Churchill, Manitoba.

☻ Hiking the West Coast Trail, a week-long jaunt on Vancouver Island's wild side, where the raging Pacific smashes the shore and meets a brooding, mist-coated forest.

☻ Kayaking the Northwest Territories' Slave River Rapids, which have six times the volume of the Grand Canyon; they froth with O'ahu-sized whitecaps and seethe with Class VI holes.

HOT TOPICS OF THE DAY

☻ Economic growth versus environmental protection: Canada's oil and natural gas reserves are helping the economy to kick ass. But extracting and developing the resources comes at a high ecological price, especially with regard to greenhouse-gas emissions.

☻ Immigration: Canada takes in the world's largest per capita immigration numbers each year. While this makes for wonderfully multicultural

cities, can the country maintain its high-calibre social and physical infrastructures if it stays this course?

RANDOM FACTS

☻ Break out the parka: Canada is the world's coldest country, with a frosty average temperature of -5.6°C. Ottawa is the second-chilliest national capital, after Ulaanbaatar in Mongolia.

☻ The entire population of Canada is less than that of Tokyo and its suburbs – but Canadians get 9,970,610 sq km to sprawl out in versus Tokyo's 13,500 sq km.

☻ Fifty-three Aboriginal languages are spoken in Canada, with the three most prevalent being Cree, Inuktitut and Ojibwa.

☻ Fifteen percent of the world's diamonds come from Canada, mostly mined from the Northwest Territories. The country's bauble production ranks third, after Botswana and Russia.

EUROPE

GEORGIA

NORTH AMERICA

ASIA

AFRICA

SOUTH AMERICA

AUSTRALIA

'…here is a fascinating culture, a realm where the welcome is spontaneous, where the landscape is breathtaking, and where travel is still a challenge…'

By Will Gourlay

GEORGIA

POPULATION 4.7 MILLION ✪ **CAPITAL** TBILISI ✪ **LANGUAGE** GEORGIAN ✪ **UNIT OF CURRENCY** LARI (GEL)
✪ **COST INDEX** BOTTLE OF BEER 1.50GEL (US$1), MASSAGE AT THE ORBELIANI SULPHUR BATHS 5GEL (US$3.20), BOTTLE OF KAKHETI WINE 7.50GEL (US$4.70), DOUBLE ROOM 95GEL (US$60), TAXI RIDE FROM TBILISI AIRPORT 20GEL (US$12.50), INTERNET ACCESS PER HOUR 2GEL (US$1.25)

THE LAND OF PROMETHEUS & THE GOLDEN FLEECE

Georgia has long been regarded as on the periphery of Europe. It was a place of exile for Prometheus, who was chained to Mt Kazbek for stealing fire from the gods. It was the land of mythical treasures for Jason and the Argonauts in search of the Golden Fleece. Today there's no question of exile to Georgia. For the canny traveller, there are countless unexpected treasures – geographical, cultural and sensual – to be discovered. Georgia's location, where western Asia crashes into Europe, creates much of its appeal. Soaring mountains and an incredible diversity of landscapes will appeal to walkers, skiers and mountain climbers. And over long centuries, a cauldron of cultural influences – Caucasian, Persian, Russian, Turkish – have created a distinctive society with rich artistic traditions and idiosyncratic architecture. Now, lustily embracing democracy and shaking off the 70-year-old Soviet yoke, Georgia's determined to place itself in the European consciousness, declaring itself open for business and touting its little-known tourism attractions.

WINE, WELCOME & SONG

The country's other claim to fame – according to Georgians at least – is that it invented wine. Whether or not that's true, wine plays a big part in Georgian life. Eating and drinking is an art form. Georgian cuisine presents distinctive dishes created from the freshest local produce. Foodies will have a field day tucking into innovative combinations of aubergines, pomegranates, walnut paste and local fruits. Meals consist of many courses, washed down with ebullient toasts and spontaneous bursts of song, all indicative of the Georgians' passionate approach to life; their tradition of hospitality is second to none.

There is more than a whiff of adventure awaiting the traveller to Georgia: here is a fascinating culture, a realm where the welcome is spontaneous, where the landscape is breathtaking, and where travel is still a challenge and all the more rewarding for it.

DEFINING EXPERIENCE

Savour the buzz and faded grandeur of Tbilisi, climbing to the Narikala Fortress for a bird's-eye view of the city, then enjoying a night of revelry (starting, of course, with a long and convivial Georgian meal, washed down with local wine). Head westward, stopping briefly at Mtskheta, the country's spiritual centre, before continuing to Batumi on the sultry subtropical coast, with its *belle époque*

A NAHAPETIAN COUPLE WELCOMES GUESTS TO VIEW THEIR DOLL COLLECTION AT HOME IN AKHALKALAK

architecture and botanical gardens. Make your way to remote Svaneti, spotting the distinctive stone towers and walking in the hills around Mestia. While in a mountain frame of mind trundle along the Georgian Military Highway to sight the peak of Mt Kazbek, then head through the wine country of Kakheti to the mysterious monastery city of Davit Gareja in the semidesert near the Azerbaijan border.

RECENT FAD

Once the favoured holiday destination for Soviet functionaries, Georgia is now the spot for trekkers who want vast stretches of untouched mountain scenery, culture buffs with a yen for the unfamiliar and overlanders on the way to or from Central Asia.

FESTIVALS & EVENTS

☼ Easter Sunday is a solemn and poignant celebration, flush with Orthodox ritual and spiritualism.

☼ Enjoy a tipple or six at the Sighnaghi Wine Festival, a celebration of the fruit of the vine in October.
☼ During Tbilisoba, the festival of wine and the city's founding, on the last weekend in October, the capital gears up for fun and partying.

LIFE-CHANGING EXPERIENCES

☼ Eating and drinking to your heart's content at a *supra* (feast) – just remember you should never try to out-drink a Georgian.
☼ Succumbing to a vigorous massage at Tbilisi's pungent sulphur baths.
☼ Watching the sun set over Mt Kazbek and the Tsminda Sameba Church.

WHAT'S HOT…

☼ Tbilisi nightlife: the hottest live music, clubs and theatres in the Caucasus.
☼ Skiing in Gudauri or Bakuriani.

…WHAT'S NOT

Overbearing Russian neighbours.

HOT TOPICS OF THE DAY

☼ Georgia had the Rose Revolution but things aren't so rosy now – do Georgians really want democracy and is mass public protest the best way to change governments?
☼ What does Kosovo's declaration of independence mean for Georgia's breakaway regions?

RANDOM FACT

Georgians love to toast with wine or vodka, but to raise a glass of beer to someone in Georgia is to signify that they are your enemy.

MOST BIZARRE SIGHT

The death mask of Josef Stalin in the Stalin Museum in Gori, the town of his birth.

GREENLAND

'With out-of-this-world scenery, iceberg-filled fjords and mesmerising pure light, the experience is worth every penny...'

By Mark Elliott

GREENLAND

POPULATION 56,648 ✪ **CAPITAL** NUUK ✪ **LANGUAGES** GREENLANDIC (KALAALLISUT), DANISH ✪ **UNIT OF CURRENCY** DANISH KRONE (DKR) ✪ **COST INDEX** BOTTLE OF CARLSBERG BEER FROM SUPERMARKETS DKR14 (US$2.80), IN BARS DKR40 (US$8), 100G OF DRIED CARIBOU MEAT DKR100 (US$20)

EDGING TOWARDS INDEPENDENCE?

Known as *ullortuneq* in Greenlandic, the longest day (June 21) might seem rather irrelevant in a country whose north sees constant daylight all summer long. However, Ullortuneq is also Greenland's National Day, when its distinctive red-and-white flags flutter from virtually every building. The day is going to be especially significant in 2009, the 30th anniversary of Home Rule, with excitement brewing that this year a new level of 'self rule' will bring further autonomy from Denmark and take Greenland one step nearer to independence.

COMING CLOSER

As it escapes politically, so improved transport brings Greenland closer. As noted by the intrepid Vikings, Greenland has never been the most accessible place. However, with new e-ticketing possibilities and a recently introduced flight to the US (Baltimore), Air Greenland, the 'national' airline, is helping to make the world's biggest island a little easier to reach (previously, the only air access was from Denmark or Iceland). Distances are huge though, and internal transport is limited to boat, plane or thrilling helicopter rides, so you'd be advised to book in advance. An increasingly popular alternative is to join a cruise from Iceland. Either way it'll cost a packet. But with out-of-this-world scenery, iceberg-filled fjords and mesmerising pure light, the experience is worth every penny.

DEFINING EXPERIENCE

Sipping coffee in comfortable mutual silence at an Inuit *kaffemik* (Greenlandic coffee party) in a colourful timber cottage overlooking a jagged-edged fjord.

On the waters, blue-white icebergs spontaneously explode as the brilliant sunshine finally causes thousand-year-old gas bubbles to expand that little bit too much.

RECENT FAD

Photographing Greenland's diminishing glaciers to 'prove' the reality of global warming, just in case there's anyone left who actually doubts it. Arsuk Fjord's glacier has retreated a whopping 5km since 1985.

FESTIVALS & EVENTS

✪ At the Ice Golf Championships held in Uummannaq from 19 to 24 March 2009, balls are red and greens are white. The dress code is definitely 'well wrapped'.

✪ The Arctic Circle Race, 24 to 31 March 2009, is a series of events focussed on an ultratough three-day cross-country skiing challenge

LIGHT UP YOUR MORNING WITH A STINT OF ICEBERG SPOTTING AT ONE OF GREENLAND'S ENTICINGLY REMOTE TIMBER-HOMED VILLAGES

covering 160km. Or just 100km in the 'easy' version.

⚙ On the first day of the school year (early August) the first-grade pupils (and many parents) dress up in colourful traditional costumes and sealskin boots. Each child, welcomed by the school principal, arrives to applause, flag waving and perhaps a shower of coins thrown into the crowd.

LIFE-CHANGING EXPERIENCES

⚙ Gaping at the mesmerising, sky-throbbing lights of the aurora borealis on a clear, moonless night.

⚙ Cruising down surreal southern fjords where toothy fangs of rock soar over a kilometre up from the icy waters.

⚙ Being awed by the Ilulissat icefjord where the northern hemisphere's most prolific tidewater glacier continuously calves its massive icebergs.

⚙ Crossing endless untamed wilderness by dog sled, whether from

accessible Sisimiut or middle-of-nowhere Ittoqqortoormiit.

⚙ Experiencing the utter solitude of hiking in one of the world's last true wildernesses.

HOT TOPIC OF THE DAY

With Home Rule moving towards self rule, should Greenland sell its rich mineral soul to balance its books? Currently around half of the Greenland's income arrives in grants from Denmark, and without financial independence how can true political independence follow? Providing infrastructure for a tiny population so widely spread across huge distances is expensive, as was underlined in 2006 when Arctic Umiaq Line, the main passenger shipping line, nearly went bankrupt.

RANDOM FACTS

⚙ Greenland is the only 'country' to have left the European Union.

⚙ The central ice sheet that covers most of Greenland is up to 3km thick. If it melted, the water produced would raise global sea levels by around 7m.

⚙ The only 'intercity' road is a 5km track between Grønnedal and the ghost town of Ivittuut.

⚙ The oldest rocks ever to have been found on earth (3.8 billion years) come from the Isua supercrustal belt, northeast of Nuuk, Greenland's pint-sized capital.

MOST BIZARRE SIGHTS

⚙ Seal carcasses hanging out to dry on washing lines on the balconies of ugly 1960s apartment blocks.

⚙ The vast bright-red post box in Nuuk holding letters that arrive addressed to 'Santa Claus, Greenland'. (All get answered come December!)

⚙ Drunken, toothless old women sexually harassing young men in seedy Wild West–style bars.

⊕ KYRGYZSTAN

'…the country that your inner nomad has secretly been dreaming about all these years.'

By Bradley Mayhew

KYRGYZSTAN

POPULATION 5.3 MILLION ✪ **CAPITAL** BISHKEK ✪ **LANGUAGES** KYRGYZ, RUSSIAN ✪ **UNIT OF CURRENCY** SOM
✪ **COST INDEX** HOTEL DOUBLE 360-1080SOM (US$10-30), HOMESTAY 252SOM (US$7), SHORT TAXI RIDE 72SOM (US$2), INTERNET ACCESS PER HOUR 36SOM (US$1), KYRGYZ HAT 108-216SOM (US$3-6)

THE SWITZERLAND OF CENTRAL ASIA

Kyrgyzstan may be tagged the 'Switzerland of Central Asia', but don't worry, it's a lot more interesting than that. With a hospitable, horsebound culture that still carries faint echoes of Genghis Khan and stunning mountain landscape dominated by the valleys and peaks of the Tian Shan, Kyrgyzstan is the country that your inner nomad has secretly been dreaming about all these years.

BORAT'S YOUNGER BROTHER

Kyrgyzstan's descent in recent years from fledgling inner Asian democracy to political basket case has been watched carefully by both the American and Russian military bases that face each other uneasily outside the capital Bishkek. Yet despite some democratic teething problems, Kyrgyzstan remains every traveller's favourite 'stan', refreshingly free of the grim authoritarianism of neighbouring Uzbekistan, the flash petro-corruption of Kazakhstan and the still-smoking Kalashnikovs of Afghanistan.

COMMUNITY-TOURISM HEAVEN

The key to unlocking Kyrgyzstan is its world-class network of grassroots community-tourism projects, which ensures that the tourism dollars you spend go directly to herdsmen, villagers and taxi drivers across the country. The fact that Asia's best-value adventures come with a warm, fuzzy ecotourist glow is one of Asia's best-kept secrets; and, for the time being at least, the Kyrgyz countryside is still all yours for the exploring. Whether you're set on trekking out to ancient petroglyphs, taking the high passes to China or riding with eagle hunters, now is the time to plan your big Central Asian adventure.

DEFINING EXPERIENCE

Waking up in a yurt and riding on horseback out to the high pastures to watch horse racing and kok boru (rugby on horseback, with a dead goat), then back to your yurt to share tea, fresh yogurt and a steaming plate of beshbarmak (meat and noodles) with nomadic hosts, before snuggling up in a sleeping bag under a lush blanket of Central Asian stars.

RECENT FAD

More travellers are using the network of rural homestays to organise anything from a horse trek in the high pastures to an afternoon of serious felt-making. Kyrgyzstan's colourful shyrdaks (felt carpets) are becoming chic – pick one up from a woman's cooperative in Kochkor or Naryn.

A LOCAL ARRIVES EARLY TO BEAT THE CROWDS AT A COVERED MARKET IN KYRGYZSTAN'S CAPITAL, BISHKEK

FESTIVALS & EVENTS

✪ The At Chabysh (Horse Racing) Festival, held in Barskoön in early November, is the place to watch such traditional Kyrgyz horse games as *kyz-kumay* (kiss the girl) and *udarysh* (horseback wrestling).

✪ Independence Day parades take place across the country on 31 August 2009, though the most elaborate are in the capital, Bishkek.

✪ The Birds of Prey Festival at Manzhyly-Ata, in August, features displays of eagle hunting on the shores of Lake Issyk-Köl, 12km from Bokonbayevo.

HOT TOPIC OF THE DAY

Local relief that Sacha Baron Cohen (Borat) chose instead to lampoon their neighbours, the Kazakhs, has given way to the hope that the political turmoil and clan divisions of recent years will settle in 2009.

LIFE-CHANGING EXPERIENCES

✪ Watching from your tent as the sun sets blood red on the perfect pyramid peak of Khan Tengri.

✪ Listening to the oral epic poem *Manas* performed on the high pastures, its style and content a direct line back to the nomadic past.

✪ Sharing a long-distance taxi ride with a Kyrgyz family, and stopping halfway to pile into a relative's house, or yurt, for delicious tea, mare's milk and vodka.

✪ Trekking through the alpine meadows of the Tian Shan, passing the occasional yurt or herding camp.

✪ Feeling the weight of a full-grown eagle on your arm during an outing with a Kyrgyz eagle hunter.

RANDOM FACTS

✪ The Kyrgyz national epic poem *Manas* is 20 times longer than Homer's *The Odyssey*.

✪ A Swedish logistics company recently recommended that Santa Claus relocate from the North Pole to Kyrgyzstan, pinpointing the Tian Shan mountains as the most efficient location from which to deliver Christmas presents to the world's children in just one night.

✪ The Kyrgyz flag represents the stylised *tyndyk* (roof opening) of a yurt, surrounded by flames that represent the nation's 40 main clans.

MOST BIZARRE SIGHT

✪ A group of Kyrgyz men all sporting the elfin, white, felt national hat known as an *ak kalpak*.

✪ The world's only three-story yurt, erected outside Osh's Silk Road Museum.

✪ The two leaky, mothballed boats anchored off Lake Issyk-Köl that make up the 'Kyrgyz navy'.

'The difference here is that the words of welcome, the spirit of religious tolerance, the preservation of the past…are the real deal.'

By Jenny Walker

OMAN

POPULATION 3.2 MILLION ✪ **CAPITAL** MUSCAT ✪ **LANGUAGE** ARABIC ✪ **UNIT OF CURRENCY** OMANI RIYAL (OR) ✪ **MAJOR INDUSTRY** OIL AND NATURAL GAS ✪ **COST INDEX** MIXED FRUIT JUICE OR1 (US$2.60), 1L BOTTLE OF WATER 150 BAISA (US$0.40), DAY'S HIRE OF 4WD OR27 (US$70), INTERNET ACCESS PER HOUR OR1 (US$2), HAND-REARED PRIZE-WINNING RACING CAMEL OR70,000 (US$180,000), PENALTY FOR A DIRTY CAR OR5 (US$13)

THE REAL DEAL

Watching people queue for visas at immigration, you can't help but notice that Oman has started to attract a different kind of visitor. There are the families and friends of expats on repeat trips to a country that has a habit of luring its visitors back; there are the independent travellers, in the know about Oman's pristine desert and mountain wilderness; and now there are the shoppers.

These aren't ordinary shoppers making a beeline for Oman's famously gossipy, garrulous *souqs* (markets). These are shoppers who've heard of Oman's newly relaxed property laws, who've come to buy into a slice of the good life.

Residential and tourist developments like The Wave, a US$800 million scheme in Muscat, have brought Oman into competition with neighbouring Gulf States trying to sell beachfront acreage to a discerning buyer. Each country advertises its credentials as a heritage-rich reincarnation of the Arabic Orient that appealed so strongly to Western sensibilities in colonial times. Not to be outdone, Oman is currently quite literally moving mountains (the world's deepest rock cut linking the Yitti development with Muscat) to attract foreign investment. The difference here is that the words of welcome, the spirit of religious tolerance, the preservation of the past, together with the rugs thrown over the walls for an airing, are the real deal.

DEFINING EXPERIENCE

Four wheels on the wild side: inching into the blue sky on a 1:3 incline, hoping the brakes hold; being flagged down for cardamom coffee by a dagger-wielding *sheyba* (old man) whose goats eat your egg sandwiches; padding off for a proverbial on the treeless summit and discovering a pavement of fossils; winding back down to sea-level with the call to prayer hanging in the air; ending a perfect day by finding a carwash before the police find you.

BLACK IS BACK

In cities, current women's fashion dictates that clothing can be any colour as long as it's black, marking a departure from the traditional riot of beetroot reds and indigo blues. One senses the new austerity won't last long: already, coloured spangles are making an appearance on *abeyyas* (overdresses), and the occasional outrageous handbag shows a hankering for the good old days.

FESTIVALS & EVENTS

✪ Qurm Natural Park provides the venue for the Muscat Festival held annually in January; the Omani public

KEEPING UP WITH THE DHOW JONESES IS IMPORTANT TO ANY SELF-RESPECTING OMANI FISHERMAN

brings most of the rest, setting up stall in ad hoc *souqs* and breaking into spontaneous poetry, song and dance.
☺ The Khareef Festival, held annually in Salalah some time from July to August, marks the greening of the Dhofar hills. It attracts caravans of picnickers, barbecuing in the rain.

LIFE-CHANGING EXPERIENCES
☺ Slipping off-road in the terraced Hajar Mountains or tracing oryx hoofprints in the great desert.
☺ Swimming with psychedelic squid in Oman's numerous coral gardens.
☺ Dangling over the void in the Majlis al-Jinn – a 158m rappel into the world's second largest cave.
☺ Tasting the dawn dew as it brings life to the Empty Quarter, before the sun lays all to dust again.
☺ Looking for leopards on Jebel Samhan as part of a volunteer programme.

NO SMOKE WITHOUT FIRE
One night it's there in all its percolating Alice-in-Wonderland, velvet-sleeved, apple-flavoured glory, and the next night it's vanished. The smoking of *sheesha* (water-pipes) is one of those hot public vices that spills onto the streets from coffeehouses and cafés; the authorities periodically try to ban it, but it soon returns to full flavour.

RANDOM FACTS
☺ In 2008 Oman signed an agreement with Microsoft to launch the world's first collaborative e-learning resource for the country's 230,000 high school students – not bad for a country that had only two schools in 1970.
☺ Muscat has been dubbed the 'eagle capital of the world' since up to 100 raptors per day started calling in for a snack at the local abattoir during the winter migration.

☺ Approximately 30,000 loggerhead turtles nest on just 14km of beach on Masirah Island, making it the largest labour and delivery unit in the world – at least for loggerheads.

HOT TOPIC OF THE DAY
Pause over aubergines in the super-market or lean on someone's half-built wall and you'll hear this lament: the cost of living has shot through the roof, taking the price of turbans with it.

MOST BIZARRE SIGHT
☺ Everyone knows that camels are the ships of the desert: what is less known is that camels these days are less 'ships' than 'shipped' – generally seated comfortably in Toyota pickups.
☺ You're not hallucinating if you spot a man dressed in orange walking alongside a 400km road to nowhere – this is the municipality's answer to automated garbage collection.

'...falling asleep in a hammock as you float away down the Amazon, waking up just in time to catch dawn over the world's second-longest river...'

By Sara Benson

PERU

POPULATION 28.7 MILLION ✪ **CAPITAL** LIMA ✪ **LANGUAGES** SPANISH, QUECHUA ✪ **UNIT OF CURRENCY** NUEVO SOL (S/) ✪ **COST INDEX** BOTTLE OF INKA KOLA S/0.5 (US$0.17), SHORT TAXI RIDE (EXCEPT IN LIMA) S/4 (US$1.38), ONE-STAR HOTEL DOUBLE US$20-40

ALL SHOOK UP

For a country that experienced two decades of civil war and instability during the late 20th century, the most surprising thing about Peru is how good things look lately: low inflation, a stable exchange rate and robust economic growth.

At least, that is until an earthquake of magnitude 8.0 hit the south coast on 15 August 2007. The next month a meteorite from outer space crashed near Lake Titicaca. Recently protests have erupted on the streets again, including against the sale of deforested Amazonian land to international investors and a new tourism law that will expand hotels and allow foreigners to buy prime real estate near fragile cultural-heritage sites.

GHOSTS FROM THE PAST

As it tries to exorcise the demons of its political past, Peru has been haunted by all-too-familiar ghosts. In 2005 ex-president Alberto Fujimori returned to Chile from self-imposed exile in Japan, only to be extradited to Lima to face charges of human rights abuses. His ongoing trial has stirred up mixed emotions for many Peruvians, proving that his cult of personality still has its share of worshippers.

Equally uncomfortable questions linger about an estimated 10,000 people who 'disappeared' and died violently at the hands of the army, paramilitary groups and guerrillas between 1980 and 2000. Although President García's government has formed a reparations council, many of the victims' families have no proof of their loved ones' identity, so compensation will never be made.

THE TIME IS NOW

Tourism growth is exponential here; now's the right time to visit. Trek to famous sites such as Machu Picchu before, as Unesco's warned, they're loved to death. Visit Amazon-basin villages before climate change alters indigenous ways of life. Cruise Lake Titicaca before pollution diminishes its sparkle. The peaks of the Cordillera Blanca, part of South America's tallest mountain chain, are not overcrowded with trekkers and peak-baggers yet but it's only a matter of time.

DEFINING EXPERIENCE

A rickety bus ride from the rural highlands down to the *selva* (jungle) after a trek to ancient Inca ruins in the shadow of the mighty Andes, then falling asleep in a hammock as you float away down the Amazon, waking up just in time to catch dawn over the world's second-longest river.

TAKE MY ADVICE, THERE'S NOTHING SO NICE AS MESSIN' ABOUT ON LAKE TITICACA

RECENT FAD

Kate Middleton, Prince William's on-again-off-again sweetheart, plans to compete in the extreme 132-mile Great River Amazon Raft Race, for which participants build their own rafts from jungle logs and vines.

FESTIVALS & EVENTS

✪ Ayacucho holds Peru's most famous celebrations: during Semana Santa (Holy Week), spectacular religious pageantry, blending Catholic and indigenous rituals, leads up to Easter.
✪ On 24 June Inti Raymi re-enacts Inca winter solstice celebrations at Saqsaywamán fort, outside Cuzco.
✪ Around Candlemas (2 February) and Puno Day (5 November), the town of Puno, on the shores of Lake Titicaca, bursts with marching bands and costumed revellers (often wearing grotesque mask-heads) dancing in the streets.

✪ Semana de Andinismo, held in June in high-altitude Huaraz, is a week-long festival of climbing, skiing and snow sports, attracting elite athletes.

LIFE-CHANGING EXPERIENCES

✪ Forgetting the Inca Trail and trekking to more remote Inca ruins, or to the massive cloud-forest fortress of Kuélap.
✪ Floating in a banana boat down the Rio Amazonas to the region where Peru, Bolivia and Brazil meet.
✪ Dragging your board up the coast in search of that elusive perfect swell, finding it at Puerto Chicama or Huanchaco, near the jet-set beach resort of Máncora.
✪ Visiting a *brujo* (shaman) or *cuandero* (healer) on the lakeside around Huancabamba.

HOT TOPIC OF THE DAY

The burning question: will a US free-trade deal bolster Peru's economic growth, or will it flood the country with cheaper imports, causing economic strife Peruvians can't afford?

RANDOM FACTS

✪ *Huaqueros* (tomb raiders) are still active in Peru, digging up (and, thereby, often destroying) pre-Columbian ruins at recently discovered archaeological sites.
✪ Almost 4000 native varieties of potatoes are grown in Peru.
✪ Arequipa province boasts the two deepest *cañons* (canyons) in the world, each of which is more than twice as deep as the USA's Grand Canyon.

MOST BIZARRE SIGHT

Biting into an unusual local delicacy – roasted cat – during the Fiesta de Señora del Rosario, held in October in the village of Huari.

'…the tough terrain will be nothing more than a distant memory once you find yourself face to face with a 200kg silverback.'

By Matthew Firestone

RWANDA

POPULATION 9.9 MILLION ✪ **CAPITAL** KIGALI ✪ **LANGUAGE** KINYARWANDA, FRENCH, ENGLISH, SWAHILI ✪ **UNIT OF CURRENCY** RWANDA FRANC (RFR) ✪ **COST INDEX** TRACKING MOUNTAIN GORILLAS (NOT GUERRILLAS) RFR272,000 (US$500), FRESH FISH DINNER RFR2700-5450 (US$5-10), 100KM BUS RIDE 1000RFR (US$2), ROOM AT THE ACTUAL HOTEL RWANDA RFR 54,500 (US$100)

A BRUTAL PAST

Mention Rwanda to just about anyone with a political consciousness, and images of one of the 20th century's most horrific genocides immediately comes to mind. On 6 April 1994, the assassination of President Juvénal Habyarimana ignited a powder keg of ethnic tensions between the Hutu and the Tutsi. In the approximately 100 days that followed, extremist Hutu formed two death squads known as the Interahamwe and the Impuzamugambi, which systematically butchered Tutsi men, women and children using nothing more than crude farming implements. While the soil of this tiny speck of a country ran red with the blood of the innocent, much of the world simply sat back and ignored the genocide. By mid-July, at least 500,000 Tutsis and thousands of moderate Hutus died, though some estimates for the total death toll are as high as one million.

A BRIGHT FUTURE

Although some scars will never fade away, much of Rwanda's wounds have healed over the past 15 years, and the country has done a remarkable job of getting back on its feet. While regional neighbours such Burundi and the Democratic Republic of Congo are struggling to maintain political stability, Rwanda is relatively safe and secure. As a result, tourists are once again returning to Le Pays des Milles Collines (Land of One Thousand Hills) and discovering lush jungles, towering volcanoes, and the 'gorillas in the mist' of Dian Fossey fame. Monkey business aside, the shores of Lake Kivu are home to some of the best inland beaches on the continent, while the montane rainforests of Parc National Nyungwe Forest are home to rare species of flora and fauna. Even in the capital city of Kigali, which was once the site of the some of the country's most brutal massacres, travellers are discovering an increasing number of sophisticated hotels, restaurants and nightlife spots.

DEFINING EXPERIENCE

No other experience in Rwanda is as definitive as trekking through Parc National des Volcans in search of the endangered mountain gorilla. Before you can lay eyes on this charismatic creature, you will need to navigate the bamboo- and rain-forested slopes of ancient volcanos. The trek is hard work, but the serene beauty of this primordial landscape is Africa at its best. And of course, the tough terrain will be nothing more than a distant memory once you find yourself

THE COWS WATCH THE BOYS WHILE THE GIRLS WATCH THE BULLS WHO WATCH THE WORLD GO BY, AT AKAGERA NATIONAL PARK

face to face with a 200kg silverback. Intimidating though they may be, gorillas are surprisingly tolerant of human visitors, though you're certainly going to want to give them the space (and respect) they deserve.

DIAN & HER GORILLAS

No discussion of Rwanda's mountain gorillas is complete without mentioning the name of Dian Fossey, the American zoologist who is largely to thank for their continued existence. In 1967 she established the Karisoke Research Center, a remote camp in the Virunga mountains, and began living amongst these gentle giants. Three years later, after a photograph of Fossey appeared on the cover of *National Geographic*, the plight of the endangered gorilla was thrust into the international spotlight. Although she was successful in breaking down the harmful King Kong image of the

gorilla, and was one of the great pioneers of the wildlife conservation movement, Fossey was brutally murdered in 1985. She was found dead in her cabin, her skull split open by a *panga*, a crude tool that was used at the time to poach gorillas. Today, she is buried next to Digit, a male gorilla that was killed and beheaded by poachers only a few years prior to her death.

FESTIVALS & EVENTS

✪ The Rwandans are not a particularly festive group of people, though this shouldn't come as a surprise given the dark history of the country. One exception is the annual Harvest Festival, which takes place on 1 August, and is celebrated with songs, dances, food, drink and a ritualistic ceremony known as Umuganura. If you can time your visit to Rwanda to coincide with this festival; it would be

an opportunity to see a more festive side of the country.

WHAT'S HOT...

The African sun: trekking though the rainforest is anything but a walk in the park, especially since you'll have to traverse mountains as high as 3000m. If you're planning a trip to Rwanda, it's best to come prepared for hot and sticky weather, rugged terrain and a whole assortment of creepy-crawlies.

...WHAT'S NOT

Tribal division: in modern-day Rwanda, there are no Hutus and Tutsis, only Rwandans. Idealistic it may be, but this is the only realistic hope for the future of the country.

'We know what you're thinking.
Blood Diamonds. Child soldiers. Summary amputations.
But that was then; this is now.'

By Tim Bewer

SIERRA LEONE

POPULATION 6.1 MILLION ✪ **CAPITAL** FREETOWN ✪ **LANGUAGES** KRIO, MENDE, TEMNE, ENGLISH
✪ **UNIT OF CURRENCY** LEONE (LE) ✪ **COST INDEX** MODERN BEACHFRONT CHALET LE120,000-190,000 (US$40-63),
HELICOPTER RIDE FROM LUNGI AIRPORT TO FREETOWN LE210,000 (US$70), BOTTLE OF STAR BEER LE2500 (US$0.85),
INTERNET ACCESS PER HOUR LE2500 (US$0.85)

ARE YOU SERIOUS?

Yeah, we know what you're thinking. Blood Diamonds. Child soldiers. Summary amputations. But that was then; this is now. Peace was declared back in 2002 and the country has been in reconciliation and under reconstruction ever since. That's not to ignore the problems – Sierra Leone ranks last in the United Nation's Human Development Index – but there is real reason for optimism.

In a development that could prove more important for the country's future than the end of the civil war, September 2007 brought about a peaceful change of government via the ballot box – an event that is, unfortunately, rather uncommon in Africa. And, so far anyway, President Koroma appears to be following through on his campaign pledge to tackle the country's culture of corruption. Though the election did largely follow ethnic lines, overall there is little discord between the various groups or between Muslims and Christians – in fact, mixed marriages are quite common. Sierra Leone has a mountain to climb, but it's on the way up.

BRAGGING RIGHTS

Before the war Sierra Leone was a steady player in Europe's packaged-holiday scene; and with some of the continent's most perfectly palm-lined sands - not to mention superb wildlife watching and other eco-tourism opportunities upcountry – it's bound to be the next Gambia. Changes are already under way with small, charming resorts popping up around the Freetown peninsula, and rumours swirling about far bigger projects. But right now you can easily have the white sands of Sussex, River Number Two, Kent and other lovely seaside spots or the riverside bungalows at Outamba-Kilimi National Park nearly, and sometimes completely, to yourself.

At some point we've all gone green with envy listening to some lucky bastard regale us with tales about what a place was like back in the day. Well, Sierra Leone is still in the early morning of its 'day'. So, whether you are here for the birds or the beaches, now is *your* chance to be the one who got there first.

DEFINING EXPERIENCE

Sip a fruit-infused cocktail from a hammock along the white-sand beaches of the Freetown peninsula one day, clear a path with a machete to track elephants at Outamba-Kilimi National Park or count primates at Tiwai Island Wildlife Sanctuary the next.

GIRLS HEADING TO SCHOOL IN FREETOWN SHOW WHAT YOU CAN DO WITH A HANDFUL OF HAIRBANDS

RECENT FAD

Electricity. Freetown hasn't had a steady supply of it since the 1980s (all hotels have generators), but the new government has made it a top priority. New generators have improved things immensely and locals are loving it. Good news for everyone except, that is, the people who sell candles.

FESTIVALS & EVENTS

✪ For some people Easter is all to do with hunting for chocolate bunnies and kaleidoscopic eggs but for the Sierra Leoneans Easter fun is all about kites – and on Easter Monday Lumley Beach in Freetown is packed with free-flying families.

✪ Impressive illuminated processions light up the Freetown night during the country's beloved Lantern Parade competition. The 2009 edition will snake through the streets on 27 April.

LIFE-CHANGING EXPERIENCES

✪ On Bunce Island, walking in the footsteps of slaves destined for Europe and the Americas.

✪ Seeing wild chimpanzees use stones as hammers to crack open nuts at Tiwai Island Wildlife Sanctuary.

✪ Watching the Single Leg Amputee Sports Club football team or other para-athletes, most of whom are war victims, in action.

RANDOM FACTS

✪ Freetown's Fourah Bay College, founded in 1827, became the first Western-style university in sub-Saharan Africa.

✪ The slaves aboard the *Amistad*, who revolted and commandeered the ship in 1839, were originally abducted from southern Sierra Leone.

✪ Mende society is one of the few in Africa where women do masked dances during sacred ceremonies.

✪ Over 660 species of bird have been recorded in Sierra Leone.

✪ Humpback whales can be seen off the Freetown peninsula in October and November.

✪ Life expectancy is just 41.8 years.

MOST BIZARRE SIGHT

Freetown's 500-year-old Cotton Tree isn't bizarre at all, but it is a little peculiar that this majestic shade-maker is one of the country's most important (and by far its most beloved) historic site. The first repatriated slaves settled around the tree; and before that people were bought and sold from this spot. There will be national mourning if it ever tumbles.

034
**BASQUE
COUNTRY,
FRANCE & SPAIN**

036
**BAY OF FIRES,
TASMANIA,
AUSTRALIA**

038
**THE ISLANDS OF
CHILOÉ, CHILE**

040
**HAWAI'I (THE
BIG ISLAND),
HAWAII**

042
**KO TAO,
THAILAND**

044
**LANGUEDOC,
FRANCE**

046
**NAM HA NATIONAL
PROTECTED AREA,
LAOS**

048
**SAN ANDRÉS &
PROVIDENCIA,
COLOMBIA**

050
**SVALBARD,
NORWAY**

052
**YUNNAN,
CHINA**

○ BASQUE COUNTRY,
FRANCE & SPAIN

'It's a country that's so complicated
its borders are marked on no maps…'

By Stuart Butler

BASQUE COUNTRY,
FRANCE & SPAIN

POPULATION 2.75 MILLION ○ **LANGUAGES** EUSKARA, SPANISH, FRENCH ○ **UNIT OF CURRENCY** EURO (€)
○ **MAJOR INDUSTRIES** TOURISM, CHEMICAL INDUSTRY ○ **COST INDEX** COFFEE SPAIN/FRANCE €1.50/2.50 (US$2.20/3.70),
MIDRANGE HOTEL DOUBLE/DORM BED €60/16 (US$90/25), SHORT TAXI RIDE €10 (US$15), INTERNET ACCESS PER HOUR €4
(US$6)

MODERN CAVEMEN

One country, two countries, seven provinces, one language, two languages –
this is the Basque Country. It's a country that's so complicated its borders are
marked on no maps, and when its name is spoken most of the world think
only of a saucy piece of lingerie. Yet this delicious chunk of mountain- and
ocean-fondled land is so ancient that its people claim, not unreasonably, to
be the oldest Europeans. These proud people have learnt to appreciate the
best of yesterday while embracing tomorrow, and by doing so they have
developed a nation, shared between France and Spain, in which almost
anything is possible.

FIESTA, FIESTA

Walkers fall head over heels for the Pyrenean vistas where huge vultures
soar on the thermals, art fans trip out on the futuristic fantasy of Bilbao's
Guggenheim Museum, as well as a flurry of more stately galleries, and
everyone loses control at all-night street parties a million people strong. It's
such a heady cocktail of fun, sun, culture and beauty that every other person
in Europe seems to want to be a part of it. With more and more budget
airlines connecting the region to the rest of the continent, 2009 looks set to be
the biggest year yet for tourist arrivals

DEFINING EXPERIENCE

The enviously green valleys of its mountains, home to spine-chilling witches
and ghosts, make for some of the most blissed-out walking in Europe.

On the higher slopes, punk-rock
snowboarders whiz off-piste in the
morning, before racing back to the
gorgeous beaches for an afternoon
in the sun sipping Perrier on Biarritz's
Grande Plage and surfing the best
waves in Europe.

RECENT FAD

Thanks both to epic waves and
a serious Hollywood makeover,
wannabe surfers from across Europe
are flocking in their thousands to the
numerous surf schools and camps
that have popped up everywhere
along the Basque coast.

FESTIVALS & EVENTS

○ Bilbao BBK in June is a three-day
music festival which was headlined in
2008 by *The Police*.
○ Los Sanfermines, in Pamplona from
6 to 14 July, is one of the world's most
outrageous, and famous, festivals.

THEY'RE HERE! THEY'RE ALIVE! LOUISE BOURGEOIS'S MASSIVE *MAMAN* SPIDER SCULPTURE OUTSIDE BILBAO'S GUGGENHEIM MUSEUM

More than just bull runs, drinking and naked people – it's also about choir singing and candlelight processions. Pass us another drink!

✪ For music lovers, the San Sebastián Jazz Festival blasts its bluesy tunes out in July.

✪ San Sebastián International Film Festival, one of Europe's most important film festivals, held in September, offers you the chance to try and woo a star or starlet.

LIFE-CHANGING EXPERIENCES

✪ Gorging on Spain's best tapas in San Sebastián.

✪ Hurtling over fresh powder, strapped to a snowboard, in the excellent, but relatively unknown ski-resorts.

✪ Cascading down a swirling mountain river in a kayak or raft.

✪ Swallowing half the Atlantic Ocean while attempting to surf Mundaka.

✪ Staring in awe at the impossibly pampered poodles of Biarritz.

✪ Indulge in the world's sexiest chocolate in Bayonne, the city that invented this culinary seventh heaven.

HOT TOPIC OF THE DAY

The region's popularity means that, for many, a simple two-week holiday isn't enough; locals are up in arms about rising house prices caused, partly, by *madrileños*, Parisians, English, Dutch and Germans snapping up second homes and holiday houses.

MOST BIZARRE SIGHT

The *encierro* of Pamplona is where hundreds of drunk men prove their manliness to the watching girls by getting mowed down by a herd of very large and very annoyed bulls charging through the streets. The girls just regard the men as very silly. In protest to the running of the bulls, the running

of the nudes, in which drunken men prove their manliness to the girls by running naked down the streets, also takes place in Pamplona. The girls just regard the men as a 'little' silly. Bayonne also hosts a particularly absurd *encierro* in which a nicely camouflaged black bull is released into the crowd in the pitch black of night...

LOCAL LINGO

It's said that the Basque language is a country. Certainly Euskara defines this country, and learning a few words of it will win you many friends. Except that mastering Euskara isn't simple – regarded by all and sundry as one of the hardest languages in the world to learn, it bears no relationship to any neighbouring language and nobody knows where it comes from – the Atlas mountains of North Africa have been mooted, as has Japan and the lost island of Atlantis!

'This is the Bay of Fires: the secret edge
of Tasmania, laid out like a pirate's treasure map…'

By Gabi Mocatta

BAY OF FIRES,
TASMANIA, AUSTRALIA

BAY OF FIRES, ✪
TASMANIA, AUSTRALIA

POPULATION 300 ✪ **LANGUAGE** AUSTRALIAN ✪ **UNIT OF CURRENCY** AUSTRALIAN DOLLAR (A$)
✪ **MAJOR INDUSTRIES** TOURISM, FISHING ✪ **COST INDEX** WHOLE CRAYFISH A$60 (US$55.20), BOTTLE OF BAY OF FIRES
TIGRESS RIESLING A$27 (US$24.80), DIVING CHARTER PER PERSON A$175 (US$161), NIGHT FOR TWO IN A BEACH HOUSE
A$150-250 (US$138-230), BEACHSIDE CAMPING WITH MILLION-DOLLAR OUTLOOK – FREE

PRIVATE PARADISE

White beaches of hourglass-fine sand, Bombay Sapphire–blue sea, an azure sky – and no one. This is the Bay of Fires: the secret edge of Tasmania, laid out like a pirate's treasure map of perfect beach after sheltered cove, studded with lichen-orange rock gardens and fringed with green forest. It's where you can always find a beach to yourself, and where the key ingredient is tranquillity.

LOW KEY OR NO KEY

You'll find no seaside high-rises or ice-cream vans here. The Bay of Fires has just two small fishing-and-holiday settlements, a tall granite lighthouse, and a 29km coastline of sand and surf. At bonny Binalong Bay there's a handful of low-key places to stay. This is just the spot for sunkissed beach holidays; a place to let one's hair get wind-tousled, and to grow salt crystals on the skin.

FAIREST OF THEM ALL

It's not long since this picture-perfect slice of coastline came to international attention. *Condé Nast Traveler* has named Bay of Fires one of the two best beaches in the world (actually the bay itself is made up of a string of superb beaches) so the crowds are bound to flock. Now is the time to visit this place of peace and dazzling beauty. Don't forget to pack your bathers.

DEFINING EXPERIENCE

The Bay of Fires Walk, a four-day guided beach hike that traces its way down the coastline and then arrives at the architectural wonder of the Bay of Fires Lodge. Both ardent epicures and hardened outdoor lovers catered for.

FESTIVALS & EVENTS

✪ The Swimcart Beach Fishing Championship, held April/May each year, is an exuberant community event – a weekend of beach camping, barbecues and Aussie mateship, where the beer flows freely and the catch of fish is almost incidental. The fish-off runs over two days and right through the night, and there prizes for almost anything, from the biggest fish to the unluckiest fisherman.

LIFE-CHANGING EXPERIENCES

✪ Watching your first Bay of Fires sunrise turn the sea to molten gold.
✪ Scuba diving in the crystalline waters of the Bay of Fires.
✪ Walking the bay's wild beaches, either on a multiday guided hike or a quiet afternoon's wanderings.

WINEGLASS BAY: WATERS AS DELICIOUS AS A BLUE MARGARITA, AND ICING-SUGAR SANDS ON THE SIDE

✪ Surfing the beach breaks at Binalong Bay.
✪ Kayaking the lagoons of Ansons River.
✪ Eating crayfish you've caught, or abalone you've just dived for.
✪ Falling asleep to the sound of the waves at a peaceful beachside camp.

HOT TOPIC OF THE DAY

Development. Now the Bay of Fires is hot, development by city slickers is on the cards. A block of land that cost A$20,000 in 1990 costs A$500,000 today. Locals are afraid of being edged out of their edge-of-the-world domain and fear the Bay of Fires will lose its down-to-earth character and blissful serenity.

MOST BIZARRE SIGHT

An underwater dragon. The strange weedy sea dragon – all fin and filigree – disguises itself as a frond of seaweed in the giant kelp forests of the Bay of Fires. Often spotted by divers.

LOCAL LINGO

The word 'abs' here refers not to the rippling muscles of your torso, but to blacklip abalone *(Haliotis rubra)* a marine delicacy that's abundant in the Bay of Fires.

REGIONAL FLAVOURS

Seafood, seafood and seafood. The rocky gulches Bay of Fires are home to large and succulent rock lobsters (known here as crayfish), oysters, mussels and, of course, abalone. Surf fishing yields Australian salmon, flathead and skate. Locals cook them on the beach – or they'll direct you one of Australia's best restaurants, Angasi, a surprising find at Binalong Bay. Come here for every sort of marine delicacy – or simply the heart-stopping views over the bay.

WHAT'S IN A NAME?

When he saw the fires lit by Aboriginal people on his visit in 1773, explorer Tobias Furneaux gave the bay its evocative name. Aboriginal people called the bay Larapuna. The Leenerrerter, Pinterrairer and Panpekanner tribes lived here for perhaps 30,000 years – evidence of their way of life is seen in the shell middens and artefacts scattered all along the coast.

WINTER: WILD & WONDERFUL

With all this talk of sand and sunshine, you might think the Bay of Fires is worth a visit only in summer. One of the joys of the Tasmanian winter is its preponderance of still, bright days, and freezing, starry nights. This is the time to wrap up warm for long beach walks, drink rich pinot noirs, stoke up the fire and watch shooting stars before bedtime.

'This misty archipelago with splendid emerald curves is the distilled, 80-proof version of traditional Chile.'

By Carolyn McCarthy

THE ISLANDS OF CHILOÉ, CHILE

THE ISLANDS OF CHILOÉ, CHILE

POPULATION 180,000 ✪ **CAPITAL** CASTRO ✪ **LANGUAGES** SPANISH, HUILLICHE ✪ **UNIT OF CURRENCY** CHILEAN PESO (CH$) ✪ **MAJOR INDUSTRIES** SALMON AND MUSSEL FARMING, SUBSISTENCE AGRICULTURE ✪ **COST INDEX** FERRY RIDE FROM THE MAINLAND CH$7000 (US$16), PLATE OF OYSTERS CH$4300 (US$10), FOUR DAYS KAYAKING THE ARCHIPELAGO CH$229,000 (US$530)

OF POETS & POTATO FARMERS

With a newly inaugurated ecological reserve and the country's oldest agro-tourism network, Chiloé has adventure on tap. This misty archipelago with splendid emerald curves is the distilled, 80-proof version of traditional Chile. Just ask the potato farmer selling his poetry chapbooks at the village fair.

MODERN FOLKLORIC

Go with your raingear and a sense of adventure but shuck romantic notions. Witches and ghost ships may go bump in the night, but modernity is on the march. There's good and bad: circular salmon cages have replaced the *pincoya* (a seductive, ship-sinking mermaid) out in the bay, but Castro's cool Museo de Arte Moderno de Chiloé is a worthy heir to Chiloé's shingled churches – the latter Unesco World Heritage sites that fuse European and indigenous influences.

FROM RECOVERY TO REDISCOVERY

In hard times Chilotes deserted their homeland in droves to find work as craftsmen, cowboys and sailors. But budding industry and tourism see new generations returning and reclaiming Chiloé as a creative space. That mythology and mysticism still thrive is the true wonder. Find it for yourself – walk the windy western coast, watch village weavers and meet taciturn locals. This place is about survival.

DEFINING EXPERIENCE

Breaking a sweat at a *minga* – a community effort that means transporting a house with pulleys, oxen and all the muscle in the barrio. Your reward? Taking part in the massive pig roast that typically follows, dancing with old men in fedoras and sipping moonshine cider.

RECENT FAD

Think old school with a twist: artisan collectives, renovated *palafitos* (stilt houses) and recycled alerce hardwood. For visitors, connect with cultural roots: try a family homestay, outdoor lamb roast, or island-hopping via wooden fishing boat.

FESTIVALS & EVENTS

✪ Semanas Costumbristas (cultural weeks) take place in summer, in January and February. Slurp steamed shellfish and get jiggy with the locals.
✪ La Feria de Biodiversidad brings rural folk to Castro to trade seeds and share prize pigs, weavings and poetry chapbooks, from 11 to 15 February.
✪ Cucao's Full Moon Festival is on 20 February in 2009.

ALL WHITE IS ALL RIGHT AT THE SOLEMN GOOD FRIDAY PROCESSION ON THE ISLANDS OF CHILOÉ

❂ Noche de San Juan, in Castro on June 23, offers a glimpse of traditional culture and the syncretism of Chilote mythology and Catholicism.

❂ The Festival de Caguach celebrates the Franciscan effort at making peace in hostile islands via a travelling party that featured a statue of Christ. The journey from Tenaun to Caguach is re-created on 30 August.

LIFE-CHANGING EXPERIENCES

❂ Paddling on foggy waters via kayak to remote outlying islands.

❂ Galloping the mist-soaked coastline of Parque Nacional de Chiloé on horseback.

❂ Grooving to jazz-infused Mexican ranchera music at Cucao's Full Moon Festival.

❂ Spotting the largest animal on earth – the blue whale – as well as penguins near the rocky coast of Puñihuil.

DEFINING DIFFERENCE

Rain, the thick cover of mist and vivid imaginations forge a world of its own. Fatherless babies are known as the children of *trauco*, a virgin-seducing forest troll in island mythology.

LOCAL LINGO

Chilotes say, *'Yo no creo en brujos pero que los hay, los hay.'* (I don't believe in witches, but they do exist.)

WHAT'S HOT...

Protecting primary resources. The newly inaugurated Parque Tantauco is the latest addition to Chile's red-hot private conservation trend. Hiking trails explore 120,000 hectares of virgin forest and remote coastline.

...WHAT'S NOT

Broken promises. Locals clamour for improved infrastructure, but the whopping US$930-million price tag on a proposed Chacao Channel bridge to the mainland forced the Chilean Public Works to renege on an old promise.

HOT TOPIC OF THE DAY

A bridge or a tunnel to the mainland would undoubtedly mean improved services, but some locals worry that easy access would corrupt island culture.

RANDOM FACTS

❂ Chiloé has 43 islands – many of which still don't have electricity.

❂ Chiloé produces almost half the fish for Chile's US$2.2 billion salmon-farming industry.

REGIONAL FLAVOURS

It doesn't get more local than *curanto*: shellfish, meat, poultry, sausages and potatoes wrapped in table-sized nalca leaves and steamed in the earth.

' …this oversized, "hang loose, brah" place has all the necessary tropical delights (plus lava-spewing volcanoes!), and it's less crowded and less expensive.'

HAWAI'I
(THE BIG ISLAND), HAWAII

By Jeff Campbell

HAWAI'I (THE BIG ISLAND), HAWAII

POPULATION 171,200 ✪ **LANGUAGES** OFFICIAL, ENGLISH AND HAWAIIAN; UNOFFICIAL, PIGDIN ✪ **UNIT OF CURRENCY** US DOLLAR (US$) ✪ **MAJOR INDUSTRY** TOURISM ✪ **COST INDEX** HOTEL HILO-SIDE/KONA-SIDE US$90-110/110-135, ALOHA SHIRT US$20-70, SNORKEL RENTAL PER WEEK US$15-20, PINT OF KONA BREWING COMPANY PIPELINE PORTER US$5

PARADISE TO DA MAX

If the four main Hawaiian islands were siblings, O'ahu would be the responsible elder brother, Maui the sexy flirt, Kaua'i the earnest artist, and the Big Island the underachieving pigdin-spouting goof-off, cracking wise at the back of class. All offer compelling takes on paradise, but you know who keeps it real and has the most fun. Seriously – the Big Island often gets dismissed because it's less polished and less glam. But this oversized, 'hang loose, brah' place has all the necessary tropical delights (plus lava-spewing volcanoes!), and it's less crowded and less expensive. Isn't that what everyone's looking for in a Hawaiian adventure?

HOT LAVA, SNOWY MOUNTAINS

Variety defines the Big Island. It's stargazing from wintry Mauna Kea, riding horses over grassy ranch land, hiking to rainforest-shrouded waterfalls and tripping across blackened lava wastelands until you're face to face (if you're lucky) with glowing magma – oh, and baking to a crisp on white-sand (and black-sand and green-sand!) beaches. Scruffy, workaday Hilo is an authentic experience of multicultural Hawaii, as are lost-in-time plantation towns, where friendly locals still offer travellers a *shaka* ('hang loose') now and then.

FESTIVALS & EVENTS

✪ Think hula is grass skirts and coconut bras? Attend Hilo's Merry Monarch Festival, a week-long event that starts Easter Sunday, to witness serious hula competitions and true Hawaiian dance.

✪ From late August to early October, all of Hawaii celebrates the Aloha Festival. On the Big Island, the series of cultural events includes a royal Native Hawaiian procession on the rim of Halema'uma'u Crater.

✪ In late October, over 1700 spandex-clad athletes descend on the Big Island to prove their mettle (metal?) in the Ironman Triathlon, one of the world's ultimate endurance contests.

✪ For a fortnight during the November coffee harvest, the Kona Coffee Cultural Festival is when java lovers raise a jittery cup to the Big Island's famous bean: tasting competitions, coffee-picking races, parades, tours and more.

LIFE-CHANGING EXPERIENCES

✪ Hiking across the goddess Pele's ruinous home, the ominously steaming, still-living Kilauea Caldera in Hawai'i Volcanoes National Park.

LAVA NEVER LOOKED SO GOOD: GETTING UP CLOSE AND PERSONAL WITH KILAUEA AT THE HAWAI'I VOLCANOES NATIONAL PARK

✪ Getting drunk on the pulsing spiritual mana of magical Waipi'o Valley: emerald cliffs, waterfalls and a thunderous black-sand beach.

✪ Standing atop the 4170m volcano Mauna Loa, lost for breath.

✪ Night diving with manta rays, swimming with sea turtles, snorkelling with *humuhumunukunukuapua'a*.

✪ Pondering ancient fates in the shadows of tikis at the Native Hawaiian place of refuge, Pu'uhonua o Honaunau.

HOT TOPIC

The three biggest island issues – affordable housing, environmental impacts and sustainable tourism – are interrelated. Locals can't afford their own piece of paradise anymore, which is threatened daily by invasive species, rampant construction and travellers' feet.

RANDOM FACTS

✪ There are only 12 letters in the Hawaiian alphabet.

✪ Hawaii is the most isolated spot on earth, over 2000 miles from any continent.

✪ Hawaii has no ethnic or racial majority. Everyone is a minority.

STRANGEST PLACE

Puna, hands down. From cinder-cone saunas filled with naked hippies to lava-buried neighbourhoods, from Native Hawaiian sovereignty activists to the rambling Maku'u Farmers Market, Puna is a kooky mashup of eccentric personalities and hallucinatory scenery.

NO TALK LI' DAT

Eavesdrop on locals 'talking story' and you'll hear them slip into syrupy, fun-loving pigdin. A legacy of Hawaii's multiethnic sugar plantations, pigdin sounds like broken English but is considered a language. Here's some common slang: *brah* (buddy, friend); *grinds* (food); *haole* (Caucasian, or foreigner); *howzit* (what's up?); *lolo* (crazy stupid); *ono* (delicious); *rubbah slippah* (sandals); *shaka* (right on!, or a Hawaiian hand greeting).

REGIONAL FLAVOURS

From greasy local *grinds* to traditional Native Hawaiian food to gourmet Hawaii regional cuisine, you are in for nonstop culinary fun. For local treats and tastes, ask anyone to point you to the nearest *loco moco, laulau, kalua* pork, *poke*, ice shave, Spam *musubi, malasadas,* Japanese *mochi* and crackseed. Or just go to Hilo.

For Pacific Rim-Hawaiian sustainably farmed fusion delicacies of the highest order, make sure you reserve a table at Merriman's in Waimea.

'...tiny Tao sure knows how to pack it in – there's something for everyone, and nothing is in moderation.'

O KO TAO, THAILAND

By Brandon Presser

KO TAO, THAILAND

POPULATION 5000, AND GROWING FAST ✪ **LANGUAGE** THAI (ENGLISH COMMONLY SPOKEN) ✪ **MAJOR INDUSTRY** TOURISM ✪ **UNIT OF CURRENCY** THAI BAHT (B) ✪ **COST INDEX** OPEN WATER DIVING CERTIFICATION 3½-DAY COURSE 9800B (US$300), SNORKELLING EQUIPMENT RENTAL PER DAY 150B (US$5), MOTORBIKE 24-HOUR RENTAL 200B (US$6), AIR-CON BUNGALOW 1500B (US$46), GREEN CURRY 80B (US$2.50)

(KO) TAO-ISM

First there was Ko Samui, then Ko Pha-Ngan; now, the cult of Ko Tao has emerged along Thailand's crystalline Gulf Coast. Today, thousands of visitors come to worship the turquoise waters offshore, and quite often many of them stay. The secret to Ko Tao's undeniable appeal? Simple: although the island is only a quarter the size of Manhattan, tiny Tao sure knows how to pack it in – there's something for everyone, and nothing is in moderation. Diving enthusiasts cavort with sharks and rays in a playground of tangled neon coral. Hikers and hermits can re-enact an episode of *Lost* in the dripping coastal jungles. And when you're Robinson Crusoe-ed out, hit the bumpin' bar scene that rages on until dawn.

It's been several years since the first backpacker came to the scrubby island and planted a flag in the name of self-respecting shoestring travellers everywhere. But fret not, there's still plenty of time to join the tribe. Ko Tao has many years to go before corporate resort-owners bulldoze rustic seaside cottages, and the chatter around private infinity pools replaces musings about sea creatures and mixed drinks.

TOO COOL FOR SCHOOL

The shallow bays that scallop the island are the perfect spot for virgin divers to take their first stab at scuba. On shore, over 40 dive centres are ready to saddle you up with some gear and teach you the ropes in a 3½-day open-water certification course. We know, we know, homework on a holiday sucks, but the intense competition among scuba schools means that certification prices are unbeatably low, and the standards of service are top-notch.

A WHALE OF A TIME

Wake up at the crack of dawn to be the first diver hitting the waves at Chumphon Pinnacle or Sail Rock; arguably the two hottest scuba spots in the Gulf of Thailand. Lucky divers will chance upon a school bus–sized whale shark. After a day of blowing bubbles, grab a sunset cocktail and swap exaggerated stories of seeing a shark 'THIS BIG!', then stumble back to your beachside bamboo hut to lather, rinse and repeat.

ALWAYS A REASON TO CELEBRATE

✪ On the eve of every full moon, everyone hops next door to the island of Ko Pha-Ngan, joining other party pilgrims as they trance the night away with body paint and glow sticks.

MAKE LIKE THE LITTLE MERMAID IN KO TAO'S WIDE BLUE YONDER

✪ Hidden jungle parties are all the buzz. Check out the flyers posted on the walls at the 7-Elevens in Sairee (Sai Ri) Village; there's usually a gathering every few weeks in the steamy rainforest, celebrating nothing in particular.

✪ When someone finishes their lengthy Divemaster certification (usually every few days somewhere on the island), a graduation celebration always ensues. There are cocktails by the bucketful (literally) and drinking games using snorkels in creative ways.

RANDOM FACTS

✪ The little island certifies more divers than any other place in the world.

✪ Ko Tao was once a penal colony for Thailand's fiercest criminals.

✪ Pirates used the island as a hidden hangout as recently as 40 years ago.

✪ Ko Tao means 'Turtle Island', although no one's quite sure why – some people think the island is shaped vaguely like a tortoise, others attribute the moniker to the crowds of nesting turtles that used to spawn along the shores.

HOT TOPICS

✪ Taste the rainbow. Ko Tao's inexplicable magnetism encourages loads of visitors to permanently hang up their rucksack. In the past, freshly minted expats became diving instructors, but as the market becomes saturated many newcomers are using their native savoir-faire to start up their own restaurants and bars. Now, in addition to the usual Thai faves, there's a palette (and palate) of exciting international flavours, from traditional French and Italian cuisine to more exotic African and Mexican fare.

✪ Water conservation. Rapid development has put a strain on the island's natural resources; expats are banding together to push forth legislation promoting grey water renewal and refiltration.

LOCAL LINGO

Due to the steady influx of international visitors, English is spoken just about everywhere. However, the locals on this scuba-savvy island regularly incorporate diving sign-language symbols into common parlance – especially at the bars. Here are a few gestures to get you started:

✪ I'm OK – make a fist and tap the top of your head twice.

✪ Cool – bring together the tips of your index finger and thumb forming an 'O'.

✪ I'm finished/I'm ready to go – hold your hand tight like a karate chop and quickly swing it back and forth perpendicular to your neck.

LANGUEDOC, FRANCE

'Spiky interior versus coastal plain;
deep chestnut forests against vast rolling vineyards;
fisherfolk and shepherds…'

By Miles Roddis

LANGUEDOC, FRANCE

POPULATION 2.5 MILLION ✪ **MAIN TOWN** MONTPELLIER ✪ **LANGUAGE** FRENCH ✪ **UNIT OF CURRENCY** EURO (€) ✪ **MAJOR INDUSTRIES** WINE, TOURISM ✪ **COST INDEX** 1L OF PETROL €1.30 (US$2), HOTEL DOUBLE/DORM ROOM FROM €50/15 (US$75/22), DONKEY TO CARRY YOUR TREKKING GEAR PER DAY/WEEK €45/245 (US$67/365), CANOE HIRE PER DAY €20 (US$30)

COMING OF AGE

Languedoc, sometime Cinderella of the south, was once overshadowed by its Midi sisters: gorgeous, mature Provence and the brash Côte d'Azur. Not any more. Now she stands as their equal, displaying a discreet charm that her flaunting, more-visited siblings long ago lost.

THE HIGH & LOW OF IT

Spiky interior versus coastal plain; deep chestnut forests against vast rolling vineyards; fisherfolk and shepherds: Haut- (high) and Bas- (low) Languedoc could scarcely contrast more sharply. Bas-Languedoc, stretching inland from its long, sandy beaches and shallow lagoons has the only sizeable towns: Montpellier, dynamic city of high-tech industry where one in three inhabitants is a student, Sète, France's largest Mediterranean fishing port and Nîmes, whose Roman heritage regularly pokes through. Haut Languedoc, split by deep gorges and topped by wild, upland plateaus, is for outdoor fun. It's a place for dissenters, from the medieval Cathars and Protestant Camisards of the 18th century to José Bové, wrecker of McDonalds, destroyer of genetically modified seed, folk hero to some and charlatan to others.

DEFINING EXPERIENCE

Drifting down the Gorges du Tarn in canoe or kayak, pulling in for a riverside picnic and feeling oh so superior to the perspiring motorists as they inch their way along the narrow road above you.

FESTIVALS & EVENTS

✪ On the third Sunday in January, gourmets flock to the Journée de la Truffe, in Uzès, the little hill town known for its truffle fair.
✪ In May, France's slickest breakdancers and freestylists compete in the Zenith arena, in Montpellier, at the Battle of the Year.
✪ On 14 July Carcassonne blazes with fireworks that rival Paris' own pyrotechnics at L'Embrasement de la Cité (Setting La Cité Ablaze).
✪ At Sète's Fête de la St-Louis, in August, there are six frantic days of *joutes nautiques*, where the crews of competing boats try to tilt their rivals into the sea.

HOT TOPIC OF THE DAY

As the French quaff less wine and the competition internationally becomes keener, how can Languedoc – for too long now regarded as a gushing

WITH WALLS LIKE THESE, WHO CARES ABOUT THEIR ENEMIES? THE FORTIFICATIONS AT AIGUES-MORTES KEEP THE CITY'S CASSOULETS SAFE FOR ITS RESIDENTS

fountain of cheap and plentiful plonk – upgrade its image?

MOST BIZARRE SIGHT

A scruffy mongrel dog padding along a trail in the Parc National des Cévennes, its provisions strapped to its back.

OCCITAN

Once spoken widely in southern France (it gave its alternative name, *langue d'oc*, to the region), Occitan is nowadays severely in decline and used mostly by older people in rural areas.

CASSOULET

Three towns claim the origin of this lipsmacking stew of white beans, sausage and hunks of duck and pork. To settle the dispute, a 19th-century writer proclaimed 'Cassoulet is the god of Occitan cuisine. The Castelaudary version is God the Father, that of Carcassonne is God

the Son, while Toulouse's is the Holy Spirit'. This truly divine dish gets its name from the *cassolo*, the Occitan term for the glazed earthenware bowl in which it gently simmers.

RANDOM FACTS

✪ When Levi Strauss was making tough trousers for Californian gold miners, he imported blue *serge de Nîmes* – named after Languedoc's second city, now known as denim.

✪ A workforce of 15,000 shifted seven million cubic metres of earth in only 15 years to build the 17th-century, 240km-long Canal du Midi.

✪ The Perrier factory near Nîmes fills 400 million stubby green bottles of mineral water each year.

✪ An astounding 2250 different plants have been logged in the Parc National des Cévennes.

✪ More than a third of France's grapes ripen in Languedoc.

✪ In high summer, the naturist village at Cap d'Agde has around 40,000 naked bodies.

LIFE-CHANGING EXPERIENCES

✪ Following in the footsteps of Robert Louis Stevenson and his wayward donkey, Modestine, as you trek the long-distance trail that bears his name.

✪ Slipping down to the massive, three-tiered Pont du Gard Roman aqueduct at night, once the last of its 15,000-daily summertime visitors have moved on.

✪ Whizzing down the Causse Méjean, the wind howling in your ears and the chain of your mountain bike singing with you.

✪ Getting butterflies as you peer down the near-vertical drop from the Cathar mountain-fortress of Peyrepertuse.

✪ Tying up, at the end of a day's lazy cruising, along the Canal du Midi.

'Die-hard adventurers can tackle leeches and thigh-destroying slopes on a true jungle trek…'

NAM HA NATIONAL
PROTECTED AREA, LAOS

By Justine Vaisutis

NAM HA NATIONAL PROTECTED AREA, LAOS

POPULATION LUANG NAM THA TOWN 35,400, LUANG NAM THA PROVINCE 145,000 ✪ **LANGUAGE** LAO ✪ **UNIT OF CURRENCY** LAO KIP ✪ **MAJOR INDUSTRY** ECOTOURISM ✪ **COST INDEX** 660ML BOTTLE OF BEERLAO 9300 KIP (US$1), HOTEL DOUBLE 46,500 KIP (US$5), INTERNET ACCESS PER HOUR 16740 KIP (US$1.80)

ECOTOURISM IN A FINAL FRONTIER

Preserved in time by the mighty Mekong to the west and China's great girth to the north, Luang Nam Tha, the northwesternmost province of Laos, shelters shattered fugitives of urban routine and flips them back into the world with a renewed love for the unknown. The gem in this rugged pocket is the Nam Ha National Protected Area (Nam Ha NPA) – 222,400 hectares of untamed forest which occupies around one-third of the province. The jungles, mountains, waterfalls, rivers and lofty plateaus of Nam Ha NPA, coupled with the culture of some 30 ethnic groups, creates the ideal landscape for trekking; in this conservation area, ecotrekking is the speciality. Paying the concept more than just lip-service, the local tourism board controls visitor numbers via organised trek–access only, in order to ensure the biodiversity of this precious region is preserved for as long as possible. This provides the visiting trekker with a small-group experience (six to 10 people), accompanied by two local guides who can provide insight into the flora, fauna, people and folklore of the area. The multilingual guides are recruited from a pool of 30 or so, and each leads one trek a month. This ensures that guides don't abandon their traditional source of income, and the distribution of the tourist dollar is as equitable as possible. Pretty enlightened, yeah?

DEFINING EXPERIENCES

✪ Die-hard adventurers can tackle leeches and thigh-destroying slopes on a true jungle trek, departing from Luang Nam Tha town in the north of the province.

✪ Budding anthropologists can people-watch by ambling through ethnic villages, on a tour from Muang Sing village in the west.

✪ Those who want it all can combine both by taking in a tour from Vieng Phoukha in the south, and indulging in an even mix of village visits and trekking.

FESTIVALS & EVENTS

✪ On the full moon of the 12th lunar month each year (which is due to fall in December in 2009), the bucolic and sedate village of Muang Sing goes nuts during the That Xieng Tung Festival. Half the entire province floods into town to celebrate, and the sound of dancing, dining, music and fire crackers endures well into the night. The festival combines Theravada Buddhism and animistic elements of worship and proves that monks certainly know how to party!

A BIT OF HOLY PEDAL-POWER, IN KEEPING WITH THE EMPHASIS ON ALL THINGS ECO, IN LUANG NAM THA

LIFE-CHANGING EXPERIENCES

✪ Staying overnight in an Akha mountain village (the Akha are woodsmen whose affinity with the forest gives them legendary status), a one-day walk from the nearest road and a good five years from running water and constant electricity.

✪ Dining on the feathered meal that was running around your feet several hours prior but has since been cooked by the village gentlemen.

✪ Ending the evening with a traditional Akha massage from budding apprentices under the age of 10.

✪ If you're *truly* lucky...OK, miraculously lucky, you might spot a clouded leopard or an Asiatic elephant.

OOPS, THERE GOES ANOTHER RUBBER TREE...

Rubber planting has made incursions into Nam Ha NPA despite its status as an Asean Natural Heritage Site.

The biodiversity of Nam Ha NPA and its surrounding forests is some of the richest in Southeast Asia. Clearing tracts of this forest to plant rubber trees erodes the soil and impacts on the flora and fauna. In some areas these monocrop plantations have resulted in flooding (the indigenous landscape would previously have absorbed the heavy rains) that has caused death and environmental devastation.

So what is hot? Contributing to the financial clout of the ecotourism industry and practising responsible traveller behaviour to ensure a more sustainable future for all of the region's living inhabitants.

REGIONAL FLAVOURS

A jungle trek in Nam Ha generally involves a lunch of grilled fish, vegetable salad, roasted peanuts and lashings of sticky rice. The whole lot is served on freshly cut palm leaves,

and the dining table is a patch of cleared earth. In the restaurants of Luang Nam Tha's towns and villages, the unadventurous can tuck into *super* fresh chicken and Laos staples like *láap* (shredded meat served with lime juice, garlic, green onions, mint leaves and chilli). *Fŏe* (hot rice-noodle soup served with lettuce, mint, basil, coriander, lime and chilli) is also a core menu item. For the brave there's a host of new consuming experiences, particularly in smaller towns and villages. Don't be surprised if you're offered barbecued dog (with a dipping sauce made from the liver) or lower-intestine soup. Protein comes in the form of civets (think a cross between a cat and a ferret) and other wild meat, including birdlife. Tempting though it may be to sample the game of Luang Nam Tha's forests, bear in mind that much of it is endangered and you'll only be reducing the already dwindling numbers.

'Clamber up to the hammock swaying over the sea and soak it all in.'

By Michael Kohn

SAN ANDRÉS & PROVIDENCIA, COLOMBIA

POPULATION 80,000 ✪ **CAPITAL** SAN ANDRÉS TOWN ✪ **LANGUAGES** SAN ANDRÉS AND PROVIDENCIA CREOLE, ENGLISH, SPANISH ✪ **MAJOR INDUSTRIES** TOURISM, FISHING ✪ **UNIT OF CURRENCY** COLOMBIAN PESO (COP) ✪ **COST INDEX** DINNER AT A DECENT RESTAURANT COP 28,500 (US$15), BUDGET DOUBLE ROOM COP 44,000 (US$23), INTERNET ACCESS PER HOUR COP 2000 (US$1), BOTTLE OF ÁGUILA BEER COP 2000 (US$1), SCOOTER HIRE PER DAY COP 47,500 (US$25)

PAVING PARADISE

Had Joni Mitchell visited San Andrés instead of Hawaii, the lyrics to *Big Yellow Taxi* might have gone something like: 'They paved paradise and put up a duty-free shopping mall'. Fortunately, commercialisation of San Andrés and Providencia was restricted to the island capital, leaving the rest of the archipelago mercifully underdeveloped. These two main islands have a yin and yang quality. San Andrés, the main commercial centre, offers jet skis, submarine rides, Segway tours and plentiful booze. Providencia is content with giving away dreamy seascapes and genuine island hospitality. In the end they balance each other out, giving visitors a cut of the urban fabric and beach activities, plus a good dose of *Castaway*.

THE YIN

Colombians get giddy at the thought of duty-free shopping and head straight for the high street on San Andrés. Improvements downtown include a new beachside promenade and renovated resorts, but the inland neighbourhoods remain rough and ramshackle. There are good deals at the seaside resorts but foreign tourists invariably make a beeline for San Luis, a laid-back settlement 15 minutes down the coast. The paved road continues right round the island: a 30km loop along the shore and through the hilly, forested interior.

THE YANG

If San Andrés feels slightly overdeveloped, hop on a flight to Providencia. Fifteen minutes are all that's needed to cover the 90km between the islands. Lush, sparsely populated and welcoming, Providencia feels like Fantasy Island sans Mr Roarke and Tattoo. All 4500 residents seem to know each other and visitors are taken in like family. Activities include scuba diving, chilling out at the famed Roland Roots Bar and daydreaming on the palm-fringed beaches. Transport consists of hopping on the back of any passing motorbike until you've worked your way round the island. It's that kinda place.

DEFINING EXPERIENCE

A fish dinner at Roland Roots Bar at Bahía Manzanillo on Providencia – think Robinson Crusoe's pad and throw in a bandstand. What makes it special is Rastafarian host Roland, a ball of energy who scampers up the trees for ripe coconuts, dives into the sea with his dog, plays Frisbee against the wind, carves driftwood and belts guitar riffs into the jungle. Clamber up

MACAW BLIMEY: WHAT'S A MAN WITHOUT HIS PARROTS ON A SAN ANDRÉS BEACH?

to the hammock swaying over the sea and soak it all in.

RECENT FAD

Segway guided tours of San Andrés. We're not kidding.

FESTIVALS & EVENTS

✪ In April, the islands hold the Festival de la Luna Verde (Green Moon Festival), which features reggae music, colourful costumes, dancing and late-night beach parties.

✪ The flower festival, held in San Andrés in August, has street performers and a parade with decorations filled with (can you guess?) colourful flowers.

✪ Colombian Independence Day, on July 20, is another excuse for music, food and merrymaking. In 2007, Colombian President Álvaro Uribe sent 1200 Colombian troops to march in the parade; a little reminder about who runs the islands.

HOT TOPIC OF THE DAY

Independence. The home-grown nonviolent separatist movement known as the Archipelago Movement for Ethnic Native Self-Determination wants to cede from Colombian rule. In June 2007 the group symbolically replaced Colombian flags around the island with the flag of the Raizal independence movement.

RANDOM FACTS

✪ In 2000, San Andrés and Providencia were declared a Unesco World Biosphere Reserve.

✪ In 1670 lpirate Henry Morgan based himself on Providencia, launching raids on Panama and Santa Marta.

✪ Nicaragua periodically stakes a territorial claim on the island chain. San Andrés is only 225km east of Nicaragua.

✪ The population of San Andrés and Providencia includes 35,000 Raizals (as the English-speaking locals are known).

MOST BIZARRE SIGHT

Hoyo Soplador. This natural hole in the rock over the sea spouts water 20m into the air when the tide is right. Come at sunset, when the orange background adds to the beauty of the sight.

REGIONAL FLAVOURS

Seafood is a way of life; get used to an abundance of fish, conch and lobster. The local delicacy *rondón* consists of fish, sea snails, cassava, yams, pigtail, conch, plantain and coconut milk. On Providencia don't miss Café Studio, run by a Canadian woman named Mary. Her baked conch and key lime pie are so well known that a Colombian businessman once flew a private jet to the island to pick up 12 orders for a party back on the mainland!

○ SVALBARD, NORWAY

'Svalbard ("cold coast" in Norwegian) is Europe's most northerly land mass and the planet's northernmost permanently inhabited spot.'

By Miles Roddis

SVALBARD, NORWAY

POPULATION 2600 ✪ **ONLY TOWN** LONGYEARBYEN, HOME TO 2100 OF THOSE 2600 ✪ **LANGUAGES** NORWEGIAN, RUSSIAN ✪ **MAJOR INDUSTRIES** TOURISM, COAL MINING ✪ **UNIT OF CURRENCY** NORWEGIAN KRONE (NKR) ✪ **COST INDEX** GLASS OF BEER NKR40 (US$7.50), HOTEL DOUBLE/DORM ROOM NKR1500/300 (US$280/55), FOUR-HOUR DOG SLEDDING NKR800 (US$150), DAY SNOWMOBILE SAFARI NKR2050 (US$385), 11-DAY CRUISE FROM NKR23,800 (US$4500).

THE NORTHERN SUPERLATIVE

This sprawling archipelago, which is about the size of Ireland or West Virginia, is barely 1300km – a mere snowball's throw, in relative terms – from the North Pole.

Svalbard ('cold coast' in Norwegian) is Europe's most northerly land mass and the planet's northernmost permanently inhabited spot. Belonging to Norway, it's also the most readily accessible hunk of polar north for visitors. Here too, the world's northernmost busts of Lenin still stand proud in the Russian mining settlements of Barentsburg and the now-abandoned Pyramiden!

HOSTILE LAND, BOUNTEOUS SEA

Well over half of Svalbard's islands and skerries are blanketed permanently in snow and ice. Except for the jungle greenness in the cosy glasshouse of Mary-Ann's Polarigg restaurant, you won't find a single plant taller than your ankle (but what variety if you stoop to look during the brief summer flowering). By contrast, the surrounding sea, watery home to seals, walruses and polar bears, is a soup of maritime riches, from microscopic plankton to beluga whales.

START SAVING

Norway is Europe's most expensive destination and Svalbard hurts even more. Seek consolation in alcohol, here free of all duty, as you watch your bank account haemorrhage.

DEFINING EXPERIENCE

Your first glimpse through the aircraft porthole of craggy peaks, dark fjords, glaciers and snow of the purest white.

FESTIVALS & EVENTS

✪ Polar Jazz is a long weekend of jazz in January
✪ Week-long celebrations at Sunfest, in early March, dispel the polar night.
✪ A chromatically appropriate five-day jam session in late October, the Blues Festival marks the onset of winter.

LIFE-CHANGING EXPERIENCES

✪ Scudding over the snow in the bruise-purple winter light as the huskies yap and strain.
✪ Spotting, from the safety of a boat (the nearest you'll get), a mother polar bear and her roly-poly cub.
✪ Crunching your crampons on Longyearbreen glacier, then fossicking for fossils just below the ice line.

BRIGHTLY PAINTED HUTS LIGHT UP THE GLOAMING IN LONGYEARBYEN, WHICH SITS THROUGH MORE THAN THREE MONTHS OF DARKNESS EACH YEAR

✪ Experiencing dawn on 14 February, when the sun peeks above the horizon for the first time in more than three months.

✪ Gazing over the reassuringly deep valley to the spot where, your guide tells you with unnecessary relish, a polar bear last ate a human.

HOT TOPICS OF THE DAY

✪ How long will the ice last? In the last 30 years, average temperatures have increased by 6°C. Will there be any summer snow cover in 50 years' time?

✪ Will there still be polar bears? It's far from a rhetorical question; worst case scenarios predict their extinction within half a century.

✪ Can Svalbard exploit its untapped mineral wealth (gold reserves that may be as rich as South Africa's, plus rich oil and gas deposits) while retaining its pristine, wilderness quality?

MOST BIZARRE SIGHT

Fresh-faced teenage trekking-guides with a rifle nonchalantly slung over the shoulder in case of polar-bear attack.

DEFINING DIFFERENCE

Svalbard is Norway enhanced: colder, purer (but for its scruffy, limited coal mining legacy), more sparsely populated, more expensive – and a cool 1000km nearer to the North Pole. It's also the only place in Europe where polar bears roam.

THE SVALBARD GLOBAL SEED VAULT

Beneath the permafrost outside Longyearbyen, a manmade cavern can store up to 4.5 million seeds from around the world, slumbering there in deepfreeze at a constant temperature of -18°C. So, if a species becomes extinct in its native habitat, it can be revived, reproduce and live on.

RANDOM FACTS

✪ Svalbard has more polar bears than people.

✪ In Longyearbyen, Thais are the second most numerous inhabitants after Norwegians.

✪ Svalbard inches towards the North Pole by 2mm per year.

✪ The lowest recorded temperature is -46°C, not counting the wind-chill factor.

✪ Before it cut loose and drifted way north of the Arctic Circle, Svalbard was once lush and tropical.

✪ The permafrost is more than 300m deep.

✪ In Longyearbyen, construction is carefully controlled – down to the colour you can paint your house.

✪ Svalbard's vast Svea Nord coalfield has estimated reserves of over 30 million tonnes.

'Yunnan is China distilled into one superlative province and offers more variety (culturally, topographically, or whatever) than any other place in China. Period.'

○ YUNNAN, CHINA

By Thomas Huhti

YUNNAN, CHINA

POPULATION 44.5 MILLION ✪ **CAPITAL** KUNMING ✪ **LANGUAGES** A DISTINCTIVE YUNNANESE DIALECT OF MANDARIN, DOZENS MORE FROM SINO-TIBETAN AND TIBETO-BURMAN FAMILIES ✪ **UNIT OF CURRENCY** YUAN (Y) ✪ **PER CAPITA INCOME** KUNMING Y12,083, RURAL AREAS Y4003 ✪ **MAJOR INDUSTRIES** TOBACCO, METAL SMELTING/ PRESSING, ELECTRICITY, CHEMICALS, AGRICULTURE ✪ **COST INDEX** A CUP OF *REAL* COFFEE Y15 (US$2.10), A BOWL OF ACROSS-THE-BRIDGE NOODLES (THE LOCAL SPECIALITY) Y10-60 (US$1.40-8.40), DORM BED Y20-40 (US$2.90-5.80)

EVERYONE'S SHANGRI-LA

Becoming every traveller's 'secret' Shangri-la, Yunnan is China distilled into one superlative province and offers more variety (culturally, topographically, or whatever) than any other place in China. Period. Oh-so-remote Yunnan was ironically once a place of banishment for disgraced court officials (who likely chuckled and said 'Thanks, chums' upon arrival). Now? China's *it* destination: Yunnan's always first or second (behind Beijing) as a 'dream destination' for travellers in China, domestic tourist numbers growing at an astonishing 12% per annum. Foreign tourists numbers grow at a mere 1% (since almost all foreigners are here already).

ENOUGH ALREADY?

The Yin to touristic popularity's Yang is overdevelopment (or, clueless development). Airports, highways, rail lines, dams and ports are being thrown up every which way to make China one node of a China-India-Southeast Asia economic free-for-all zone. And bring in tourists. Loads of 'em. (Indeed, given the first sybaritic city-state resorts are now going up, the jet set and their moolah can't be far behind.)

Trickle-down economics hasn't worked nearly as well for Yunnan's poverty-rife rural areas as for other provinces in southwest China; Unesco has even threatened to de-list World Heritage–site status for some of Yunnan's amazing landscapes unless authorities knock off extortive and destructive development. One unavoidable annoyance: entrance fees in particular are (gallingly) pricey – higher than those in the West.

ALL THAT SAID...

This is the one province in China you must visit.

FESTIVALS & EVENTS

✪ The Torch Festival, on 14 August 2009 and 4 August 2010, is held throughout the province. Take your cameras for torch parades, endless fireworks and general celebratory hoo-hah.
✪ Kunming has been hosting a few small, but worthy, film festivals; hopefully Lijiang will continue its Jade Dragon Snow Mountain music festival (China's Woodstock), the highest music festival in the world at nearly 3000m.
✪ Otherwise, hope you enjoy metallurgical conferences and such.

DEFINING EXPERIENCES

✪ Spiritually recharging sunsets along the famed Tiger Leaping Gorge trek, or sunrises atop the Yuanyang rice terraces.

✪ Back-alley meanderings in the time-warp towns of Lijiang and Dali.

✪ Ice-cold beer in Xishuangbanna, after a jungle trek.

DEFINING DIFFERENCE

The Yunnanese can't really get worked up about much. It is charming to see officialdom here attempt, in their gee-whiz way, to build the province an image that's 'hip', 'cutting edge' and other such marketing nonsense.

RECENT FADS

✪ For the Yunnanese, buying a car.

✪ Taking the ass-busting bus rides into western Sichuan from northwestern Yunnan. Take note that due to 2008 riots in Tibetan regions this backdoor is occassionally closed off to foreigners, so check first.

✪ Travellers bitching about how many other tourists are here.

✪ The government changing town names to maximise tourism potential (Zhongdian is now Shangri-la; and Simao is Pu'er, after the legendary tea).

HOT TOPIC OF THE DAY

Water, or lack thereof (as you'll note when your hostel's water is shut off) and, thus, many controversial dam projects in northern Yunnan. And traffic.

HOT TIP

Meander carefully, oh intrepid one – sneaking into Tibet still pisses off The Man. You're in deep doo-doo if caught crossing illegally, even by accident on a bike ride, into Laos, Vietnam or, especially, Burma (where you'll be presumed to be a drug smuggler).

RANDOM FACTS

✪ Dali is building one of Asia's largest solar-power plants.

✪ Kunming is known as the Spring City, but it's becoming a bit foggy from the 500 cars *per day* added to the streets (one reason for no-car days).

✪ The lion's share of China's cigarettes come from this province.

✪ Starbuck's (China) uses Yunnan coffee.

DO MENTION

✪ The ubiquitous flowers – easy to do!

✪ The extraordinary fruit, tea and coffee here – ditto!

DON'T MENTION

How *cool* it is that Yunnan's so much less developed than Beijing or Shanghai.

MOST BIZARRE SIGHTS

✪ The otherworldly karst peaks of the Stone Forest.

✪ The mind-boggling throngs of tourists jamming into Lijiang's square.

✪ Or, possibly, that yak head on the bus seat next to you.

056
ANTWERP,
BELGIUM

058
BEIRUT,
LEBANON

060
CHICAGO,
USA

062
GLASGOW,
SCOTLAND

064
LISBON,
PORTUGAL

LONELY PLANET'S
TOP 10 CITIES

066
MEXICO CITY,
MEXICO

068
SÃO PAULO,
BRAZIL

070
SHANGHAI,
CHINA

072
WARSAW,
POLAND

074
ZÜRICH,
SWITZERLAND

ANTWERP, BELGIUM
EUROPE

'...there's much more to this city than the world's best variety of beer.'

By Ryan Ver Berkmoes

ANTWERP, BELGIUM

POPULATION 455,000 ❂ **LANGUAGE** FLEMISH, AKA *VLAAMS OR NEDERLANDS* ❂ **UNIT OF CURRENCY** EURO (€)
❂ **COST INDEX** GLASS OF SUPERB BEER €3 (US$4.60), HOTEL DOUBLE/DORM ROOM €100/20 (US$154/30.80), SHORT
TAXI RIDE €5 (US$7.70), CONE OF *FRITES* €2.50 (US$3.85), BIKE HIRE PER DAY €10 (US$15.40)

TOPS BEYOND THE TAPS

Belgium's about consumption: beer, mussels, *frites* (fries) and chocolates are just some of the iconic oral pleasures. You'll find these in Antwerp, but there's much more to this city than the world's best variety of beer. There's ModeNatie, home to MoMu (the modern art museum), the Flanders Fashion Institute and the fashion department of the Royal Academy of Fine Arts, which has spawned legions of hot designers. On the surrounding streets you'll find the salons and shops of the Antwerp Six, the half-dozen local designers who exploded on the world's catwalks in the 1980s, as well as the scores more who've followed.

DIAMOND IN THE ROUGH

While politicians in Brussels dither about the country's future, Antwerp zips along as the heart of thriving Flanders, the region straddling the Dutch-speaking north of Belgium and the south of the Netherlands. Appearances have always been big, from today's designers and world diamond markets to as far back as Pieter Paul Rubens, the 17th-century baroque painter whose works grace local venues, including the city's soaring Onze Lieve Vrouwekathedraal (Cathedral of Our Lady). The mix of ancient alleys and modern venues pulse with clubs and shops; ancient-timbered bars and cafés offer respite.

DEFINING EXPERIENCE

Drinking your way to the bottom of the fabulous beer lists, while avoiding the literal meaning of brews with names like Mort Subite (Instant Death) and Delirium Tremens (Loss of Mind).

RECENT FAD

What's another word for fad but fashion and Antwerp's once dowdy image is as yesterday as wide ties. Scores of hot designers like Antwerp Sixers Walter Van Beirendonck, Dries Van Noten and Ann Demeulemeester have shops in St Andries, on and around Nationalestraat. The tourist office sells a book with not one but five fashion walks here. See works by the latest stars at Louis, on Lombardenstraat.

FESTIVALS & EVENTS

❂ Surprise! A big draw locally is Beerpassie Weekend, a sudsy blast late in June when some of the region's best brewers – including many of the smallest and most sought after – offer tastings of hundreds of beers.
❂ September heaves with parties fronted by the best DJs. Antwerp Is Burning, Laundry Day and Illusion

pulse with house, trance, techno – and other beats of the moment.

LIFE-CHANGING EXPERIENCES

✪ Proclaiming 'I've found my favourite beer!' at the Beerhuis Kulminator, a pilgrimage spot for Belgian beer-lovers, with over 700 varieties.

✪ Buying a cheap diamond at a gem mart next to the train station, and then hightailing it.

✪ Finding the club-of-the-moment before almost anyone else.

HOT TOPIC OF THE DAY

Four out of five diamonds in the world once passed through Antwerp. That number's plummeting as regulations to rein in the blood-diamond trade send business to Dubai.

RANDOM FACTS

✪ It's not just beer. *Jenever*, a type of gin long popular in Belgium and the

Netherlands, gets its due in Antwerp. De Vagant, a cosy old bar near the Cathedral has 200 kinds.

✪ Fast trains from stunning Centraal Station put Paris and London less than three hours away, Amsterdam less than two and Brussels less then one.

✪ Antwerp has over 200 *frituren* (chip shops) which produce treats that are the Rubens of the deep-fried world. Local potatoes are dipped twice in hot oil and served in a paper cone with a vast choice of sauces (mayo being the perma-fave).

STROLL OF PLENTY

More evidence that Antwerp has its pleasure priorities right? The Sunday market on Hoogstraat doesn't really get going until 2pm. Sleep off last night's beer and this morning's clubbing, then crawl out to one of the many heaving cafés along this street, which stretches several hundred metres from

the 16th-century Grote Markt south to trendy St Andries. Scores of vendors sell everything from dodgy antiques to real treasures. Browse, stroll, then plop down for a restorative drink.

CLASSIC RESTAURANT EXPERIENCE

For centuries Antwerp earned its keep as a port, and North Sea scents flavour the air. The long-running Gin-Fish eschews tired menus for an ever-changing line up of fresh fish. It jumps like a net full of eel.

CLASSIC PLACE TO STAY

Antwerp's style finds a home at Hotel Julien. Here, designer Mouche Van Hool transformed two ancient townhouses into an understated 11-room dream.

'Despite its weakness for all that's new and swanky, Beirut's not entirely about the hottest, priciest and glitziest.'

By Amelia Thomas

BEIRUT, LEBANON

POPULATION 1.2 MILLION ✪ **LANGUAGES** ARABIC, FRENCH, ENGLISH ✪ **UNIT OF CURRENCY** LEBANESE LIRA (LL), PRICES OFTEN IN US DOLLARS (US$) ✪ **COST INDEX** STRONG BLACK COFFEE FROM AN ITINERANT COFFEE-WAGON LL1000 (US$0.70), FIVE-STAR HOTEL SUITE US$1800, DORM BED NEAR THE BUS STATION US$6, SHARED SERVICE-TAXI RIDE TO AND FROM ANY POINT IN TOWN LL1500 (US$1), GLASS OF LOCAL ARAK LL2000 (US$1.30), BOTTLE OF CHAMPAGNE AT CRYSTAL NIGHTCLUB US$3000

CITY ON THE BRINK

Beirut's always on the verge of something happening – covert political assassinations, airborne invasions by foreign powers, the opening night of the hippest new beach bar in the Middle East – and any or all of them might happen in 2009. Despite the uncertainty in the air and armed troops on the streets, the city clings tenaciously to its sybaritic appeal, with supercool clubs attracting top name European DJs, swanky restaurants churning out delectable fusion sushi, cool underground jazz joints, tip-top designer-clothes shopping, and even a friendly, familiar Starbucks or two, for that priceless 'Starbucks Beirut' souvenir coffee mug.

OLD TIMERS

Despite its weakness for all that's new and swanky, Beirut's not entirely about the hottest, priciest and glitziest. Squeezed in between century-old coffee shops, where ancient patrons, enveloped in clouds of nargileh smoke, serenely clack backgammon counters, the weathered remains of the Roman Cardo Maximus, the Ottoman-era Grand Serail, the 19th-century Jewish cemetery and 12th-century Al-Omari Mosque offer visual and cultural respite amid a mess of modern city construction.

DEFINING EXPERIENCE

Sip a perfect martini in a swanky, silicone-heavy beach club watching weathered pole-fishermen battling the waves on the Corniche rocks, then stroll past bomb-craters and city-centre Hezbollah encampments to munch on a divine eggs Benedict brunch with the artsy crowd in Beirut's funky Gemmayzeh district.

FESTIVALS & EVENTS

✪ Twice this year, in either May or November, hunt for hidden treasure at the Souk el-Bargout, a week-long city-wide flea market during which everyone hauls the junk they bought at the last one back out onto Beirut's streets for your purchasing delight.

✪ In October the Beirut International Film Festival showcases the pick of the crop of new films from across the region.

✪ Docudays, held just before Christmas, is a world-class documentary film festival, attracting flocks of international filmmakers and pensive, bearded locals.

✪ Pound Beirut's streets with the dedicated and professional at the Beirut Marathon in October – or opt

A MARONITE CHRISTIAN PARADE IN A BEIRUT SUBURB ADDS A DASH OF COLOUR TO THE CITY'S WAR-WEARY CONCRETE EXPANSES

for the 10km fun-run with other, saner, individuals.

LIFE-CHANGING EXPERIENCES

✪ Touring a city-limits Palestinian refugee camp with a local Palestinian guide.

✪ Exploring the cavernous Jeita Grotto, just north of the city, one of the most impressive subterranean displays of stalactites and stalagmites on the planet.

✪ Taking up the quintessential Lebanese challenge of swimming in the Med in the morning, then hitting the slopes of the Faraya Mzaar ski resort, above Beirut, in the afternoon.

HOT TOPIC

Though politics is never far from people's minds in volatile Beirut, the current talk of the concrete-laden town is green, green, green. As the city and its shoreline succumb to air pollution and waste mismanagement, manifold groups are springing up to protect Lebanon's fragile environment and promote eco-everything, from hiking the Lebanon Mountain Trail, to defending the capital's stray cats and dogs, to taking to Beirut's streets – albeit precariously – on two person–powered wheels instead of four Hummer-sized ones.

MOST BIZARRE SIGHT

Though many might claim they've already stayed at the world's worst Holiday Inn, this Beirut landmark beats them all. Built towering and earthquake-proof in the heady 1970s, it was the talk of the town for just a few weeks before the civil war turned it into a prime sniper post. The hotel still dominates the Beirut skyline, complete with gaping mortar holes, fluttering shreds of bedroom curtains, and resident flocks of pigeons.

CLASSIC RESTAURANT EXPERIENCE

After splurging on fine dining, the best place to come down is Le Chef, a 'blue collar' institution since the 1950s. Hefty plates of good old-fashioned Arabic food are brought to your Formica table by loquacious waiters, and don't miss the *moolookhiye* if it's on the day's specials: a gloopy, soupy mix of mallow leaves, lamb, rice and chicken – believed to be a powerful aphrodisiac.

SLEEP WITH A LOCAL

Swap your pastel-shaded hotel room for the spare bedroom of a born-and-bred Beiruti, to experience legendary Lebanese hospitality. B&B specialists L'Hote Libanais (www.hotelibanais .com) arranges home-comfort lodgings in the city, the best way to dive beneath Beirut's sometimes glistening, sometimes murky surface.

CHICAGO, USA

'If you want your finger on America's pulse, don't head to New York or LA. The heart beats in Chicago.'

By Karla Zimmerman

CHICAGO, USA

POPULATION 2.83 MILLION ✪ **LANGUAGE** ENGLISH ✪ **UNIT OF CURRENCY** US DOLLAR (US$)
✪ **COST INDEX** PUBLIC TRANSIT FARE US$2, DOWNTOWN HOTEL ROOM US$159, GREEN MILL MARTINI US$7.50, BLUES CLUB COVER CHARGE US$15

SECOND IN NAME ONLY

If you want your finger on America's pulse, don't head to New York or LA. The heart beats in Chicago. That's why businesses have come here for decades to test new products, be they Broadway shows or Costco caskets. Whether they make it for mass consumption depends on the Windy City's opinion.

Yes, Chicago determines the future of American retailing, and thus popular culture. No surprise that both McDonald's and Oprah base themselves in town. If Chicago really is merely a 'Second City', as a New York columnist once dismissed it, would people around the world be eating egg McMuffins and writing about it in their passion journals? Don't think so.

THINK BIG

Big things are on Chicago's horizon in 2009 – literally. Über-architect Santiago Calatrava is constructing the Chicago Spire to twist 610m into the clouds; only the United Arab Emirates' Burj Dubai will be taller. The Donald pops the top on his new Trump Tower, which rises to Chicago's third-tallest rank (after the Spire and Sears Tower). The penthouse costs around $25 million, but consider it an investment. If Chicago wins its 2016 Summer Olympics bid (determined in October 2009 after a smackdown with Rio, Tokyo and Madrid, among others), it'll all be worth it.

DEFINING EXPERIENCE

Looking up at steely skyscrapers and puzzling over the burnished Bean, Picasso and other public art in the morning; eating hot dogs, drinking Old Style beer and watching baseball's Cubs get clobbered by afternoon; and squashing into a sweaty blues, jazz or rock club by night. Or say to hell with noise and crowds, and go to a café and to a play instead.

FESTIVALS & EVENTS

✪ After the St Patrick's Day Parade rolls downtown in mid-March, the local plumbers' union dyes the Chicago River shamrock green with a secret, biodegradable colouring. Then everyone drinks beer.

✪ The free Blues Festival amps up four days of the fret-bending licks that made Chicago famous. More than 750,000 people unfurl blankets in the park to listen, party and picnic in early June.

✪ Lollapalooza celebrates its fifth year of Windy City–based body-surfing in 2009. The rock fest toured around the States for a decade, until it decided Chicago would make a sweet home.

MY KIND OF TOWN, CHICAGO IS…ENJOY THE RAZZLE-DAZZLE AND ALL THAT JAZZ AMID THE BRIGHT LIGHTS OF THE WINDY CITY

Now 130 bands spill off seven Grant Park stages the first weekend in August.

RANDOM FACTS

✪ Chicago received its Windy City nickname in the 1880s not because of its blustery weather but because of its big-mouthed politicians who constantly bragged about the town's greatness.

✪ Chicago has wowed the world with more than architectural ingenuity. The city also invented roller skates (1884), Hostess Twinkies (1930), the pinball machine (1930) and Lava Lites (1965).

✪ The faces projected on Millennium Park's Crown Fountain are all native Chicagoans who agreed to strap into artist Jaume Plensa's dental chair, where he immobilised their heads for video filming. Each mug puckers up and spurts water, a look Plensa modelled on the gargoyles atop Notre Dame Cathedral. A fresh set of non-puckering faces appears in winter, when the fountain is dry.

✪ When Mrs O'Leary's cow kicked over the lantern that burned down the city in 1871, it created the blank canvas that allowed Chicago's mighty architecture to flourish. Chicago put up the world's first skyscraper in 1885, and hasn't looked down since.

CLASSIC RESTAURANT EXPERIENCE

Let Hot Doug's acquaint you with a Chicago superfood: the hot dog. Chef Doug serves many dog styles (Polish, bratwursts, Chicago) cooked many ways (char-grilled, deep-fried, steamed). Confused? Doug will explain. He also serves 'haute dogs' – say, blue-cheese pork with cherry cream sauce, or sesame-ginger duck – for a seamless merging of highbrow and lowbrow cuisine.

CLASSIC BAR EXPERIENCE

Glamorous, dark and curvy, the Green Mill Jazz Club earned its notoriety as Al Capone's favourite speakeasy (the tunnels where he hid the booze are still underneath the bar), and you can feel his ghost urging you on to another martini. Top-flight local and national artists perform seven nights per week; on Sunday there's the nationally acclaimed poetry slam.

BEST SHOPPING

Follow that queue of frenzied suburban housewives into The Oprah Store. Located next to Oprah Winfrey's TV studio, the shop is filled with her favourite things. Get a passion journal, 'live your own dreams' coffee cup, or pair of Manolo Blahnik pumps – just like Oprah wears! If you lack cash, you can ogle the celeb photos and wall-mounted TVs re-running O's shows.

GLASGOW, SCOTLAND

'Forget about castles, kilts, bagpipes and tartan – you come to Glasgow for the cocktails, cuisine and designer chic (plus the legendary native wit).'

By Neil Wilson

GLASGOW, SCOTLAND

POPULATION 581,000 ✪ **LANGUAGE** ENGLISH, WITH A STRONG GLASGOW ACCENT ✪ **UNIT OF CURRENCY** POUND STERLING (£) ✪ **COST INDEX** PINT OF BEER £2.75 (US$5.50), HOTEL DOUBLE £60-100 (US$120-200), DORM BED £12-19 (US$24-38), SHORT TAXI RIDE £5 (US$10), ADMISSION TO LIVE-MUSIC GIG £5-10 (US$10-20)

SCOTLAND WITH STYLE

Scotland's biggest city has shaken off its shroud of industrial soot and shimmied into a sparkling new designer gown. Ten years on from being named UK City of Architecture & Design 1999, Glasgow is flaunting its reputation as a capital of cool, branding itself 'Scotland with Style' (a lot snappier than Edinburgh's insipid 'Inspiring Capital'). Like London, Glasgow has rediscovered the river that made its fortune, with modern architecture, luxury apartments and snazzy bridges springing up along the Clyde waterfront. With visitor numbers rising rapidly, it won't be long until Glasgow draws neck and neck with the Scottish capital.

CHIC & CHEERFUL

Forget about castles, kilts, bagpipes and tartan – you come to Glasgow for the cocktails, cuisine and designer chic (plus the legendary native wit). Long famous for the Art Nouveau elegance of Charles Rennie Mackintosh, the city is still turning out world-class designers such as Jonathan Saunders, the Glasgow School of Art graduate who has taken the women's fashion world by storm (Madonna, Kylie and Thandie Newton are fans), and the Timorous Beasties design duo whose hugely fashionable wallpaper and textile designs – without which no self-respecting style bar or boutique hotel would be complete – span the spectrum from surreal to subversive.

DEFINING EXPERIENCES

✪ Cruise the Clyde by powerboat or paddle steamer, marvel at the Mackintosh-designed Glasgow School of Art, and dally in designer boutiques in the streets of the Merchant City before sipping cocktails for two in a Bath St bar.

✪ Add your voice to the Hampden roar at an international football match, then down a pint or six in the Horseshoe Bar before catching the 'next Franz Ferdinand' at King Tut's Wah Wah Hut. Finally, stagger off for a late-night curry in the West End.

FESTIVALS & EVENTS

✪ The biggest item on Glasgow's 2009 calendar is Homecoming Scotland, a year-long, nationwide programme of events celebrating the 250th anniversary of the birth of Robert Burns. It's aimed at attracting the Scottish diaspora back home for a holiday in the old country.

✪ Laugh along with the natives at the 18-day Glasgow International Comedy Festival, the city's annual chuckle-fest in March 2009.

THE DUKE OF WELLINGTON AND HIS TRUSTY STEED RECOVER FROM A NIGHT ON THE TOWN OUTSIDE GLASGOW'S GALLERY OF MODERN ART

✪ Check out the latest offerings from Glasgow's (and Scotland's) innovative art and design community at the Glasgow International Festival of Contemporary Visual Art in April, and the Six Cities Design Festival in May/June.

WHAT'S HOT...
James McAvoy. Pan-fried scallops. Charles Rennie Mackintosh.

...WHAT'S NOT
Billy Connolly. Deep-fried Mars Bars. Wearing a mackintosh.

MOST BIZARRE SIGHT
The equestrian statue of the Duke of Wellington outside the Gallery of Modern Art. For almost two decades, despite the best efforts of the city fathers, the duke has sported a jaunty traffic cone for a hat – an enduring symbol of Glasgow's irreverent sense of humour. (On good days the horse wears a matching titfer.)

CLASSIC RESTAURANT EXPERIENCE
It may have been around for 35 years, but the Ubiquitous Chip is still setting the pace in Glasgow's frenetic restaurant scene. In the '70s and '80s the Chip almost single-handedly created Modern Scottish cuisine, with the emphasis on top-quality, locally sourced produce. These days it's more of a culinary complex than a single restaurant – you can choose to eat in the airy cobbled courtyard surrounded by tumbling greenery and a tinkling fountain, retire to the candlelit confines of the cosy dining room, or down a dram in one of the three bars.

BEST SHOPPING
Glasgow offers the UK's biggest shopaholic fix outside of London, with classy designer malls such as Princes Square and the Italian Centre complemented by innovative boutiques along Great Western Road, and quirky little shops selling vintage clothing, secondhand books and antiques in the lanes around Byres Road. Good buys include cutting-edge jewellery and eccentric accessories designed by graduates of the Glasgow School of Art, available at the Brazen gallery: anyone for a pair of handmade, printed ceramic nipple tassels?

CLASSIC PLACE TO STAY
A darkly decadent retreat amid the tree-lined terraces of the West End, Glasgow's original boutique hotel, One Devonshire Gardens, has been refurbished and resurrected as the Hotel du Vin. Voted Scotland's most stylish hotel in 2007, it's the first choice of visiting celebs.

⊕ LISBON, PORTUGAL

'While a lesser girl would have developed bags under her eyes after all this partying, Lisbon has simply become better with age.'

By Stuart Butler

LISBON, PORTUGAL

POPULATION LISBON CITY 565,000, GREATER LISBON 1.9 MILLION ✪ **LANGUAGE** PORTUGUESE ✪ **UNIT OF CURRENCY** EURO (€) ✪ **COST INDEX** COFFEE €1.50-2.50 (US$2.20-3.70), MIDRANGE HOTEL DOUBLE/ DORM BED €60/18 (US$90/27), SHORT TAXI RIDE €10 (US$15), INTERNET ACCESS PER HOUR €3 (US$4.50)

YOU SEXY MERMAID

Back in the early '80s, when sexy meant fluorescent orange socks and big hair, or the early '90s, when sexy meant not washing for six months, Lisbon was considered a boring and unfashionable backwater in comparison to nearby Spain's sangria cities. Nobody gave her a second glance. But that was then, and now this seaside city has transformed herself into the sultry, seductive mermaid of Iberia.

THE BEAUTIFUL GAME

The transformation started with a makeover in '94 when Lisbon was named European City of Culture, flowed through to Lisbon's hosting of Expo 98 and hit overdrive when she took centre stage for the Euro 2004 football tournament. While a lesser girl would have developed bags under her eyes after all this partying, Lisbon has simply become better with age. As 2009 dawns she has matured into a cultured, sophisticated – and still slightly dirty – temptress. Catch her now while she's at her most enticing.

DEFINING EXPERIENCE

It's the Festas dos Santos Populares, so, in this order – dress up in an outlandish costume, stuff your face with sardines, down a barrel of sangria and then, when you're suitably inebriated, take a pot of basil, a paper carnation and the best love poem you can write (you had better make that two barrels of sangria) to your secret lover. We guarantee she (or he) will love you for it!

FESTIVALS & EVENTS

✪ Late April ushers in the start of IndieLisboa, the country's premier independent film festival.
✪ Festas dos Santos Populares takes place on various dates in June and is the city's big knees-up – and those knees really do go up!
✪ Arrail Pride, also in June, is the big event for the city's gay community. There are parades and parties galore for everyone.
✪ The amusingly named Super Bock Super Rock Festival is held in late June/early July and is the most prestigious of various music festivals.
✪ Joggers, for which Portugal certainly isn't renowned, come out of the woodwork for the Lisbon Marathon in December.

LIFE-CHANGING EXPERIENCES

✪ Catch a ferry over the Tejo River and pretend you're the great explorer Vasco

TRUNDLE PAST THE TRIUMPHAL ARCH ON YOUR WAY BETWEEN PUBS AND PARTIES IN *FADO*-FILLED LISBON

da Gama sailing back to port after discovering the sea route to India. All right, it's not quite the same...

✪ Fear for your life as a huge shark bears down on you at the world-class Oceanarium.

✪ Search for a princess (or a prince) locked away inside one of the palaces of Sintra, Byron's glorious Eden.

✪ Learn what bathroom tiles should really look like at the quirky Museu Nacional do Azulejo.

HOT TOPIC OF THE DAY

The Portuguese like nothing better than parking their bums on a bar stall and setting the world to right. Currently bar-stall bums are fiercely debating the upcoming national elections due to be held in October 2009. Topics on the menu include solving the age-old problems of sky-high taxes, low wages and high unemployment.

MOST BIZARRE SIGHT

For the lazy (after one lung-bursting hike up a Lisbon hill, that'll include you) the Elevador de Santa Justa, a surreal industrial-age iron lift, will act as a flying carpet from the sea-level Lisbon of the Baixa to the upper-crust shops of the Chiado.

RANDOM FACTS

✪ Almost all of central Lisbon was destroyed by an earthquake in 1755.

✪ The result of the first ever SL Benfica and Sporting clash (Lisbon's big two football clubs) in 1907 was Sporting 2 SL Benfica 1.

✪ The city's best *pastéis de nata* (custard tart) is at Antiga Confeitaria de Belém, west of the centre.

CLASSIC RESTAURANT EXPERIENCE

Lisbon is a gourmet's dream – the range of places to eat is huge and prices reasonable. The seafood is especially good – and so fresh you'll probably be handed a rod and reel and told to catch your own. One of our favourite places is A Travessa. Set inside a renovated 17th-century convent, it has flamed monkfish and duck dishes that would set any convent girl's heart racing.

BEST PLACE TO MAKE LIKE A DANCING QUEEN

Kick your groovy night off in the bars of the ancient Barrio Alto district before moving on to the megafashion club Lux in the Santa Apolónia district. If this isn't for you, perhaps then a late-night *fado* session. *Fado*, which translates as 'fate', is Portugal's homespun blues with a flamenco kick; it's so full of nostalgia and pain it'll get even the biggest of us crying into our beers. Senhor Vinho is one of the most reliable venues.

✪ MEXICO CITY, MEXICO

'Crossing the street in Mexico City plays
out like a scene from Death Race 2000. No kidding.'

By John Hecht

MEXICO CITY, MEXICO

POPULATION MEXICO CITY PROPER 8.8 MILLION, METROPOLITAN AREA 20 MILLION ✪ **LANGUAGES** SPANISH, NÁHUATL, OTHER INDIGENOUS DIALECTS ✪ **UNIT OF CURRENCY** PESO ✪ **AVERAGE TEMPERATURE** JANUARY DAILY HIGH 21°C, JULY DAILY HIGH 23°C ✪ **COST INDEX** SHOT OF TEQUILA 50 PESOS (US$4.50), SHORT TAXI RIDE 30 PESOS (US$2.70), HOTEL DOUBLE/DORM 590/130 PESOS (US$54/12), SERVING OF TACOS 50 PESOS (US$4.50), MARIACHI SONG 50 PESOS (US$4.50)

SAVOUR THE FLAVOUR

Looking for an alternative to Mexico's touristy beach destinations? Edgy Mexico City is the hot ticket. After all, we're talking about the so-called 'Manhattan of Latin America', a city so fast and invigorating that sleep is a mere afterthought. Cultural and entertainment options abound in the sprawling capital. It's simply a matter of choosing your pleasure among the slew of trendy bars, live-music venues, museums and fine restaurants. Boredom is not an option.

DON'T BELIEVE THE HYPE

Truth be told, Mexico City gets a bad rap. Sure, the city has a fair share of crime, but nothing like the sensationalist media reports would have you believe. Just use some of that proverbial common sense and you should be fine. And what of the city's infamous smog? In recent years, tighter emissions standards have considerably reduced air pollution. Contrary to popular thought, blue skies are not a rarity here.

THE MEXICAN MECCA

Also known as the Distrito Federal, present-day Mexico City has been a political, cultural and religious centre for nearly 700 years. The architecture, which runs from pre-Hispanic ruins to modern skyscrapers, is a crash course in Mexican history. At first glance, even an experienced city slicker may find the vehicular and pedestrian traffic overwhelming; for locals, however, it's just another day in the Western Hemisphere's most populated metropolis.

DEFINING EXPERIENCE

Wandering among the hurrying throngs on the narrow streets of the Centro Histórico and discovering an Aztec temple, striking colonial monuments and old-school cantinas.

RECENT FAD

Long considered the ugly cousin of tequila, *mezcal* is making a strong comeback these days, especially in the überhip bars lining the streets of the Roma and Condesa neighbourhoods.

FESTIVALS & EVENTS

✪ For the first time ever, Mexico City will host the World Baseball Classic from 8 to 23 March. Did someone say soccer?

✪ The Festival de México en el Centro Histórico in March offers a two-week-long cultural smorgasbord of live bands, theatrical groups and dance troupes from Mexico and abroad.

HE KNOWS HIS ATZECS FROM HIS INCAS: COMMEMORATING THE 483RD ANNIVERSARY OF CUAUHTEMOC, THE LAST AZTEC EMPEROR, IN MEXICO CITY

✪ On 15 September, the eve of Independence Day, tens of thousands of people descend on the city's main square for the biggest fiesta of the year, Grito de la Independencia.

LIFE-CHANGING EXPERIENCES

✪ Visiting the ruins at the Templo Mayor, a site the Aztecs believed to be none other than the centre of the cosmological universe.

✪ Taking a gondola ride through the canals of Xochimilco amid colourful floating gardens.

✪ Tossing back tequilas and listening to balladeers belt out tunes into the wee hours of the morning at the famed mariachi square.

HOT TOPIC OF THE DAY

In an effort to make Mexico City more 'livable', the government provides urban beaches in summer, one of the world's largest ice rinks in winter, and year round women-only buses to protect female riders from would-be gropers.

RANDOM FACTS

✪ Crossing the street in Mexico City plays out like a scene from Death Race 2000. No kidding, some drivers will actually accelerate when they sight oncoming pedestrians.

✪ Mexico City is sinking fast. Perched atop a drained lake bed and rapidly depleting aquifers, the capital sank about 30ft last century.

✪ The city's metro system transports some 4.5 million passengers a day: one of the busiest underground rail networks in the world.

CLASSIC RESTAURANT EXPERIENCE

Waiters and regulars at the Hostería de Santo Domingo swear that a hooded monk haunts this former 16th-century convent at night. Converted into a restaurant in 1860, it's Mexico City's oldest eatery. The house specialty is the stuffed *chiles* bathed in a walnut sauce. The ghost apparently hasn't scared off anyone's appetite.

MOST BIZARRE SIGHTS

Some of the city's roughest neighbourhoods have creepy altars dedicated to St Death, a female grim reaper figure who receives petitions from those who have lost faith in the Catholic religion. Many of her devout followers are career criminals.

MOST UNUSUAL PLACE TO VISIT

El Chopo, an alternative flea market held every Saturday, brings together local punks, metalheads and goths seeking rare CDs and a dose of live music. People-watching doesn't get any better than this.

'Once typecast as the bad-boy city of crime and pollution, São Paulo has reinvented itself in recent years, emerging as Brazil's cultural behemoth.'

By Regis St. Louis

SÃO PAULO, BRAZIL

POPULATION 11 MILLION, METROPOLITAN AREA 20 MILLION ✪ **LANGUAGE** PORTUGUESE
✪ **UNIT OF CURRENCY** BRAZILIAN REAL (R$) ✪ **COST INDEX** GLASS OF *CHOPE* (DRAFT BEER) R$3.50 (US$2),
MIDRANGE DOUBLE R$150 (US$88), METRO TICKET R$2.40 (US$1.40), ADMISSION TO MASP
(MUSEU DE ARTE DE SÃO PAULO) R$15 (US$8.80)

URBAN DYNAMO

One of the world's great metropolises, São Paulo is a vast city of skyscrapers and hypermodern design, with a financial industry helping to fuel Brazil's strong economic growth. Once typecast as the bad-boy city of crime and pollution, São Paulo has reinvented itself in recent years, emerging as Brazil's cultural behemoth. The art and music scene here is world class, and there's great shopping and nightlife.

RESIDENTS OF THE WORLD

Paulistas (São Paulo residents) have a long history of immigration. Italians, Spanish, Japanese, Lebanese, Greek, Syrians, Germans and other communities have put down roots in the last 100 years, making the city a rich melting pot. Its diverse neighbourhoods (31 districts at last count) provide fascinating wandering – and highly rewarding dining at any of over 12,000 restaurants.

DEFINING EXPERIENCE

✪ Joining the festive drinking and live-music scene in Vila Madalena, São Paulo's nightlife centre.
✪ Strolling the boutiques and cafés of the tree-lined Jardim Paulista neighbourhood.

RECENT FAD

The preferred mode of transport of São Paulo's wealthiest is neither the luxury sedan nor the clean, efficient metro system. Instead, the elite prefer the helicopter, bypassing the gridlocked streets as they zip through the skies to get across town. Boasting more than 300 heliports, São Paulo has more helicopter traffic than any other city on the planet. Those who can't afford their own chopper join collectives, sharing in the cost and upkeep of a helicopter with fellow members.

FESTIVALS & EVENTS

✪ São Paulo's Carnaval (which runs from 20 to 24 February) is a brilliantly colourful event, featuring all-night parades and numerous parties across town. Paulistas claim the *festa* (party) keeps getting better every year, though it still remains undiscovered by tourists.
✪ Hosting the world's biggest Gay Pride parade, São Paulo attracts over three million gays and *simpatizantes* (gay-friendly straights) who come to party in the streets in mid-June.

SAMBA LIKE THE DEVIL HIMSELF AT SÃO PAOLO'S SMOKY, SEXY, SIZZLING ANNUAL CARNAVAL

✪ Held in late April or early May, Virada Cultural is a 24-hour cultural marathon, featuring free events all over town. There are concerts, film screenings, dance parties, book readings, and museum and gallery openings.

RANDOM FACTS

✪ São Paulo is one of the world's great melting pots. Its Japanese population is the largest outside of Japan.

✪ The population has grown enormously in the modern era, going from 32,000 inhabitants in 1880 to more than 20 million today.

✪ One of the city's more unusual sights is the Instituto Butantan, a renowned biomedical research institution with the largest collection of snakes on earth (over 50,000) – the snake venom is used to make antidotes to snake and spider bites, and to research other medicines.

CLASSIC RESTAURANT EXPERIENCE

Brazil's undisputed culinary capital, São Paulo boasts an incredible restaurant scene that owes much to its cultural diversity. You'll find great Italian fare in the Bela Vista district while the Asian enclave of Liberdade has fantastic sushi and ramen spots. Brazil, of course, has its own great cuisines, and you'll find superb steaks and seafood dishes at the legendary Figueira Rubaiyat.

CLASSIC PLACE TO STAY

The boutique Hotel Unique, designed by award-winning architect Ruy Ohtake, is one of São Paulo's icons. The striking building resembles a half moon or a two-dimensional ship, with porthole-like windows. Inside, the wild design continues with retractable windows in the bathrooms and floors that curve up to the ceiling on outer rooms. If you'd rather not spring for the US$600 a night, you can stop in for an evening cocktail instead. Head up to the rooftop bar for fabulous views of the city skyline.

BEST SHOPPING

São Paulo is a city of options when it comes to shopping. Bargain-hunters head outdoors on the weekends to take in the impressive market scene. Top choices include the Sunday antique fair in front of MASP, São Paulo's famous modern art museum, and the Saturday Feira Benedito Calixto with handcrafts, food stalls and live music. Those shopping at the high-end should chopper over to Daslu, a glittering palace of luxury goods and top designs, with elegant restaurants and cafés amid the gilded boutiques.

'Racy architecture, charming side streets and European verve meet the clamour and energy of the Chinese.'

By Damian Harper

SHANGHAI, CHINA

POPULATION 18.45 MILLION ✪ **LANGUAGE** PUTONGHUA (MANDARIN), SHANGHAIHUA ✪ **UNIT OF CURRENCY** YUAN (Y) ✪ **COST INDEX** CUP OF COFFEE Y10-25 (US$1.40-3.50), GLASS OF BEER Y25-45 (US$3.50-6.30), BOTTLE OF WINE FROM Y25 (US$3.50), HOTEL DOUBLE Y150-4000 (US$21-560), DORM BED FROM Y45 (US$6.30), SHORT TAXI RIDE Y11 (US$1.50), INTERNET ACCESS PER HOUR Y3 (US$0.40)

SHANGHAI SURPRISE

Few world cities exude such a tangible sense of up-to-the-minute cachet and cool as Shanghai. Everyone – from your dentist to your best friend and their old flame – has a trip planned here. With visitor numbers exploding faster than a strip of Chinese New Year bangers, to overlook Shanghai is to miss out on *the* big travel destination – China – and its most dazzling city.

THE GREAT MALL OF CHINA

In no other mainland Chinese city are the fruits of consumerism displayed so ostentatiously. China's commercial and shopping capital, Shanghai celebrates the yawning contradictions between Karl Marx and Adam Smith with a gusto that makes the rest of this rapidly developing land look simply catatonic.

CHINA IN YOUR HANDS

Racy architecture, charming side streets and European verve meet the clamour and energy of the Chinese. Cosmopolitan maybe, but Shanghai is China to the core, without the Middle Kingdom's stubborn mustiness or mind-boggling size. The city's history as a foreign concession still defines Shanghai – but the language, culture and psyche of Shanghai is pure Chinese.

DEFINING EXPERIENCES

✪ A nocturnal cocktail from the Bund bar terrace, with the neon glow of Pudong drenching the skyline.

✪ Putting a crick in your neck looking up the side of the Shanghai World Financial Center – the world's third tallest building.
✪ White-knuckle Shanghai taxi rides: vehicles defy the laws of physics.

LIFE-CHANGING EXPERIENCES

✪ Travelling on the maglev train at over Mach 0.3, wondering why there are no seat belts.
✪ Discovering the true meaning of population density in the rush-hour metro at People's Square.

RECENT FAD

The desirable Bund area sparked a frantic last-minute tussle for land among five-star hotels, from the Hyatt on the Bund (completed) to the Peninsula Shanghai (under construction). Car horns have been banned within the confines of the outer ring road; in only a few days

SHANGHAI'S OTHERWORLDLY ORIENTAL PEARL TV TOWER SEEMS TO BE BEAMING OUT TO MORE THAN JUST THE LOCALS

cars took to annoyingly flashing their headlights instead.

FESTIVALS & EVENTS

✪ Chinese New Year (Spring Festival), is celebrated with a commercial frenzy of Christmas proportions, staking claim to seven days of festive mayhem. In 2009 the New Year falls on 26 January, announced with fireworks at midnight.
✪ Shanghai International Literary Festival: Bundside Glamour Bar March/April fixture for the literati and glitterati.
✪ Formula 1, a mass congregation of petrolheads and speedfreaks, sends room prices up to the ozone layer.

HOT TOPICS OF THE DAY

✪ The proposed extension of the maglev to Hongqiao has people bothered. Middle-class Shanghainese have taken to the streets in protest.
✪ Everyone's talking about *disanzhe* (extramarital lovers) and the havoc

they wreak on high-profile marriages; runaway divorce rates have old-timers stupefied.
✪ Affordable housing remains a perennial headache.
✪ With the Beijing Olympics over, the spotlight is on Shanghai for World Expo 2010.

RANDOM FACTS

✪ Shanghai is the world's largest cargo port.
✪ Number plates in Shanghai are more expensive than a small car.
✪ The Grand Hyatt in Pudong houses the world's longest laundry chute.
✪ Bicycles in Shanghai: 9 million.
✪ Crossing guards in Shanghai: 8000.
✪ Dogs in Shanghai: more than 400,000.

MOST BIZARRE SIGHTS

Locals wandering the streets in pyjamas or the fantastic variety of

peculiar sunhats donned by cyclists appear natural after a while, but the signature Oriental Pearl TV Tower, in Lujiazui, is always going to be an acquired taste. The fairyland turrets of Moller House, rising up south of roaring Central Yan'an Road, create a sense of enchantment.

CLASSIC PLACE TO STAY

Astor House Hotel: copious doses of old Shanghai charm and history temptingly coupled to a fantastic north Bund location. The iconic Peace Hotel on the Bund is set to reopen in 2009 after a major, and long overdue, refit.

BEST SHOPPING

Taikang Road Art Centre/Tianzifang: for funky fashion boutiques, cafés and art studios in a where-time-stood-still *shikumen* (literally, stone-gate) setting, all without the overdone and overvisited mania of Xintiandi.

○ WARSAW, POLAND

'Warsaw still has its work cut out to become a world-class capital...but any visitor willing to spend some time here will find its energy and vibe infectious.'

By Neal Bedford

WARSAW, POLAND

POPULATION 1.7 MILLION ✪ **LANGUAGE** POLISH ✪ **UNIT OF CURRENCY** ZŁOTY (LITERALLY 'GOLDEN'; ZŁ) ✪ **COST INDEX** BOTTLE OF ZYWIEC BEER 15ZŁ (US$6.20), 1L OF VODKA 40ZŁ (US$16.60), TRAM TICKET 2.40ZŁ (US$1), MIDRANGE HOTEL DOUBLE 200ZŁ (US$80)

CAPITAL OF THE NEW EUROPE

Eastern Europe is the new Europe, and Warsaw is its new capital. Long the punching bag for invading powers – and after WWII a Soviet backwater built on rubble – this indestructible city has in recent years shaken off the shackles that restricted its self-expression and begun to forge a fresh identity.

THE PRESENT...

This identity is melding past and present, and creating a city both glamorous and gritty. Warsaw can now boast a contemporary cultural scene without par in these parts – thumping clubs cater to an invasion of international DJs, designer bars fill with street models and styled suitors, and jazz aficionados are spoiled for choice. Art galleries are filling derelict shops, even in some of Warsaw's poorest neighbourhoods, and café culture is booming (forget Starbucks, Varsovians have gone gaga over their own particular style of café, the café-bookshop).

...AND THE PAST

Despite the forward focus, the city and its citizens haven't lost their connection to the past. And it's easy to see why, for it confronts them at almost every turn. The stark reminders of a tumultuous past – holocaust memorials, war museums, socialist realist architecture – dot the city. For many they are a source of inspiration rather than an obstacle to change. Warsaw still has its work cut out to become a world-class capital and at times it can appear all too rough and ready, but any visitor willing to spend some time here will find its energy and vibe infectious. Catch it before the stag parties take over.

DEFINING EXPERIENCE

Stumbling into daylight after partying all night in one of Warsaw's progressive clubs, grabbing a quick breakfast on Nowy Swiat, the city's übercool avenue, before taking the lift to the 30th floor of the Palace of Science & Culture to drink in the views.

RECENT FAD

The rise of Praga. Warsaw's rough neighbourhood, east of the Vistula River, is the current fave with the city's art crowd who are slowly infiltrating it with galleries, bars and clubs.

FESTIVALS & EVENTS

✪ The Old Town makes a picturesque backdrop for the highly acclaimed Jazz in the Old Town International

HOP ABOARD THE 19TH CENTURY FOR A HORSEDRAWN MEANDER AROUND WARSAW'S PECULIARLY NEW OLD-TOWN

Open-Air Festival, which runs from July to mid-August.

✪ Catch off-the-wall street theatre and a large dollop of anti-pop-culture sentiment in early July at the International Streets Arts Festival.

✪ Held over 10 days in September, the Warsaw Autumn International Festival of Contemporary Music provides Varsovians with the chance to hear the best of avant-garde music from around the world.

✪ Held in mid-October, the Warsaw International Film Festival showcases the best of independent world cinema. Its side event, Warsaw Screenings, specialises in new Polish films.

LIFE-CHANGING EXPERIENCES

✪ Marvelling at the reconstructed Old Town which, despite looking 200 years old, is only 40 years young.

✪ Paying homage to the Varsovians who lost their lives in defence of the city during WWII at the Warsaw Rising Museum.

✪ Wandering through the neglected Jewish cemetery, home to over 150,000 graves.

HOT TOPIC OF THE DAY

The effect of mass migration to the West. With skilled labour leaving in droves for better pay in the UK and Ireland, who will be left in Warsaw, and who is going to build the stadiums for football's 2012 European Championships?

RANDOM FACTS

✪ Almost 20% of the population is less than 17 years old.

✪ The world's first public library was opened here in 1747.

✪ Despite being miles from any sea or ocean, Warsaw's symbol is the mermaid.

✪ 85% of the city was destroyed in WWII.

MOST BIZARRE SIGHT

The mingling of old and new: country girls well into retirement selling bunches of freshly picked flowers to bright young things dressed in designer clothes and clutching the latest mobile phone.

BEST SHOPPING

Quality handmade craftsmanship is alive and well on Warsaw's back streets. Hunt down the likes of an exquisite chandelier or wall lamp from Wyrobów Oswietleniowych (ul Emilii Plater 36), a made-to-fit corset from Aniela (ul Zurawia 26), or a bronze candle holder or picture frame from Bracia Łopienscy (ul Poznanska 24).

CLASSIC PLACE TO STAY

Hotel Rialto. Its Art Nouveau décor is exceptional, and its restaurant regularly ranks in the city's top five.

✪ ZÜRICH, SWITZERLAND

'…this is one city that definitely changes its face after dark. That's when the pinstripe brigade yields the streets to glam bar-hoppers and clubbers…'

By Becca Blond

ZÜRICH, SWITZERLAND

POPULATION 351,700 ✪ **LANGUAGES** SWISS GERMAN, GERMAN, ENGLISH (FOR BUSINESS)
✪ **UNIT OF CURRENCY** SWISS FRANC (SFR) ✪ **AVERAGE HIGH TEMPERATURE** AUGUST DAILY HIGH 22°C, JANUARY DAILY HIGH 3°C ✪ **COST INDEX** BOTTLE OF ABSINTHE SFR50 (US$50), HALF PINT OF BEER SFR4 (US$4), HOTEL DOUBLE/DORM BED SFR150/SFR35 (US$150/35)

SPLIT PERSONALITY & PLENTY OF ENERGY

There's electricity in the air in Switzerland's most fun city, a vibrancy not found anywhere else in the country. Sure the city is home to all the typical Swiss stereotypes – banks, chocolate shops and plenty of places to buy a watch – but it's also party to art galleries and trendy bars. Hours pass easily by day, wandering the 13th-century old town's twisting cobbled streets or having an espresso with a bit of people-watching at one of the elegant cafés lining the Limmat riverfront. Zürich has two faces, old and new. The wide, placid Limmat River runs through it; elegant clock-faces and 800-year-old churches grace one side, while Züri-west, home to some of Europe's hippest nightlife, sprawls out on the other. No matter what side you're on, this is one city that definitely changes its face after dark. That's when the pinstripe brigade yields the streets to glam bar-hoppers and clubbers, and Zürich quickly becomes the poster girl for Europe's hip club scene, on par with Berlin and London.

WORK HARD, PLAY HARD

Work hard, play hard, that's this Swiss city's mantra it seems. During the day Zürich is a relatively sedate place. Those stereotypes involving straight-laced banker types bedecked in pinstriped suits who check their handcrafted Movado wristwatches regularly while dipping into a power lunch of *rösti* and sausage at a trendy old town café are definitely valid. But come dark, the city lets her hair down and becomes a totally different girl. When night falls, the suits and heels come off and the adults come out to play. The entire city hums quietly, like a well-oiled Swiss train, and effortlessly transforms into a club kid's fairy tale.

DEFINING EXPERIENCE

✪ Wandering the cobbled streets of the old town on a warm spring day when the city is green and flowering, popping down a hidden alley and discovering a homeopathic pharmacy sharing space with a doner kebab stall and retro boutique, or a cosy café in a 16th-century chateau.

✪ Indulging in cocoa sweets at Sprüngli, the mother of all chocolate shops and a Zürich institution. Sample a range of truffles and cakes downstairs, or head up to the elegant 1st-floor tea rooms to mingle with the well-heeled crowd over rich hot chocolate and crumpets.

FESTIVALS & EVENTS

✪ Zürich's wild trance-and-techno Street Parade became Europe's largest block party, overtaking London's Notting Hill Carnival a few years ago. Street Parade takes place in August

WHAT, NO TOBLERONE? REVELLERS POSE AT ZÜRICH'S TECHNO-HEAVY STREET PARADE

and attracts well over half a million ravers. All-night parties around the city follow a three-hour parade.

✪ Parades and costumes mark Fasnacht, an all-night carnival-style party held just after Ash Wednesday.

✪ Spring is celebrated on the third Monday in April with Sechseläuten when guild members, dressed in traditional costume, parade the streets and guild halls.

UNIQUELY ZÜRICH

Head to Letten for lake-swimming in summer, it's where Zuri-west trendsetters come for splashing, skateboarding, barbecues and drinking at the always crowded Bar Offen, one of the city's favourite summer-only bars

RANDOM FACTS

✪ Zürich's underground bank vaults are crammed with gold and silver.

✪ Both absinthe and LSD were invented in Switzerland.

✪ Protestant preacher Huldrych Zwingli first spread his message of 'pray and work' during the Reformation in the 16th century at the Grossmünster cathedral in the old town.

✪ During Sechseläuten, a fireworks-filled snowman (the Böögg) is blown up to symbolise the coming of warmer weather! Supposedly, the time it takes from the Böögg being lit to its head exploding determines the coming summer: a quick explosion means a warm summer, a slow one means a cold one.

CLASSIC RESTAURANT EXPERIENCE

Zeughauskeller. Definitely a Zürich institution, this favourite haunt manages not to feel too cheesy-touristy. An atmospheric beer hall, it

offers Swiss-German food at its most traditional – there are 20 different types of sausage on the menu! Other Swiss specialities are also featured, including treats for vegetarians.

BEST SHOPPING

Wander down Zürich's world-famous Bahnhofstrasse, where the shops are as posh as the banks – if you've got the cash, you can open a private Swiss account, then pop across the street for a credit-card binge at Louis Vuitton.

MOST BIZARRE SIGHT

If you're in town on Sunday morning head straight for the lake. On the Christian Sabbath, it seems as if all of Zürich takes an afternoon stroll around this large lake. Make sure to join in. There are sometimes human traffic jams, but it is definitely a worthwhile cultural experience.

BY SARAH BAXTER

THE ULTIMATE WATER TRAVELLER

IT'S GLOBAL AND ESSENTIAL

SARAH BAXTER grew up in England's flattest county, Norfolk (highest point: 100m), which goes some way to explaining her love of mountains. She's spent the past six years writing, trekking and travelling the world for *Wanderlust*, where she's currently deputy editor. She's fond of water in all its forms, having snorkelled with killer whales in Arctic Norway, floated among glow-worms in New Zealand's caves and touched the snows of Kilimanjaro (highest point: 5895m). But nothing, she reckons, beats standing on a cliff, pasty in hand, after hiking a chunk of Cornwall's South West Coast Path.

AND OFTEN A LOT OF FUN. RIGHT NOW IT'S THE MIRROR REFLECTING THE STATE OF THE PLANET

We always ought to think about water – but mostly we don't. Without it we wither; the average human body is 60% water and requires a constant supply. Yet our need for it is so fundamental that, unless facing a life-threatening shortage or surplus, we barely give it a thought. But now is the time every traveller needs to be more conscious of the world's water. As man and nature combine to alter the planet's ebb and flow – creating floods here, droughts there, eliminating countries and whipping up storms – the globe we're wandering across is changing.

We need to consider our impact on the planet's waterways, and do our utmost to protect them. We must tread carefully, consume less, and understand what water means to others: how it conveys Mali's traders to the markets of Timbuktu, brings in the New Year with a splash across Southeast Asia and cleanses the faces of Muslims before Allah. From the hot springs of Japan to the crash-and-flip of a raft-ride down the Zambezi, water is exhilarating, tranquil, terrifying and purifying. It's global, essential – and often a lot of fun. Right now it's the mirror reflecting the state of the planet.

In 1867 Mark Twain set sail aboard one of the world's first passenger cruises, a five-month trans-Atlantic odyssey costing $1250. Twain was enthralled by the idea: 'the bold originality, the extraordinary character, the seductive nature...of the enterprise...Who could read the program without longing to make one of the party?'

Today we can fly across the Atlantic in seven hours, but where's the romance in that? Would Twain have been so thrilled if he were boarding a 747 at JFK? It was embarking on a journey across the sea, into the unknown like Cook or Columbus, that excited, with the getting there as significant as the ports he docked at. Slow travel at its best.

WATER MOVES US

Water is essential to quench our thirst and nourish our crops, but our relationship with it goes far beyond such practicalities. Water has inspired travel and discovery, transporting the world's intrepid to mysterious realms in search of alien peoples, treasures and vegetables.

Way before Twain, Southeast Asians set off for Polynesia, the Polynesians for New Zealand, the Vikings across the Atlantic – not knowing what wonders, or dangers, they might encounter. From the 15th century the 'Great Age of Exploration' saw European seafarers venturing ever further until, in 1522, Ferdinand Magellan's depleted crew completed the first circumnavigation of the globe.

Today, as we consider the environmental impact of travel and the joy of the journey, we're nostalgic for past pioneers, eager to experience anew some of Twain's water-bound wonder. The Antarctic alone has seen

tourist numbers more than triple in the past 10 years.

It is not just a physical transport though: water moves us emotionally. In the 1880s cruising was encouraged by the British Medical Journal for its restorative qualities; it simply feels healthier to breathe when you're near water. Unsurprisingly, many of the world's great travel experiences – crossing Hong Kong's harbour by ferry, rafting the Colorado through the Grand Canyon, diving into the Great Barrier Reef – involve journeying on, in or to water.

WATER IS ALWAYS MOVING

We might hitch a brief lift, but water travels more than we ever could. Covering 70% of the planet – 97% of that in the oceans – the cycle of evaporation, condensation and precipitation means a Pacific Ocean droplet could become an Amazon downpour, an Andean lake, an Inca Trail trekker's coca tea...

Powerful natural forces help water along its way. The Gulf Stream whips water from the Gulf of Mexico across to northern Europe – helping its west coast stay mild. The Humboldt Current draws cold water from south Chile to the equator, and with it a profusion of marine life. And the monsoon winds from the Indian Ocean ensure the subcontinent gets a dousing between June and September.

Water's peregrinations – from glacier to fjord, river to sea, cloud to ground and kettle to cup – are essential. We need it to stay alive, but also to inspire, to remind us how small and relatively ineffectual we are. We may be meddling in the ways of water right now, but water's never-ending nomadism will continue around us, always tempting, always promising another adventure.

(TOP LEFT) » A CANADIAN COASTGUARD ICE-BREAKER PLOUGHS CHANNELS OF PASSAGE FOR THE REGION'S CONTROVERSIAL SEAL HUNTERS

(BOTTOM LEFT) » EGYPT'S SUEZ CANAL, OPENED IN 1869, CREATED A DIRECT 163KM CHANNEL FOR SHIPPING GOODS BETWEEN EUROPE AND ASIA

(TOP RIGHT) » POLAR BEAR FAMILIES, UNTIL RECENTLY A COMMON SIGHT IN THE NORTHWEST PASSAGE, ARE SLOWLY FALLING PREY TO ITS SHRINKING ICE COVER

(BOTTOM RIGHT) » KICKER ROCK IN THE GALAPÁGOS ISLANDS, WHERE A US$110 ENTRY FEE HELPS FUND CONSERVATION WORK ON FRAGILE ECOSYSTEMS

GO WITH THE FLOW

THREE GREAT OCEAN JOURNEYS FOR THE NEW CENTURY

NORTHWEST PASSAGE

The fabled shortcut from Europe to Asia via Arctic Canada, which teased explorers for four centuries, was finally traced by Roald Amundsen in 1906. But only in 2007 – due to melted ice clearing the route – was it deemed a commercially viable waterway. Good news for shipping, bad news for the region's ice-dependent polar bears.

GALÁPAGOS ISLANDS

2009 marks the 200th anniversary of Charles Darwin's birth, at a time when the archipelago that inspired his evolutionary theory is facing its greatest test. The Ecuadorian president has declared the islands 'in danger'; restrictions may be implemented to protect the unique animal inhabitants. Go – just tread carefully.

ROUND THE WORLD

Ferdinand Magellan's crew took three years to circumnavigate; today it takes 120 days. Board a cargo vessel in the UK, zip through the Panama Canal, across the Pacific, round Asia, up the Suez Canal, through the Med and back to Britain. Andrew Weir Shipping sails freighters on this route, with space for 12 travellers – but there's none of the quoits-and-cabaret hoo-hah of glammed-up cruise ships.

THE TURNING TIDES

In 2000, Ismail Serageldin, then World Bank vice-president for special programmes, declared: 'The wars of the 21st century will be fought over water.' As the planet's population rises – but the quantity of water on it doesn't – the disparity between demand and supply could be the powder-keg of the new millennium.

In an effort to supply water to earth's 6.7 billion people – already far more than our water cycle can sustain, and growing fast – we have dammed and diverted rivers and caused dramatic changes to the lay of the land. You need only travel to Central Asia's Aral Sea for evidence: this inland reservoir has shrivelled from 68,000 sq km in 1960 to just 16,525 sq km today.

Exacerbating this population upsurge is climate change: opinions on its causes and significance vary, but it's likely that ice caps will melt and seas will rise; warm, dry places will get drier, wet places wetter and floods more frequent. The Intergovernmental Panel on Climate Change (IPCC) predicts that, by 2080, up to 3.2 billion people will experience water shortages.

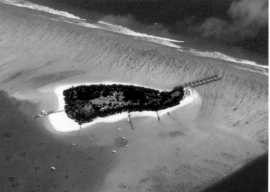

‘ **…IN 2006, REMOTE LOHACHARA – PRECARIOUSLY SITUATED IN THE FLOOD-PRONE INDIAN SUNDARBANS – WAS THE FIRST INHABITED ISLAND TO GO UNDER, CREATING THE PLANET'S FIRST CLIMATE REFUGEES.** ’

But haven't the world's water levels always fluctuated? Well, yes: previous millennia have seen both planet-wide Ice Ages and times so toasty that palm trees grew at the poles – think Costa del Svalbard. The Italian Dolomites, now poking more than 3000m above sea level, were once a coral reef; marine fossils are frequently found there.

You don't even have to go so far back: when Henry VIII came to the English throne in the 16th century the census recorded 139 vineyards in his kingdom. A subsequent 'Little Ice Age' chilled the UK, killing its viticulture and ensuring that Europe's foremost wine-tasting tours are today conducted on the other side of the Channel.

So it's always all change. As Greek philosopher Heraclitus stated: 'you can't step into the same river twice'. Water is constantly flowing, freezing, surging and receding on its journey to nurture life on the planet. And the state, rate and whereabouts of each drop have never been more important.

MAKING WAVES

'The unique problem we face now is the sheer rapidity of the change in climate, due to human interference', says Dr Sophie Nicholson-Cole of the Tyndall Centre for Climate Change Research. 'The temperature rise is happening at a much faster rate than has ever happened naturally, leading to a huge uncertainty as to how sea levels will respond.'

Some things *are* certain, however: Kiribati has already lost islands to the mounting Pacific and, in 2006, remote Lohachara – precariously situated in the flood-prone Indian Sundarbans – was the first inhabited island to go under, creating the planet's first climate refugees.

These lost lands aren't alone: the dreamy shores of the Maldives, Tuvalu and Vanuatu all face imminent submersion. Either that, or they must adapt – just like the pigs of Pacific-threatened Tokelau, which have learned to swim and fish as their beach-set pens have become swamped. Such species adjustment offers hope, as well as an unconventional and accidental tourist attraction.

But while we're losing some islands, we're gaining new ones. If the real Australia is submerged by

'...BUT TO WITNESS THE FRONT LINE OF WATER-GONE-HAYWIRE, HEAD TO ARCTIC CANADA AND HANG OUT WITH THE INUIT. '

a rising Pacific, buy a new one – the initial development stage of Dubai's 'The World', a vast, manmade, globe-resembling archipelago of artificial sandbanks, has just been completed. 'Greece' island sold for $15.5 million; the top-end 'Asian mega-island' is up for $263 million.

Land reclamation from the sea is nothing new – think London's Embankment, New Orleans, Hong Kong, most of the Netherlands – but the audacity of this project and the skill involved (including the construction of massive offshore breaks to protect the islands from

the elements) are mind-boggling. A tasteless attempt by the super-rich to tame nature, maybe, but could technology used to protect the mansions on 'China' and 'Ireland' be utilised to defend the shores of real-life Bangladesh?

For the people (formerly) living on the shores of the Aral Sea, land reclamation has been rather more inadvertent. While the damming of the Amu-Darya and Syr-Darya rivers in the 1960s successfully fed the cotton fields of Kazakhstan and Uzbekistan, the sea began to recede – drastically. The fish within

it, unable to adapt to such swift salt-concentration increases, died, ruining the livelihoods of the dependent fishermen. The tourism industry was also hit: once-seaside Muynak used to be popular with holidaymakers for its watery views; now travellers stop off only to wonder at the rusting hulls of redundant ships, tilting forlornly in the sand of the former docks, the sea now 100km away.

But to witness the front line of water-gone-haywire, head to Arctic Canada and hang out with the Inuit. Climate change – more pronounced at the poles – is challenging the

(LEFT) » ICE FISHING IN UNALAKLEET, ALASKA, MAY ONE DAY BE A THING OF THE PAST: INUIT COMMUNITIES ACROSS ALASKA AND CANADA HAVE BANDED TOGETHER TO FIGHT CLIMATE CHANGE AND THEIR POTENTIAL EXTINCTION

(TOP RIGHT) » A MOTORWAY DIKE IN IJSSELMEER, THE NETHERLANDS, WHERE LAND RECLAMATION HAS BEEN AN EVERYDAY PART OF LIFE FOR CENTURIES AND RECLAIMED LAND COMPRISES AROUND 20% OF THE ENTIRE COUNTRY

(BOTTOM RIGHT) » CRITICS OF THE THREE GORGES DAM SAY THAT ARCHAEOLOGICAL SITES AND IMPORTANT HABITATS FOR ENDANGERED SPECIES HAVE ALREADY BEEN LOST, AND MILLIONS OF LOCAL PEOPLE DISPLACED

centuries-old traditions of these supremely adapted survivors. Warmer temperatures are melting the permafrost their homes are built on and the ice they hunt on, whipping up more ferocious storms and eroding their coasts – the land they know intimately is starting to become alien and unpredictable.

Their animal cohabitants are facing an even sterner challenge. Polar bears, walruses and seals are struggling to survive as the ice they live on melts; caribou and reindeer are being caught out by shorter winters, returning to their spring feeding grounds too late to munch the early blooming grasses. Previously iced-up passages may now be more easily navigable for expedition ships, but will travellers rush to sail them if there's no wildlife left to watch?

Travelling today, water's fluctuations are increasingly evident. Lounge on a Caribbean beach from June to September (though these dates are becoming less reliable) to witness the increased rage of the Atlantic hurricane season. Or sail along China's Yangzi River and wonder at what you're missing – the Three Gorges Dam has flooded the valley, submerging hundreds of archaeological sites: 1300 will be engulfed by the time the dam is fully operational in 2011. All around, the planet is reacting to water's flux.

Adaptation is key to coping, but it's all happening so fast – for Arctic deer, Pacific pigs and humans alike. As little as five years ago, few travellers would have given a second's thought to their aviation carbon emissions, yet now tour operators are falling over themselves to be more ethical than their competitors. If the future is green, the present is more pale-mint,

❝ AS THE WATERY FACE OF THE PLANET CHANGES, SO WILL OUR TRAVEL PATTERNS, THE MOST DRASTIC OF WHICH BEING THE DISAPPEARANCE OF POTENTIAL DESTINATIONS. ❞

as we start to take on board the way water is changing, and gradually substitute planes for trains, hotels for eco-lodges. There's still a long way to go; the majority are *talking* green but acting global-warming red – after all, we've only just got used to the novelty of $2 flights! – but the tides are starting, quite literally, to turn.

AND THE FORECAST IS…
As the watery face of the planet changes, so will our travel patterns, the most drastic of which being the disappearance of potential destinations. Bangladesh (and its resident tigers), Indonesian islands, Hungary's Lake Balaton, the Amazon rainforest, California's Pacific Coast Highway (possibly the planet's coolest roadtrip?) all face extinction

as water ebbs here, rises there.

The urban landscape may change too, as water laps at some of the world's biggest conurbations. Cities including Kolkata, Mumbai, Shanghai and Miami are all, according to the Organisation for Economic Co-operation and Development (OECD) research, vulnerable to the increased flooding predicted for this century. One study suggests even the money men on Wall Street are vulnerable to the ravages of rising sea levels, with the Hudson and East Rivers predicted to subsume Manhattan's financial district. While rich economies such as the USA may be able to devise and fund strategies to safeguard their at-risk populations, the majority of the effects of climate change will be felt by those least able to pay their way out.

So as water rises and recedes, some parts of the planet might not make it through the century, forcing travellers to adopt a 'get there quick' attitude, with increasing interest in trips to at-risk destinations: the 'climate tourist' is born. Greenland's ice caps, the snows of Kilimanjaro, Andean glaciers (Argentina's Upsala alone is making a hasty retreat of 200m a year) – all will be high on the wish-list of intrepid travellers.

Coral reef devotees in particular may have to book soon if gloomy IPCC forecasts are correct: the organisation reckons up to 18% of the world's reefs will be gone by 2030, while the Worldwide Fund for Nature (WWF) estimates Australia's Great Barrier Reef could lose 95% of its coral by 2050 if sea temperatures

(TOP LEFT) » MOORE REEF, PART OF AUSTRALIA'S SPECTACULAR GREAT BARRIER REEF, WHICH STRETCHES FOR AN INCREDIBLE 2600KM: CLIMATE CHANGE, COMBINED WITH POLLUTION, IS ITS GREATEST ENEMY

(BOTTOM LEFT) » TOURISTS PHOTOGRAPH A MOUNTAIN GORILLA AT THE DEMOCRATIC REPUBLIC OF CONGO'S VIRUNGA NATIONAL PARK, WHOSE NORTHERN EXTENT INCLUDES PART OF AFRICA'S LARGEST GLACIAL REGION

(RIGHT) » LARGE STRETCHES OF THE CONGO RIVER AND ITS ENVIRONS ARE NOW PROTECTED BY LAW, ENSURING IT REMAINS PRISTINE FOR THOSE WHO MAKE A LIVING PLYING ITS WATERS

' IN OTHER GOOD NEWS, 13% OF THE WORLD'S LAND SURFACE

rise by 1.5°C. The glass-half-full perspective on these disastrous statistics is that we now *know* – as travellers aware of the most pessimistic predictions, we can look out for and encourage ecofriendly dive operators, sailing boats and beachfront accommodation. Indeed, in recognition of this vital link between well-managed tourism and the future welfare of the environment, the Great Barrier Reef Marine Park won the Destination award in the 2007 Tourism for Tomorrow Awards, the Oscars of the sustainable travel industry.

In other good news, 13% of the world's land surface now falls within designated protected areas. New national parks are being mooted all the time, and in countries not previously known for their green credentials. For instance, on World Wetlands Day 2008, the Congo designated four conservation areas, including 5.9 million hectares around the Congo River, now the world's second-largest protected wetland. With eco-issues very much on the world agenda, travellers will find more national parks safeguarding more environments (including

marine habitats) cropping up on green itineraries. Rather than high-rise resorts or villa-villages blighting seashores, swathes will be left pristine under the protection of ecolegislation.

It's not only travel destinations that will alter: perceived wisdoms will skew. Malaria, endemic in hot, humid countries, could spread as other areas develop ripe conditions – some doom-mongers say malarial mosquitoes could be causing havoc in southern Spain as soon as 2020. By the end of the century will we need prophylaxis for holidays in

NOW FALLS WITHIN DESIGNATED PROTECTED AREAS...IN COUNTRIES NOT PREVIOUSLY KNOWN FOR THEIR GREEN CREDENTIALS. "

Scandinavia? Heat-waves, cold-snaps and increased incidence of water-borne diseases could also get travellers thinking harder about their health before they head off.

Travel insurance costs will alter too as policymakers accommodate climate-change-induced phenomena, such as extreme weather and coastal flooding. Insurer Lloyds is already urging the industry to assess new risk levels so premiums can be adjusted – no doubt upwards. Perhaps it will be impossible to be covered for travel to certain areas based on the heightened risks from drought or drenching.

So it's all change in travel as well as in water, with some destinations demanding immediate attention and others falling off the map completely. Oddly, some spots may 'benefit' from the climatic shift. The coastlines of the north – Norway, Canada, the UK – could host the beach resorts *du jour* as their temperatures become more appealing. As the Mediterranean, Caribbean and Africa become unbearably hot and dry, travellers may change their tune – altogether now: 'We're all off to sunny Siberia...'

TRAVEL WATER-WISE

So mounting ecomessages will force us to travel differently. Do you really *need* an infinity pool in the arid African bush? Or a lushly tended golf course in dry-as-a-bone Dubai? Desert-stranded Las Vegas (average water consumption: 1162L per person per day, the highest in the world) will certainly have to bung up its act (though a colossal water theme park, Las Vegas Wet, is due to open in 2011).

Travellers will need to take personal responsibility, choosing to avoid water-guzzling destinations and

' TRAVELLERS KEEN TO WITNESS WORLD WONDERS WILL HAVE TO BECOME SAVVY TO NATURE'S ALTERATIONS. '

activities in favour of spending their dollars, dinars or yuan where they will be most useful. There may be a move towards explicitly philanthropic travel, where volunteering forms a large part of the itinerary. With extreme weather events and flooding on the up, such services and donations – akin to the global aid contributed after the 2004 tsunami – may be essential.

The onus will be on travellers to consume less. Reusing our hotel-room towels (after a speedy nonpower-shower) is the least we can do. We should limit our use of an area's resources and always buy local produce – surely a cinch, given how much better a homemade watermelon shake tastes on a Thai beach than a lukewarm imported Coke.

Travellers keen to witness world wonders will have to become savvy to nature's alterations. It may be that some areas are completely off-limits at certain times of year so as not to stretch limited local water resources. In other areas, seasons may shift, precipitation patterns dictating that, for example, February is no longer wet season in Botswana or that the Alps won't offer guaranteed snow – as recent winters are already testifying. While August might be the month to spot Monarch butterflies in Mexico in 2009, warmer weather might decree that, come 2109, July or September will be the months for migration – if they bother migrating from their newly warmer northern homes at all.

This increased unpredictability will make wildlife harder to see,

their patterns becoming erratic like the seasons. At worst, floods and droughts could lead to extinction. Brazil's Pantanal, for one, sits on a knife-edge: a proposed dam on the Río de la Plata is threatening to drain the world's largest wetland, at present home to a profusion of wild and wonderful species.

Also, the IPCC predicts that by 2020 between 75 and 250 million people in Africa will be exposed to increased water stress due to climate change. So where does that leave the wildlife? You only have to look to Saharan cave paintings to understand a worst-case scenario: desert etchings there depict giraffes, hippos and lions, indicating that animal-rich savannah used to be where now there is just inhospitable sand.

❛ ULTIMATELY WE'LL MOVE TO SLOWER TRAVEL, TAKING TRAINS, BUSES, BOATS OR BIKES TO OUR TRAVEL DESTINATIONS WHEN POSSIBLE. ❜

Flying is a tricky one. While we should be looking to decrease our air kilometres (aviation-pumped CO_2 is the most publicly vilified cause of water-level rising), flying will be easier than ever, with more routes on offer all the time. China alone is planning to construct 97 new airports by 2020. It will cost more though – as green issues become increasingly prevalent, higher taxes will be levied on flying, waving goodbye to the bargain-basement deals of today.

When you do fly, there are measures you can take to lessen your impact. Choose daytime flights during brighter months (when aeroplane contrails reflect sunlight and decrease warming effects) on more fuel-efficient aircraft. Offsetting your flights – paying an organisation a fee to 'neutralise' your carbon emissions by planting trees or setting up renewable-energy projects – is not an excuse to travel more. It also has its detractors: the industry is currently unregulated and sceptics argue that some of its schemes are fruitless or even exploitative. But as offsetting develops, it may truly help to mitigate the negative effects of your trip.

Ultimately we'll move to slower travel, taking trains, buses, boats or bikes to our travel destinations when possible. While the time outlay will be significant, the benefits – total and sustained cultural immersion, longer breaks – will make for a more satisfying travel experience. Not to mention recapturing an air of exploration; a smidgen of the sense of adventure that the Cooks and Columbuses of the past must have felt when they first set off on their boat journeys into the unknown.○

BOTTLED WATER – JUST SAY NO!

Quite aside from the results of a survey by Decanter magazine, which rated humble tap juice as more palatable than almost all of the mineral waters under scrutiny in a blind taste-test, the bottled water industry is one of the planet's most wasteful and destructive.

First, it's expensive. While tap water is free, one litre of top-end New Zealand 420 Volcanic sells for £50. Then there's the environmental impact: plastic containers made in fossil-fuel-belching factories are transported worldwide (think emissions), refrigerated (more emissions) and left to mount in unsightly landfill. The bottled water industry also creates a reliant culture, allowing the wealthy in societies supplied with impure, inadequate water to survive regardless,

weakening the demand to clean-up tap water and depriving millions of their basic right.

So what can travellers do? Always carry a refillable water bottle and top up from the mains. In countries with less sanitary supplies, use iodine or chlorine purification tablets, boil water if you can, and look out for coolers or jugs in hotel or hostel lobbies – many supply purified water for guests.

Finally, when you treat yourself to a slap-up meal at the end of a long trip, and the crisply dressed waiter approaches bearing crystal glasses, his neatly twizzled moustache twitching as he enquires: 'Still or sparkling?', reply with a firm and unashamed: 'Tap!'.

01 BEST FOR...SPARKLE
Kayak off Puerto Rico and watch the glow of bioluminescence in your wake – like a liquid version of the Northern Lights

02 BEST FOR...MIRACLES
Make like Moses and head to South Korea's Jindo Island, where the seas part in biblical fashion to reveal a footpath snaking across the seabed

09 BEST FOR...MOONBOWS
Time your trip to Victoria Falls with the full moon to see ghostly spray rainbows in the lunar light

10 BEST FOR...A GOOD SOAK
Penetrate the Japanese psyche – and get naked with strangers – in a traditional *onsen* (hot spring)

03 BEST FOR...DISCOVERY
Journey through the jungle to Peru's Yumbilla Falls – only 'found' in 2007, and alleged to be the world's third-tallest cascade

04 BEST FOR...SMELL SENSATION
Descend below Paris for that *Phantom of the Opera* feeling on a tour of the city's historic (and haunted?) sewers

05 BEST FOR...CONTINENT CROSSING
Sail from Europe to Asia in less than 10 minutes across the Bosphorus in divided Istanbul

06 BEST FOR...UNDERWATER BALLET
Snorkel with tens of thousands of gracefully pulsing (and stingless) jellyfish in South Pacific Palau

07 BEST FOR...ICEBERGS
Head to Newfoundland between March and July to watch icy monoliths from the Arctic float by

08 BEST FOR...GOING UNDERGROUND
Blackwater rafting in New Zealand's Waitomo Caves, or a boat trip through its glow-worm grottoes

11 BEST FOR...REFLECTION
Head down the road from the Rockies' postcard Lake Louise to less-visited Moraine Lake for mirror-image mountains in the glassy water

12 BEST FOR...HIDDEN DEPTHS
Hop off the Trans-Siberian Railway for a dip in pristine Lake Baikal – at 1637m, the planet's deepest plunge

13 BEST FOR...EXERCISE VOYEURS
Stroll along the Bund, Shanghai's iconic waterfront, before dawn to see a legion of t'ai chi-ers, fan dancers and various oddballs limber up before the city awakes

14 BEST FOR...PARTYING
Dance on the Danube in June at Vienna's vibrant island music festival

15 BEST FOR...DROPPING ANCHOR
Cruise to Australia's outer Great Barrier Reef to dive the top drops of this 2300km-long curve of coral

16 BEST FOR...STRANGE SURF
Ride the weird waves of the Amazon – the *pororoca* (tidal bore) roars at the mouth of the river, creating breaks of up to 6m

THE WORLD OF
WATER

WATER SAFARI

MEET THE BIGGEST STARS OF THE WORLD'S OCEANS
AND WATERWAYS

✪ MANTA RAYS

'Manta' is Spanish for blanket, but these titanic rays are more like magic carpets, gracefully swooping through the water. Though vast – their wingspan can top 6m – and sporting devilish horns (actually extra limbs), manta rays are gummy, stingless and no threat to humans. In fact they are curious creatures, often approaching divers for close encounters. Just don't touch – contact causes damaging lesions on their delicate skin.
WHERE? Night dives with mantas are possible off Big Island, Hawai'i. They are widespread in tropical waters: try dive sites off Mexico, the Maldives and Southeast Asia.

✪ WHALE SHARKS

Up to 14m long, with a mouth as wide as a car, the world's biggest fish looks pretty menacing. But whale sharks are filter feeders and have no interest in chomping on humans – indeed, they are the endangered ones, classified as 'vulnerable' by the World Conservation Union. This harmlessness makes them humbling to snorkel with: nothing reinforces your own insignificance like finning as fast as you can to keep up with a fish the size of a bus.
WHERE? Western Australia's Ningaloo Reef attracts large concentrations from April to June; also try Baja California and Djibouti's Gulf of Tadjoura.

✪ MANATEES

It was a short-sighted sailor indeed who mistook the chubby and somewhat aesthetically challenged sea cow

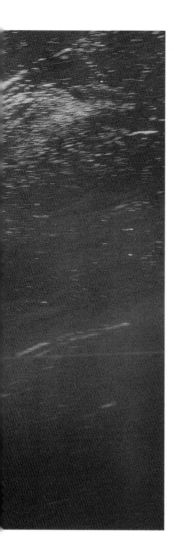

– think whiskery and woebegone tuskless walrus – for an alluring, fishtailed maiden. Nonetheless, it's thought manatees gave rise to mermaid legends; on seeing 'mermaids' in the New World, Columbus reportedly commented that he thought they'd be more attractive. But what the manatee lacks in looks, it makes up for in love. Snorkel with them and they'll likely snuffle over and give you a hug. WHERE? Head to Crystal River National Wildlife Refuge, Florida, from November to March.

✪ HAMMERHEADS

The hammerhead isn't like most sharks. There's its unconventional but acutely sensitive head, designed to sniff out the most diluted prey trail.

Its a sociable sort, too – while many sharks skulk alone, the hammerhead shoals (to find mates, it's thought): several hundred of them may glide together. They make a nerve-jangling mob but, while deemed the sea's seventh most dangerous shark, attacks on humans are extremely rare.

WHERE? Board a dive boat and anchor off Cocos Island, Costa Rica; also try Darwin Island, Galápagos.

✪ HUMPBACK WHALES

In just two locations worldwide it is possible to snorkel with a 14m-plus humpback, to get close to their bumpy heads and slender pectoral fins as they sashay through tropical waters. Hunted to near extinction,

the population is recovering and now 70,000 of these baleen feeders fill the oceans, both with their bulk and their song: the strange and sonorous tunes of a male humpback are unique to the species and can last for hours, the purpose as yet unknown. WHERE? Snorkel with humpbacks in Tonga, where they calve between July and September, and off the Dominican Republic, where they mate from January to April.

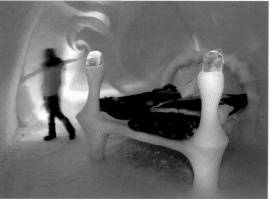

By Penny Watson

BELOW-ZERO GLOBAL

YOU WON'T BE ABLE TO SHAKE OFF THAT COLD – BUT WHY WOULD YOU WANT TO?

✪ SPOT THE NORTHERN LIGHTS – ALASKA (USA)

Light might be scarce during the winter months in Fairbanks, Alaska, but that's what makes this northern interior city an ideal place to set eyes on the aurora borealis, otherwise known as the northern lights. Typically this visual night-sky spectacular, taking place 80km to 320km above the earth, can be seen on an average 200 days per year, more if you head out of the city away from those other lights, the electric ones.

✪ CARVE UP THE ICE – HEILONGJIANG PROVINCE (CHINA)

Anywhere further north than Vladivostok, Russia, is bound to be cold, so it stands to reason Harbin, the capital of China's Heilongjiang Province, plays host to the International Ice and Snow Festival, a teeth-chattering event of extreme Disney-esque proportions held in January each year. The city's average winter temperature is -17°C, but the mercury can sink to -38°C – ideal temperatures for cutting massive blocks of ice from the

Songhua Jiang River and using them to carve 30m-high larger-than-life sculptures.

✪ SLEEP IN AN ICE HOTEL – JUKKASJÄRVI (SWEDEN)

Pieced together each December from the frosty ice blocks of the Torne River in the Swedish Arctic Circle, Jukkasjärvi's huge Icehotel will make your teeth chatter. To counteract below-zero temperatures, guests don woolly overalls, hats, mittens and boots and sleep under reindeer-fur blankets. Still cold? The toilet seats are heated.

✪ FLOAT ON AN ICEFIELD – FINNISH LAPLAND (FINLAND)

Kemi, in Finnish Lapland, offers an icy reception to those who dare dip into freezing water. With the help of a

specialised thermal suit, guests aboard the world's only tourist icebreaker, the *Sampo*, can step off the boat into the middle of Europe's largest icefield and bob around like an iceblock amid sheets of frozen Arctic water.

✪ WALK A FROZEN RIVER – CHADAR ICE TREK (INDIA)

At the end of January for a few short weeks, India's Zanskar River freezes over, opening the way for an epic icy river-gorge trek through the isolated high passes of the Zanskar mountains. The Chadar Ice Trek, as it's known, is not for the faint-hearted. Temperatures can plummet to -30°C. When this happens the only way to warm up is to keep walking at least until you reach cave accommodation and campfires are lit. Cold comfort?

✪ GO COLD CAMPING – NEW SOUTH WALES (AUSTRALIA)

Follow the oversized footsteps of your snow-shoed guide into the gum-spotted Snowy Mountain scenery surrounding Australia's Thredbo ski resort. Here, an insulated tent, a boiling billy and a survival skill or two are essential ingredients for an overnight camp on one of Australia's snowiest peaks. Sleep serenely under the Southern Cross while the snow flutters down around you.

✪ DRINK IN AN IGLOO – HOKKAIDO (JAPAN)

On Japan's northernmost island of Hokkaido, Niseko's bizarre Ice Bar is in fact an igloo where the barmen wear more ski gear pouring drinks than they need on the powdery slopes. Finish off a day's backcountry

snowboarding with an ice-cold beer or a whiskey on the rocks. Actually, make that a mulled wine.

✪ DIVE BELOW THE ICE – FRENCH ALPS (FRANCE)

If the cold doesn't make your teeth chatter, the fear factor will. Ice diving under the frozen surface of Lake Tignes in the French Alps pushes the limits of extreme activity. Don a thick drysuit, gloves and mask, attach the rope then descend through an Eskimo-style hole into an icy playground where bubbles dance to the surface through turquoise sunlit water.

✪ LAND ON A GLACIER – FOX & FRANZ JOSEF GLACIERS (NEW ZEALAND)

The sheer scale of New Zealand's low-lying Fox and Franz Josef Glaciers, on the west coast of the South Island, is

best observed from the hot seat of a helicopter. The giddy highs achieved by flying the length of these rivers of frozen ice – across glacial icefalls, plateaus and crevasses – are only topped by actually landing on one. Circle the peak of magnificent Aoraki (Mt Cook) on the way back to base.

✪ TAKE A HUSKY RIDE – FINNMARK PLATEAU (NORWAY)

On the Finnmark Plateau, north of the Artic Circle, husky safaris make the journey along ancient frozen routes, once the highway of the Sami people. Be guided by a local musher in a dog sled led by a crew of energetic Alaskan huskies as you travel through the Arctic silence across frozen lakes and snow-white tundra. Sleep in cosy wooden huts, tucked up under reindeer pelts as the snow falls outside.

FABULOUS FERRIES

BOAT JOURNEYS THAT ARE SO MUCH MORE THAN A TRIP FROM A TO B

THE INSIDE PASSAGE
(CANADA & ALASKA)

The words 'spectacular' and 'public transport' are seldom mentioned in the same breath, but the ferry that glides along the island-flanked and glacier-fed coast of British Columbia and Alaska – around 2000km of scenic, sheltered waterway – deserves both. There is no need to splurge on a cruise ship; Alaska Marine Highway ferries spend four affordable days threading the channel from Belling-ham to Juneau year round. Book a cabin, or hunker down on deck – the perfect vantage for surveying this realm of pristine and largely inaccessible temperate rainforest, where spirit bears roam on shore, whales and orca feed in the waters and bald eagles hover above.

✪ RMS ST HELENA
(SOUTH ATLANTIC)

There is not much time left to embark on one of the planet's longest ferry journeys. The last remaining Royal Mail Ship – which delivers both cargo and the curious to the remote South Atlantic – will be retired when the island of St Helena finally gets an airport, slated for 2010. The ship sails just 12 times a year from South Africa (and once a year from the UK) to the isolated island; it takes seven days from Cape Town, during which time its 128 passengers dine on some of the sea's finest suppers, limber up for onboard cricket and mourn the loss of a maritime institution.

✪ DOWN THE NIGER TO TIMBUKTU (MALI)

The overburdened ferry that wheezes downriver from near Bamako to the planet's most alluring (in name at

least) city isn't a boat – it's a seething, clucking mass of humanity, bursting at the bulwarks. There's nothing much to do for the five days you're on board – this is top-notch slow travel. Discuss politics with businessmen and banana-sellers, lean overboard to buy supplies from pirogue-punting hawkers and sip tea boiled by praise-singing ladies as villages, hippo nostrils and Saharan dunes bob by.

⭐ LAKE MALAWI (MALAWI)

You wouldn't set your watch by the *MV Ilala*. Though she's been chugging the length of the world's ninth-largest lake, a three-day amble from Monkey Bay in the south to northern Chilumba, for 50-odd years, she hasn't become any more punctual. But relax: let the sandy bays soothe you to African time... until you enter port. This boat is the lifeblood for lakeside communities and all hell breaks loose when the *Ilala* drops anchor. Passengers, their kids, their kid's goats, their goat's kids, maize bags, wheelbarrows, bicycles – all are loaded and unloaded in a cacophony of waving, shoving and shouting. It's Malawi in microcosm.

⭐ RÍO PARAGUAY (PARAGUAY)

There are no creature comforts – just creatures – on the ferries that delve from capital Asunción (the world's cheapest city) into one of the least-populated patches of South America: the Gran Chaco. Try the two-day run from crumbling Concepción to Puerto Vallemi, where the Río Paraguay disappears into the Brazilian Pantanal – here, river traffic peters out and the banks crawl with capybara, caiman and monkeys. Sling your hammock with Guaraní Indians, slurp a bowl of piranha-head soup and enjoy.

WATER WORSHIP

THE WORSHIP OF WATER IS OFTEN THE CENTREPIECE OF RELIGIOUS ACTIVITY AROUND THE WORLD

A Hindu in Mumbai, a Catholic in Milan, a Klamath Indian in the USA: all hold water sacred. It's simultaneously life-sustainer, purifier, healer and destroyer, revered and feared down the centuries by cultures worldwide.

It's impossible to travel without noticing this liquid devotion. Arrive in the Rajasthani town of Pushkar

and it's thrust upon you. Hugging a holy lake, Pushkar is brimful of sadhus who whisk you shoreside to perform a watery *puja* (prayer) – for a 'donation'. If motives may be suspect, consider that this lake is a major pilgrimage site for Hindus, a faith that venerates water more than most. For proof, stand on the banks of the Ganges – at Rishikesh,

Haridwar, Varanasi – and watch. Here, devotees immerse themselves, certain its blessed flow will wash away their sins.

Visit any mosque to see a most labour-intensive form of purification. Islam dictates that feet, forearms and faces must be cleaned before praying to Allah, resulting in a five-washes-a-day ritual for strict Muslims, and

(LEFT) » THE WHOLE FAMILY GOES FOR A DIP DURING THE HOLY WATER CEREMONY AT THE SPRING WATER TEMPLE IN TAMPAKSIRING, BALI

(TOP RIGHT) » THE BISHOP OF BARNAUL BLESSES AN OPEN-AIR FONT IN THE OB RIVER, ON EPIPHANY DAY IN RUSSIA

(BOTTOM RIGHT) » ALWAYS HAVE YOUR BEST IDEAS IN THE SHOWER? TWO JAPANESE BUDDHIST MONKS MEDITATE BENEATH AN ICY WATERFALL

SIX LOCATIONS FOR A
LIQUID BLESSING

BETHANY BEYOND THE JORDAN (JORDAN) – it was supposedly here that John baptised Jesus; thanks to excavations only begun in 1996, you can now visit the site's churches and baptismal pools.

LOURDES (FRANCE) – roll up, roll up for all your religious kitsch. The miracle-working spring has been curing the Catholic sick since 1858, and flogging them tasteless souvenirs for almost as long.

LAKE TITICACA (BOLIVIA/PERU) – sail across the high-altitude blue, where Inca god Viracocha created civilisation, to Isla del Sol; here, Inti (the Sun God) made his water-based home.

CAPE REINGA (NEW ZEALAND) – watch the Tasman Sea and Pacific collide at Reinga ('underworld'), where Maori believe dead souls enter the afterlife.

PAMUKKALE (TURKEY) – paddle with old artefacts in the healing pool of ancient Hierapolis ('sacred city'), then watch water dribble onto the brilliant-white travertine terraces that give Pamukkale ('cotton castle') its new name.

MIYAJIMA (JAPAN) – take the ferry from Hiroshima to Miyajima Island where a wooden temple, dedicated to the Shinto goddesses of the sea, stilt-stands in the water as if floating.

some beautiful fountains at mosques. Likewise, Japan's Shinto shrines contain troughs where adherents rinse before worshipping, and Jews perform mikvah ablutions before special occasions.

> **THIS SPIRITUAL CLEANSING CAN EXTEND TO PHYSICAL HEALING, WITH MANY BELIEVING A DIP IN, OR DRAM OF, THE RIGHT WATER ABLE TO CURE EVERYTHING FROM HEADACHE TO HIV.**

This spiritual cleansing can extend to physical healing, with many believing a dip in, or dram of, the right water will cure everything from headache to HIV. Ethiopia's Christians flock to Mt Entoto, the peak looming over Addis Ababa, to be cured in its sacred stream, now flanked by churches. The *huaringas* ('sacred lakes') near Huancabamba in Peru's Andes attract shamans who

perform hallucinogen-fuelled rites and direct the hopeful sick to then bathe in the lake most fitting for their ailment. And pagans, Romans and Christians alike have dallied in Bath for 7000 years to partake of England's most efficacious waters – though what early man would make of the recently renovated spa facilities encasing the superspring today is anyone's guess.

Some water sources are übersacred: the rivers cascading from divine Mt Kailash and the gush from Mecca's Zamzam Well take some out-holy-ing. But you don't need to go to such hallowed examples – in the simple font of every church, in a small celebration to welcome the monsoon rain, in the raising of a glass to toast your host's health, water worship has flooded every part of the planet.

✪ GRAND PRISMATIC SPRING (USA)

The colour competition's stiff in Wyoming's Yellowstone National Park: Emerald Lake, Rainbow Pool, Pink Cone Geyser – flamboyant show-offs all. But Grand Prismatic Spring takes the technicolour title. Pigmented bacteria grow in microbial mats surrounding the planet's third-largest hot spring, creating a steaming splat of graduated indigo-blue-green-yellow-orange-red water. For the best view, go just beyond Fairy Falls Trailhead and look down on the broiling fantasia below.

✪ KAMCHATKA (RUSSIA)

The brown bears (all 12,000 of them) are the dullest thing about Kamchat-ka's hard-to-reach landscape. Hugging the Pacific Rim of Fire, the rumbling peninsula's 300 volcanoes ensure an unconventional colour palette. Lakes aren't blue – they're gaudy turquoise or shocking green. Burping mud holes are white, grey or rust-red. Geysers, fumaroles and hot-water scorch-marks are variously yellow, cobalt, umber or lime, accompanied by a stink of sulphur and school-boy fart noises. It's an eight-hour flight from Moscow but, with all its weirdy wonders, it could be another world.

✪ KELIMUTU (INDONESIA)

Make sure you drag yourself up early for the 45-minute *bemo* (minibus) ride so that you reach Inspiration Point by 5.30am. Watching the sun rise over the moonscape of volcanic Kelimutu will make it worth the effort: the darkness peels back to reveal three deep crater-lakes – each a strikingly different colour. Folklore has it that these sacred cauldrons are where the spirits of the dead go: the young to turquoise Tiwa Nuwa Muri Koo Fai; the old to brown Tiwi Ata Mbupu; the wicked to black Tiwi Ata Polo. However, given that the lakes change colour with the year and the season – oxygen and mineral levels sending them purple, red, chocolate and green by turn – you have to hope those souls don't get confused.

✪ NILE CONFLUENCE (SUDAN)

Arabian poets call it the 'longest kiss in history' – which, admittedly,

(LEFT) » AROUND 49M DEEP AND DISCHARGING ABOUT 2000L OF WATER PER MINUTE, THE GRAND PRISMATIC SPRING'S BUBBLING TEMPERATURES MAKE IT A LITTLE TOO TOASTY TO DIP YOUR TOES

(TOP RIGHT) » THE WATERS GO WAY BEYOND BLUE IN THE CRATER LAKE ATOP THE MALY SEMIACHIK VOLCANO ON RUSSIA'S 1250KM-LONG KAMCHATKA PENINSULA

(BOTTOM RIGHT) » I'M SURE I SAW A FLAMINGO HERE SOMEWHERE…A SOLITARY SPOTTER GAZES DOWN AT THE LAGUNA COLORADA, TO WHICH JAMES'S, ANDEAN AND CHILEAN FLAMINGOS – ALONG WITH INTREPID TRAVELLERS – ARE IRRESISTABLY DRAWN

sounds much nicer than 'confluence' and does more to convey the import of this river collision. The pale-silt-carrying White Nile, rushing up from Uganda, and the soily Blue Nile, on its way west from Ethiopia, get it on in Khartoum – meeting, flirting for a stretch (their coloured waters flowing together but still visibly separate) before entwining for a monotone future together, watering farmers and pharaohs all the way through Egypt. Take a ferry to rural Tuti Island, in the middle of the city, and look back on the liquid love story.

✪ LAGUNA COLORADA
(BOLIVIA)
Tinged by the algae and plankton in its mineral-dense waters, blood-red

RAINBOW WATER
GO BEYOND BLUE – MEET THE LAKES, SPRINGS AND RIVERS THAT DARE TO BE DIFFERENT

Laguna Colorada epitomises the harsh, inhospitable terrain of Andean Bolivia. Inhospitable, that is, to almost everything but flamingos, three species of which flock to feed here in their thousands to add their pink plumage to the

mix, despite the 4000-plus-metre altitude and icy temperatures. If red's not your colour, move on: nearby a selection of blue-green Laguna Verde, wine-hued Laguna Guinda and milky Laguna Blanca add to the cocktail.

✪ SHACKLETON'S FOOTSTEPS (SOUTH GEORGIA)

In 1916 explorer Ernest Shackleton – bedraggled and exhausted from five months marooned on pack ice, then 16 days sailing for help on a tiny boat – took just 36 hours to tramp across the never-before-penetrated interior of South Georgia. Today visitors to the near-Antarctic island will more likely need three or four days to get from King Haakon Bay to deserted (save for seals) Stromness whaling station, via craggy peaks, crevasse-riven glaciers and an enormous huddle of king penguins. Global warming has increased the difficulty but, as you strap on your crampons and haul yourself through the perilous terrain, you'll still be astonished by Shackleton's mighty achievement.

✪ CAMINO REAL (PANAMA)

There aren't many walks that cross continents and join oceans. But Panama's 'Royal Road' leads you from Pacific to Atlantic in just five – albeit sweaty, strenuous, viper-infested – days. This is the route the conquistadors used to haul their pilfered Inca gold back to Spain (once they'd learned the shortcut from the local Indians). Its alleged that there's treasure still hidden along its jungly depths – though you're more likely to find bare-breasted Emberá tribeswomen, languid sloths, a rainbow of birds and, perhaps, the flash of a resident jaguar.

✪ CHADAR TREK (INDIA)

In freezing midwinter the only way to reach Zanskar – one of the most isolated inhabited valleys in Ladakh's Himalaya – is to walk on water. The iced-over Zanskar River provides a solid (mostly) and sparkling catwalk for locals taking their butter to market

WALKING ON WATER

TOP TREKS TO TAKE YOU OVER, ALONGSIDE OR RIGHT ON TOP OF THE WORLD'S BEST WET BITS

in Leh and trekkers brave enough to camp out in -30°C temperatures. This is a serious five- to eight-day expedition, but the rewards are caves, monasteries and towering mountain viewpoints where everyone else isn't.

✪ THE GREAT OCEAN WALK (AUSTRALIA)

The Great Ocean Walk embraces the 91km of coastal Victoria that the Great Ocean Road just couldn't reach. Totally untamed, this bulge of blue gum and eucalyptus, rocky headlands and Southern Ocean-slapped beaches is also known as the Shipwreck Coast:

more than 700 vessels have come a cropper here, some leaving anchors as evidence on the wide strands. It takes six to eight days to walk the lot, carrying your own supplies (there's little civilisation en route), or get a local operator to set up your camp each night, leaving you to look out for roos and koalas unencumbered.

✪ SOUTH WEST COAST PATH (ENGLAND)

England's longest walking trail is a beauty. Originally blazed in the 1820s by foot-patrolling coastguards eager to thwart hiding smugglers, it traces

the coast for 1000 torturous, up-down kilometres from Minehead in Devon to Poole in Dorset. Eight weeks should cover the lot, but many attempt it in shorter sections. However you try, it won't disappoint: along its route you'll find Mediterranean-turquoise bays, historic ruined tin mines, a rock-hewn abbey on its own island, surf beaches, deserted beaches, grey seals and basking sharks, and the best Cornish pasties in the land.

WATER WHERE?

OCEANS ARE OBVIOUS, BUT DESERTS? SOMETIMES WATER APPEARS IN THE MOST UNLIKELY PLACES

✪ CENOTES (MEXICO)

Despite its forested luxuriance, you won't see many rivers on the Yucatán Peninsula – the water here gushes unobserved beneath the surface. The only windows to this subterranean aqua-park are cenotes, circular sink-holes exposed following the collapse of the rock above. Some of the area's 7000-plus cenotes make nature's best swimming pools: secluded, fish-full and draped with vines. Others lead deep into eerie caverns of stalactites, stretching off into 100km-long cave networks – believed by the Maya to be the entrance to the underworld.

✪ SIWA OASIS (EGYPT)

A crumble of mud-brick houses, date palms swaying around desert pools, a domineering ruined fortress and donkey carts on dusty tracks – Siwa makes a fair bid for the 'Most Stereotypically Oasis-y Oasis' title. Marooned in Egypt's far western sand-sea, sealed road only reached Siwa in the 1980s, though Alexander the Great stumbled on its welcome springs and was pronounced pharaoh here in 332 BC. Still, being so isolated has had a profound effect: Berber-descended Siwans have their own language, tribal system and intricately embroidered outfits – recently seen on the catwalks of Milan.

✪ LAKE VOSTOK (ANTARCTICA)

It's one of the biggest freshwater lakes on the planet. And probably the least spoiled – because it's been hiding 4000m below the surface of

the Antarctic ice cap for the past 25 million years. Welcome to Lake Vostok, the most massive of the 140-odd subglacial lakes that lurk, against the odds, full of liquid water beneath the White Continent. Knowledge of these buried reservoirs is sketchy, but it's believed that cleverly adapted organisms may exist down there. And given the lake's similarity to the subsurface of Mars, discovery of life in Vostok could just point to the possibility of life on the red planet.

✪ HEXI CORRIDOR (WESTERN CHINA)

Traders on a strand of the ancient Silk Road found welcome relief in this 1000km-long passageway snaking between the sinister Taklamakan Desert (meaning 'go in, don't come out') and the vast Gobi. The Hexi Corridor's oases became key hubs for the exchange of goods and cultures in China's wild west. Bleakly stranded Jiayuguan fort and the Buddhist-art-crammed Mogao Caves near Dunhuang hint at the area's past glories, while gradually shrinking Crescent Moon Lake, today just a third of its former size as the dunes drink it up, illustrates the desert's water rapacity.

✪ THE GREAT MAN-MADE RIVER PROJECT (LIBYA)

Thirsty Libya – 90% desert – is one of the planet's driest countries; in some areas rain doesn't fall for decades. But deep beneath the arid undulations of the Sahara, where temperatures can soar up to 57°C, a massive, pre–Ice Age aquifer gurgles. In possibly the most audacious (or just mad?) engineering scheme in history, a colossal network of under-sand pipes stretching 4000km from the country's far south to its water-short coastal cities is being constructed. Turn on a tap in cosmopolitan Tripoli to wash in the results, made possible by what Qaddafi's dubbed 'the eighth wonder of the world'.

(LEFT) » SOME CENOTES ARE MEANT FOR MARVELLING AT; SOME ARE DIVINE FOR DIVING; STILL OTHERS SPORT RESTAURANTS: THERE'S SOMETHING FOR EVERYONE IN YUCATAN'S SUBTERRANEAN FAIRYLAND

(TOP RIGHT) » THE HEXI CORRIDOR'S CRESCENT MOON LAKE NEAR DUNHUANG, WHOSE NAME MEANS 'GRANDEUR AND PROSPERITY', REFLECTING ITS HISTORICAL IMPORTANCE AS A PITSTOP ON THE SILK ROUTE

(BOTTOM RIGHT) » THE ORACLE TEMPLE AT SIWA, WHERE A PENCHANT FOR ECO-TOURISM IS NOURISHED BY ECOLODGES LIKE ADRER AMELLAL, WHICH AIM TO SAFEGUARD SIWA'S STUNNING OASIS ENVIRONMENT

WATER FESTIVALS
GET WET AT THE PLANET'S BEST SOAKING CELEBRATIONS

✪ FESTA DE AGUA (SPAIN)

Way, way back in the, er, 1980s, worshippers stood dutifully under the merciless August sun as the effigy of San Roque processed around the scorched streets of Vilagarcía de Arousa. As the heat intensified, the devout called for water – and onlookers obliged, drenching the crowds from the windows above. Thus a modern tradition was born, and since the early 1990s, water throwing (in biblical quantities) has become an official component of the town's holy day (on 16 August). You just have to abide by the rules: no drop can be flung until San Roque is safely inside his chapel, to protect him from the watery cross-fire now launched in his name.

✪ OMIZUTORI (JAPAN)

Who needs Botox? Head to Nara's Todai-ji temple in March for an ancient water-drawing ritual instead, where the Wakusa Well's contents reputedly heal the process of aging. At 2am on the 13th day of the festivities, which run from 1 to 14 March, a torch-lit procession of softly chanting priests scoops water from the well as an offering to the people and the 11-headed goddess of mercy, Kannon. The lustral liquid is poured into two pots, one of which holds water from all previous ceremonies, dating back to AD 752.

✪ NEW YEAR (SOUTHEAST ASIA)

It's the world's biggest water fight: call it Songkran (Thailand), Bpee Mai (Laos), Chaul Chnam (Cambodia) or

MAKE LIKE THE MILLIONS BY TAKING A DIP IN THE HOLY GANGES, WHICH MANY CONSIDER TO BE THE LIFEBLOOD OF MOTHER INDIA HERSELF

Thingyan (Myanmar), come mid-April (the region's hottest month) Southeast Asia picks up its water pistols to wash off the old and welcome new year. A time of cleansing, locals bathe Buddha statues and sprinkle water on the hands of loved ones to show respect; except sprinkling has evolved into a damned-fine dousing as bucket- and balloon-armed masses take to the streets with soggy gusto.

✪ KUMBH MELA (INDIA)

In January 2007 more than 70 million Hindu pilgrims converged on Prayag (Allahabad) for the Kumbh Mela – the world's largest gathering. That's the population of the UK, plus 10 million extras, assembled in one city for an en masse sin-purging dip at the sacred confluence of the Ganges, Yamuna and Saraswati Rivers. Thanks to a god-versus-demons fight over the *kumbh* (urn) of immortal nectar several thousand years ago, drops were spilt on four now superholy Hindu cities: Prayag, Haridwar, Ujjain and Nasik. The *mela* alternates between the four, with the main Maha Mela occurring every 12 years, and a mini *mela* taking place every three years between. Head to Haridwar in March/April 2010 for the next big bath – if you dare.

✪ KU-OMBOKA (ZAMBIA)

When the fertile plains of the Upper Zambezi River begin to flood – around Easter – the king of the Lozi knows it's time to shift. The king, or Litunga, leads his people to higher ground, with three mammoth drums heralding his departure in a zebra-striped barge. While the Litunga wears a dapper suit, his 96 polers sport headdresses topped with tufts of lion mane and row the regal vessel to the boom and ululations of accompanying musicians. The queen, local dignitaries and lucky, right-place-right-time travellers follow, gliding towards Limulunga for a right royal knees-up.

A STRETCH OF AMAZON NEAR MANAUS, BRAZIL, WHICH PROSPERED HISTORICALLY THANKS TO TRADE FLOATING IN ON THE MIGHTY RIVER

MAKES A CHANGE FROM A PET RABBIT...CHAM MUSLIM BOYS DISPLAY THE CATCH OF THE DAY ON THE MEKONG RIVER IN PHNOMH PENH

WORLD RIVERS

WHERE THEY GO AND WHERE TO SEE THEM

NILE
From Greek 'Neilos' – 'River Valley'
LENGTH (WORLD RANKING) 6695km (ranked 1 – allegedly; in 2007 researchers claimed the Amazon is actually 6800km)
COURSE From Lake Tana (Ethiopia) and south of Lake Victoria (Tanzania/Uganda), the Blue and White Niles converge in Sudan before charging north through Egypt to the Med.
WHERE TO EXPERIENCE IT At Tis Issat (Blue Nile Falls) in **Ethiopia**; white-water rafting around Jinja in **Uganda**; or in **Egypt**: temple-bagging at Aswan, felucca-sailing from Luxor or on the deck of a chaotic Cairo river bus.

AMAZON
From the Greek legend of women warriors
LENGTH (WORLD RANKING) 6516km (ranked 2 – but largest by volume)
COURSE Starting in the Peruvian Andes, tributaries join from Ecuador, Bolivia and Colombia to rush across Brazil into the Atlantic.
WHERE TO EXPERIENCE IT At seriously remote Kapawi rainforest lodge in **Ecuador**; floating past the macaw-busy claylicks of Manu Biosphere Reserve in **Peru**; or sailing on a riverboat from Manaus, **Brazil**, to the Peru–Colombia triborder.

YANGZI
From Chinese 'Chang Jiang' – 'Long River'
LENGTH (WORLD RANKING) 6380km (ranked 3)
COURSE East from the Tibetan Plateau through China to Shanghai.
WHERE TO EXPERIENCE IT At **Shigu**, the river's dramatic first bend; in cavernous **Tiger Leaping Gorge**, saved (for now) from controversial damming; or sailing the **Three Gorges**, though the associated dam (due for completion in 2011) will increase water levels by up to 100m.

MEKONG
From Thai 'Mae Khong' – 'Mother of all Rivers'
LENGTH (WORLD RANKING) 4425km (ranked 11)
COURSE From the Tibetan Plateau through China, Myanmar, Thailand, Laos, Cambodia and Vietnam.
WHERE TO EXPERIENCE IT On the two-day slow boat from Huay Xai to Luang Prabang, **Laos**; river-dolphin-watching around Kratie, **Cambodia**; or haggling at Can Tho floating market, **Vietnam**.

ALL ABOARD THE TIGER LEAPING GORGE FERRY WHILE YOU STILL CAN: CHINA'S PLANS FOR A DAM HERE HAVE BEEN SCRAPPED BUT MAY RESURFACE EVENTUALLY

KAZUYOSHI NOMACHI » CORBIS | ROBERT HARDING WORLD IMAGERY » CORBIS | NEIL McALLISTER » ALAMY

MISSISSIPPI

From Anishinaabe 'Misi-ziibi' – 'Great River'

LENGTH (WORLD RANKING) 3766km (ranked 14; but ranked fourth as the combined Mississippi-Missouri)

COURSE South from Minnesota through 10 states to the Gulf of Mexico.

WHERE TO EXPERIENCE IT Loon-spotting on Lake Itasca (the river's source) in northwestern **Minnesota**; Elvis-impersonating (a-huh-huh) in **Memphis**; or cycling – a 3000km-long riverside trail is being constructed.

YUKON

'Great River' in Gwich'in

LENGTH (WORLD RANKING) 3184km (ranked 20)

COURSE From British Columbia, into the Yukon and out through Alaska to the Bering Sea.

WHERE TO EXPERIENCE IT In **Canada**, kayaking from Whitehorse to Dawson City like a gold-rush pioneer; or scenic salmon-fishing anywhere in **Alaska**.

INDUS

From Sanskrit 'Sindhu' – 'Ocean'; the name given to part of Pakistan

LENGTH (WORLD RANKING) 3180km (ranked 21)

COURSE From the Tibetan plateau through India and Pakistan to the Arabian Sea.

WHERE TO EXPERIENCE IT At sacred Lake Mansarovar, **Tibet**, one of the planet's highest freshwater lakes (4556m) and the river's source; or along the Karakoram Highway, which coils with the river through **Pakistan**, between three mighty mountain ranges.

DANUBE

From Danuvius – Celtic for 'flow'

LENGTH (WORLD RANKING) 2850km (ranked 29)

COURSE From Germany's Black Forest east through Central and Eastern European before pouring into the Black Sea.

WHERE TO EXPERIENCE IT In the public steam baths of Budapest, **Hungary**; in clubbing capital Belgrade, **Serbia**; or bird-ogling afloat the Danube Delta, **Romania**.

ZAMBEZI

Tonga for 'Great River'

LENGTH (WORLD RANKING) 2574km (ranked 31)

COURSE Loops around Zambia, skirting Zimbabwe, and out to Mozambique and the Indian Ocean.

WHERE TO EXPERIENCE IT Peering into Victoria Falls; rafting the hippo- and croc-infested rapids; or spotting wild dogs in even wilder Lower Zambezi National Park, **Zambia**.

GANGES

From Hindi 'Gang Ma'

LENGTH (WORLD RANKING) 2510km (ranked 39)

COURSE From the Indian Himalaya, south-east into Bangladesh and the Bay of Bengal.

WHERE TO EXPERIENCE IT On the six-day pilgrimage to Gangotri Glacier, the river's sin-purging source, by the burning ghats of holy Varanasi, **India**; tiger-spotting among the mangroves of the Sundarbans in **Bangladesh**.

HOLD ONTO YOUR HAT AS YOU PLUNGE OVER THE ZAMBEZI, AFRICA'S FOURTH-LONGEST RIVER, ON A SEAPLANE SAFARI

FLOAT YOUR BOAT ALONG THE MILES CANYON ON CANADA'S YUKON RIVER, ONCE THE SOLE PRESERVE OF GOLD-RUSHERS AND GRIZZLIES

A TRAVELLER'S GUIDE TO WATER WORDS

BAYOU Creek of scarcely moving water, most often in the steamy swamps of the Mississippi basin (think Cajun jambalaya and blues).

BILLABONG A dead-end river-channel or torpid backwater, made famous in Aussie anthem 'Waltzing Matilda'; one of the biggest is Cullyamurra Waterhole (South Australia), near where explorers Burke and Wills waltzed their last.

BOG A squishy quagmire. Good for preserving corpses; some of the millennia-old bodies discovered in bogs still have skin (see stubbly Tollund Man in Denmark's Silkeborg Museum).

FJORD GLACIER Carved sheer-sided inlet, often gorgeous (see costal Norway or South Island, New Zealand, for goodies).

GEYSER Ferociously erupting hot spring, geological equivalent of a whale's blowhole; named after Iceland's original Geysir at Haukadalur, which inter-mittently spews water 60m skyward.

LAGOON Shallow lake isolated from the sea by a sand bank or coral reef; often paradisiacal (see superblue Aitutaki, Cook Islands).

MEANDER Snaking loops of a river, caused by build-ups of sediment; named for the Meander River, a particularly bendy example near Izmir, Turkey.

OASIS A miracle of green in the desert; for a Hollywood-perfect version (used in *Star Wars*) see Tunisia's canyon-side Tamerza.

WADI A mostly dry riverbed; Jordan's Wadi Rum is an epic example.

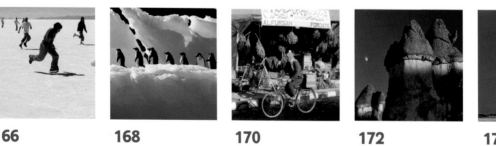

LONELY PLANET'S
TOP TRAVEL LISTS

136
BEST ECOTRIPS

138
CLASSIC TRAVELLERS' TOTEMS

140
GREAT TURNING POINTS

142
TOP 10 PLACES TO STEAL A KISS

144
I CAN'T BELIEVE IT'S NOT THE CAPITAL

156
BEST PLACES FOR DEEP THINKING

158
BEST CHRISTMAS CRACKERS

160
LOST CITIES OF THE WORLD

162
BEST THINGS TO THROW YOURSELF OFF

164
HAPPIEST PLACES

176
BEST ARCHITEC-TURE & PLACE COMBINATIONS

178
BEST CYCLING ADVENTURES

180
BEST PLACES TO TAKE A BATH

182
MOST EXTREME ANCIENT SITES

184
ECCENTRI-CITY

MOST SPINE-TINGLING
COMMUTES

FROM NEW YORK TO OLD DELHI, RUSH HOUR NEVER LOOKED BETTER

01 GRAND CENTRAL TERMINAL, USA

Morning rush hour at New York's Grand Central is one of the most beautiful commuting moments in the world. The sun spills across the great echoing main concourse, a giant stage under the four-faced clock. The massive windows are worthy of a cathedral, and below them scurrying figures cast long, long shadows, interspersed with golden light. The beaux-arts station dates from 1903, the heyday of the railroads; and it's still busy – around 150,000 commuters pass through here every day.

02 FERRY ACROSS SYDNEY HARBOUR, AUSTRALIA

The best way to see the beauty of Sydney Harbour is from its ferries, which are sleek, efficient and cheap. This is a commute to raise goose bumps. With its many coves and bays; the harbour has an incredible 240km of coastline, the landscape varying from awesome skyscrapers to sandy beaches. Two iconic landmarks greet the boats as they zoom towards the city – the graceful iron arch of the Sydney Harbour Bridge and the armoured petals of the Sydney Opera House.

03 VESPA IN ROME, ITALY

Epic traffic blights this epic city, and the best way to commute is by scooter. As well as making it easier to park, it's hard to beat the cool factor of navigating ancient cobbled roads on a Vespa. Sunglasses are essential. The highlight of any scooter trip is zooming down alongside Circo Massimo, the mammoth chariot racing track in Rome's historic centre, today a lozenge-shaped grassy park. Perched above, on the Palatino, are the ruins of the great imperial palaces.

⭐ VAPORETTO IN VENICE, ITALY

Aside from walking, the vaporetto (steamer) is undoubtedly the finest way to get from A to B in the floating city, with surroundings of extraordinary beauty and services every few minutes. Spot the locals by their easy nonchalance, standing (not even clutching the rail), talking and texting. The vaporetto might not have the glamour of a gondola – it's more of a floating bus – but it feels much more *autentico* and is a lot cheaper.

⭐ EXPRESS FERRY ALONG CHAO PHRAYA IN BANGKOK, THAILAND

In a city where gridlocked tuk tuks and cars belch out fumes and it feels like you're never going to get anywhere, the river offers thrilling freedom.

masters of sleeping on the commute, so you might have to move a fellow passenger's head gently from your shoulder before getting off at your stop.

⊛ RICKSHAW IN OLD DELHI, INDIA

A Wacky Races–style jamboree fills the narrow, bumpy streets in the confusing mayhem that is Old Delhi. Rickshaws, bicycles, handcarts, cars and pedestrians all narrowly, and incredibly, miss each other in a meandering onward dance. It's an intense experience, especially when the sun is beating down. The traffic creates a chorus all of its own: hooting horns and ringing bells is important, not only to warn other road users, but for the sheer joy of being noisy.

⊛ WALKING ACROSS LONDON BRIDGE, ENGLAND

Here's your chance to feel immersed in a piece of epic modernist poetry. Join the sea of dark-suited figures streaming over London Bridge in the morning – workers coming in from the suburbs by train, then walking the last 15-minute stretch to work in the City, the capital's financial centre. TS Eliot describes the commute in his seminal poem *The Wasteland* (1922). It evokes faceless figures flowing across London Bridge, their eyes downcast – and the modern city haunts the poem like a miserable spectre. It might not be the most cheerful of commutes, but it's poetic.

⊛ TRAM 28 FROM MARTIM MONIZ TO PRAZERES CEMETERY, PORTUGAL

The legendary tram 28 winds through the narrow, hilly streets of Moorish Alfama district in Lisbon. It is sunflower-yellow, trimmed in wood, endearingly rounded and old fashioned, and is always chock-a-block with enraptured tourists, as well as casual commuters. Despite its age it trundles up and down with impressive tenacity. It twists and turns to expose views down narrow streets, past washing lines, ornately tiled facades, and over the electrifying blue waters of the Tagus.

There's no better way to get around Bangkok than the hop-on, hop-off express ferry along the Chao Phraya – stop off and see the Grand Palace, with its magical gardens and gold-leaf spires. The only problem is that boats are scarily full during rush hour – if you can, commute at a time when other people are not.

⊛ THE STAR FERRY, HONG KONG

Like floating through a scene from Blade Runner in a 19th-century boat, crossing Victoria Harbour in Hong Kong is one of the world's most surreal and amazing journeys. The Star Ferry Company was founded in 1898. The fixtures – all varnished wood and rows of life buoys – resonate with another era, a dramatic contrast with the concrete, neon and steel that surround the harbour. Prices seem from another, gentler, time as well. The harbour crossing costs HK$2.20 (US$0.30) in 1st class (upstairs, with posher seats away from the diesel fumes), HK$1.70 (US$0.20) in 2nd class (downstairs on wooden benches).

⊛ TOKYO SUBWAY, JAPAN

Rush hour is the ideal time for indulging in some social observation. Sardines don't get crammed closer than Tokyoites on the subway, yet people are notably considerate of others – the result of being a polite race living in a crowded space. Some people wear face masks to prevent the transmission of colds. Uniformed attendants in white gloves help pack people in before the doors close. The Japanese are

THE BEST
PLACES OF REST

ABOVE GROUND OR SIX FEET UNDER, THESE ARE PRIME
SPOTS FOR BOTH THE LIVING AND THE DEAD

KHUFU, KHAFRE AND MENKAURE POSE FOR A PICTURE

DOGON WOMEN PLAY MUSIC TO WAKE THE DEAD IN DOUENTZA, MALI

01 TAJ MAHAL, INDIA

The Taj Mahal in Agra is surely the world's most beautiful place in which to push up daisies. The 17th-century Mughal emperor Shah Jahan built the mausoleum in memory of his favourite wife, Mumtaz Mahal, using white marble from Rajasthan, crystal from China, turquoise from Tibet and sapphire from Sri Lanka. It's a monument to love, one of the world's most famous buildings and represents the pinnacle of Mughal architecture. But such beauty came at a price: the mammoth cost helped lead to the fall of Shah Jahan and the Mughal empire.

02 PYRAMIDS OF GIZA, EGYPT

These pyramids on the outskirts of Cairo may be ancient (dating to around 3200 BC) but they're as space age as tombs get. They pierce the sky, unperturbed by crowds of hustlers, camels and camcorder-toting tourists. An estimated 20,000 to 30,000 workers built the pyramids, the largest of which is constructed from over two million blocks. Once covered in white limestone, they would have gleamed dazzling white. Inside, the pharaohs were equipped with everything from mummified cats to boats to ferry them into the afterlife.

03 DOGON TOMBS, MALI

A craggy mass rears up from the sun-bleached plain, one of West Africa's most stunning sights. This is where the remote Dogon tribe lives. Most extraordinary in this extraordinary place are the tombs. These are tiny buildings set into the cliffs, often halfway up, with no discernible method of approach. They look like they were built by aliens, but were constructed by the Tellem tribe, who lived here before being driven away by the Dogon. Now the Dogon use the inaccessible structures to house their dead, hauling the bodies up on ropes.

✪ THE NON-CATHOLIC CEMETERY, ITALY

This overgrown garden is a surprise, in a busy corner of Rome. Romantic poets Keats – who died at the unripe age of 26 – and Shelley are buried here. The garden is dominated by a sharp-tipped pyramid: the fanciful tomb of a Roman general with a penchant for Egyptology. The evocative, verdant cemetery is usually deserted, and there seems no more fitting spot for Romantic poets. Seek them out, read the inscription on Keat's grave – 'Here lies one whose name was writ on water' – and weep.

✪ HOLLYWOOD FOREVER CEMETERY, USA

These immaculate lawns and stately memorials are the final picture for much of Hollywood royalty. The glamorous graves at the back of Paramount studios are a veritable Milky Way of departed glitterati, including Rudolph Valentino, Fay Wray, Douglas Fairbanks, Harvey Henderson Wilcox (who founded Hollywood on his ranch), Mel Blanc (the voice of Bugs Bunny; his tombstone reads: 'That's all folks') and cenotaphs to Jayne Mansfield and Johnny Ramone, amongst others. In summer, Angelenos come armed with deckchairs and picnics to watch old movies projected onto a blank wall. So, it's weird – this is LA.

✪ THE CATACOMBS OF ROME, ITALY

Ancient Roman law forbade burial within Rome city limits. Most Romans were cremated, but early Christians were buried in a series of endless, echoing, underground tunnels, out near the old Roman road, the Via Appia. This underground death complex is Rome's most haunting sight – now empty of bodies but retaining early Christian frescoes, altars and icons. Three sets of catacombs are open. The largest, di San Callisto, has over 29km of tunnels, and once housed St Cecilia, the patron saint of music, while the martyr St Sebastian was buried in his eponymous catacombs.

A FISHERMAN BOATS PAST THE TAJ MAHAL, RUDYARD KIPLING'S 'EMBODIMENT OF ALL THINGS PURE', ON INDIA'S YAMUNA RIVER

✪ PÈRE LACHAISE CEMETERY, FRANCE

The world's most-visited cemetery has a star-studded afterlife gathering, with residents as diverse as Edith Piaf, Marcel Proust, Oscar Wilde, Honoré de Balzac and Isadora Duncan. It was founded in 1804, but languished until the management had the bright marketing plan of moving here the remains of famous people, such as Molière, to attract business. Follow the graffiti and crowds to the most notorious tomb, that of Jim Morrison – lead singer of The Doors, who died in Paris in 1971. A security guard is posted to prevent excessive rock-and-roll tributes (previously, fans would take drugs and even have sex on the tomb).

✪ TOMB OF PACAL, MEXICO

In the foothills of the Chiapas mountains lie the remains of the ancient Mayan city of Palenque, set in a tangle of jungle. It's a place of cinematic splendour, complete with rolling mist and thick undergrowth. The city's most famous monument is the Tomb of Pacal (Pacal was the city's 7th-century founder-king). The secret opening to the tomb was discovered, by chance, within the glorious Temple of the Inscriptions, a steep, stepped pyramid. Inside is a limestone sarcophagus, sealed with a lid weighing over 4.5 tonnes, inscribed with the now-famous Mayan depictions of Pacal falling into the underworld.

✪ HARTSDALE PET CEMETERY, USA

In 1896 Dr Samuel Johnson, a vet, offered his apple orchard to a bereaved friend as the burial place for his dog. Today Hartsdale, in New York, has 70,000 graves, including those of some famous war dogs, and a memorial to the Red Cross dogs that served during WWI. Famous owners who have had their pooches interred here include Mariah Carey and Diana Ross. The headstones make fascinating reading ('Sport: Born a dog, died a gentleman'). Among the endlessly entertaining names are Bum, Grumpy, Jerk, J Edna Hoover, and a surprising number of pets called Peggy.

✪ THE CITY OF THE DEAD, EGYPT

This is the most curious cemetery in the world: not only a city of the dead, but of the living. Chronic housing shortages in Cairo have driven families to live in tombs in the large cemeteries on the city's outskirts. Traditionally, Egyptians buried their dead surrounded by rooms, so that relatives could live in them during the long mourning period. These are now occupied by squatters – often large families – who use the gravestones as tables, and dry their laundry on lines between tombstones.

ELEMENTAL TRAVEL

WHETHER IT'S SOMETHING IN THE AIR OR BUBBLING UNDER-
GROUND THERE'S PURE CHEMISTRY IN THESE DESTINATIONS

✪ SILICON (SI) – GRAVITY-DEFYING LOS ANGELES, USA

Stretched across the California desert lies the world's most elementally enhanced city, the silicon capital of the United States, lusty and busty Los Angeles. Under all that plastic fantastic, the earth's crust is the same here as anywhere, sporting more oxygen than silicon. But in LA it's all about what's on show and, above ground, silicon certainly tips the balance. Catch LA's silicon-bolstered inhabitants strutting their stuff along the city's famous boulevards and beaches or skip the amateur prospecting and tap straight into the mother lode, Hef's Playboy Mansion.

✪ CARBON (C) – DIAMOND MINES, SOUTH AFRICA

Inconspicuous carbon pulls off one of nature's most impressive magic tricks deep below the earth's surface in southern Africa. Here, due to high pressure and high temperature, close to 50% of the world's most sought after and glorified jewels have been born and raised. These little beauties don't come easy. The history of diamond mining in southern Africa is fraught with corruption, violence, dirty politics and racism. Take a trip to the Cullinan Diamond Mine about 50km from Pretoria, where the world's largest diamond, the Cullinan Diamond, was unearthed.

✪ SODIUM (Na) – LAC ASSAL, DJIBOUTI

Assal is the saltiest body of water on earth. Found at the lowest point on the African continent, in one of the harshest deserts in Africa, just thinking about it has you reaching for a glass of water. Take a trip to the capital, also called Djibouti, then grab a 4WD for a 70km drive to the barren moonscape of the lake. The salt plains that surround it tell the story, and you won't find any rivers feeding into it – part of the reason for its high salinity. Assal is a crater lake and seismic activity is prevalent – nearby Ardoukoba Volcano last erupted in 1978.

✪ ALUMINIUM (Al) – ARNHEM LAND, AUSTRALIA

Beneath the red earth and unrelenting heat of the Northern Territory lies a seam of bauxite, the ore from which aluminium is extracted. Befitting the giant landscape, the toys used to dig up the earth are enormous. Great yellow trucks with tyres as tall as a house, wheel nuts like Olympian barbell weights, conveyor belts that run for kilometres to the attractive sea (a joke in this hot climate, given the abundance of crocodiles, sharks and deadly jellyfish). Mine tours can be arranged from Gove on the Gulf of Carpentaria. It's a site guaranteed to live large in your memory.

✪ GOLD (Au) – FORT KNOX, USA

It's well-known by name to many, and it's synonymous with gold, that yellow metal that's sent humans into a spin for much of our history. Fort Knox is actually a US Army base in Louisiana and the nearby United States Bullion Depository is where you'll find your fortune. If you could get in, that is. It's the epitome of security, and the five tonnes of gold that lie beneath the granite-lined walls are protected by army units. No visitors permitted, but you could look longingly from a distance, and enjoy the General George Patton Museum at the base – though that might be more about lead...

✪ HELIUM (He) – BALLOONING ABOVE THE FALLS, ZAMBIA

The second-lightest element has been putting us into the air and bringing us advertising for what seems like eternity. A quiet helium-balloon ride like this is the way to appreciate the roar of Victoria Falls from Zambia. It feels safer knowing that all the hydrogen, as used in the doomed *Hindenburg* airship, is mostly below you in the water.

✪ IRON (Fe) – A NEW AGE

The Iron Age – defined as the time iron smelting and use became prevalent in a society – refers to varying dates, depending on where you are. In Britain the Iron Age is said to have commenced in the 5th century BC – in India, this date is much earlier, between the 12th and 18th centuries BC. It's not easy to pin down the dates, but pay a visit to Lahuradewa in Uttar Pradesh and get a feel for perhaps 4000 years of iron-working history. Actual dates for human settlement go many thousands of years past that.

01 NEON (NE) – BRIGHT LIGHTS OF TOKYO, JAPAN

Welcome to the future. No city on earth fulfils our fantasies of a futuristic city quite like Japan's neon capital, Tokyo. This city doesn't sleep – it can't sleep, somebody left all the lights on. Besides, who'd want to sleep when you can shop at Shibuya-ku, dine like an emperor on more than 20 different varieties of Japanese cuisine, sling back sake in Roppongi and belt out that power ballad in any one of thousands of karaoke bars. The future's so bright, you gotta wear shades.

02 SULPHUR (S) – STEAMY SPRINGS OF ROTORUA, NEW ZEALAND

If you arrive in Rotorua thinking this town sure does like its egg sandwiches, you'd be forgiven – but off the mark entirely. The smell of sulphur isn't due to the inhabitants' penchant for gas-inducing gastronomy, it's just the earth letting off a little steam. Bubbling potholes of mineral-rich mud dot the local landscape and the numerous lakes surrounding the town are all craters formed by extinct volcanoes. The land in Rotorua is alive: it rumbles, gurgles, spits and hisses like a prehistoric creature of sorts. And the smell? Well, it smells like the cave of a prehistoric creature after a long winter hibernation.

03 KRYPTON (KR) – A FANTASTIC ELEMENT

Let's not cloud romance and adventure with reality, let's visit Superman's secret sanctuary, more than likely located deep in the icy Arctic. Here, in his secret lair, he would work on the science of defending himself against the remnants of his home world, Kryptonite. The precise address is unknown, but you'd look for an ice mountain. There may be a giant door, a giant lock and a giant key. You'd need to be Superman to lift the key and open the lock, for what it's worth. Otherwise, enjoy the trek through the polar expanse, marvel at spectacular ice formations, and enjoy your solitude…before global warming makes a fiction of our northern ice cap.

BRIGHT LIGHTS, BIG CITY IN TOKYO, JAPAN

BEST PLACES FOR
DEADLY SINS
(& CARDINAL VIRTUES)

OUR TOP PICKS FOR BEING NAUGHTY AND NICE

SOCCER FANS GO WILD AT MILAN'S SAN SIRO STADIUM

MONEY MAKES THE WORLD GO ROUND IN TOKYO'S SHIBUYA DISTRICT

01 GREED – LAS VEGAS, USA

Vegas's slogan could almost be 'greed is good'. The bandits here may be one-armed, but they're reaching for your money all the same. It's not just the casino owners – everywhere, glazy-eyed gamblers try to defy the odds and pile up the pennies. Come here to connect with your inner kitsch: acres of neon, rhinestone-encrusted showgirls and outrageously opulent casinos. There's even a museum to the ultimate showman – Liberace. This capital of capitalism is unlike anywhere else on earth – after all, there's no exceeding excess.

02 WRATH – MILAN, ITALY

It's easy to mistake the red flares burning at big Italian soccer matches for the red mist of rage – so fierce are some local encounters. Packed in amid seething crowds, you'd be excused a frisson of fear as decibels surge to ear-numbing proportions and the teams trot onto the pitch. For years some of the most wrathful rivalry has been at the San Siro stadium, where Milan take on their local arch-enemies Inter. When they do, the whole city is a riot of red and blue. Watching the big match on the telly at home will never be quite the same again.

03 ENVY – TOKYO, JAPAN

Shoto in Tokyo's Shibuya district has some of the most expensive real estate in the world. At around US$1800 per square foot, it recently pipped Barker Road in Hong Kong, Eaton Square in London's Belgravia and New York's Fifth Avenue to the title. Along with love hotels, gigantic street TVs and super-chic shops, you're likely to encounter a few green-eyed monsters in the district's frenetic neon-lit bustle. Soak up culture-shock Japan – but don't count on buying a home.

✪ SLOTH – CARIBBEAN ISLANDS

When it comes to laid-back chilling out, many minds turn languidly to the Caribbean. In this place limin' (watching the world go by) is a way of life. While away some lazy, hazy days in relatively undeveloped Tobago. Calypso music drifts by on the breeze, azure seas lap at pristine sands and turtles glide silently across coral reefs. When you've exhausted all your options for doing nothing, hike through ancient forests, get drenched at a cascading waterfall or join in the fun at a local festival – if you're here at Easter, watch out for the crab and goat racing.

✪ LUST – AMSTERDAM, THE NETHERLANDS

Amsterdam is as notorious for its red-light district as for its tolerant approach to soft drugs. Despite plans to close down a third of the city's sex venues, the scantily clad women in the Wallen's well-lit 'window brothels' are still a big draw for the curious coach-party crowd. If all that risqué posing falls rather flat for you, develop a burning passion for Amsterdam's waterfront architecture instead. Some of the best canal-fringed streets in this city of 90 islands are in the Jordaan district – tiny and winding, they are crammed with funky clothes shops, markets and bars.

✪ PRIDE – LOS ANGELES, USA

Los Angles: land of big hair and small noses. Displaying more nips 'n' tucks than a street full of couture houses, this is a city that appears to have more plastic surgeons than palm trees. Cruise the boutique shops of Beverly Hills for some people-watching of the people who just loved to be watched. Giorgio, Jimmy and Ralph would love you to drop by. Or simply head to Hollywood for a burst of celebrity-spotting, then road test the old theory that unless you look a million dollars it is very hard to get a smile out of the shop assistants on Rodeo Drive.

VIVA LAS VEGAS: A COUPLE FLASH THEIR CASH AT HARRAH'S CASINO

✪ CHASTITY – VATICAN CITY, ROME

Where better to witness cardinal virtues than in a city full of virtuous cardinals. Only around 900 people live in this state within a city, but a fair few of those have forsworn the temptations of the flesh. The Holy See (Vatican City) is only just over 1000m long and 850m wide but there's a wealth of riches crammed into its tiny dimensions. Be dazzled by the beautifully baroque St Peter's Basilica, the artefact-packed Vatican Museums and Michelangelo's awe-inspiring creations in the Sistine Chapel. Here the visual journey from Genesis to the Last Judgment is via a vast vaulted, fresco-laden ceiling.

✪ CHARITY – KOLKATA, INDIA

One of the iconic figures of the 20th century, Mother Teresa was legendary for her compassion for the homeless, sick and starving – her order still has more than 4000 nuns worldwide. This diminutive 'saint of the gutter' began working in the slums of Kolkata (Calcutta) in the 1950s. Her legacy is marked by a statue on Mother Teresa Sarani, formerly named Park St, in the heart of town. It's slap-bang in the midst of modern India: shopping malls and museums mingle with multiplex cinemas and exquisite Raj-era architecture – all in a city caught up in an IT boom.

✪ TEMPERANCE – KENTUCKY, USA

Forgo the sore head and take a temperate approach to drinking in one of the USA's 'dry counties'. Here in an echo of Prohibition-era speakeasies and bootleggers, local laws limit (to various degrees) the sale of alcoholic tipples. These days Kentucky is less wet than most – 53 of its 121 counties are completely dry; partial restrictions in 38 others see them dubbed 'moist'. Best make sure you know what you can buy, and where, in time for the classy Kentucky Derby in early May – tradition dictates a bourbon-laced mint julep is raised to toast the riders as they take off.

✪ GLUTTONY – PARIS, FRANCE

For centuries the epicentre of epicurean delight, the restaurants of Paris risk making gluttons of us all. Although Tokyo sometimes trumps the French capital for sheer numbers of Michelin stars, dining by candlelight in a back-street bistro in the Latin Quarter is still divine. Guzzle a galette in even the humblest creperie and you'll wonder how they manage to make buckwheat pancakes taste so sublime. Or do what the locals do – pack a picnic and lunch alfresco in the playful Jardin du Luxembourg, where you can work off the calories with a Gallic game of boules.

BEST PLACES TO
SKY WATCH

WE BRING YOU A STAR-STUDDED GUIDE TO DARK SKIES, SUNRISES AND AN UP-CLOSE VIEW OF THE HEAVENS

01 MCDONALD OBSERVATORY, USA

For a night-time event like no other, head 2040m above sea level to the top of Mt Locke. The McDonald Observatory, at Davis Mountains in Texas, enjoys some of the best dark skies in the continental United States, ensuring jaw-dropping views of celestial splendour. It also holds regular star parties, allowing you to look through the kind of massive telescopes that make astronomers rub their hands together with glee. Even the rest of us will marvel at the unrivalled views of planets, stars and galaxies – there's a whole universe out there waiting to be glimpsed.

02 STONEHENGE, ENGLAND

Thought by some to be a giant, primitive observatory, Stonehenge suggests that going 'wow' at the heavens' twinkling bits is nothing new – they began building this monumental circle of standing stones around 5000 years ago. It's still a good place to star gaze today – out in Salisbury Plain in Wiltshire there aren't many lights around interfering with nature's display. Wander the path around the site during the day, find a vantage point nearby, wait for the sun to go down, then think millennia-old mystic thoughts.

03 ABU SIMBEL, EGYPT

Even in a country crammed full of awesome ancient sites, Abu Simbel – one of the most important ancient observatories in the world – inspires. Its four 20m statues of Ramses II and monumental main hall were laid out to honour sun gods. The whole shebang was moved lock, stock and statuary during the construction of the Aswan High Dam and then rebuilt, still precisely aligned. On the anniversaries of Ramses' birth and coronation (around 22 February and October) the first rays of the morning sun still pierce the length of the main hall to shine on the statues at the end.

VOYAGE TO ANOTHER GALAXY AT JUST 6700 FEET: MCDONALD OBSERVATORY, TEXAS, WHERE YOU CAN BOLDLY GO WITHOUT EVER HAVING TO LEAVE THE GROUND

CARIBBEAN ISLANDS

Where better to gaze at a bejewelled blanket of stars than islands where the breeze is warm, the night air is fragrant with frangipani and the rum is sweet. Find a romantic beachside, palm-fringed spot, lie back and stare into the velvety darkness. You and your significant other can even find and name a constellation of your very own. In some islands the view is made all the more intense by the not-infrequent power cuts – proving a great dark-sky maxim: lights go off, stars come out.

PISAC, PERU

For the Incas gazing at the heavens was about much more than horoscopes and romantic views. Instead the firmament featured a celestial roadway – the Milky Way. Priests possibly used this wide band of diffuse light as a route map for parallel terrestrial pilgrimages. Tap into this mindset at Pisac, near Cuzco, with its sky-high complex of temples, citadels and terraces. While you're there have a close look at the Milky Way. The Incas saw negative patterns in it; dark cloud constellations are the gaps *between* the stars. See if you, like them, can spot a fox, a snake and a baby llama.

CALDERA DE TABURIENTE NATIONAL PARK, CANARY ISLANDS

Flung out into the sea off west Africa, the Canary Islands are the last chunk of land before a whole lot of ocean. La Palma is the island furthest west, and right at its tip is the Caldera de Taburiente National Park. It's such a good spot for star gazing that it's home to the Roque de los Muchachos Observatory, which has one of the most extensive fleets of telescopes in the world. When you're not staring at the night sky, hike the pine-clad, stream-scored slopes of the park's massive crater, then head to the beach to soothe those hamstrings.

SHERBROOKE, CANADA

Once the global hub of ice-hockey-stick manufacturing, Sherbrooke, Québec, didn't, until recently, have many other claims to fame. Visitors tend to use this French-speaking city as a springboard for the pristine rivers, mountains and lakes of the nearby Mont-Mégantic National Park. But there is another reason to visit: both the park and the city have been designated the world's first International Dark-Sky Reserve. It's resulted in some 2500 light fittings being replaced – neatly cutting light pollution by a quarter. Look up and see much less of a city glow bleeding into the night sky.

SLOVENIA

As Oscar Wilde put it: we are all in the gutter, but some of us are looking at the stars. In theory you should be able to see a lot more stars in Slovenia – the country recently passed its first light-pollution law. A trip here would include memories of Prague-like Ljubljana's charming architecture, skiing at speed down Slovenia's alpine slopes – and recollections of carefully shaded street-lamps, low-glow public lighting and flipping the switch on unnecessary illuminations. The International Dark-Sky Association reckons the law will save Slovenia €10 million a year, and the planet some hefty greenhouse gas emissions.

HAWAI'I (THE BIG ISLAND), HAWAII

You may plan to explore the smoking, steaming landscape around Crater Rim Drive, crawl through the lava tubes at Kaumana Caves or simply snorkel and sunbathe on the perfect white sand of Kauna'oa Bay. But it'd be a shame to leave the Big Island without at least one long look at the night sky – Hawai'i's altitude and isolation give it a distinct astronomical advantage. Twelve domed telescopes dot the 4300m-high summit of Mauna Kea. But your best bet is the visitors centre 1500m lower down, where they'll let you gaze through telescopes and gasp at constellations after dark.

SARK, GREAT BRITAIN

Get out of the cities to see more stars. Urban light pollution means you'll usually only see 100 with the naked eye; in a dark-sky zone you can pick out 1000. For a beautiful nightscape head to Sark, in the Channel Islands. This high plateau of granite is nearly 5km long, 2.5km wide, has few houses and no cars or street lights. Cycling its pock-marked, unpaved lanes by moonlight is magical – but bring a torch. Then gaze up from vertiginous cliffs above an inky expanse of sea and do some serious star counting.

BEST
ECOTRIPS

NO FLYING REQUIRED. CHOOSE FROM NOMADIC TRAILS, RUNNING THE RAILS AND SPOKE-SPINNING ADVENTURES ACROSS THE GLOBE

YUKON DO IT: CANOEISTS PLY NORTH AMERICA'S LONGEST RIVER   CROSS-COUNTRY SKIERS MAKE LIGHT WORK OF IT IN NORWAY

01 SOUTH AMERICA BY TRAIN

For classic South American adventure, you can't beat running the rails. Trace the Andes on the *Old Patagonia Express*. Then visit the Incas on the journey from Arequipa to Cuzco, but watch the altitude on the world's highest train ride. For a three-week epic, take the Quito–Caracas route from Ecuador to Venezuela, visiting protected jungle, colonial cities and World Heritage sites. The section of track through little-visited Columbia is a treat – the beaches of Islas del Rosario National Park and the crater of the Totumo mud volcano are two great highlights.

02 KAYAK THE YUKON RIVER, CANADA

At the dawn of the 20th century prospectors flocked to Dawson City, drawn by the Klondike Gold Rush. The 3770km Yukon River, flowing from northern Canada to the Bering Sea, was the principal trade route for exporting the booty but became heavily polluted. Now, with most of the miners long gone, the river has fought back and its Grade 1 waters make for great wilderness paddling. The 315km trip from Minto to Dawson takes 10 days; camps are struck on sandbanks and islands. You might not strike gold but the memories will be priceless.

03 CROSS-COUNTRY SKIING IN KAMBEN, NORWAY

For the uninitiated, cross-country skiing can be torture. Burning calves, freezing limbs and crossed blades seem more like pain than pleasure. But stick with it and Norway's favourite winter pastime invigorates. The country's telemark region has some of the finest skiing, with hundreds of kilometres of self-guided trails through forest and open terrain. Clean air, pristine snow and the serenity of a wilderness cabin can't fail to put you at ease. And even if your technique's more amateur than marathon champion, embrace the spirit of it and the Norwegians will love you. Skintight Lycra body-stockings are optional.

✪ BEDOUIN TRAILS, JORDAN

Budding Lawrences of Arabia won't be able to resist following in the footsteps of Jordan's Bedouin nomads. Travel south from Amman to Dana Nature Reserve with its stunning array of endemic plant and animal life. Bunk down in a local ecolodge before pressing on to Petra, carved city of Nabataean splendour and junction of ancient Chino-European trade routes. Bugged by the crowds? Then skip on down to the eerie Dead Sea, exploring spectacular desert canyons en route. Round your trip off with a therapeutic soak in the unique mineral-rich sea; at 410m below sea level, it's the lowest point on earth.

✪ ISLAND-HOPPING, GREECE

For years travellers have flocked to the Greek islands in search of sun, sand and good times – the last stop on the pilgrimage through Europe, and it's so hard to leave! In the blink of an eye, days become weeks and weeks turn to months. So island-hopping seems the best way to go – a laid-back approach and an attitude that says, 'Yeah, we're late, but we'll get there when we get there.' From Mykonos to Tinos, and Naxos to Santorini, the Cycladic islands offer deep blue seas, sleepy villages and powder-sand bays. Why would you want to rush home?

✪ MOUNTAIN-BIKING, NEW ZEALAND

If zorbing, jet-boating or extreme-ironing aren't your cup of tea, hit the trails for spoke-spinning adventures. At the top of New Zealand's South Island, the fabled Queen Charlotte Track is a 71km two-day ride through the scenic Marlborough Sounds, an intricate maze through lush coastal forest. On the North Island head to Tongariro National Park, blessed with some of the country's premium routes and epic *Lord of the Rings* territory – the 42 Traverse is one of the top rides, famous for adrenaline-filled downhill sections. And if you want to party after peddling, Queenstown remains NZ's number one adventure-sports resort.

ALL ABOARD IN ARGENTINA, ON THE TRAIN TO THE CLOUDS

✪ HORSE RIDING IN PATAGONIA, CHILE

Torres del Paine National Park, in Chilean Patagonia, is a vast land of jaw-dropping vistas; there's only one way to see it, and that's on foot. Or four equine feet to be exact. So hop in the saddle and steer your Criollo steed beneath the looming granite pinnacles of the Paine Massif, crossing rivers and skirting the park's glaciers. Bunk down under canvas to experience the wonder of Patagonia by night – you'll sleep like a baby, with 10-day trips clocking up over 40 hours of riding. If you're going to get saddle sore, what better place to do it?

✪ SCUBA DIVING, TURKS & CAICOS ISLANDS

Caribbean diving used to be all about Bonaire and the Cayman Islands, but head to Turks and Caicos for lesser development and pristine coral reefs, where visibility of up to 60m reveals a marine world abundant in vivid flora and fauna. Princess Alexandra National Park offers protected diving off the main island of Providenciales, encompassing some of the islands' most spectacular sites in a 320km-long reef system. Out of the water, seek solitude on untouched powder beaches that are regularly voted the world's best, or just dream of rubbing shoulders with the wealth of millionaires who flock to this island paradise.

✪ WALK THE PENNINE WAY, GREAT BRITAIN

Pull on your boots and don your waterproofs for Britain's premier long-distance path, 429km of unrelenting sole-destroying trekking. Originating at Edale in Derbyshire's Peak District, the path heads north through the Yorkshire Dales on its way to Northumberland and Kirk Yetholm in the Scottish Borders. It's a slog: few walk the full length, which averages three weeks. The route is served by youth hostels, as well as great bunkhouses and country B&Bs. But for the true British experience, try a night or two in a traditional pub – a few pints of real ale make all the difference to those blistered feet.

✪ CYCLE THE ÅLAND ISLANDS, FINLAND

Cycling in Finland? Well, not the big bit of Finland but the autonomous Swedish-speaking Åland Islands in the Baltic Sea. Comprising more than 6000 islands, 80 of which are inhabited, the flat terrain, climate and laid-back lifestyle are perfectly suited to cycling. From Mariehamn, the islands' capital, head to Osnäs for the Northern Archipelago route: six days of rolling hills and winding lanes. Free ferries link the various islands – just plan ahead or you'll find yourself with nothing to do but pitch your tent, kick back and look at the view.

CLASSIC
TRAVELLERS' TOTEMS

A BRAGGER'S GUIDE TO GOING FROM ONE EXTREME TO THE OTHER

✪ THE ANTARCTIC CIRCLE – ANTARCTICA

A visit to Antarctica means you can beat most travellers' tales – it's hard to top icebergs, pack ice and a polar plateau. This inhospitable continent is the coldest, highest and driest in the world. It's also the breeziest; parts of it have an average wind speed of 70km/h. In theory it's also the most peaceful – the 42 member nations of the Antarctic Treaty pledge to use Antarctica for nonmilitary purposes only. Take a tour in summer (November to February) and delight in cute and courting penguins, spouting whales and almost perpetual daylight.

✪ HIGHEST SEAT OF GOVERNMENT – LA PAZ, BOLIVIA

A dizzy 4000m above sea level, La Paz is likely to leave you gasping for breath. This city's skyscrapers really do scrape the sky. They also line up with sprawling shanty towns and elegant cathedrals in front of the snow-capped peaks of the Cordillera Real. This high you'll spot two classic creatures of the Andes: condors and llamas (rarely seen below 3050m and 2300m respectively). All this altitude might make you a little queasy – locals go to La Paz's 'Witches' Market' for folk cures and good-luck charms. Dried llama foetus anyone?

✪ LOWEST ELEVATION – DEAD SEA

The waves of this landlocked salt lake lap at the shores of Israel and Jordan a remarkable 410m below sea level – the lowest elevation on earth. The briny expanse is just short of 1036 sq km and sits in the middle of a desert. The high-density saline water makes the sea incredibly buoyant (go on, try sinking), and a visit isn't complete without staring at your toes as you float. Head to one of the luxury spas, get plastered in dark, mineral-rich mud and ponder exactly how a sea can be below sea level.

✪ TROPIC OF CANCER – HAWAII

It's the kind of totem most travellers have heard of but few can define. This virtual, latitudinal line is all to do with the sun's position at the time of the summer solstice – if you want to really understand declinations and ecliptics ask a brainy astronomer. Alternatively, head for Hawaii, fall off a surfboard, let the sand tickle your toes and say aloha to a whole new way of life. Luxuriate in tropical seas or clamber up a volcano – either way, you'll forget all about being 23°27' north of the equator.

✪ TROPIC OF CAPRICORN – ALICE SPRINGS

Australia is in places a dusty, fiery country and at its dusty, fiery heart sits Alice Springs. This settlement is at the centre of life in the Red Centre (260,000 sq km of rock and desert at the continent's core). Visit in relatively mild April and team up with parties of adventurers itching to tramp dry river beds on an Outback expedition. The Alice is also plum on the Tropic of Capricorn – try boring the local barflies about being 23°27' south of the equator, then drop in the news that Hawaii is exactly the same distance north.

✪ HOTTEST TEMPERATURE – LIBYA

A trip to Libya bags you the bragging rights to having been in the hottest place on earth – not surprising as the bulk of this vast country is the Sahara Desert. The record-breaker was coastal L'Aziziyah where, on 13 September 1922, the thermometer registered a stultifying 57.7°C. The relatively mild October and November months are the best time to saddle up a camel and head into the desert. If you visit in April expect the ghibli desert wind to whip up sand from the Sahara, turn the sky russet and cut visibility to 18m.

✪ INTERNATIONAL DATE LINE – KIRIBATI

All atolls, white sand and turquoise sea, this artful scattering of 33 coral islands fringes the International Date Line. The line used to run right through the country, but was rerouted around it in 1994 (the same thing happening in the same country on different days tended to cause confusion). The change meant Kiribati became the first nation to say *mauri* (hello) to the third millennium. This sprinkling of reefs and lagoons is now 12 hours ahead of GMT and 22 hours ahead of Honolulu. Phone a friend there and arrange to go snorkelling. How does noon, yesterday, sound?

NORWAY'S LOFOTEN ISLANDS, PRISTINE WILDERNESS ON THE EDGE OF THE ARCTIC CIRCLE

A SIBERIAN NOMAD AT OYMYAKON, THE WORLD'S COLDEST SETTLEMENT

QUITO'S GUAGUA PICHINCHA VOLCANO HAS AN EARLY-MORNING SMOKE

01 ARCTIC CIRCLE – LOFOTEN ISLANDS

Catch a ferry from the Norwegian port of Bodø and surge across the sea to the sheer peaks of the Lofoten Islands. This enchanting archipelago rears from the waves more than 100km north of the Arctic Circle. A mass of jagged mountains, the islands are scenically stunning; and sometimes slightly stinky – thousands of white fish are caught and air-dried here. Emerge from a cosy *rorbuer* (fisherman's shack) and come eye to eye with racks of the pungent offerings wafting in the breeze. On the way to Bodø the train whistle hoots as you cross the Arctic Circle and notch up a travellers' totem.

02 COLDEST TEMPERATURE – SIBERIA

Northern Siberia may be a tad warmer than Antarctica (which notched up a mind-numbing -89.2°C) but it's still pretty darn chilly – snow covers the icy earth for nine months of the year. It also has one of the coldest towns in the world – in Verkhoyansk the January average is around -50°C, although temperatures can plummet to -67°C. For a taste of tundra and bleak expanses try the Trans-Siberian Railway. It crosses far, far south of Verkhoyansk, but they still have to break ice from the carriages with an axe.

03 EQUATOR – QUITO

Slap-bang in the middle of earth, Ecuador's location is defined by its name – Republic of the Equator. The capital Quito is just 23km south of the globe's virtual belt – the line of 0° latitude. It's a city worth seeing in its own right: soaring, snowy volcanoes circle the ancient town; labyrinthine streets snake around colonial architecture, palaces, plazas and parks. There's also the chance for pseudo-scientific studies of the direction in which water swirls down plug holes. Stare at a few and see if you can bust that myth which says it goes anticlockwise in one hemisphere, clockwise in the other.

GREAT
TURNING POINTS

WE MAKE TIME TRAVEL LOOK EASY. VISIT A MOMENT IN HISTORY –
FROM PLACES OF PITCHED BATTLE TO THE LAUNCH SITE OF AIR TRAVEL

01 FLYER 1, USA

Putting aside debates about how 'first' the Wright brothers actually were, the launch of Flyer 1 in 1903 was certainly the catalyst for popular enthusiasm for taking to the air. At Kill Devil Hill in North Carolina (where a memorial stone and museum stand today), Orville Wright assumed the prone position and let fly. The powered glider was propelled along rails until its wings bit into the air and Orville found himself airborne. Just 36m later he brought the plane back to earth, having ushered us on the way to mass global tourism (not to mention novel forms of warfare and the space age).

02 BATTLE OF HASTINGS, ENGLAND

For the English speakers out there – want to get in touch with your French roots? Head out to Senlac Hill, 10km from Hastings, and picture two massive armies pitted against each other, one led by William the (soon-to-be) Conqueror, the other King Harold II. It's 1066. The ensuing melee spelled the end of Harold's reign (and his life, as it happens, which ended famously with an arrow through the eye) and the commencement of life under Norman rule. During this time, French influence dominated all aspects of life, particularly at the upper echelons – high culture, government, academia, cuisine, language, all bear the hallmarks of the Norman invasion, forever changing the face of Anglo Saxon Britain.

03 ATOMIC BOMB, HIROSHIMA, JAPAN

When the atomic bomb left a US bomber on its downward course for Hiroshima, irradiating and disintegrating hundreds of thousands of people on 6 August 1945, the world became mesmerised by the prospect of total annihilation. Although the first atomic device was detonated in the New Mexico desert, it was with Hiroshima that the world understood the deal. Standing by the A-bomb Dome at the Hiroshima Peace Memorial Park you feel the power of recent history come hurtling over you. And if that's a little abstract, inside the nearby museum are images of the personal devastation suffered by both victims of the bomb and victims of Japanese wartime atrocities.

ALL WE NEED TO DO IS HEAD IN THE WRIGHT
DIRECTION...HALF OF THE FAMOUS BROTHERS
TAKES TO THE SKIES IN NORTH CAROLINA, 1903

☼ THE PRINTING PRESS, GERMANY

Bringing together a number of technologies of the time, Johannes Gutenberg's development of the printing press around 1640 set off a cascade of effects that revolutionised human interaction. The printed word became widely available to the masses, literacy and learning became more common, knowledge more widely circulated. It was then just a small step to another massive turning point in global history, the internet. But to get back to words on paper, pay a visit to Mainz. In the centre of the town you'll find the Gutenberg Museum where the complete history of printing can be explored, and you'll even see a couple of those original printed bibles, hot(-ish) off the presses.

☼ GROUND ZERO, USA

It's hard to imagine a more momentous act of terrorism in recent years than the attack on the two towers of the World Trade Center in New York on 11 September 2001. It saw the commencement of war in Afghanistan and Iraq, and gave terrorism – a not uncommon feature of late-20th-century history – a real presence in the popular consciousness, setting the tone of politics throughout the Western world for the first decade of the new millennium. While plans are well under way to build a new skyscraper to replace the fallen ones, the experience of those tower lights – ghostly apparitions in the New York night, lit on the anniversary of the attack – are a chilling way to connect with the tragedy.

☼ THE BATTLE OF SEKIGAHARA, JAPAN

For those who know Japanese history, and perhaps fans of the '80s novel and TV series *Shogun*, the battle of Sekigahara in 1600 marked the end of the shogunate in Japan. The Tokugawa clan won the battle and took control, but the victory planted the seeds for a long-brewing revenge which, 200 years later, saw the fall of the clan and the rise of Japan as an empire, launching it into the modern world and paving the way for its military supremacy in Asia. Visiting the sleepy town of Sekigahara now, it's difficult to imagine 150,000 men in a pitched battle that lasted only six hours – imagine the ferocity!

☼ THE LONG MARCH, CHINA

Such a grand title for what was in fact a retreat, but the fleeing communist armies were rallied by one Mao Zedong, who gained critical popularity and power. This 'march' was in fact a series of retreats which lasted about a year as Chiang Kaishek and his Kuomintang attempted to destroy Chinese communism. Regrouping in Yan'an in 1935, the communist forces were able to rebuild and, through WWII, develop an army that would later chase out the Kuomintang, establishing the China we know today. Yan An in Shaanxi province is home to a number of monuments, memorials and museums. Start at Yan'an Revolutionary Memorial Museum and make your own march around the city.

☼ THE TET OFFENSIVE, VIETNAM

A classic case of losing the battle but winning the war. The Tet Offensive in 1968, by the combined Viet Cong and North Vietnamese Army, brought home to the USA that things might not be going so well in Vietnam. The attack took place on the morning of 31 January, the first day of the lunar new year. More than 100 towns were attacked, causing initial surprise, but most were contained quickly; the angst went far deeper though. It was the attack on the US Embassy in Saigon, deep in the city's heart, which perhaps did the most telling damage. Images broadcast throughout the world showed just how fragile the position of the USA and its allies was in Vietnam.

☼ THE CROSSING OF THE RUBICON, ITALY

Julius Caesar set Rome on its path to superpower status in 49 BC when he and his forces defied the orders of the senate to return to Rome and instead, in a deliberate act of war, crossed into Italy over the Rubicon river near Ravenna, a border that no standing army was allowed to cross. Civil war ensued, with Caesar eventually winning (after three years) and being declared dictator. The Republic of Rome was lost and a 500-year empire began, spanning Europe, Africa and the Middle East.

☼ SALT SATYAGRAHA – GANDHI'S MARCH FOR LIBERATION, INDIA

It's difficult to nominate just one event of significance in a country as diverse as India, but in 1930 when Gandhi led thousands of people on a 400km march to the coast protesting the introduction of the British salt tax, the world paid heed and India's claims for independence gathered understanding and support globally. Gandhi symbolically harvested his own salt from the sea (an act of *satyagraha* – the term coined for his method of nonviolent civil disobedience), making light of the British salt tax and prompting millions to do the same; this had *Time* magazine declaring Gandhi 1930's 'Man of the Year'.

TOP 10 PLACES TO
STEAL A KISS

IT'S ALL IN THE LIPS – PUCKER UP FOR EVERYTHING FROM PASSION TO CHOCOLATE

✪ KISSING, GERMANY
The act of puckering up was invented here, in 1808. We jest, of course; Kissing is a quaint Bavarian hamlet decked with steeples and spires. The origin of this delightful moniker remains a mystery, although history first mentions the village in 1050, when it was a minor capital called Chissingin. If things start getting hot and heavy during your visit, it's only 185km to – dare we say it – Fucking, Austria (although we recommend swinging by the lovely village of Condom, France, first).

✪ NEW YORK CITY, USA
New York's history is filled with memorable kisses. From 1892 to 1954 Ellis Island was the main entry point for immigrants entering the United States. During its prime, the checkpoint employees dubbed a baluster 'the kissing post', as it was here that freshly minted Americans would reunite with their estranged families. In 1945 tonsil tennis in Times Square was immortalised by Alfred Eisenstaedt's definitive photograph of an American sailor planting a wet one on a young woman. And in 1973 this gritty metropolis was home to Gene Simmons and Paul Stanley when they formed the rock band KISS.

✪ KIRIBATI
Island destinations are always a great choice for a romantic getaway, but this tiny nation of rugged atolls offers a little something extra. Kiribati's 33 isles are in the cerulean waters of the South Pacific, just west of the international dateline, making it the first place in the world to welcome the new day. If you ring in the New Year on one of Kiribati's Line Islands, you and your special someone could be the first people on earth to steal a kiss in 2009.

✪ RIO DE JANEIRO, BRAZIL
'Tall and tan and young and lovely' pretty much describes every frolicking sun-aholic on scintillating Copacabana Beach. Antonio Carlos Jobim, a native of Rio, wrote the sultry *The Girl from Ipanema*, which perfectly captures the longing for a beachside romance under the tropical sun. Even when played as instrumental elevator Muzak, the heartbreaking bossa nova elicits a quixotic desire to immediately pack one's bags and head to Brazil, where a kiss on both cheeks comes with every friendly 'hello'.

✪ VENICE, ITALY
The charming canals of Venice have been synonymous with romance since long before Shakespeare and the Renaissance. Local legend maintains that lovers will find eternal happiness if they share a kiss while passing beneath the Bridge of Sighs on a sunset gondola ride. Many believe that the bridge was named for romantic exhalations, but the term was actually coined because the limestone overpass connected a courtroom and a prison, and criminals would often sigh as they took a final look at the beautiful city before being locked away.

✪ HERSHEY, USA
Only in tiny Hershey, Pennsylvania, would the main thoroughfare be called Chocolate Avenue. This quiet township is home to the Hershey's factory, which produces the infamous Hershey's Kisses. Wrapped in silver foil, these delicate drops of chocolaty goodness have been responsible for over a century's worth of cavities. Travellers to Hershey can check out Chocolate World, the on-site visitor centre, and embark on a Willy Wonka–style adventure through the plant. There is a 3D musical show, a simulation ride, singing trolley tours and a tasting booth where you can steal all the kisses you want.

✪ CASABLANCA, MOROCCO
'Kiss me, kiss me as if it were the last time' was just one of Ingrid Bergman's indelible phrases that catapulted the movie *Casablanca* to cult status, and forever gave the Moroccan metropolis a certain *je ne sais quoi*. Although Humphrey Bogart's smoky Café Americain was a figment of the writer's imagination, there are plenty of hectic hangouts to use as a backdrop for your own re-enactment. Gaze into your lover's eyes and whisper 'we'll always have Paris' (our number one place to steal a kiss).

GO WILD FOR WILDE AT HIS GRAVE IN PÈRE LACHAISE

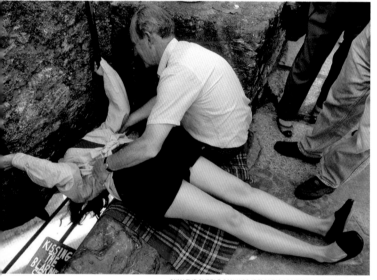

ONLY THE SUPPLE CAN KISS IRELAND'S LEGENDARY BLARNEY STONE

SMOOCH A STORMTROOPER AT WALT DISNEY WORLD

01 PARIS, FRANCE

Our 'pecking order', so to speak, would be incomplete without the City of Lights and Love. Heck, we could come up with a completely separate list just featuring places to pucker up in Paris. Without besmirching the other classic places to be smooching, our favourite spot is Père Lachaise Cemetery, the final resting place of some of the most passionate people that ever lived. Steal a kiss at the apocryphal tombs of lovelorn Abelard and Heloise, and don't forget to visit Oscar Wilde's burial place to add your mark to the mosaic of fading lipstick ovals left by other admirers.

02 BLARNEY, IRELAND

All those who seek the 'gift of gab' flock to Blarney Castle, near Cork, to get intimate with a celebrated chunk of bluestone. No one is quite certain how the tradition began but, according to legend, those who give the rock some lovin' will be rewarded with uncanny eloquence and the ability to flatter even the surliest characters. It's not that simple. To kiss the stone, visitors must lie on their back, arch their head back into a deep crevice, and kiss the stone upside-down while gripping two iron railings.

03 KISSIMMEE, FLORIDA, USA

The home of Walt Disney World announces its smoochability via its name. Kissimmee attracts millions of tourists looking to re-enact an assortment of magical fables involving valiant princes waking their sleeping beauties with a delicate embrace, or would-be princesses planting kisses on a warty toad hoping he'll transform into their lover. Cinderella's castle, the hallmark of the Disney brand, sits at the centre of the theme park – this rambling fortress of twisting turrets is the perfect place for a fairytale kiss.

I CAN'T BELIEVE IT'S
NOT THE CAPITAL

THESE CITIES DON'T NEED A LABEL. THEY *KNOW* HOW GOOD THEY ARE

☼ ISTANBUL, TURKEY

Istanbul has had a hard time coming to terms with the fact that it's no longer the Turkish capital, and who can blame it? The centre of two world-class empires (Byzantine and Ottoman) which lasted over 1500 years, it holds an embarrassingly large number of monuments worthy of any great capital – embarrassing, that is, for Ankara, the dusty Anatolian town that became the nation's capital in 1923. And today it's those same monuments – the Aya Sofya, the Blue Mosque – that continue to convince tourists and locals alike that the real heart of Turkey is still Istanbul.

☼ AMSTERDAM, THE NETHERLANDS

OK, we're cheating a bit here as Amsterdam is kind of joint capital city of the Netherlands. But that doesn't mean it's full of dreary parliamentarians. Oh no. While they're discussing the political issues of the day over in Den Haag, Amsterdam enjoys all the splendour and culture of a capital but without the boring governmental stuff. One of the city's great draws is its laid-back attitude to most things,

best demonstrated on 30 April every year when Queen's Day sees the whole place go wild.

☼ AUCKLAND, NEW ZEALAND

'He's a JAFA, mate' is something you hear a lot travelling round New Zealand and it's easy to see why the rest of the population refers to the inhabitants of the country's largest city as Just Another Fucking Aucklander – they're jealous! Auckland has the best weather, the fanciest restaurants, and the coolest bars. So what if Wellington has the famous Beehive parliament building and an internationally acclaimed film industry, Auckland's got the tallest building in the southern hemisphere. So there!

☼ CAPE TOWN, SOUTH AFRICA

Take a magnificent setting at the point where the Indian and the Atlantic Oceans meet, a suitably impressive backdrop of one of the world's most famous mountains, a vibrant mix of nationalities from around the globe, and a range of architecture, cuisine and nightlife second to none in Africa and you'd think you'd have the best darn capital in the world. Instead you

get Cape Town which, though South Africa's legislative capital, has to share the title with Pretoria (administrative) and Bloemfontein (judicial). We know which one we'd prefer to visit.

☼ MARRAKESH, MOROCCO

When your name is good enough not just for you but for the region you're located in, you'd think you deserved some recognition. But while it's been Morocco's capital on and off over the years and is still the country's most popular destination, Marrakesh has to be content with containing Africa's busiest square, Djemaa el-Fna, and with being the burial place of the Seven Saints, Muslim holy men who brought pilgrims to the city from the late 17th century on. And if it's good enough for saints…

☼ TORONTO, CANADA

If you've heard of one Canadian city, it's likely to be Toronto. The nation's largest urban centre is like a major US city without the crime. With an amazing 49% of the population born outside Canada, this is the most diverse city on the planet. Ironically, in light of its contemporary multiculturalism, Toronto's lack of capital status today is due to the fact that back in 1857, when the capital was chosen, Toronto was just too English for its Francophone compatriots in Québec to accept. Still, it can content itself with being the Canadian city everyone's heard of.

☼ MUMBAI, INDIA

If population size, cultural importance and financial clout were gauges to judge what makes a capital city then Mumbai (formerly Bombay) would be up there with the best of them. Remnants of British imperialism, such as the Gateway of India, contrast with slums that house many of the city's 13 million inhabitants. Bollywood, the world's biggest movie industry is here, and the city controls most of India's booming economy. Not bad for a city that's a relative latecomer in terms of India's history.

ADRENALINE'S NOT THE ONLY RUSH IN NYC

01 NEW YORK, USA

When you're the cultural and financial centre of a country who cares if you're not actually the seat of government? New York certainly doesn't. The melting pot of the United States has over 160 languages spoken across its five boroughs by 8.2 million inhabitants. Visitors are attracted by skyscraping architecture that struts across the skyline like an international supermodel and nightlife that puts most actual capital cities to shame. The city is home to the UN – who needs to be the national capital when you can justifiably claim to be capital of the world?

SAY 'QUEIJO': POSING FOR A CARNAVAL SNAP IN RIO DE JANEIRO

02 RIO DE JANEIRO, BRAZIL

Sometimes losing your status as capital city can be a liberating experience. Take Rio de Janeiro which waved *adeus* to the national politicians in 1960 when they decamped to the jungle and newly built Brasília – and said *olá* to what the Cariocas (Rio's inhabitants) do best: partying. Whether it's two million people seeing in the New Year on Copacabana beach, or neighbourhood *blocos* and traditional samba schools thrilling the Carnaval crowds, locals know how to celebrate. With everyone invited, there's nothing stopping you packing your smallest piece of swimwear and heading to the party capital of the world.

STAYING COOL'S IMPERATIVE IN SYDNEY

03 SYDNEY, AUSTRALIA

Like its American counterpart, Sydney doesn't lose any sleep about the fact that it's not the Australian capital. Manufactured Canberra is a dull, suit-wearing place filled with scheming politicians, while Sydney is the kind of town that heads for the beach to top up its tan and catch a few waves before inviting a few mates round for a barbie. The original (in terms of European settlement) and still the best, Sydneysiders will happily extol their city's virtues to the visitor. Just ask the visitor what they think, and they'll undoubtedly agree. Canberra who?

WEIRDEST PLANTS
(& WHERE TO SEE THEM)

DON'T FORGET TO STOP AND SMELL THE ROSES…
OR NOT. SOME OF THESE FLORA ARE, LITERALLY,
BREATHTAKING

FEED ME, SEYMOUR: AN INDONESIAN RAFFLESIA ARNOLDII

THE TITAN ARUM STANDS PROUD AT KEW GARDENS, LONDON

01 WELWITSCHIA MIRABILIS, NAMIBIA

Resembling an alien life form in the Namibian desert, this plant is thought to be a living relic of the Jurassic era. Along with a short stem and roots, it consists of two leaves (the only leaves it ever grows) – and never sheds – making it unique among plants. Long and leathery, the leaves spill onto the ground, getting torn and split over the years. And it can be many years – a *Welwitschia* plant is thought to live for between four and 15 centuries.

02 RAFFLESIA (RAFFLESIA ARNOLDII), INDONESIA & MALAYSIA

This parasitic plant wins the title of world's biggest flower. In fact it's all flower, having no leaves, stem or roots. The huge, fleshy bloom, with its acne-like white spots, grows to over 1m across – and smells of putrefying road kill. Seeing one in its natural habitat can be a challenge as they usually grow in steep, leech-infested jungle. Your best bet is the Rafflesia Sanctuary in the Rimba Pati Nature Reserve, West Sumatra. In Malaysia, the Orang Asli people, who traditionally used the plant for healing after childbirth, now take tourists to see the blooms.

03 TITAN ARUM (AMORPHOPHALUS TITANUM), INDONESIA

Its Latin name means 'gigantic misshapen penis'. This more or less describes its appearance. Its local name is 'corpse flower', which more or less describes its smell. This delightful specimen has a central shaft that grows taller than a man and emits the scent of rotting meat to attract pollinating insects. It's native to the rainforests of Sumatra, but it only flowers in the wild once every couple of years so you may have to get yourself to the botanic gardens of Sydney, Bonn or Washington DC, to see one in its full glory. Just don't forget your gas mask.

✪ ROSE OF JERICHO (ANASTATICA HIEROCHUNTICA) MIDDLE EAST

The rose of Jericho (actually nothing like a rose) survives in the desert by curling up into a tight, dry ball and waiting for the next rainy season, when it revives and unfurls with the first raindrops. This curling up and drying out can occur repeatedly over many years, leading to its alternative name: the resurrection plant. This miraculous ability, together with its origins in the Holy Land, have given the rose of Jericho religious significance, and individual plants have been passed down generations of families, stored in their dry state and brought out at special occasions for a brief comeback appearance. A bit like the Rolling Stones.

✪ PITCHER PLANT (NEPENTHES RAJAH), BORNEO HIGHLANDS

A plant that consumes frogs and small mammals sounds like something you don't want to stumble over in a dark Borneo jungle. In fact, the pitcher plant prefers to eat insects, and is generous enough to share its bounty. Monkeys drink rainwater from the plant's tube-like funnel, whose slippery sides are designed to catch small critters; and diving spiders attach a line to the lip of the cup, abseil down into the liquid and use a bubble of air as a scuba tank while they fish for prey.

✪ LIVING STONES (LITHOPS), SOUTH AFRICA & NAMIBIA

In southern Africa, especially in the Karoo desert, you might stumble over a strange-looking brown or grey stone with a split across the surface. On closer inspection this will turn out to be a succulent plant, which has evolved so well that it can be hard to distinguish from the sand and rocks of its surroundings. *Lithops* survive the harsh conditions by growing partly underground and devoting most of their size to water storage. In autumn and winter the plant suddenly shrugs off its disguise and shows its true nature by sprouting daisy-like flowers.

A WELWITSCHIA MIRABILIS SPRAWLS ACROSS THE NAMIBIAN DESERT SANDS

✪ GIANT SEQUOIA (SEQUOIADENDRON GIGANTEUM), USA

Giant sequoias are the planet's largest living things (by volume). You can pay your respects to the record holder, nicknamed General Sherman, in the Giant Forest of Sequoia National Park, California. Estimated to be over 2000 years old, the General measures 83.8m tall and 31.3m in circumference at the base, which makes it neither the tallest (the accolade belongs to another species of sequoia, the coast redwood) or the thickest (many African baobabs have greater girths) – but it's probably one of the most impressive living things you'll ever see. Wandering through the grandeur of the Giant Forest and observing its scale is quite a humbling experience.

✪ WOLFFIA GLOBOSA, THAILAND

Unlike a camel, a single one of these tiny round green blobs could easily pass through the eye of a needle. Hundreds of them will fit on your fingertip. This is the world's smallest plant. It can be found floating in slow-moving streams and ponds throughout the tropics. In Thailand it's known as *khai-nam* (water eggs) and has been harvested as a vegetable for generations. *Khai-nam* looks like a dark green dip, and is a good source of protein.

✪ MIRACLE FRUIT (SYNSEPALUM DULCIFICUM), WEST AFRICA

The red berries of this shrub, known in its native tropical West Africa as *taami*, *asaa*, or *ledidi*, are completely tasteless. However they have the seemingly miraculous power of changing the taste of other foods eaten after them. Any acidic food, like lemon, lime or vinegar, suddenly tastes sweet. The berries contain a glycoprotein called miraculin, which in the presence of acid activates the tastebuds responsible for sweetness. A word of warning though: if you try miracle fruit, go easy on the acid, or you'll end up with a sore mouth and stomach.

✪ SQUIRTING CUCUMBER (ECBALLIUM AGRESTE), GREECE

The fun thing about this plant is that its fruit, which look like small bristly cucumbers, explode violently when ripe and squirt their juicy content and seeds a considerable distance. In the plant world this just about qualifies as fastest gun in the West. The liquid can cause skin irritation, but also has anti-inflammatory properties and is traditionally used to aid sinusitis. Squirting cucumbers grow in sandy and stony areas throughout Greece, Malta and Turkey – a good place to watch one go off is on the slopes of Mt Pelion in Thessaly.

BEST LOCATIONS FOR
SIGHTING CRYPTIDS

FROM LOCH NESS TO THE CONGO, THERE ARE PLENTY OF PLACES LEFT TO
SEEK OUT YOUR VERY OWN PRIMEVAL PREDATOR

01 SCOTLAND

Cryptozoology's poster monster, Nessie is the long-necked lake beast lurking in
Loch Ness. Loch Ness's massive volume – the lake is 37km long, with a maximum depth
of 230m – leaves lots of hiding space for an elusive cryptid. All the better for Nessie's
neighbours, profiting from the multimillion-pound industry she has spawned. The big
question: could she be a plesiosaur, the otherwise extinct aquatic reptile? And what about
her sister monsters, such as Mòrag, Muc-sheilch, Seileag and more in Scotland's sister
lochs, watched over by big brother Fear Liath Mor, the giant paranormal Big Grey Man of
Scotland's Cairngorm range?

02 AFRICAN CONGO BASIN

The Likouala swamp just might be the real *Land of the Lost*, minus the silly Sleestaks.
An immense expanse in the north of the Republic of Congo, it is hot, humid and thick with
forests and wetlands. According to one report, more than 80% of it is unexplored. Where
better for reptilian survivors of the Jurassic to remain undocumented? So it is with the
Mokele-mbembe, a Lingala name that refers to hypothetical but oft-reported prehistoric
wildlife (such as Emela-ntouka, Mbielu-mbielu-mbielu and Nguma-monene) all fitting the
description of a sauropod dinosaur – elephant-sized, with a long neck and long tail.

03 AMAZON RAINFOREST

The planet's most likely cache of undetected large mammals is the vast unexplored
Amazon rainforest. Hidden therein could be countless beasts, both fantastical and credible.
The latter includes the Tapire-iauara, or *onça d'água* (water jaguar). Cow-sized and donkey-
legged, with glossy, water-repellent, red-gold fur, it is said to have the face of a jaguar with
drooping ears. The remote swamps it inhabits suit its semi-aquatic needs and carnivorous
nature, and keep it away from the slow but ferocious Mapinguari, a legendary slothlike Bigfoot of the Amazon, and the Minhocão, a scaly, black giant-worm bugaboo up to 20m long.

⊕ PACIFIC NORTHWEST, NORTH AMERICA

Sasquatch, from *sesquac,* a Coast Salish Indian word meaning 'wild man', is just one of many Native American terms to describe our favourite, but unverified, large, hairy, bipedal primate – Bigfoot. This secretive, nocturnal cryptid who refuses to sit for a portrait has seriously challenged both sceptics and proponents. Although believed to be present all across North America, its frequent appearances in the extensive forests of Washington state and British Columbia draw the curious from around the globe. Perhaps there, sasquatch swaps human-encounter stories with Ogopogo, the serpent-like presence in Lake Okanagan, the wolf-like Waheela and any folkloric Thunderbirds alighting nearby.

EAST AFRICA

The Nandi people of forested western Kenya have a beast they call Kerit, aka the Nandi Bear. As large as a lion, like a hyena on steroids, with high and broad front shoulders, thick dark-brown fur and the gait and face of a bear, it is said to be ferocious, and craves human blood. Having eluded capture through centuries of sightings, it must also be smart; after all, according to the Nandi, its favourite food is brains. Not the kind of cryptid to cuddle. The area's enigmatic, hairy, humanlike Agogwe and maneless Buffalo Lion must be watching their backs.

⊕ THE HIMALAYAS

Although tamed by Tintin, Scooby-Doo and Hermey the Elf (from *Rudolph the Red-Nosed Reindeer*), the 'real' abominable snowman has yet to be substantiated. With many sightings registered and footprints photographed (the latter as recently as December 2007), including by mountaineering greats Eric Shipton and Sir Edmund Hillary, the yeti appears to be alive and well, though still only on the desolate snowbound slopes of the high Himalayas. If chased by a yeti, why not turn your pet Nyalmo (a 5m-tall, four-toed primate-like Himalayan cryptid) on him, or summon up a Tibetan mystical Tulpa energy being?

⊕ MONGOLIA

Something elongated, reddish and deadly may lurk beneath the sun-baked rocky plain of the southern Gobi Desert. Known to the local Mongolian tribesmen as the *allghoi khorkhoi* ('intestine worm'; it looks like living cow entrails), cryptozoologists call it the Mongolian Death Worm. The thick-bodied invertebrate is said to emerge after rain in June and July, spitting lethal acid from its front end and emitting an immobilising electric charge from its tail. The local reddish brown–haired wild hominid called the Alma and the mysterious Mongolian Goat-Antelope best beware. As should anyone wearing yellow, supposedly the death worm's favourite colour.

⊕ INDONESIA

Sleepless nights may be routine for children of Seram Island in the Moluccas archipelago of eastern Indonesia. Folklore and several contemporary run-ins tell of nocturnal winged monkeys that abduct and feed on young flesh. The fearsome Orang-bati (winged men) supposedly dwell in a cave network deep within Mt Kairatu, a dormant volcano. Its humanlike torso, complete with blood-red skin, bat wings and a long tail, is covered with short black fur; its shrill wail is naked terror. Could it be a distant kin of Java's Ahool, a cryptid giant bat with a 4m wingspan?

⊕ AUSTRALIA

Australia is known for its unusual fauna of monotremes (egg-laying mammals) and marsupials (pouched mammals) with uncommon names (quoll, quokka, numbat), and also for the unfortunate extinction of the thylacine (Tasmanian Tiger). Are there really none left? Maybe not. Maybe too there's still a thylacoleo (Queensland Tiger), conjectured to be the marsupial equivalent of a predatory feline. Or the fabled bunyip – could there be a surviving prehistoric diprotodon? Or maybe they're all examples of the Australian deadpan humour evident in tales of spurious beasts like the Yowie, Australia's yeti; the Drop Bear, a large, vicious and carnivorous cousin of the koala; or the Jackalope, Hoop Snake and Wild Haggis. Fair dinkum.

OCEANS OF THE WORLD

For many, fear of what lies fathoms below date from the first haunting dah-dum of *Jaws* or Captain Nemo's battle against a giant briny tentacle. What's actually out there in the liquid unknown covering 71% of the planet's surface and accounting for 80% of living things? Lots, including the oft-spied cadborosaurus sea serpent, the most famous of which is Caddy of British Columbia; or the giant monsters of the deep such as Kraken and Lusca (octopuslike sea beasts); megalodon (shark); biblical leviathan (whale); or any of the globsters (unidentifiable organic mass washed up on a beach).

BEST PLACES TO HAVE A
MIDLIFE CRISIS

FORGET THE RED SPORTS CAR. HERE ARE OUR
RECOMMENDATIONS FOR HOW TO AGE DISGRACEFULLY

✪ A BLINGTASTIC NEW LOOK – DUBAI

It's time for a new outfit, which means an expedition to Dubai. Fashion is serious business in this shopping-mall heaven, and flashy togs can be had in designer-handbags full. To finish the look, eye-punishing displays of glittering gold line the streets of Dubai's gold souq. Over 25 tonnes of the stuff are on display in the city's jewellery-shop windows. Take your pick from earrings, rings, necklaces or bracelets – the more ostentatious the better.

✪ SAY 'OM' – RISHIKESH

If your crisis is one of faith and you're feeling life should have more meaning than meandering, take your pick of places in which to have a spiritual epiphany: St Peter's in Rome, Lhasa in Tibet or Mecca in Saudi Arabia could help you find your calling. But we reckon the ideal spot is Rishikesh, on the banks of the sacred Ganges in the foothills of the Himalaya. It's lined with ashrams, and holy men mingle with tourists and the odd celeb. This was the Beatles' favourite centre of Hindu philosophy and learning, as well as being nicknamed yoga capital of the world.

✪ SAY 'I DO', NOT 'WHO ARE YOU?' – LAS VEGAS

You've realised what your first wedding was missing: an Elvis impersonator, matching polyester pantsuits and a partner you'd only just met. So it's time to take a gamble of a different sort with a second/third/seventh wedding in Vegas. It offers more than 30 places to say 'I do', and over 100,000 couples say their vows here each year, including more than a handful of celebs. The Little White Wedding Chapel is open 24 hours, so when your eyes meet over a crowded poker table, there's no need to bother waiting before tying the knot.

✪ TIME FOR A NIP AND TUCK

Fed up of peering in the mirror, jiggling your wobbly bits and wishing everything was a little further north? Considering a little nip and tuck or two, but worried about showing your post-op bruises in public? The attraction of cheap prices coupled with recuperating in the sun is making surgery in Phuket, Kuala Lumpur or Manila increasingly popular. India is the daddy of them all – after all Shiva attached an elephant's head to his son's body around 4000 years ago. Today state-of-the-art facilities make a facelift or hip replacement a short inconvenience before relaxing by the beach.

✪ ROUND THE BEND – SILVERSTONE

It's not too late to fulfil that dream of being a racing driver, temporarily at least. Crowds have watched heroes like Senna, Prost and Stewart hurtle around the legendary Silverstone track, home of the British Grand Prix, since the 1950s, and you can recreate it with a power test drive. Imagine the cheers as you burn rubber in a Ferrari, slide into corners in an old single-seater or test a 4WD on something more taxing than the streets of Islington. Just don't try this on the school run.

✪ JAWS INDOORS – SYDNEY & MELBOURNE

For centuries, man has pitted himself against beast to prove his manliness and worth, from rather one-sided trophy hunting to careering down side streets at the running of the bulls in Pamplona, Spain. Something a little more equal and up close is diving with sharks, and for that it has to be Australia. For those with no diving experience, tank dives in Melbourne's aquarium and Sydney's oceanarium give a chance to watch these predators glide past soundlessly, eyeing you up as a potential meal. Friends and family can watch your bravery/barely concealed terror via a glass viewing screen.

✪ GET YOUR KICKS – ROUTE 66

Search for freedom on the open highway with a road trip across America. It requires a Harley or classic convertible, and plenty of 'issues' to resolve. Take your pick from a multitude of interstate routes, but to travel in the footsteps of film, literary and music legends it has to be well-worn and iconic Route 66, from Chicago to Santa Monica. Do take a movie camera to record your trip. Don't forget to fill up with gas.

GET UP TO SPEED WITH SCHUMACHER AT THE MONACO GRAND PRIX

PUT IT ALL ON RED AT MACAU'S CASINO LISBOA

PETRA: 'ROSE-RED CITY, HALF AS OLD AS TIME', ACCORDING TO POET JOHN WILLIAM BURGON

01 SHAKEN, NOT STIRRED – MONTE CARLO

Dust off your tux and brush up on the slick one-liners as you join the jet set, Bond-style, in Monte Carlo. The beautiful people out-glamour each other from their million-euro yachts moored along the harbour, as international businessmen monitor their investments from this secure tax haven. Visitors to the casino glint with gold, like the sun on the Med. The Monte Carlo Rally in January and Monaco Grand Prix in May offer adrenaline-fuelled breaks from spending cash.

02 GAMBLE AWAY YOUR KIDS' INHERITANCE – MACAU

Cashing in the pension fund and re-mortgaging the house might just be enough to get you in the door of Crown Casino, Taipa Island, Macau. Boasting six stars and over 200 gaming tables, the casino's not shy about the number of noughts involved. For those with pockets smaller than China, there are another 27 casinos to choose from. These include the grandly decked-out Emperor Palace Casino on the penin-sula – featuring plenty of marble and as much gold on the brick floor as on the gamblers themselves – or the famous, lively Casino Lisboa.

03 ADVENTURE, BEATING BADDIES & GETTING THE GIRL – PETRA

Petra, setting for much of *Indiana Jones and the Last Crusade,* looks like it should only exist in films. A narrow canyon winds to its iconic entrance, carved from deep rose–coloured sandstone. As you enter, you're greeted by the intricate facade of the famous Khazneh ('treasury'), fictional home of the Holy Grail. The site contains plenty more to explore, includ-ing the Temple of the Winged Lions, still in the process of excavation. Today the only hazards are bumping shoulders with the other 3000 visitors; poisoned arrows, rolling balls of rock and snake pits are usually avoidable.

BEST
BIG TRIPS

CITY SLICKER? RUGGED MOUTAIN TREKKER? TRAIN
TRAVELLER? THERE'S NO LIMIT – NOT EVEN THE SKY –
WHEN IT COMES TO MAKING THAT JOURNEY OF A LIFETIME

WODAABE-BORORO LOCALS DON THEIR BEST FACEPAINT IN NIGER   TAKE ME HOME, COUNTRY RAILS: AN OVERLAND ALBERTA ODYSSEY

01 THE SILK ROAD

Some explorers earned celebrity far beyond the journeys they made. Step forward Marco Polo, whose record of the Silk Road propelled him to adventuring superstardom. His father and brother travelled the overland route from Europe to Asia before him, but it was Marco's 17 years' service to Kublai Khan that gilded his inspiring tales. Modern-day pilgrims still follow the ancient trade roads from Turkey to China. If you've a few spare months, take the train from Istanbul to Tehran and then on to Ashgabat, Tashkent and Almaty before arriving at ancient Xi'an.

02 LONDON TO CAPE TOWN

Take a Land Rover, six months' supplies and a passport. Mix with the spirit of adventure for a classic overland journey. Heading south from London, take the western route to hit as many countries as possible. Political sensitivities allowing, this will lead you through Morocco, Western Sahara, Mauritania, Senegal, Guinea, Sierra Leone, Liberia, Mali, Côte d'Ivoire, Burkina Faso, Ghana, Niger, Nigeria, Cameroon, Equatorial Guinea, Gabon, the Congo, Angola, Namibia and, finally, South Africa. As the crow flies it's 9681km; by road it's as long as you want.

03 VANCOUVER TO HALIFAX

The world's finest single-country journey takes in over 6000km of Canada's natural splendour. Plan your route in Vancouver's hip cafés before taking the train to Jasper, in the Rockies. Pick up a car and drive the stunning Icefields Parkway to Banff, then south to Dinosaur Provincial Park – the scorched badlands hide the bones of prehistoric monsters. Arrive in Edmonton by Greyhound, then back on the train to travel east. Montréal's vibrant nightlife awaits, with gentle Nova Scotia beyond. Drive the coastal Cabot Trail before winding down in the pubs of Halifax.

✪ FOLLOW THE ANDES

Looking for an epic mountain journey? Then how about the 7000km range that comprises the Andes? From Venezuela to Patagonia, South America's defining landmark draws tourists the world over, many flocking to Peru to visit Machu Picchu. But don't restrict yourself. For the definitive adventure pick your way south from Caracas to Bogotá, Quito to Lima and La Paz to Santiago. The further you go, the better it gets: at 6962m Aconcagua, in Argentina, is the highest peak outside Asia, and hints at the wild grandeur that awaits in Patagonia.

✪ MOSCOW TO THE KAMCHATKA PENINSULA

The volcanoes and geysers of the Kamchatka Peninsula are an awesome attraction of Russia's far east. Closer to Tokyo than any of Europe's major cities, Kamchatka's volcanic belt comprises 29 craters and forms part of the greater Pacific Ring of Fire. It's a tough place to visit. Hardcore travellers take the Trans-Siberian Express from Moscow to Khabarovsk before catching a flight to Petropavlovsk-Kamchatsky, the peninsula's capital. Choose a local guide to meet your needs – fishing on the Bystraya River, diving in Avacha Bay or hiking to the Valley of Geysers.

✪ SINGAPORE TO BEIJING

Singapore's shiny, Westernised skyscrapers might not seem like the obvious place to begin an adventure, but the overland route to Beijing takes in some of Southeast Asia's top attractions: the beaches of Terengganu in Malaysia, Thailand's mountainous Khao Yai National Park, the Unesco-listed Angkor Wat temple complex in Cambodia and the rich Buddhist history of Vientiane, Laos' capital city. Beyond it all lies China. The route to Beijing goes one of two ways – north for Xi'an, the Terracotta Army and the Yangzi River, or the eastern coastal roads via Hong Kong and Shanghai. When you arrive in Beijing, the city's wonders will match anything you've seen.

SOLITARY SILK-ROAD SPLENDOUR AT THE 12TH-CENTURY MAUSOLEUM OF SULTAN SANJAR, IN ANCIENT MERV, TURKMENISTAN

✪ EXPLORE CENTRAL AMERICA

Few places in the world offer the diverse culture, nature and wildlife of Central America. If you want a blue-water diving paradise, head to Belize. For stunning Mayan history, try the ruins of Guatemala. Looking for un-spoilt beaches, active volcanoes and primary rainforest? Try Costa Rica's lush national parks. Panama's Bocas del Toro archipelago region is a hiking paradise, whilst surfers head to Nicaragua in search of the perfect wave. Combine the countries of Central America, often overlooked as the bridge between North and South America, for a spine-tingling adventure.

✪ INTERRAIL EUROPE

The gap-year student's favourite adventure has taken a hammering in recent years, as budget airlines battle it out to make air travel more afford-able. But everyone gets misty eyed over the romance of train journeys, so why not get out there and do it? With a bit of planning it's possible to travel from northern Scotland to southern Turkey, covering all the points between. The re-cent expansion of the EU means there's never been a better time to see eastern countries like Slovenia, Slovakia, Roma-nia and Bulgaria. Grab a map, check the timetables and get planning.

✪ NORWEIGAN COASTAL VOYAGE

The fabulous slow boat from Bergen to Kirkenes wows travellers with the most stunning vistas of Norway's majestic coast. Some of the world's longest fjords await, where calm waters sit below towering peaks and colour-ful fishing villages cling to the rocky shores, all 21,342km that face the full force of the North Atlantic. Keep your eyes peeled for majestic sea eagles as you sail towards the midnight sun, leaving time to explore Trondheim and the Arctic capital of Tromsø. In a land dominated by the sea, boat travel seems the perfect way to go.

✪ OUTER SPACE

For the tourist who's been everywhere and got all the T-shirts, a $12.5 million space flight could be the final fron-tier. A select group of big-spending intergalactic adventurers have already made the International Space Station their ultimate destination. But you'll need deep pockets – at an average of 400km above the earth's surface, it works out at a cool $31,250 per kilometre. If your pockets don't quite stretch that far, start saving for a seat on one of the proposed commercial flights. For around $200,000 you can book a place on a rocket bound for the Kármn Line, the arbitrary boundary of space at an altitude of 100km.

COOLEST CAMPS

LEAVE YOUR TWO-MAN TENT AND PARAFFIN STOVE AT HOME – THESE CAMPSITES ARE ABOUT EXPERIENCING WILDERNESS WITHOUT BANGING IN PEGS

✪ CAMEL CAMP, INDIA

Something of the regal splendour of the maharajahs is recreated at the India Safari Club's Camel Camp. Located near Osian, known for its ancient Hindu and Jain temples, the luxurious permanent tents are fully carpeted, decorated in sumptuous fabrics, furnished with antique furniture and have elegant ensuite bathrooms. There are also 50 mobile tents that can be taken on camel safari into the dunes of the Thar Desert. Camels are well padded to protect human posteriors, and there's a good chance of seeing wildlife such as gazelles and peacocks, as well as local artisans at work in the surrounding villages.

✪ CAMP ATTA, MOROCCO

At the edge of the Sahara in southeast Morocco is the territory of the Aït Atta, a tribe of seminomadic Berbers. This is a starkly beautiful region of golden dunes, canyons and flat-topped mesas softened by date palms and almond groves. Here, not far from the village of Merzouga, a camp has been created based on traditional Saharan design and lifestyle, including strict waste, water and energy management. Nomad-style goat-hair tents surround a large communal tent where local artists sometimes come to perform.

✪ TIPI CAMP, CANADA

On the shores of Lake Kootenay on the traditional lands of the Ktunaxa Nation is this peaceful, low-impact camp. The cosy, conical tipis are the ultimate in basic back-to-nature accommodation, with sleeping pallets and a central fireplace. Vegetarian meals are laid on. Access to the camp is by boat or a hike through the forest, so the only noise you'll hear is the cry of loons, the chatter of chipmunks or the distant call of a coyote. In summer the camp hosts various spiritual retreats and youth programs aimed at connecting people to nature.

✪ SHIELINGS, SCOTLAND

Shielings were shelters used by Highland shepherds while grazing their flocks in summer pastures. The shielings on the Isle of Mull are large canvas tents with tiled floors, basic beds and gas cooking facilities, some with bathrooms. They're a novelty to sleep in but the location is the real attraction, with stunning views across the Sound of Mull to Ben Nevis. There's even otters frolicking in the water below. Too close to nature for comfort? The local pub's a short stroll away.

✪ DOMWE ISLAND CAMP, MALAWI

Africa's the home of the luxury tented camp, but Domwe Island at the southern end of vast Lake Malawi is something special. The permanent, thatched-roof safari tents are ecologically designed to blend into the surrounding national park. Kayaking is the star attraction here – there's also top-notch freshwater scuba diving, and wildlife spotting on the nature trails. From the hammock on your private deck you can watch the sun set behind the mountains on the far side of the lake; as night falls the fishermen's lamps come out like fireflies, their distant voices carrying across the water.

✪ KOOLJAMAN, AUSTRALIA

Cape Leveque on the north coast of Western Australia is spectacular, with deserted palm-fringed beaches and stunning red cliffs backed by incredibly blue sky. In this idyllic location, eco-tourism award-winning Kooljaman has accommodation ranging from luxury safari tents with panoramic views to basic thatched humpies on the beach. The resort is jointly owned and run by two Aboriginal communities – visitors receive an insight into their culture through the display of artworks and artefacts, and tours of the communities.

✪ PLANET BAOBAB, BOTSWANA

You'll know you're almost there when you see the huge concrete aardvark. It marks the turn-off to funky Planet Baobab, a community-run lodge in the Makgadikgadi Pans National Park. Pitch a tent beneath the shade of an eponymous baobab tree or choose between Bakalanga-style 'mud huts' and San-style 'grass huts' (both are much more plush than they sound). The highlight of the lodge, however, is the open-air bar, complete with vaulted wooden ceilings, cowhide barstools, beer-bottle chandeliers and framed memorabilia celebrating the glory days of African travel.

TRAILER TRASH IT 'AINT: SHADY DELL, ARIZONA

01 THE SHADY DELL TRAILERS, USA

At quirky and nostalgic Shady Dell, you can relive the heyday of the American trailer by spending the night in your choice of one of several 1950s Airstreams and other vintage models. Each is lovingly refitted with period furnishings and decorated with astonishing attention to detail. Some trailers have black-and-white televisions playing Elvis movies, and phonographs with a selection of vintage records. Also on site is Dot's Diner, a restored 1950s diner serving up grits and biscuits with gravy. Nearby is the quaint, historic copper-mining town of Bisbee, Arizona, where you can indulge in yet more retro kitsch.

GET BACK TO NATURE IN A WHITEPOD AT LES CERNIERS, SWITZERLAND

02 WHITEPOD ECOCAMP, SWITZERLAND

A 'whitepod' is a chic, space-age structure designed to blend with the pristine snowy majesty of the Swiss Alps. Perched at an altitude of 1400m, the camp is only accessible by ski or snowshoe – and the occasional dog sled. The insulated igloo-shaped pods use no electricity – they are heated with a wood-burning stove and lit by the soft glow of oil lamps; there's no need to emerge from the comfort of your organic bedding unless you're tempted by the private ski run. It's hi-tech, ecofriendly and designer cool.

03 YURTS, TAJIKISTAN

Known as the 'roof of the world', the snowcapped Pamir region of Tajikistan has a history of being inaccessible and is still largely undiscovered by tourists. But it is possible to join the summer camps of nomadic yak-traders in the flowering mountain pastures. The Murgab Ecotourism Association has revolutionised independent travel in the area by linking together travellers and locals, and organises accommodation in genuine yurts throughout the area. The facilities are few, but the cost is negligible, the economic benefits that tourism brings to the region are great and the warm hospitality you'll experience is as about as authentic as you can get.

NO TAJIK YURT'S COMPLETE WITHOUT SATELLITE TV

BEST PLACES FOR
DEEP THINKING

HAD ENOUGH OF CONTEMPLATING YOUR NAVEL?
TRY OUR DIFFERENT TAKES ON DEEP THOUGHT ALL
AROUND THE WORLD

ILLUMINATING THE LEFT BANK LUMINARIES · CECI N'EST PAS UNE PIPE

01 BEIJING, CHINA – MAO ZEDONG

It battled the bourgeoisie in the Cultural Revolution, now get your head around today's capitalism-meets-communism blend of 21st-century Beijing: skyscrapers, flyovers and glitzy shopping plazas. It's a short step, but a far cry, from the imposing Chairman Mao Memorial Hall in Tiananmen Square. Take in the hammers, sickles and communist icons that surround the embalmed leader, then hop back to Wangfujing Dajie to see Maoism meet MTV.

02 PARIS' LEFT BANK, FRANCE – EXISTENTIALISM

Catch a whiff of scandal and deep early-20th-century thought in a café on Paris' Left Bank. Boho-chic, scuffed wooden floors and worn wooden tables conjure the existentialist world of Jean-Paul Sartre and Simone de Beauvoir. They argued that we create the meaning in our own lives (ie make your own rules) and applied 'free thinking' to their personal relationships. Once wreathed in a fug of cigarette smoke, the cafés and individual freedoms are now governed by health laws. If you want to light up a Gauloise, you'll have to go outside.

03 BRUSSELS, BELGIUM – SURREALISM

Best summed up by René Magritte's iconic *Ceci n'est pas une pipe*, surrealism began as an antiwar art movement which produced anti-art, works which questioned the nature of art. Why? Good question. Or rather, bad question – the surrealists opposed conventional thinking, arguing that rationalism had led to the terrible, destructive effects of WWI. Instead, we should act because of beliefs or emotions. To see for yourself, visit the intensely quirky house in Brussels, which used to be Magritte's home. Discover a train in a fireplace, and see if that 'window' really is a window. Or – don't decide to go there; do it on impulse.

✪ VIENNA, AUSTRIA – SIGMUND FREUD

Vienna's architecture is monumental. Everywhere, massive creamy constructions signal the Habsburgs' penchant for self-glorification. Freud used to like it too – every afternoon the man who brought us the Oedipus complex and penis envy walked the entire length of the city's Ringstrasse. Soak up some statuary then duck into a cosily elegant Kaffeehaus where intellectual types sip coffee, nibble pastries and peruse the paper. Next hop on a rattling tram to the State Opera House – some fork out hundreds to sit in the opera house's red-and-gold opulence; the cognoscenti opt to stand, for just a few euros.

✪ ATHENS, GREECE – THE GREATS

The Ancient Greeks kick-started the things that shape our modern world: democracy, mathematics, politics and drama. A lot of deep thinking went on in the era of Plato, Aristotle and Socrates, and it's written large in the wealth of friezes and columns on show in Athens. Pick up a copy of Plato's *Republic*, clamber up to the Parthenon and, in between reading, feast your eyes on its gleaming Doric colonnades. Linger until the crowds have gone, then gaze down through the early evening haze at a view that encompasses 2400 years of history: a sprawling buzzing city, dotted with temples.

✪ HIGHGATE CEMETERY, ENGLAND – KARL MARX

Born in Prussia, revolutionary in Russia, Karl Marx is buried in the most English of cemeteries. London's Highgate is the final resting place of around 850 famous people. The leafy, creepy western cemetery features mausoleums, gothic crosses, Victorian vaults and catacombs draped with ivy. On the east side the massive bust of Karl Marx bears the inscription 'workers of all lands unite'. If you don't like his train of thought, try dropping by on fellow inhabitants Douglas (*Hitchhiker's Guide to the Galaxy*) Adams and George Eliot. Highgate is also home to a very modern Russian: the poisoned former KGB agent Alexander Litvinenko.

THE LAST OF THE MOHICANS SEE THE SIGHTS OF BEIJING

☼ RED SQUARE, MOSCOW, RUSSIA – VLADIMIR LENIN

For decades in the frosty grip of the Cold War, Russia continues its rapid thaw. The trappings of the hardline thinking that saw it pitted against entrenched Western views are best seen in the massive granite mausoleum of Lenin's Tomb in Red Square. Here thousands still queue up to file past the waxy, mummified body of the man who lead the Bolshevik Revolution and inspired countless other leaders worldwide. But the Kremlin, that byword of communism, also houses evidence of much older beliefs: the icons, gables and golden domes of the Archangel, Assumption and Annunciation Cathedrals.

☼ DELHI, INDIA – GANDHI

Delhi's profoundly rich culture more than makes up for its famous chaos and pollution. The old city is laced with winding streets, bazaars and pungent aromas; the leafy, open vistas of New Delhi are lined with relics of the British Raj. Nestling amid the imperial architecture is Birla House, the home of Mahatma Gandhi. The man who sparked Indian independence and inspired nonviolent civil rights movements around the world strolled the gardens here each night. Follow suit, then visit his room to see his meagre possessions. Birla House is also where this man of peace died, shot by an assassin in 1948.

☼ WASHINGTON DC, USA – RIGHTS & PEACE

Washington's Reflecting Pool is a place of deep thoughts and shallow waters. This limpid stretch of water is 610m long and only 46cm deep in places. It lies between the Lincoln Memorial and the Washington Monument, neatly linking two of America's great thinkers. The area was the venue for Martin Luther King's rousing 'I Have a Dream' speech and intense anti-Vietnam war demonstrations. A short walk leads to the searing simplicity of the Vietnam Veterans Memorial – poignantly, its mirrorlike black granite stretches into the distance, etched with more than 58,200 names.

☼ STADE DE FRANCE, PARIS, FRANCE – FOOTBALL AS PHILOSOPHY

For the moody French philosopher Albert Camus, kicking a ball about was thought-provoking business. This keen goalkeeper practically invented the concept of the angry young man in his 1942 novel *L'Étranger* (The Stranger), and famously said, 'what I know most surely about morality and the duty of man I owe to sport'. Mull it all over at the home of French soccer, the Stade de France. As 80,000 voices chant *La Marseillaise*, ponder the cryptic words of the French Manchester United striker Eric Cantona: 'when the seagulls follow the trawler, it's because they think sardines will be thrown into the sea.'

BEST
CHRISTMAS CRACKERS

YULE LOVE IT. SNOW, SANTA, STORYBOOK SCENES AND A MENAGERIE
OF FANTASTIC BEASTS RING IN CHRISTMAS

o1 REINDEER RACE, NORWAY

When rock-and-roller Chuck Berry belted out *Run, Run Rudolph*, he surely had
these guys in mind. On a bitterly cold morning in February, Tromsø hosts its annual
reindeer-racing championships, where the locals compete on a short course through
snowy streets. North of the Arctic Circle, between the frosted Norwegian fjords and
peaks, the setting is pure winter wonderland. The hot breath of the reindeer as they
gallop at speeds of up to 60km to the finish line, the swoosh of skis and the cheering
crowds make for a wildly exciting event.

o2 SANTA CLAUS WORLD CHAMPIONSHIPS, SWITZERLAND

Picture the scene: a sleepy village in the Swiss Alps, a thick blanket of snow and
100 pseudo-Santas in all their red-cloaked glory. On the first weekend in December,
Father Christmas wannabees descend on Samnaun to vie for the coveted title of world's
best Santa. This is no mean feat, with disciplines that include climbing a 5m chimney
schlepping a sack full of pressies, delivering gifts by donkey, decorating gingerbread and
horn-sled sprinting. It's an utterly bonkers event for getting into the Christmas groove
with Santa, schnapps and a helluva lot of ho-ho-ho-ing.

o3 GENGENBACH ADVENT CALENDAR, GERMANY

Remember the anticipation of opening those tiny windows in the countdown to
Christmas? Set in the enchanting Black Forest, Gengenbach conjures up such childhood
memories when its Rathaus (town hall) morphs into one of the world's largest Advent
calendars. Every evening at 6pm, one of its 24 windows opens to reveal a festive scene
painted by artists or children's-book illustrators, such as Tomi Ungerer. The giant calendar
can be admired until Epiphany (6 January) and is complemented by carol singing, brass
bands and a twinkling Christmas market for a gluhwein pick-me-up.

November to December (closed Christmas Eve and Christmas Day).

✪ THREE KINGS PARADE, SPAIN

Always up for a fiesta, it's little surprise that the Spaniards celebrate long after other folk have chucked out the tree and begun their post-Christmas diet. Held across Spain, the Cabalgata de los Reyes Magos (Three Kings Parade) is an incredible spectacle; nowhere more so than in Barcelona. On the eve of Epiphany, Caspar, Melchior and Balthazar arrive by boat in Moll de Fusta harbour to a cacophony of foghorns and fireworks. This kicks off a huge parade, where characters aboard the decorated floats shower the crowds with sweets and confetti en route to Montjuic.

✪ GREAT CHRISTMAS PUDDING RACE, ENGLAND

Decorated with holly, doused with brandy and momentarily set alight – pudding has long been a staple of the British Christmas dinner. But the suet-and-currant calorie bomb was never the stuff of competitions until some bright sparks devised this race to raise cash for Cancer Research UK. Nowadays teams in fancy dress tear across London's Covent Garden, balancing trays laden with puddings. Sounds a piece of cake? Not when you consider that participants must negotiate bollards and squirty cream to win the trophy: a perfectly inedible Christmas pud.

✪ SINGING CHRISTMAS TREE, SWITZERLAND

Zurich's top-of-the-tree attraction during the festive season is the all-singing tree on Werdmühleplatz. Yuletide spirit, whiffs of gluhwein and a blast of nostalgia drive the Swiss city totally cuckoo. And so it is that this square is dwarfed by a tiered tree made up of young carol singers; their faces aglow, voices sweet and red bobble hats resembling baubles when viewed from the front. The carolling youngsters, strings of fairy lights and inviting glow of log huts at the Christmas market below capture all the enchantment of a Dickens novel.

✪ KRAMPUSLAUFEN, AUSTRIA

On 5 December, the eve of St Nicholas' Day, the devilish Krampus runs riot through Igls' streets to the clatter of cowbells and the crack of whips. Goat-horned and hairy, the character is the absolute antithesis of good guy St Nick. Around 70 of the menacing ghouls stampede through this alpine village near Innsbruck, scaring anyone (the smaller the better!) who dares cross their path. The pre-Christmas tradition is fun for kids who enjoy screaming at the top of their lungs and grown-ups keen to indulge in Krampus' sinful treats: schnapps and Krapfen (sugary doughnuts).

✪ TURKEY FESTIVAL, FRANCE

Stuffed into the Trois-Pays region of Nord-Pas de Calais, Licques' claim to fame is as one of France's most prolific turkey-rearing towns. Come the second Saturday in December, the gobblers have fattened up nicely for the two-day Fête de la Dinde (Turkey Festival), where the spotlight is on birds soon to be plucked, roasted and stuffed with chestnuts. In spectacularly joyous fashion, dignitaries parade the condemned turkeys through the streets while locals toast their prized poultry with Licquoise liqueur. The merrymaking continues with fresh turkey tastings, farmers-market goodies and late-night soirees.

✪ ZOO LIGHTS FESTIVAL, USA

'Tis the season to nip across to Chicago's magnificently illuminated Lincoln Park Zoo. When a chill wind blows across from Lake Michigan, locals take their overexcited kids on a surreal outing. As darkness falls, the focus shifts from live critters to twinkling beasts emerging from the undergrowth. The zoo gets into the festive swing with croc encounters on Santa's Safari, Rudolph held captive in a snow globe, an endangered-species carousel – there goes a Siberian tiger! – and animal ice-sculptures. The first 1000 visitors get a free pair of dazzling 3D glasses. It happens Friday to Sunday from late

✪ SANTA VILLAGE & POST OFFICE, ARCTIC CIRCLE

Sure it's pricey and touristy, but the land of eternal Christmas is still a cracker year round. Far, far away in the Arctic Circle lies the yule-themed Santa Village. A visit takes in the post office where the big fella receives 700,000 letters every year, toy shops (all toys elf-made, of course) and a grotto, home to the *real* Santa. Go for the Christmassy overkill and you'll be singing jingle bells all the way back to Helsinki. Behind the kitsch wrapping, however, lies a place of deep snow and reindeer-dotted forests straight out of Narnia.

LOST CITIES
OF THE WORLD
WAR, WEATHER, COSMIC INTERVENTION OR SIMPLY A CASE
OF PURPOSE SERVED...NOTHING LASTS FOREVER

PALENQUE'S RESIDENTS ACT THEIR AGE

EXPLORE THE BIBLICAL BYWAYS OF IRAQ'S ANCIENT BABYLON

o1 ANGKOR, CAMBODIA
Crumbling stone temples in the python grip of jungle vines, a flash of turmeric-coloured robes disappearing into the alcoves of ancient temples. Angkor has its fair share of tourists, but its size means you'll easily find a place to get lost in the distant past. The greater city was enormous, new research suggesting it covered 3000 sq km. Built by a succession of Khmer god-kings from AD 900–1200, it had a population close to one million, and was the capital of the Khmer empire. It's been suggested that climate change (affecting water supply) caused the city to be abandoned some 500 years ago.

o2 PALENQUE, MEXICO
At the foot of the Chiapas mountains in southwestern Mexico, Palenque is an archaeologist's treasure trove. The city appears to have existed at least 100 years BC. Five hundred years later it became a major population centre of Classic Mayan civilisation, complete with myth and legend: child kings, invasions, decapitations, court intrigue and finally the abandonment of the city. The city's rich history is recorded in the hieroglyphs which adorn temple walls.

o3 BABYLON, IRAQ
Babylon, settled around 2500 BC, became a great centre of the Mesopotamian world 500 years later, when Hammurabi, the first king of the Babylonian empire, made it his capital. It was destroyed in the 6th century BC by the Assyrians, and then left to fall into ruin in the 2nd century BC, following the death of Alexander the Great. The ruins of Babylon conjure images of a biblical past: the great Tower of Babel; the beautiful hanging gardens...and there's that certain disco song that just won't leave your head...

✪ CARTHAGE, TUNISIA
It's never enough for a great city to be destroyed only once. After 900 years exerting power in North Africa and southern Europe, Carthage succumbed to the wrath of the Roman Empire (needled for so long by the elephant-led armies of Hannibal). Later rebuilt by the Romans and raised to new glory, it once again found itself at the nexus of conflict and was destroyed by Arab Muslims expanding their own sphere of control. Today, on the outskirts of Tunis, you can visit the crumbling remains of Roman baths, temples and villas, and watch the next stage of rebuilding as Carthage is absorbed by the sprawl of Tunis.

✪ HERCULANEUM, ITALY
Like neighbouring Pompeii, Herculaneum was lost to a river of Vesuvian lava and ash in AD 79. A kind of upper-class town, home to members of the imperial family, it was uncovered about 250 years ago and remains a treasure trove for archaeologists. The pyroclastic flow which enveloped the city carbonised organic matter, preserving both structures and human bodies – a number of which were found by the seafront, presumably as they were trying to escape by boat. Most enticing though are the hundreds of scrolls found in the Villa of the Papyri, ancient texts from the only ancient library to have survived into modern times.

✪ DUNWICH, ENGLAND
Here was a town basking in glory, a major seaport and one of the largest cities in medieval Britain, said to have been the capital of East Anglia; but all built on sand. In the late 13th century a storm blew in, demolishing a good part of the town. Coastal erosion chipped in and before you could say 'cursed city', only a few cottages remained (actually, a few hundred years passed as the town slipped into the ocean). Tales of haunted beaches abound, and at low tide you might well hear the muted tolling of church bells beneath the waves.

MONKS KNOW WHAT'S WAT AT ANGKOR, CAMBODIA

✪ SKARA BRAE, SCOTLAND

More a village than a city, this well-preserved prehistoric set of ruins in Orkney is of a small farming settlement over 5000 years old. It was discovered in 1850 after a wild storm revealed the stone remnants. Excavations (and more storms) showed the village had at least eight stone cottages, complete with beds, hearths and shelves. It seems erosion brought the village closer to the sea, until it was abandoned and left to the enshrouding sands for four millennia. Today, erosion continues to threaten the site, and visits in winter depend on weather conditions.

✪ TAXILA, PAKISTAN

Founded by an ancient Indian king some time around 7th century BC, Taxila (or Takshashila) is a tale of three lost cities. The first was built on a hill, later known as Bhir Mound. In an Old Testament–style confusion of begats and political intrigue, the city was lost to a new Taxila, known as Sirkap, built by Greek invaders. It enjoyed a period of significance in the world of philosophy and the arts, which continued under the Kushans, who took over and refounded Taxila as Sirsukh. Eventually, the city was lost to the Huns in the 6th century, who destroyed it and left it in ruins. Visit the site today, about 30km northwest of Islamabad. The Taxila Museum houses all manner of artefacts, which help you get a feel for the complex history of this once-great city.

✪ DARWIN, USA

Darwin, California, like many thousands of towns in late-19th-century USA, sprung up on the back of a lucky strike, in this case, of silver. But these are flash-in-the-pan places – the town became derelict just four years from its settlement in 1878, as prospectors leapt to the next lucky strike. It revived in the early 20th century as copper became a commodity. You might bump into a resident today, though chances are it'll be tumbleweed caught on a desert wind. The edge of Death Valley seems an appropriate place to visit the remnants of a Wild West town, so grab a bottle of whisky for the picnic as you head out.

✪ WITTENOOM, AUSTRALIA

Way out west, in the desert-dominated state of Western Australia, you'll find a town if not fully lost, so close to being a ghost as makes no difference. Officially no longer a town, and not receiving government services, this place supported an asbestos-mining industry until the mid-1960s, when health concerns over the lung-clogging stuff spelled its demise. A handful of residents remain but it's tough going. Made famous by Australian band Midnight Oil's hit 'Blue Sky Mine', a lot of us know of it in theory; to experience it, take a long (1100km!) drive north of the state's capital, Perth. A lonely drive to a very lonely place.

BEST THINGS TO
THROW YOURSELF OFF

AN ADRENALINE RUSH AND AN ELEMENT OF DANGER – THIS IS WHERE YOU GO FOR THE PERFECT FLING

✪ PARAGLIDING SEDONA RED ROCKS, USA

Pray that the rain has stopped by the time you reach Sedona, and breathe in the scent of the desert – juniper, red clay, limestone and wildflowers. Sedona, in Payson, Arizona, has all the characteristics of an empty desert-city, but this red town has become incredibly popular among flying and adventure enthusiasts. Flying over the rocks here has you looking down on a landscape of hellish delight – fallen, burnt rocks on the edge of the middle of nowhere. Hang-gliders and paragliders both love the place, although the latter will tell you that their machine rules the Sedona skies.

✪ ZIP LINING THE TREETOPS OF DURANGO, USA

If you're harbouring Tarzan dreams, take your very own Jane to the jungle-green forests of Durango, Colorado. Zip lining is, quite simply, a glorified flying fox; in Durango, this is an adventure that will send you high into the treetops. Durango has a population of around 15,000, and is nestled in the Animas River valley, surrounded by the San Juan Mountains. As you

zip from tree to tree, be careful not to land in the homes of the incredible bird- and reptile-life, which keep the jungle alive.

✪ HANG-GLIDING THE MOUNTAINS OF BARILOCHE, PATAGONIA

Patagonia is surely the land of the giants, and if you're looking for a horizon on the road to nowhere, Bariloche, in the heart of San Carlos, is the place to find it. Located on the south margin of Lake Nahuel Huapi, Bariloche shows its beauty from its shores to its highest peaks, and hang-gliding here has been described by many as a truly angelic experience. Ideal places for descent include Mt Otto and Mt Catedral, which are easily reached by chairlifts. Flying activities can take place all year round, but the best views will be during the summer months.

✪ PARAGLIDING MT BABADAG, TURKEY

Not every country in the world will have it's own flying festival – but the Oludeniz region in Turkey celebrates the art of flying each October with its annual Air Games week. Part of the turquoise coast, this region of Turkey

is one of the best places to have your first soaring experience. Climb your way up BabaDag (Father Mountain), taking in the cedar forests and native fauna on your way.

✪ HANG-GLIDING THE SIERRA NEVADA MOUNTAINS, AROUND GRANADA, SPAIN

Visit the Sierra Nevada (literally 'snowy range' in Spanish) and launch yourself above this southernmost tip of Europe, where the mountains meet the sea. This area of Granada is a skier's haven during the winter, but in the summer months the mountains beckon climbers and flyers to its illustrious peaks. Be warned: some of the walks up the Sierra mountains are a stretch, so put those walking legs on before launching your flying dreams.

✪ BASE JUMPING FROM SKY TOWER, NEW ZEALAND

If you want a city view before you take the big plunge, make your way back to New Zealand. In Auckland, one of NZ's most bustling cities, jumpers from all corners of the world come here to BASE jump from the tallest free-standing structure in the southern hemisphere. At 328m above ground level, the jumper can reach up to 85km/h. Just to be safe, the jump is guide-cable-controlled to prevent jumpers from colliding with the tower, in case of gusts. Now, that's bravery for you.

✪ CAVE-DIVING IN THE CAVERNS OF CENOTE DOS OJOS, MEXICO

Sixty five million years ago, a huge meteor hit Mexico's Yucatán Peninsula, leaving a 284km-wide crater in the land's surface. For years to come rainwater filled the cavities which had formed in cracks below the crater's surface, creating an incredible vascular system of underground river and pools. Today, cave divers from all corners of the earth come to the Hidden Worlds Cenote Park to swim deep in the 35m pools, all of which retain their natural appeal. Be awed by an eerie underwater world of stalactites and stalagmites.

A BASE JUMPER DESCENDS FROM AMERICA'S SECOND-HIGHEST BRIDGE ON 'BRIDGE DAY' IN NEW CREEK, WEST VIRGINIA

A GLEEFUL BUNGEE JUMPER HURTLES TOWARD THE ZAMBEZI RIVER, NEAR AFRICA'S VICTORIA FALLS

01 BASE JUMPING THE NEW RIVER GORGE BRIDGE, USA

If you can make it to the New River Gorge Bridge on the third Saturday of October, you will step right into one of mankind's only 'Bridge Days' – and meet a family of mad flyers. The bridge is the centrepiece of Fayette Country's festival, and includes demonstrations of rappelling, ascending and most notably BASE jumping. This form of flying involves the use of a parachute to jump from fixed objects such as buildings, towers and bridges, and natural formations such as cliffs. In Fayetteville, West Virginia, jumpers take their time to open their chutes in the 28,330-hectare National River range. If you don't want to jump, this is definitely the place for nail biting.

02 BUNGEE JUMPING AT VICTORIA FALLS, AFRICA

Step between the borders of Zimbabwe and Zambia and you'll hit Victoria Falls, or hear it – whichever comes first. Named after Queen Vic herself, this is also one of the most-jumped spots in the world, and during the '90s bungee fever took this area of bellowing water by storm. Jumpers are encouraged to find their own spot on the 1.7km-wide precipice, plummeting 111m into the deep curtain of water. Go in November, when the Zambezi River rapids are running at their best.

03 SKYDIVING OVER LAKE TAUPO, NEW ZEALAND

Thinking about opening that emergency exit? See if you can make it happen over the Lake Taupo, one of the last remaining active-volcano regions in New Zealand. Snow-capped volcanoes beckon flyers from all over the world. Tandem skydives here are made at around 4600m, with over one minute in freefall. Notably, it's one of the cheapest adventure falls around.

HAPPIEST PLACES

TRY ONE OF THESE CHEERFUL SPOTS.
YOU'LL BE GLAD YOU CAME

QUEBEC'S UPBEAT FÊTES DE LA NOUVELLE FRANCE PARADE   LIFE'S A BLAST AT VIENNA'S SPRINGTIME LIFE BALL

01 BHUTAN, THE HIMALAYAS

Getting life's priorities right is important. Policymakers in this country at the roof of the world are required to consider not only GDP (Gross Domestic Product) but also GNH – Gross National Happiness. It's seen things like tobacco and plastic bags being banned in this Himalayan kingdom – television was only allowed in 1999. Shopkeepers in the ancient capital Thimphu have even had to take down signs advertising Western soft drinks. Instead, the views are of carved temples and vivid prayer flags fluttering against a backdrop of snow-dusted mountains.

02 MONTRÉAL, CANADA

If laughter is indeed the best medicine they should need fewer medics in Montréal. The Francophone capital of Québec has been staging one of the world's best comedy festivals every July since 1983. In between fits of the giggles wander the squares of Vieux-Montréal or explore the tree-clad gradients of Mt Royal. You can even strap on some skis, shoot down a slope and be back in time for a gourmet supper. But if you want to tell the joke about the American, the Canadian and the grizzly in one of the city's many bohemian bars, they've already heard it.

03 AUSTRIA

Edging in at number three in the global happiness table, Austria is another country tailor-made for natural highs. You'll be grinning from ear to ear after careering down Innsbruck's bobsleigh run – 1000m in a minute. Or bowl up in Mozart-infused Salzburg and sign up for a Sound of Music tour, then round it all off with one of the most atmospheric arrivals by rail in the world. At Hallstatt the train deposits you on one side of a crystal-clear lake, a ferry whisks you to the village clinging to the base of the mountains on the other side.

✪ SWITZERLAND

Health tops the list of things that make people content, according to the world happiness map researchers. Switzerland came in second. Which is fitting – this is a country where you can zip down ski runs in the winter, hike flower-strewn mountain passes in the spring and plunge into deep-blue lakes in August. Highlights are the breathtaking Lauterbrunnen Valley, which is graced by more than 70 waterfalls, the craggy Matterhorn and skateboard-crazy lakeside Lausanne. You can even indulge in the world-famous chocolate and fondue secure in the knowledge that you'll need those calories with all that activity!

✪ ICELAND

Icelanders are the fourth most contented folk in the world and there's a wealth of warmth here despite the chilly moniker. Taking a dip in a geothermal pool tends to raise the temperature a bit – as does hiking or horse riding amid a landscape of active volcanoes, spouting geysers and vast lava fields. If you're prone to glum-inducing SAD (seasonal affective disorder), it's best to avoid the winter, when there can be as few as four hours of sunlight a day. But one of nature's most spectacular displays – the dazzling, ethereal northern lights (aurora borealis) – more than makes up for it.

✪ THE BAHAMAS

The Bahamas drifts in to bag the number five spot on the world map of happiness, beating New Zealand (number 18), USA (23) and UK (41). It's no surprise; at the rate of one a day you'd need almost two years to visit each of its 700 sun-soaked islands and six years to curl your toes in the sand at its 2500 cays. Head for the less developed Out Islands for a laid-back slice of Bahamian life; watch birds at Great Inagua (population: 924 people, 80,000 flamingos) or dive in coral seas off Cat Island, famous for its pink-and white sand.

A YOUNG MONK PLAYS PEEK-A-BHUTAN IN PUNAKHA DZONG

✪ SHANGRI-LA (1), THE HIMALAYAS

Shangri-la is a fictional paradise where the evils of the modern world are kept at bay and people live in harmony with nature and each other. This mystical kingdom was imagined by the British author James Hilton in the novel *Lost Horizon*. He set it in the Himalayas, doubtless inspired by a landscape where sculpted mountains prop up an impossibly blue sky. Add monasteries clinging to cliffs and rare blue poppies and you get the perfect place to contemplate Utopia and the true nature of happiness. Actually, it all sounds an awful lot like Bhutan.

✪ SHANGRI-LA (2), USA

It's highly unlikely you'll get into this Shangri-la. It's in rural Maryland, was established in the 1940s by President Roosevelt and has now been renamed Camp David. But the spectacular scenery nearby successfully evokes idyllic high-altitude hideaways. It also opens up the Blue Ridge Parkway; a 755km drive through the Great Smoky, Shenandoah and Blue Ridge Mountains – a lush panorama of log cabins and lakes, often turned a hazy 'blue' by mists. And there is even a ready-made road-trip soundtrack – chose from down-home bluegrass, John Denver's 'Take Me Home, Country Roads' or Laurel and Hardy's 'The Trail of the Lonesome Pine'.

✪ HAPPY, USA

If a positive outlook spreads contentment, visiting somewhere with an upbeat name should help. Test this theory at Happy, Texas – in this 'town without a frown' the kids go to Happy High, the first newspaper was *Happy News* and they even had a Happy Bank. It's also just a coyote's howl from the 193km-long and 32km-wide Palo Duro Canyon. This cinematic landscape, all vivid colours and towering rock formations, is a place for deep breaths and even deeper thinking. Rent a horse and a cabin, then drink in mind-expanding sunsets and big skies.

✪ DENMARK

Academics drawing up a 'world map of happiness' recently found Denmark is the most cheerful nation on earth. The satisfied residents of this country ensured it came out top in the poll of 178 nations. Denmark's main peninsula meets an idyllic archipelago of more than 400 islands and it's easy to pick up on its positive vibe. The ancient core of Copenhagen, the capital, is a warren of streets creaking with old buildings, and framed by canals and colourful 18th-century houses. The local *smørrebrød* (huge open sandwiches laden with cheese and meat) will also make you smile.

THE
SALTIEST SITES
OF THE WORLD

THE PLAINS, CAVES, LAKES AND TUNNELS THAT ADD
FLAVOUR TO YOUR TRAVELS

01 SALT PLAINS OF SALAR DE UYUNI, BOLIVIA

Dreaming of a white Christmas? Pack your Santa hat and make the trek to the
world's most enduring salt plains, spanning nearly 12,000 sq km in the Potosí region
of Bolivia. At some places, the salt is over 10m thick; in the wet season the plains are
covered with a thin sheet of water. Take a shot of your shadow on the sparkling plains or
visit the salt-mining area, where tons of the stuff is piled into giant mounds. When it's
time for bed don't go past a salt hotel, where you'll be handed a candy bar on entrance to
your shimmering white bedroom.

02 SALT-CRYSTAL FORMATIONS OF DEVIL'S GOLF COURSE, USA

In the centre of the Southern Californian Desert, Nevada, sit elements of nearly every
major geological era. Death Valley National Park is one of the lowest points in the western
hemisphere, one of the hottest places in the world, and also plays host to an incredible
salt phenomenon. The bizarre, moonlike field of salt crystals at Devil's Golf Course, in the
centre of the park, will take you back to the world of dinosaurs and prehistoric wonders.
The crystals are fragile to touch and should be handled with care; it's not an actual golf
course – park rangers advise that you leave the golf balls at home.

03 WHITE-SALT MOUNTAINS OF TRAPANI, ITALY

Next time you try to reach for the moon, why not get a leg-up from one of the
glistening white-salt mountains and shallow *saline* (salty pools) in Trapani, western
Sicily? These saltpans were formed by the evaporation of sea water, and sit majestically
along the coast road between Trapani and Marsala. Here, life still centres around the
ocean, with industries such as tuna fishing, coral harvesting and salt production. Take in
the sight of the 100-year-old windmills which sit alongside the *saline*, slowly fanning the
winds of salt harvesting.

✪ NAMAKDAN CAVES, PERSIAN GULF, IRAN

In January 2006 a group of Czech geology students discovered an area touted to become the largest salt-cave system in the world. The students stumbled upon the hidden treasure in the Namakdan Mountain on Qeshm Island, and could hardly believe their eyes – underground salt lakes, glistening dripstones and sparkling domes of pure salt stood majestically before them. Unlike limestone, which takes thousands of years to grow, the jewels of the salt caves grow just days or weeks after rain, forming beautiful dripstone crystals. The student discoverers named the cave The Three Naked Men (coined while bathing in its salty glory?).

✪ THE SALT CATHEDRAL OF ZIPAQUIRA, COLOMBIA

If you need a reason to go to church, the small town of Zipaquira will give you one. Several kilometres from the town, in Cundinamraca, sits one of the world's only salt cathedrals, built in a tunnel of mines from some 200-million-year-old salt deposits. As you wind your way underground, take note of the 14 small chapels on the descent, each of which illustrate the events of Jesus' last journey. Each station has a cross and kneeling platforms, several of which are carved into the salt structure. You won't be alone; more than 3000 churchgoers worship in this shimmering cathedral every Sunday.

✪ THE GREAT SALINAS, ARGENTINA

The Great Salinas in Cordoba is a collection of large salt dunes in the central northwest of mainland Argentina. It is said that the origin of these mountains lies in a large gap in the Mar, a tectonic fault which exposed the saline seafloor from which the great dunes were formed. The area is also known to be in constant hurricane; in times of flooding, a surface of saline creates a pristine mirror to the sky. This is the place to show off your extra-dark glasses with UV filter – even if your only audience is the sky.

✪ THE SALT TUNNELS OF SOLOTYVNO, WESTERN UKRAINE

Solotyvno is not the most stunning destination, but it certainly attracts thousands of visitors each year. The Soviet-looking Ukrainian mining town runs one of the most successful tourist businesses of eastern Europe, all of which takes place underground. The town's salt mine, situated near the Romanian border, offers speleotherapy – an unusual form of treatment for people with respiratory conditions. The mines have a unique microclimate because of the salt particles in the air. For US$22, patients will spend several hours a day breathing in the salty atmosphere more than 300m underground. Who said that a marble castle, where everything glistens, sparkles and twinkles, couldn't be therapeutic as well?

✪ LAKE QINGHAI, CHINA

Ever wondered whether salt lakes exist inland? Set between the snowy mountains of Tibet and the grasslands of the Qinghai region lies China's largest interior salt lake, situated some 3200m above sea level and spanning nearly 4400 sq metres. Located on the Qinghai-Tibetan plateau, this area is often looked on simply as a passage to Tibet or northwest China – indeed, the lake attracts lots of migratory birds, which stop here on their way across Asia. The main attraction is Bird Island. Huge numbers of birds congregate in the breeding season, between March and early June.

✪ CARDONA SALT MOUNTAIN, SPAIN

In the hilltop town of Cardona, some 90km northwest of the city of Barcelona, sits a group of majestic mountain masses made entirely from salt. The mountains, partner to the town's historic castles, form a solid backdrop to this picturesque city; reddish-brown and clay in parts, and in others, translucent. When you've had your mountaintop moment, make a trip to the portico of St Vincenc in Cardona, where the fragments of painted vaults will give you a strong sense of the sacred.

✪ GREAT SALT LAKE, USA

Size does matter. The Great Salt Lake, located in northern Utah, lays claim to being the largest salt lake in the western hemisphere. The lake used to be part of prehistoric Lake Bonneville, and is also known as America's Dead Sea. It's home to millions of creatures able to survive the high saline levels, including birds, waterfowl and the largest staging population of Wilson's phalarope in the world. If you're looking to get lost for a while, why not take a salty cruise to one of the lake's 11 recognised tidal islands.

TOP 10 PLACES TO
EXPERIENCE THE BLUES

FROM SKY, SEA AND ARCTIC ICE TO COCKTAILS AND COOL TUNES – FEELING BLUE DOESN'T HAVE TO BE A DOWNER

JODHPUR'S 'BLUE CITY' AND FORT MAKE FOR STUNNING SCENERY

RIO'S CHRIST THE REDEEMER STATUE EMBRACES THE WIDE BLUE YONDER

01 ANTARCTICA

With an annual average temperature of -50°C on the polar plateau, no wonder Antarctica was dubbed 'The Freezer'. In these conditions the body allows the extremities to cool in order to preserve core temperature. The result? Frostbite! To avoid this painful and potentially disfiguring condition, stick to the more northerly Peninsula region, where the mercury can regularly tip the positive side of zero. Here, bird and sea life thrives, although you'll be exposed to some of the continent's strongest winds, enough to chill those digits all over again.

02 JODHPUR – INDIA

Located in northwest India and dating from the mid 15th-century, the ancient city of Jodhpur in Rajasthan is famous for the pastel-blue buildings of its old town. Originally designed for members of the priestly Brahmin caste, the distinctive blue whitewash was thought to deflect the burning sun. Nowadays, the crumbling buildings in the city's heart are amongst Jodhpur's oldest, shared equally by humans and monkeys alike. For the best view head to the fantastic Mehrangarh Fort, located on the outskirts of the city atop a 125m hill, from where a stunning blue patchwork quilt unfolds before your eyes.

03 CHRIST THE REDEEMER STATUE – BRAZIL

Spectrometer at the ready? Got your UV filters? And what about those people over there – do they look happy? In 2006 an online survey set out to find the ultimate blue-sky destination, taking scientific measurements and soaking up the ambience along the way. Data duly analysed, it was Rio de Janeiro's *Christo Redentor* that came out tops. Paul Landowski's 40m-high concrete and soapstone marvel sits atop the 700m Corcovado mountain, affording one of the world's defining city views and, for now, the best of blue.

✪ BLUE MOUNTAIN PEAK – JAMAICA

Think Jamaica and what comes to mind? Beach holidays, rum'n'Coke and the home of reggae, Rasta and reefer? Maybe, but just 40km east of Kingston is Blue Mountain–John Crow National Park, established in 1990 to protect the island's remaining forest and largest watershed area. At 2256m, Blue Mountain Peak is the king of the mountains; hike the summit trail predawn to see the glorious sunrise. Blue mists often shroud the mountains, giving them their unique colour, so if the peak's off the agenda head out and explore the myriad trails that link the region's villages.

✪ CHICAGO – USA

For many music fans around the globe, *this* is the true meaning of the blues. The legendary musical style of hard living and even harder partying is synonymous with the 1950s American Midwest and no man typifies the genre better than Muddy Waters, the 'Father of Chicago Blues' who shot to fame alongside contemporaries such as Earl Hooker and Howlin' Wolf. Today's scene continues to revolve around the clubs of Maxwell St and is celebrated with the annual Chicago Blues Festival in early June, where what you feel is as important as what you play – to quote Waters himself, 'I been in the blues all my life. I'm still delivering 'cause I got a long memory.'

✪ LA BASILIQUE DU SACRÉ COEUR DU MONTMARTRE – FRANCE

To the north of the River Seine and the heart of Paris sits Montmartre, a romantic neighbourhood of cobbled streets, sleepy cafés and ivy-covered balconies. Overlooking it all is the magnificent 19th-century travertine stone Basilique du Sacré Coeur (Basilica of the Sacred Heart). On long summer evenings, lovers litter the steps leading to the city's highest landmark. Buskers sing of revolution, street artists perform and red wine flows. Below them all unfolds the

EVEN ANTARCTIC ADELIE PENGUINS GET THE BLUES

most spine-tingling of Parisian vistas. If you're heartbroken, lonely or just down in the dumps, what better place could there be to *really* feel blue?

✪ BLUE LAGOON – VANUATU

On the northeast coastline of Espiritu Santo, Vanuatu's largest island, lie the unspoilt beaches of Champagne Bay, lapped by crystal waters and a popular stop-off for Pacific cruise ships. The bay was used as the location for the 1980 film *The Blue Lagoon*, Randal Kleiser's controversial desert-island romance starring Brooke Shields and Christopher Atkins. Tours to the nearby freshwater lagoon of the same name command a hefty fee, so just stroll barefoot on the sand and kick your way through the surf – escapism like this doesn't cost a bean.

✪ YVES KLEIN'S IKB 79 AT TATE LIVERPOOL – ENGLAND

International Klein Blue (IKB) is one of the modern art world's most baffling creations, yet also one of the most lauded. Yves Klein, a French artist of the early postmodernist movement, spent years searching for a 'unique' hue of deepest blue to express his artistic feelings. In 1958 he finally found it, and proceeded to slap it all over anything he could find – from simple canvases to writhing naked models. 1959's *IKB 79* is his definitive work, a monochromatic rectangle of purest blue. Art critics swooned, whilst countless others scratched their heads and said 'I could do that'.

✪ BLUE RIVER – CANADA

In a land of gargantuan scale, Blue River is but a tiny speck. With a population of fewer than 300, this outpost between better-known Kamloops and Jasper offers spectacular mountaineering, glacier adventures and wildlife encounters. Sure, you could head to one of the bigger resorts, but what's the point? This is British Columbia, where less is more and isolation part of the humbling experience. For solitude on an unparalleled scale, head off by kayak to explore Murtle Lake and Wells Gray Country, where moose, bear and eagle abound.

✪ BLUE CURAÇAO – NETHERLANDS ANTILLES

Golden beaches and azure seas mark Curaçao as the definitive Caribbean retreat, famous for the liqueur of the same name. Made from the dried peel of the bitter Laraha orange, the vivid blue colour remains a mystery but suits the island's style perfectly – the red, green or orange versions just aren't the same. For the ultimate cocktail kick grab a bottle, mix with gin, top up with grape juice and *voila!* Curaçao Sunset. Head to Jeremi Beach to watch the sun go down over the rocky cove; sip, and you're in paradise.

MOST INTERESTING
TRADITIONAL
FOODS

NEVER MIND SLOW FOOD. HERE ARE THE COMMUNITIES CULTIVATING AND PRESERVING MARVELLOUS OLD FOOD

✪ IJKA CORN, COLOMBIA

We all eat corn in some form, but few of us *live* corn like the Arhuaca people of northern Columbia. Calling themselves Ijka which means 'men of corn', the Arhuaca eat corn in all their meals and also use corn's four colours (yellow, coffee, black, and white) to outline their view of the universe, and as the basis of their social structure. This holy food is used in rituals and as a therapeutic tool. Unfortunately, Western culture means that few people maintain these ancient customs.

✪ GUARANA, BRAZIL

Guarana shows up in wonderfully buzzy fruit drinks at health food stores, but few people know of its indigenous origins in the Brazilian rainforest. For the 8000 members of Brazil's Sateré-Maûé tribe, guarana is called 'the fount of all wisdom', and they still use an ancient technique of mashing the plant's potent seeds into a hard bar that is then grated over food and drink. Guarana is rich in caffeine and vitamins and helps combat fatigue and stimulate cerebral activity. Continued production relies on preserving native customs and intact rainforest.

✪ MUSTARD OIL PICKLES, INDIA

Indians preserved many of their fruits and vegetables by storing them in a mixture of mustard oil and ground spices to create flavourful batches of artisanal pickles. With this technique they were able to eat lemons, mangoes, bananas, onions and other foods throughout the year. It is easy to see why Indians honoured the mustard plant with an important ritual each spring. Every region and community developed its own unique pickle-making recipes but these are being lost as cheap industrial pickles flood the marketplace. Villages in the central eastern state of Orissa are working with the Navdanya Foundation to bring back these traditions.

✪ TXAKOLI WHITE WINE, SPAIN

First described in a document from AD 864, Txakoli white wine is traditionally seasoned in very large, very old oak barrels then drunk while it is still quite young and has a slightly sparkling feel in the mouth. Despite its ancestral roots in Basque culture, fewer than two hectares of grapes remained in production by 1988. It's a testament to the endurance of old traditions that this fresh, fruity white wine is now recognised by wine connoisseurs the

world over and has been brought back from the brink of extinction.

✪ PRE-COLUMBIAN SALT PRODUCTION, MEXICO

Salt has been collected, traded and treasured in countless ways since the dawn of civilisation, yet today most of us simply dump it from a salt shaker without second thought. In the Mexican state of Colima, they have been proudly gathering salt in a traditional way for at least 500 years. One highest-quality type is called *flor de sal* – derived from the thin layer of salt that crystallises on the surface of saltwater basins. It must be collected by hand – a process so time-consuming that production is limited to 90 tonnes a year.

✪ CHUNO BLANCO, PERU

Ever wonder who invented freeze-drying? Extreme temperature variations in the Andes present the perfect environment for this ancient method of preserving otherwise bitter and inedible potatoes. Three freezing nights, three sunbaked days, a bit of barefoot stomping in between and a two-day bath in a frigid river is a ritual still carried out by the Quechua and Aymara peoples on the border of Bolivia and Peru. Lightweight and ideal for travel but looking more like pumice stones, naturally freeze-dried potatoes are a treat to keep an eye out for in the local markets.

✪ MANOOMIN, MINNESOTA

The only grain indigenous to North America, manoomin (wild rice) has long been harvested by the Anishinaabeg tribe of the Great Lakes' White Earth Reservation. Not to be confused with commercially cultivated wild rice, manoomin grows along the shores of the Great Lakes and is hand harvested and hulled. Nearly extinct 100 years ago, this aquatic grass has made a remarkable comeback and recently received the Slow Food Award for the Defence of Biodiversity. The White Earth Land Restoration Project is helping this gracious grain fight its next battles; destruction of natural habitat and genetically engineered cultivars that threaten the heart of the wild rice genome.

THERE'S NO SHORTAGE OF DATES FOR MEN IN SIWA OASIS

01 SIWA OASIS DATES, EGYPT

In 332 BC, Alexander the Great followed birds across the scalding sands of north-western Egypt to find the legendary Siwa Oasis, one of the most remote settlements in Egypt. His goal was a private consultation with the oracle of the Sun God, Amon-Ra, who would anoint him the next Egyptian pharaoh, but there can be no doubt that he sampled the dates and olives of Siwa – among the finest in the world. Today each crop is still cultivated in small private gardens that have been lovingly tended and hand-pollinated in the traditional way for countless generations.

A PERSIMMON TREE, HEAVY WITH FRUIT, BESIDE MT FUJI

02 HACHIYAGAKI PERSIMMONS, JAPAN

These priceless honey-sweet persimmons were once given as gifts to Japanese royalty. But with the tilling under of fields for silk production, the fruit trees disappeared until the 1940s when a 20-year-old farmer launched an extensive search and finally located a single remaining 'mother tree' in the garden of an old family house. Fortunately a few elderly patriarchs in the village remembered the traditional ways of preparing these persimmons so these techniques were preserved as well. There are now 87 producers in the Gifu prefecture growing these delicate persimmons, but the techniques are so time-consuming that few young people are learning the necessary skills.

SACHSEN-ANHALT'S CHEESE IS A MITE TOO UNUSUAL FOR SOME

03 MITE CHEESE, SACHSEN-ANHALT, GERMANY

Mite cheese (Milbenkäse) is like something out of the Dark Ages. Prepared with an ancient technique from the Middle Ages that has only recently been revived, mite cheese may be one of the most unusual foods you'll ever eat. In Sachsen-Anhalt, raw low-fat cheese (quark) is placed in wooden boxes full of mites that crawl all over the cheese and poop on it. After three months the mite's excrement turns the cheese reddish-brown, and at one year it turns the cheese black, at which point it is consumed – mites and all!

BEST
UNDERGROUND EXPERIENCES

HOW TO REALLY GET UNDER THE SKIN OF A PLACE

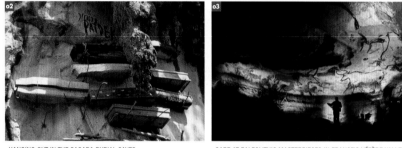

HANGING OUT IN THE SAGADA BURIAL CAVES · GAPE AT PALEOLITHIC MASTERPIECES IN FRANCE'S VÉZÈRE VALLEY

01 CAPPADOCIAN UNDERGROUND CITIES, TURKEY

You can taste the true troglodyte lifestyle in the mysterious underground cities of Cappadocia. The best known are Kaymaklı, Derinkuyu and Özlüce, though there are many more still unexcavated. Dated to 7th century BC or earlier, the cities were forts where the people could escape invaders and live for up to six months at a time. You'll find yourself in a vast, complex labyrinth of rooms and tunnels over several levels. Signs of life are everywhere: storage jars, communal kitchens blackened by smoke, stables – and holes in the ceilings through which hot oil could be poured on the enemy.

02 SAGADA BURIAL CAVES, PHILIPPINES

Sumaging Cave is an exhilarating adventure guaranteed to bring out the Indiana Jones in you. The route takes you crawling through narrow crevices, wading through water and scaling the sides of deep ravines, and in some sections the smooth limestone is so slippery you have to go barefoot. Guides light the way (and the stunning calcium formations) with gas lanterns. The connected Lumiang Burial Cave is fascinating for its eerie collection of centuries-old wooden coffins. Other, slowly decomposing, coffins can be seen hanging from the cliff-face.

03 GROTTE DE FONT DE GAUME, FRANCE

France's Vézère Valley is crammed with prehistoric rock art, but this cave is arguably the best of them, containing one of the most astounding collections of paintings still open to the public. You can get close to about two dozen of its 230 figures of mammoths, bison, horses, fish, reindeer and bears, and wonder at the meaning they held for their cave-dwelling Cro-Magnon creators 14,000 years ago. Many of the animals, carved into the rock or delicately shaded with red and black pigments, are caught in remarkably lifelike movement.

✪ BLACKWATER RAFTING IN WAITOMO, NEW ZEALAND

Imagine jumping backwards off a waterfall into darkness, feeling the shock as you hit the cold water, and then shooting through tunnels and caverns, bumping gently against rock walls until suddenly the velvety blackness above you is filled with sparkling pinpoints of blueish light – the glow-worms of Waitomo caves. Riding the underground river in a wetsuit and inner-tube raft is the magical (but oh so cold) experience of blackwater rafting. For the really adventurous, there are underground climbing and abseiling too.

✪ PATHET LAO CAVES, LAOS

Caves make brilliant wartime hideouts. In 1964 the Pathet Lao, a leading communist organisation in Laos, moved its headquarters to a series of caves near Vieng Xai. Situated inside an impressively narrow and precipitous valley, it was virtually unassailable. Six of these caves can be visited: inside are former meeting rooms, government offices, markets, temples, printing presses, hospitals, army barracks and more. Wooden walls, as well as natural formations, divide the caverns into various rooms, still decorated with images of Lenin and Che Guevara, and incongruous house facades and gardens are built onto the front of the caves.

✪ CROWN MINES SHAFT 14, SOUTH AFRICA

South Africa proudly lays claim to the world's deepest pub, 226m down a Johannesburg gold mine known as Shaft 14. This is also one of the deepest mine tours you can take, and despite being located in a kitsch theme park, it gives an authentic glimpse of gruelling mining life. When the mine opened in 1897, there was only candlelight to work by, up to 40°C heat, ear-shattering drills and dangerous gases – along with miserable wages. Migrant miners of many languages learned to send messages by slapping their boots in rhythms, the origin of the *isicathulo* or gumboot dance.

VOLCANIC 'FAIRY CHIMNEYS' IN CAPPADOCIA, TURKEY

✪ CANOEING BARTON CREEK CAVE, BELIZE

Some say the intricate cave systems of Belize offer the best spelunking in the world. For the ancient Maya, the caves were the entrance to the underworld, where the gods lived and accepted sacrifices. One of the most exciting caves to explore is Barton Creek Cave, which you traverse by canoe. You'll paddle and swim past fragments of pots and human skulls, evidence of at least 28 people who lie interred here. As your headlamp lights up spooky limestone formations and bats flit around your head you'll see why the ancients called this Xibalbá, the Place of Fear.

✪ COOBER PEDY, AUSTRALIA

Coober Pedy's *raison d'être* is opal mining. The town's Aboriginal name, meaning 'white man's hole in the ground', describes it pretty well. As well as the mines, many of the houses, hotels, the church, shops and museums are underground 'dugouts', sheltering from outback Australia's extreme climate: daytime summer temperatures can soar to over 50°C and the winter nights are freezing. With the dry, dusty lunar landscape, you'd never describe the town as attractive, but it's worth sticking around a while to hear the outrageous yarns of mining fortunes made and lost, intrigues, vendettas and crazy old-timers.

✪ THE PARIS CATACOMBS, FRANCE

In order to solve the problem of Paris's overflowing cemeteries, in 1785 the bones of the buried were exhumed and relocated to the tunnels of disused quarries, 20m beneath the city streets. This continued for around a hundred years, and 300km of tunnels are lined with almost artistically arranged stacks of skulls, tibias and femurs. In the 2km open to the public, it's estimated that six million individu-als are represented. During WWII the tunnels were used as a headquarters by the Resistance. Today they make a macabre attraction; urban spelunkers are often caught illegally roaming the unstable closed-off section.

✪ SIDI DRISS HOTEL, TUNISIA

If you've ever wished to set foot on the planet of Tatooine, the village of Matmata in the Tunisian Sahara might be as close as you can get. The Berber underground dwellings here are built around a deep sunken courtyard with cave-like rooms coming off the sides, which means they remain at a comfortable temperature year round. But Hotel Sidi Driss has an added attraction for movie buffs: the hotel was used as the set for Uncle Owen and Aunt Beru's house in the *Star Wars* movies, making it a rather surreal place to stay.

FLASHIEST
LIGHTHOUSES
THESE TOP LIGHT SPOTS ARE SURE TO DAZZLE

01 CAPE HATTERAS, USA

You'll know it by the barbershop spirals coiling around the tower. And possibly the height – Hatteras is the tallest lighthouse in the USA at 63m. An earlier incarnation was completed in 1803 but was damaged during the Civil War. The current building was first lit in 1871. Due to erosion of the shore, the Cape Hatteras lighthouse was moved, in 2000, from its original location at the edge of the ocean to safer ground approximately 800m inland. There's a visitor centre and museum at the site. It remains an active lighthouse, guiding vessels past the treacherous Diamond Shoals off the North Carolina coast, the cause of some 2000 wrecks over 400 years.

02 HOOK HEAD, IRELAND

The great granddaddy of lighthouses, Hook Head is arguably the oldest working light in the world. The site had humble beginnings, reportedly as far back as the 5th century, with monks lighting a beacon there. The structure as it stands today has existed for 800 years. It's an automated light, squat and a little…plump (they say horizontal stripes emphasise a thick waist, so it might just be an illusion). Access to the light is by tour, organised through the visitor centre. A historical teaser – have you ever wondered where the phrase 'by hook or by crook' comes from?

03 CRÉAC'H, FRANCE

The black-banded Créac'h, standing tall (seriously tall, at 54.85m) on Isle d'Ouessant (Ushant), is one of the most powerful lighthouses in the world. The French Atlantic coast is famous for its churning, storm-swept oceans, made treacherous by the numerous granite outcrops that lie off the Brittany shore. The Créac'h cuts across the waters with a beam reaching 60km. A lighthouse museum provides an insight into the workings of the light. As a bonus, a visit to the Créac'h is an opportunity to visit the nearby Stiff Lighthouse, one of the older lighthouses still in use, built in the late 17th century.

GREEN CAPE, AUSTRALIA

Where else would you expect to find a lighthouse, but at the tip of a bay bearing the name Disaster. Green Cape Lighthouse, in New South Wales, has seen a few wrecks in its time, most significantly the SS *Ly-ee Moon* which ran aground in 1886, just three years after the lighthouse was lit; 71 sailors died and 15 were rescued by the keeper. Disaster Bay is at the border of two national parks (Croajin-galong and Ben Boyd), and the light-house is perched above the epitome of an Australian bush beach: chalky, fine sand, rugged cliffs festooned with tea trees, wild blue waters and the lingering scent of eucalyptus.

EDDYSTONE, ENGLAND

The lighthouse on the Eddystone rocks is the fourth such structure to bear the Eddystone name. The Great Storm of 1703 (a hurricane that blew for a week) destroyed the first incarna-tion, lit in 1698. The second structure was a wooden wonder, lit in 1709 but destroyed by fire in 1755. The third at-tempt was made from stone and lit in 1759, but the rock it was built on was unstable, so the structure was dis-mantled 120 years later – today, you can visit the reassembled lighthouse at Plymouth. In 1882 the current struc-ture was lit, a sleek, modern-looking tower built near the stumpy remains of Eddystone III.

SLANGKOP, SOUTH AFRICA

Looking out from the infamous Cape of Good Hope, Slangkop was built in 1914 but first lit after WWI, in 1919. A few years prior to its construction, the SS *Maori* was wrecked, highlighting the need for a beacon. The brilliant white of the structure has you ponder-ing the repainting cycle, which must be constant – you can ask the keeper on a guided tour. This cast-iron light-house overlooks Kommetjie, a village about 30km from Cape Town, where you can combine your lightspotting with some crayfishing – crayfish is a local speciality.

PONDICHERRY, INDIA

In a country most would associate with English colonialism, Pondicherry is a strongly French-influenced town in the south of India. It grew from sleepy village to significant trade centre for the French East India company, which eventually replaced a log fire on a hill with a lighthouse to give ships fair warning. The lighthouse shot out its first beam in 1836 and re-mained in use for 150 years. It stands now as a monument, but is being restored as a museum to the French architecture of the town.

CAPE PALLISER, NEW ZEALAND

The 1897 Cape Palliser Lighthouse, resplendent in its wide red bands, is a cynosure to ships navigating the Cook Strait, off the southern tip of New Zealand's North Island. Inland it looks over fine wine-and-food coun-try, so it's a gourmet lightspotter's paradise and, as you'd expect in New Zealand, the adventure activities in the region are many. The light is still in service – though you can still climb up the 250 steps to get a light's eye view of ocean and land.

MARJANIEMI, FINLAND

To get a good feel for the romance of lighthouse-keeping – the storms, the constant wind, the tumult of crashing ocean – spend a night in one. The pilot station at this 1871 lighthouse is now a hotel. Getting to Hailuoto Island by ferry adds to the nautical adventure. Hurry, though; continental rebound (the earth rising back up after being compressed from the glacier-weights of an ice age) will eventually see the island join the mainland. If you can't get out there soon, a webcam is in operation, and a quick search on the internet (www.luotokeskus.fi/webcam) will give you some immediate vicari-ous adventure.

GIBBS HILL, BERMUDA

The Gibbs Hill Lighthouse stands high on a hill in Southampton, and climbing to the platform gives you a view of the entire island, with Caribbean splen-dour all around. Early in the year you might catch a glimpse of migrating whales. At such a height, the beacon can be seen up to 60km away. Back on ground it's more standard tourist fare, with a café and gift shop; the owner's grandfather was the last keeper before the lighthouse was automated, so the romance is not all gone.

BEST
ARCHITECTURE & PLACE COMBINATIONS

OUR PICK OF PLACES THAT HAVE BUILT A NAME FOR THEMSELVES

ISTANBUL'S SERENE AND SOARING BLUE MOSQUE   'I SPY' IN THE SKY, NEW YORK

01 ANTONI GAUDÍ & BARCELONA, SPAIN

High on a hill in Barcelona's Gràcia district sits Park Güell, a fairytale dream made real. Hansel and Gretel–style gingerbread houses sit amidst the trees, beyond the grand entrance that features a multicoloured lizard-shaped mosaic fountain. The architect was Antoni Gaudí, a Catalan modernist with a truly individual style. Away from the park, Gaudí's most famous works are Casa Milà (La Pedrera) in Eixample and his defining masterpiece, the unfinished Sagrada Família, still under construction a mind-boggling 126 years after construction began.

02 MOSQUES & ISTANBUL, TURKEY

Straddling the Bosphorus with one foot each in Europe and Asia, cosmopolitan Istanbul dances to the tune of the muezzin's call to prayer. One-time capital of the Byzantine Empire, the city dubbed the City of Mosques is peppered with distinctive Ottoman domes and needle-sharp minarets – there are some 3000 for a population of 12 million. Greatest of all are the early-17th-century Sultan Ahmet Camii (the Blue Mosque) and the Aya Sopya, the latter originally a church built in the name of Emperor Justinian.

03 SKYSCRAPERS & NEW YORK, USA

The Big Apple is large in every sense of the word. America's most populous city has a gregarious attitude all of its own, with a population of 20 million squeezed into some of the world's tallest buildings. Synonymous with the skyscraper, the cloud piercing structures that typified the economic boom of the American Dream, New York's energetic streets buzz below these commercial monsters. In the 1920s and '30s architects battled to build the city's biggest, resulting in landmarks such as the Chrysler and Empire State Buildings. Today, these are just two amongst a staggering 5000.

✪ BUDDHIST TEMPLES & NARA, JAPAN

The teachings of Buddha reveal a step-by-step path to lasting happiness, and there's no better place to find inner peace than ancient Nara, a 45-minute ride on the bullet train from Kyoto. Japan's capital in the 8th century, the city was politically and religiously important; a power that remained long after Nara lost its administrative control. The Historic Monuments of Ancient Nara comprise eight primordial temples and shrines, of which Todai-ji (the Great Eastern Temple) is reputed to be the world's largest wooden building, complete with its own immense bronze Buddha.

✪ INDUSTRIAL HERITAGE & LIVERPOOL, ENGLAND

Northern England's industrial revolution and burgeoning trans-Atlantic trade routes brought immense wealth to mid-19th-century Liverpool. Huge bonded warehouses were filled with cargo from around the world and immigrants bound for North America packed Cunard's liners. The docks were also the departure point for the UK's Africa-bound slave boats. In 2004 Liverpool's dock front was declared a Unesco World Heritage Site, protected for future generations and renovated for the 21st-century with a creative selection of restaurants, bars, museums and hotels.

✪ PYRAMIDS & GIZA, EGYPT

To call the pyramids of Giza 'iconic' doesn't do them justice – nowhere else in the world is architecture so instantly identifiable with a country's history and culture. Constructed around 2500 BC for King Khufu, the 146m Great Pyramid is the centrepiece of the complex, dominating the neighbouring pyramids of Khafre and Menkaure. Reaching Giza is simple. Just 20km southwest of Cairo, the town has been gobbled up by Egypt's sprawling capital and today urban development spreads all the way to the boundary of the site. If the modern world detracts from your experience, just keep your back to it.

BARCELONA'S SUMPTUOUS SAGRADA FAMÍLIA

✪ MODERNISM & HELSINKI, FINLAND

Alvar Aalto is Finland's figurehead of design and architecture. Household items such as vases and tables flowed from the Aalto production line, but it's in classic modernist buildings – melding form and function – where he made his name. On the banks of Töölönlahti, a picturesque sea inlet north of Helsinki's centre, sits the flamboyant Finlandia Hall. Considered one of Aalto's finest works, the angular concert hall is clad entirely in Carrara marble. Walking back to town, detour past the Kulttuuritalo (House of Culture), before taking dinner at the Savoy in Esplanade Park, the restaurant Aalto designed with his wife, Aino.

✪ MUD ARCHITECTURE & DJENNÉ, MALI

In the modern world of instant gratification, building with earth sounds primitive in the extreme. And it is.

Over 4000 years of history can be traced through the world's mud architecture, with examples in countries ranging from Peru to India. But nowhere is the skill better demonstrated than in Mali, and the Great Mosque of Djenné is top of the tree. Mud bricks, baked in the sun, form walls in excess of 30m, sculpted smooth as icing sugar with a coating of earthen plaster. Djenné's Old Town is a Unesco site, which together with the mosque forms one of Western Africa's most important cultural sites.

✪ THE BIRTH OF WESTERN CIVILISATION & ATHENS, GREECE

Bustling crowds, stifling heat and choking pollution. If you can see past Athens' negative press then the history makes this one of Europe's essential cities. Dating back over 3000 years, Athens gave birth to many of the ancient world's pre-eminent philosophers, and it encourages

considered contemplation to this day. From the Parthenon to the Temple of Olympian Zeus and the Temple of Hephaestus, Athens is a city break to bring out your inner classical being. Choose the central Plaka district to experience ancient Greece for yourself.

✪ THE INCAS & CUZCO, PERU

Legendary amongst backpackers seeking spirituality along the Inca Trail, Cuzco is much more than a glorified gateway to the mountains. Capital of the Inca empire, elements of the classic past can be seen in modern-day architecture, mixed with the later influence of Spanish settlers. If you're heading to Machu Picchu, take in some pre-trek research and whet your appetite with a visit to Cuzco's own Inca ruins at Sacsayhuamán, Qenko, Puca Pucara and Tambo Machay, all within easy reach of the city.

BEST
CYCLING
ADVENTURES

CRUISE THROUGH FRENCH VINEYARDS OR POWER UP
MOUNTAINS AND ACROSS COUNTRIES. WE SHOW
PEDAL-PUSHERS WHERE TO SET THEIR OWN PACE

A LONE CYCLIST PLIES EUROPE'S STUNNING MOUNTAIN ROADS   BIKE LIKE A LOCAL ON THE TOUR D'AFRIQUE

01 COAST-TO-COAST, USA

The TransAmerica trail is a cycle-touring classic. Try all or parts of the 6835km
from Astoria, Oregon, on the Pacific Ocean, to Yorktown, Virginia, on the Atlantic.
Like the great American dream, it spans the continent – its mountains (including
the 3518m Hoosier Pass in the Rockies), its prairies, its greatest river (the Mississippi) and the forests of its national parks (Yellowstone, Grand Teton). Better yet
are the farms, people and home cooking of rural America. Ground winds will catch
you eastbound and westward; the pedalling is best between May and September.

02 EUROPEAN VINEYARDS

There's magic in those hills. Squeeze it from the grapes growing in precisely planted rows and the result is the world's greatest wines. Ride it on two
wheels and the days pass in sweet wonder. Most of Europe's peerless vineyards
are accessible via public roads, often part of designated wine routes. In France,
plunge into the fields of Champagne, Burgundy and Bordeaux. In Italy, Tuscany's
hills help burn off culinary dalliances. You won't lose your way in Germany's
steep-sided Mosel River valley. Summer's best, but harvests are in autumn.

03 TOUR D'AFRIQUE

Think you've cycled it all? Looking for a challenge? How about a mountain-
bike tour of Africa? Start in northern Egypt with your handlebars pointed south;
the Cape of Good Hope is only 12,000km and 10 countries away. Not up to organis-
ing the odyssey? Join the Tour d'Afrique, the world's longest (120 days) and most
gruelling bicycle event. It next sets out in January 2009 and it's a fully supported
charity ride. Go self-propelled from Cairo to Cape Town through villages, deserts,
mountains, fertile valleys and wildlife-rich savanna. Beware of elephants!

✪ EUROPEAN ALPS

Europe's spine of snow-capped Alpine
peaks draws the national borders of
Italy, France, Switzerland, Austria and
Slovenia. Human engineering has defi-
antly incised zigzag surfaced roads –
some of Europe's highest – up and
over dividing mountain passes, dozens
thrusting up above 2000m. Here,
dedicated cyclists test their mettle,
and champions in Europe's greatest
two-wheel road races are acclaimed
and shamed. The mountain passes'
names alone are inspirational: Croix de
Fer, Galibier, Izoard, Iseron, Simplon,
Grand-Saint-Bernard, Furka, Umbrail,
Stelvio, Gavia, Grossglockner, Ötztaler.
They'll take your breath away. Literally.

✪ AMERICA'S GREAT DIVIDE MOUNTAIN BIKE ROUTE

This behemoth of a pedal, with more
than 60,000m of elevation gain, isn't
for the faint-hearted. It's a ride of
staggering remoteness and beauty,
covering areas replete with wildlife
and arresting vistas. Declared the
longest off-pavement route on the
planet, the full Great Divide Mountain Bike Route criss-crosses (up and
down every day!) the continental
divide for 4363km from Banff, Alberta,
in the Canadian Rockies to Antelope
Wells, New Mexico, on the Mexican-
American border. Limited services
mean planning, endurance, mechani-
cal proficiency and some backcountry
skills are indispensable. Travel in summer, but prepare for harsh weather.

✪ PAN-AMERICAN HIGHWAY, CENTRAL & SOUTH AMERICA

It's epic – about 14,000km through
12 countries. Although it begins in
Alaska, the Pan-American Highway
from Mexico City claws through every
kind of geography and climate im-
aginable – from lush jungles to frigid
Andean mountain passes – on its way
to Ushuaia at the Tierra del Fuegan tip
of South America. But for the impass-
able Darien Gap between Panama and
Colombia, the highway makes it possible to keep two wheels to the ground
on an extraordinary intercontinental

ONE FOR THE CYCLE-PATHIC: THE GRAND TRANSAMERICA TRAIL

trek. Expect fierce Patagonian winds, drenching rains and tar-bubbling heat, as well as the open-armed welcome of people along the way.

✪ NORTHWEST VIETNAM

Bamboo groves, mist-shrouded karst outcroppings, colourfully dressed Montagnard peoples (hill tribes), water buffalo on the roads – you must be in the northwest highlands of Vietnam. From Hanoi, Route 6 slides 490km through gorges, over mountains and past fruit and tea plantations to historical Dien Bien Phu. Then tough, unpaved roads launch another 316km, up and over Tram Tom Pass (1900m) on Vietnam's highest and most breath-taking road, before the descent, via the hill station at Sapa, to Lao Cai. It's challenging; best tackled October to mid-December or March to May.

✪ TASMANIA, AUSTRALIA

Tasmania squeezes a diversity of ter-rain into a compact area. This is ideal for cycle tourists in search of pristine beaches, Alpine high country, lush rain-forests, wild rivers, wildlife and historic villages, all without having to pedal too far. The 1000km Giro Tasmania covers the state's highlights, man-made as well as natural, on well-graded sealed roads. Experienced backcountry moun-tain bikers will love the Tasmania Trail, a 477km traverse from Devonport to Dover via fire trails and forestry roads. Remember, in the southern hemisphere ideal riding is from January to April.

✪ DANUBE BIKE TRAIL, EUROPE

Europe's second-longest river, the Danube, begins in Donaueschingen in Germany's Black Forest and flows 2850km to the Black Sea. Tracing its banks much of the way is the continent's best-beloved bike path: the Donauradweg. Its first 550km to Passau take in Bavaria, but the 320km to Vienna and 330km more to Budapest are the most famous, treating pedallers to unforgettable

nature, baroque monasteries, hilltop castles, Wachau wines and preserved medieval towns of half-timbered houses and cobblestone streets. The Austrian section is particularly notable for being car-free, flat and well signed. Go from April through September, although summer sees crowds.

✪ MAUI, HAWAII

The tropical Hawaiian island of Maui boasts a triple crown of biking – a metric century, full century and hill climb – that some say is the best in world. The 100km West Maui Loop fol-lows a coastal road skirting a phenom-enal forest reserve. The full century East Maui Loop is an even more chal-lenging littoral route of rolling hills around the base of Mt Haleakala, the island's extinct volcano. Cycle to the Sun is the annual mid-August 56.5km race (although you can do the ride anytime) from near sea level to the 3048m summit of Haleakala. The best of paradise from all angles!

BEST PLACES TO
TAKE A BATH

BUBBLE BATHS TAKE ON A WHOLE NEW MEANING WHEN YOU'RE ACTUALLY SOAKING IN BUBBLY

CHECK THE TEMPERATURE, MATE, AT BUDAPEST'S SZÉCHENYI BATHS

BATHING'S A SERIOUS BUSINESS AT ICELAND'S BLUE LAGOON

01 BEPPU, JAPAN

This town on the coast of Kyushu is associated in Japanese minds with one thing: hot springs. Millions of litres of steaming hot water spill daily out of around 3000 springs, providing a dazzling array of bath-time treats. On offer for your bathing pleasure are mammoth modern indoor spa complexes, small outdoor springs, simmering mud baths and even 'sand baths' where you can be buried up to your neck in hot sand by a lady with a shovel. When you're done getting wet, it's time to discover why Beppu is nicknamed the 'Las Vegas of Japan'.

02 SZÉCHENYI BATHS, HUNGARY

Budapest is a city famed for its thermal baths, and was dedicated a spa city as far back as the 1930s. Sample the city's bathing habits at the Széchenyi Baths – a meandering neo-baroque complex of pools, ranging from icy cold to steaming hot – smack bang in the middle of the city park. Originally a medical treatment centre, this is the place to come for a massage, a sauna and a dip in the huge open-air thermal pool filled with local families, tourists and gentlemen playing chess on floating boards.

03 BLUE LAGOON, ICELAND

Iceland's answer to Disneyland and the country's number one tourist attraction, the Blue Lagoon is sometimes dismissed as overcrowded and over-priced. But what's not to like about floating in a steaming pool of milky blue (at a spot-on 38°C), surrounded by a landscape of dark and twisted lava fields, with a futuristic geothermal plant puffing away in the background? When you're fed up of the main pools, you can have a steam bath in a lava cave, a waterfall massage or a sauna. You'll no doubt leave with your spirits renewed and baby-soft skin.

✪ HOT WATER BEACH, NEW ZEALAND

Thermal waters brew just below the sand at Hot Water Beach in the North Island. During the peak tourist season it looks like it's just been set upon by giant rabbits – for two hours, at either side of low tide, you can dig your own hole in the sand with a spade rented from the local café, then sit back, relax and warm your behind in your own natural spa. Luckily your rapidly roasting limbs will be regularly refreshed by cool waves from the incoming sea water.

✪ VINOTHERAPY, FRANCE

Being rubbed with grape seeds, slathered in honey, oil and wine yeast and submerged up to the neck in a wine-casket bath might sound like a hedonistic Roman orgy but it is, in fact, vinotherapy – a spa treatment to be had at Les Sources de Caudalie in Bordeaux using grape extracts. It seems that bathing in the stuff rather than drinking it is one of the best beauty treatments around, with the power (apparently) to reduce wrinkles, stress and even cellulite. Les Sources is set in a vineyard, so you can also ingest your grapes the traditional way with a glass or two of the local tipple.

✪ CHAMPAGNE-GLASS WHIRLPOOL BATH, USA

If you've ever dreamt of soaking your troubles away in a mammoth glass of champagne this could be your lucky day. That's right, at Pocono Palace only a couple of hours' drive away from New York City, you too could be relaxing in a 2.13m tall champagne glass whirlpool bath for two. If that's not cheesy enough for you, look around your suite and savour the faux Roman columns, the circular beds, the mirrored walls and the private heart-shaped swimming pool.

✪ LES BAINS DE MARRAKESH, MOROCCO

For a bathing experience that indulges all your *Thousand and One Nights* fantasies – think glorious sunlit court-

...AND DON'T FORGET TO WASH BETWEEN YOUR TOES: A FATHER AND CHILD BATHE IN BEPPU, JAPAN

yards, tinkling fountains, carved al-coves and scattered rose petals – Les Bains de Marrakech is just the ticket. As well as the traditional *hammam* (bathhouse) experience, involving an unceremonious scrub down with black soap and a wire mitten, you can chose from gentler options such as chocolate body massages or candlelit oriental baths for two. In between treatments you're encouraged to sprawl out on an indecently comfort-able pile of cushions and drink your own body weight in mint tea.

✪ DOGO ONSEN, JAPAN

Japan's oldest hot springs facility at a rumoured 3000 years old, Dogo Onsen is at the centre of many an old folk tale. Its centrepiece, the Honkan bathhouse, is the oldest public bath house in Japan. An intricate three-storey timber structure, it looks like a fairy-tale castle and is said to be the inspiration behind the enchanted bathhouse in Miyazaki's animated film

Spirited Away. Splash out on a first-class ticket and you'll get a hot soak, your own relaxation room, a *yukata* (kimono) and a post-bath snack of green tea and crackers.

✪ CHODOVAR BREWERY BEER BATHS, CZECH REPUBLIC

For the ultimate beer on skin expe-rience, you can relax in the Czech Republic's first underground beer spa. Large stainless steel Victorian-style tubs (including double tubs for two!) are filled with a specially brewed bathing beer and crushed herbs and topped off with a creamy foam 'head'. As you bubble away in all that malty goodness you can partake in a glass of two of the local brew from the bath-side bar. Apparently it's all excellent for the pores.

✪ THE DEAD SEA, ISRAEL & JORDAN

King Solomon, Cleopatra and the Queen of Sheba were among the early

believers in the benefits of a Dead Sea spa, one of the world's first health resorts owing to the medicinal proper-ties of the area's waters and minerals. Since then, the climate has inspired a huge array of therapies such as thalas-sotherapy (bathing in Dead Sea water) and balneotherapy (a treatment using the black mineral mud of the Dead Sea). There are resorts on both the Israeli and Jordanian sides, offering health packages to cure everything from psoriasis to arthritis.

MOST EXTREME
ANCIENT SITES

WALK THE THE INCA TRAIL, CLIMB MT OLYMPUS OR HIKE INTO THE VALLEY OF THE KINGS TO REACH THE VERY BEST PLACES THAT TIME FORGOT

✪ HADRIAN'S WALL, ENGLAND

Most walls aren't that interesting. Hadrian's is. In AD 122, this Roman bricklayer extraordinaire bowled up in Britain and decided to build a 118km barrier across northern England to keep those troublesome barbarians out. The Emperor's legacy is a some-times fragmented stone chain draped across the stunning scenery of North-umberland National Park. The craggy coast-to-coast archaeological ramble takes about seven days. On the way you'll encounter a world of ramparts, towers and fortlets – and develop a whole lot of respect for the blokes who built it 1800 years ago.

✪ MACHU PICCHU, PERU

This could be the hike of your life: a 33km, four-day trek through forest into the heart of the Inca Empire. At 2350m you'll encounter mountain passes, stoic llamas and thousands of footsore tourists. You'll also see breathtakingly beautiful Machu Picchu clinging to a ridge between two precipitous peaks at the end of the Inca Trail. This complex of palaces, terraces, temples and tombs was inhabited in the 15th and 16th cen-turies and only came to the attention of the wider world in 1911. Conservationist urge responsible trekking to ensure it's around for the next 500 years.

✪ MT OLYMPUS, GREECE

Home of fickle gods and even more fickle weather patterns, mist-shrouded Mt Olympus soars 3000m into the heavens west of the Aegean. This is the place where Zeus let off thunder-bolts, Apollo sunbathed and Dionysus dropped by for a drink. The three-day scramble to the summit takes you through lower slopes carpeted with wild flowers, and rich forests of beech, oak and cedar. It's an epic, Homeric hike to the tops which, provided the clouds haven't snuck in, reveals a god's-eye view of the mortals below.

✪ TERRACOTTA WARRIORS OF XI'AN, CHINA

What would you take with you to the afterlife? How about 8000 life-sized soldiers, horses and war chariots? China's first emperor Qin Shi Huang was buried alongside these 2000 years ago. Despite the number of these troops, he was unlikely to have asked 'haven't I seen you before?' – each terracotta figure has different facial fea-tures. It's not just the army; acrobats, strongmen, musicians and birds have also been discovered. Endless ranks of mottled, cracked figures stretch off into the distance. And that's not the end of it. It's estimated that thousands more have yet to be unearthed.

✪ VALLEY OF THE KINGS, EGYPT

Hike or take a donkey ride to 1500 BC and the tomb-laden Valley of the Kings. As the sun beats down, the dust coats your clothes and the thirst builds in your throat, marvel at past majesty. An extraordinary 62 tombs are buried be-neath the shifting sands here, includ-ing the final resting places of the boy pharaoh Tutankhamun and some of Ramses II's 52 sons. Forget talk of curses; peer down shafts, go under-ground and explore a world of cham-bers, rich murals and hieroglyphics.

✪ SILBURY HILL, UK

The biggest prehistoric man-made mound in Europe is surprisingly little known. Silbury Hill is 4400 years old, took an estimated four million man-hours to build and is made up of half a million tonnes of chalk and rubble. All that effort was possibly for a now similarly obscure character: King Zel (or Sil). Handily Silbury, in Wiltshire, is just a few miles from the infinitely bet-ter known ancient sites at Stonehenge and Avebury. So once you've cricked your neck looking up to Silbury's 30m summit, you can head off to gaze at the mystical monuments nearby.

✪ ROME, ITALY

An archaeological site with a modern city tucked into it, Rome is the ultimate ancient urban adventure. While oh-so-stylish locals perform their famous *passeggiata* (languid stroll), take a timeless walking tour of your own. Start by checking out, from the interior, the perfect dome that tops the Pantheon; debate the merits of wandering the ruins of the Imperial Forums; and end with giving a thumbs up to the stunning Colosseum. Be warned: cacophonous, chaotic and effortlessly classical – Rome can't be walked in a day.

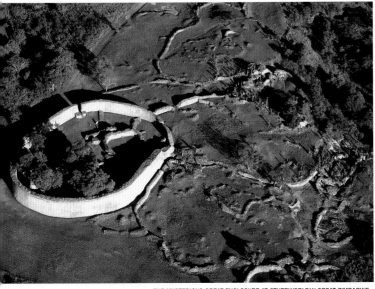

THE MYSTERIOUS GREAT ENCLOSURE AT OTHERWORLDLY GREAT ZIMBABWE

CROP CIRCLES FOR GROWNUPS: PERU'S NAZCA LINES

TRAGEDY TO TURN YOU ASHEN AT POMPEII

01 GREAT ZIMBABWE, ZIMBABWE

The first Westerners to see Great Zimbabwe were so stunned they thought they'd stumbled on King Solomon's Mines. Visitors today are equally impressed. In medieval times up to 20,000 people called this area home – today the 81-hectare central ruins are a mass of stacked granite boulders, tiny passageways and snaking walls. The best bit is the 9m high, 245m round Great Enclosure which is crowned by the Conical Tower, possibly a phallic symbol. Set in a country as renowned for turmoil as it is for ruins, just getting here can be fairly extreme.

02 NAZCA LINES, PERU

It's the kind of archaeological site you couldn't invent. A giant hummingbird, monkey and spider all traced 2000 years ago into the Peruvian desert. And the killer is they can't be seen from the ground. No one's quite sure how the ancient Nazca pulled off this artistic conjuring trick, but they mapped out an incredible 800 geoglyphs; shapes, straight lines and pictures on the plain. At ground level it looks like an unimpressive stretch of red-brown earth. But when a light airplane whisks you skywards a 60m whale, 120m condor and 275m pelican unfold before your eyes.

03 VESUVIUS & POMPEII, ITALY

The rounded cone of Mt Vesuvius punctures the horizon, towering above the Bay of Naples. A testing half-hour hike up this active volcano reveals a whopping crater, plumes of fumes and a bird's-eye view of Pompeii. The Roman city of Pompeii was famously frozen in time by the ash and burning pumice stone which spewed from Vesuvius in AD 79. The city's excavated ruins are a profound and pitiful mix of the monumental and the mundane: the imposing amphitheatre and forum sit alongside homes and bakeries. Look out for the Cave Canem (Beware of the Dog) sign, and the saucy pictures on the brothel walls.

ECCENTRI-CITY

WEIRD, WACKY OR SIMPLY WONDERFUL. YOU THINK YOU'VE SEEN IT ALL BUT THESE CITIES WILL MAKE YOU LOOK AGAIN

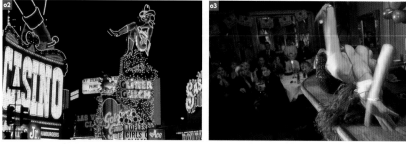

LAS VEGAS IN ALL ITS GARISH, GLITTERY GLORY

THINGS HEAT UP IN REYKJAVÍK

o1 TOKYO, JAPAN

Talking toilets and microsized pod hotels have kept Japan at the top of the eccentricity charts for years. But have you tried drinking in Tokyo? *Now* we're talking weird, for this is the city with a million themed ways to wet your whistle. Feeling a bit peaky? Try ER's hospital bar, where staff wear pristine white uniforms and administer 'doses' direct from oversized hypodermic needles. Sip cocktails in psychedelic Alice in Wonderland, marvel at the sword-wielding bartenders at Ninja or hit Office, where drinks are downed over the photocopier and filing cabinets.

o2 LAS VEGAS, USA

Where to begin? Your hotel seems to be under the Eiffel Tower, there's an exact replica of Tutankhamun's tomb down the road and the neon glare is burning your retina. Everything's big, and we mean *huge* – crowds, casinos, nightclubs, hangovers…and especially the gangs of porn-peddling pimps. No one means to gamble much but suddenly you've no idea what day it is, let alone what the time might be – somebody removed all the clocks, shut out the daylight and pumped you full of oxygen. It's all a bit of a blur and, for that reason, utterly fantastic.

o3 REYKJAVÍK, ICELAND

Partying in Reykjavík is like partying in no other city – mad, frantic and laced with Nordic energy. Cosmopolitan bars rock through the night, inhibitions disappear and alcohol flows hard. It seems like a competition, and in a sense it is because Icelanders are making up for lost time. After all, beer was illegal until 1990 and thumping all-night clubs were nonexistent. If it all seems a bit crazy, just remember this – if you spent half the year in near darkness and the other half under the midnight sun, you'd be a bit bonkers too.

✪ ASHGABAT, TURKMENISTAN

Considering he banned beards, ballet and lip-synching to music, it's no surprise that Saparmurat Niyazov became famed for eccentricity. The self-styled President for Life, Turkmenbashi (Leader of all the Turkmen) also closed every hospital outside Ashgabat, renamed the month of January after himself and presided over a trade deal in which Ukraine gave his nation 12 million pairs of galoshes in exchange for a bunch of TV sets. Niyazov died in 2006 but the memory of this odd dictator lives on at The World of Turkmenbashi Tales, an oddball Central Asian Disneyland of Ferris wheels and roller coasters.

✪ DELHI, INDIA

On first sight Delhi seems like a seething, uncontrollable mass of humanity. But once you get to grips with the tumult and a raft of unusual attractions appear, nowhere more so than in the city's architecture. Swamped by the spread of 15 million residents, some of Delhi's greatest old ruins have been pushed aside by 20th-century growth. And so historic remains are hidden under flyovers, beneath towering high-rise blocks or have been converted to modern-day mansions. It's a peculiar balance of past and present – and since Delhi doesn't stop for anyone, who knows what will change next.

✪ AMSTERDAM, THE NETHERLANDS

Try as they might, Amsterdamers just can't shake off their sex and drugs image, but the coffee shops and neon windows of the red light district generate big money. Tourists wander the elegant tree-lined streets beneath graceful canal houses, although nobody comes for the architecture. Live sex shows, erotica museums and hardcore porn shops keep the euros flowing, but it all takes place in an unthreatening atmosphere. You're just as likely to see grandma taking a photo of the huge phallus fountain as you are

PACHINKO GAMES ROOM IN SHIBUYA, TOKYO

to be offered hard drugs. And that, in itself, is more than a little bizarre.

✪ PYONGYANG, NORTH KOREA

As the world gets smaller and cultures homogenised, few places remain as unwelcoming to visitors as North Korea. But ironically, the very communism that is designed to keep the outside world at bay is attracting a growing number of curious visitors. Don't expect to go it alone, for you'll be fastidiously escorted from one weird attraction to the next. Right across the board, from huge statues of Kim Il Sung to museums of gifts donated to the country (including a stuffed crocodile from Nicolae Ceausescu) and restaurants with no menus, Pyongyang defies all accepted convention.

✪ GUANAJUATO, MEXICO

Unesco-listed Guanajuato is one of Mexico's finest historic towns, with 450 years of history and one very macabre attraction. Guanajuato Mummy Museum doesn't pay homage to Mexican matriarchs – rather, it's a gruesome collection of mummified remains exhumed from the city's cemetery. When families couldn't afford the upkeep of the crypts, bodies were removed and placed on public display, preserved for humiliation by the region's dry climate. If twisted, ash-grey corpses float your boat, the museum's collection of over a hundred modern-day mummies, including the world's smallest, make for a fascinating visit. Those of a fragile disposition should steer clear.

✪ SONGJIANG, CHINA

As modern China rushes headlong to the future in a blur of tower cranes and high-rise condos, a small area of this city near Shanghai is turning the clock backwards. Drinkers sip pints at the local Tudor-style pub, kids play on the village green, trees flutter on streets of Regency terraced homes and wedding bells chime in the cathedral. For all the tea in China, this is middle England. Except it's not. Welcome to Thames Town, Songjiang's built-from-scratch theme-park recreation of an idyllic English life. It's utterly bizarre, and about as far from real Britain as it is from frenzied Shanghai.

✪ NEW ORLEANS, USA

The Creole city that boasts individual charms such as gumbo, streetcars and a red-hot jazz scene really comes alive during Mardi Gras. The culmination of New Orleans' carnival season, the celebration goes off amid a riot of colourful parades, parties and primeval revelry. At least, it does for the visitors, who lap up the flamboyant costumes and drape themselves in strings of plastic beads. Locals might see it as a time for family, but they're not going to stop the booty-shaking excess of the French Quarter.

SCANDINAVIA

EUROPE

NORTH
ASIA

NORTH ATLANTIC
OCEAN

MIDDLE
EAST

CENTRAL
ASIA

NORTH PACIFIC
OCEAN

AFRICA

SOUTH

INDIAN OCEAN

WORLD PROFILES »

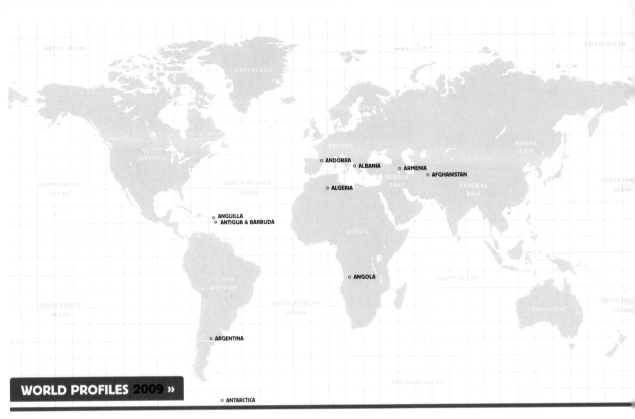

ARCTIC OCEAN
GREENLAND
SCANDINAVIA
EUROPE
○ ANDORRA
○ ALBANIA
○ ARMENIA
○ AFGHANISTAN
NORTH AMERICA
NORTH ATLANTIC OCEAN
MIDDLE EAST
○ ALGERIA
CENTRAL ASIA
NORTH ASIA
NORTH PACIFIC OCEAN
○ ANGUILLA
○ ANTIGUA & BARBUDA
AFRICA
NORTH PACIFIC OCEAN
○ ANGOLA
INDIAN OCEAN
SOUTH AMERICA
SOUTH PACIFIC OCEAN
SOUTH ATLANTIC OCEAN
AUSTRALIA
SOUTH PACIFIC OCEAN
○ ARGENTINA
SOUTHERN OCEAN

WORLD PROFILES 2009 »

○ ANTARCTICA

AFGHANISTAN

CAPITAL KABUL **POPULATION** 32.7 MILLION **AREA** 647,500 SQ KM **OFFICIAL LANGUAGE** AFGHAN PERSIAN

Except for the extremely intrepid, Afghanistan isn't shaping up to be a viable traveller destination in 2009. Some visitors were beginning to return following the ousting of the Taliban in 2001, but early 2008 saw a return to regular and devastating violence, with Taliban-linked bomb attacks rising sharply. Current president Hamid Karzai won his five-year mandate in October 2004, meaning that elections may be on the cards for 2009. For those who do decide to travel here, Afghanistan remains home to a wealth of historical and archaeological wonders, and some stunningly dramatic scenery.

ALBANIA

CAPITAL TIRANA **POPULATION** 3.6 MILLION **AREA** 28,748 SQ KM **OFFICIAL LANGUAGE** ALBANIAN

Secretive Albania is starting to emerge from its bunker – of which it still has many (courtesy of invasion-paranoid former leader Enver Hoxha), now sitting redundant and pastel-painted on its beaches. A niche destination for now, this last undeveloped slice of the Mediterranean won't stay that way. At the moment you can drive (bumpily) past unspoiled bays, but not to them. Saranda in the south is an exception, a building boom 10 years ago transforming the sleepy port. Head out to the Unesco-listed Ottoman town of Gjirokastra or the many hillside monasteries and you won't see another soul. In the north, the gorge-navigating ferry from Shkodra to Fierza is reputedly one of the world's best ferry trips.

ALGERIA

CAPITAL ALGIERS **POPULATION** 33.8 MILLION **AREA** 2,381,740 SQ KM **OFFICIAL LANGUAGE** ARABIC

This is the African continent's second- largest country, after massive Sudan. Tourists have stayed away from Algeria for the last decade or so as civil war raged wild. Though terrorist attacks do continue to occur – with suicide bombings occasionally rocking Algeria's major cities – travellers are tentatively returning to explore the vast Saharan wastes of the south and the historical remains sprinkled across the country. Assuming things stay reasonably calm in 2009, head straight to the lovely Saharan desert oasis town of Timimoun. Well set up for travellers, it currently offers a comfortable desert experience without the tourist hordes of Morocco or Tunisia. The time will come when Algeria is firmly back on the tourist map, so visit now to beat the tour buses.

ANDORRA

CAPITAL ANDORRA LA VELLA **POPULATION** 71,822 **AREA** 468 SQ KM **OFFICIAL LANGUAGE** CATALAN

Despite its minuscule population, this petite principality attracts 10 million tourists a year – impressive for a country with no airport or train station and, until recently, poor roads. But smooth highways now dissect these Pyrenean highlands (Andorra's average elevation is 1996m), and an airport is planned for 2010, just 15km over the border in Spain. Indeed, aside from shopping (this tax haven is famed for duty-free bargains), the mountains are the big draw for pleasant skiing in winter and hiking in summer – follow the Victor Hugo trail to Vianden for a mix of scenery and a peep into the exiled writer's former home.

ANGOLA

CAPITAL LUANDA **POPULATION** 12.3 MILLION **AREA** 1,246,700 SQ KM **OFFICIAL LANGUAGE** PORTUGUESE

Though still beset with problems, from malaria to poverty to unexploded ordnance, Angola is a diamond destination for the intrepid traveller. One of the best places to experience Angola's slowly growing wildlife tourism is at the Parque Nacional da Kissama. A nature reserve for 70 years, the park saw repopulation with the astonishing Operation Noah's Ark, in which elephants were airlifted in from other African game reserves. Despite its problems (including dire poverty, despite being one of the world's greatest oil exporters), Angola can be a safe destination to explore. However, elections to decide a new president and national assembly are scheduled for 2009 – the first in 17 years – so keep abreast of developments.

ANGUILLA

CAPITAL THE VALLEY **POPULATION** 13,677 **AREA** 102 SQ KM **OFFICIAL LANGUAGE** ENGLISH

Beloved by the Brits who have colonised its sunny shores since the 17th century, Anguilla is a vision of white-sand beaches and luxury-villa getaways. Though increasingly catering to a well-sandalled international crowd, Anguilla is trying to preserve its friendly local identity with a ban on foreigners purchasing land. Despite the relatively recent building boom, some spots remain low-key as ever with reggae and tempting barbecue scents wafting from seaside shacks. If you fancy catching a spot of rugby while on the island, look out for the newly formed Anguilla Eels RFC, currently taking the Caribbean rugby union scene by storm.

ANTARCTICA

POPULATION 0, EXCEPT FOR MANNED RESEARCH STATIONS **AREA** 14,000,000 SQ KM

The world's last great wilderness, there can be no wilder destination for travellers and no better time to visit than now, due to climate change. In 2007, Norwegian artist Vebjørn Sand built an ice bridge here, based on a design by Leonardo da Vinci, to turn the world's attention to global warming; in 2008, around 570 sq km of ice in Western Antarctica collapsed, putting the remaining ice of the Wilkins Ice Shelf at dire risk. Currently, just under 40,000 visitors per year make it to the world's southernmost continent, almost all by cruise ship. All tourist activities are managed by the Antarctic Treaty to ensure that tourism remains a responsible and awareness-raising blessing rather than another Antarctic curse.

ANTIGUA & BARBUDA

CAPITAL ST JOHN'S **POPULATION** 69,481 **AREA** 443 SQ KM **OFFICIAL LANGUAGE** ENGLISH

This pair of islands are the mismatched siblings of the Caribbean. Touted as having a different beach for every day of the year, Antigua is a bubbling, ultra-welcoming destination, with beautiful backdrops and stunning sunsets. Head here in April 2009 for the 23rd annual yacht regatta – the region's largest – or in August for its heady Carnival; there's some sort of cheerful, colourful event, often involving cricket, hosted by the island almost every month. Quiet Barbuda is a birdwatcher's bliss. Its huge rookery, frigate-bird sanctuary and deserted beaches, with only basic facilities, is a far cry from the rum punch and partying of Antigua. It's still unusually undeveloped for the Caribbean.

ARGENTINA

CAPITAL BUENOS AIRES **POPULATION** 40.3 MILLION **AREA** 2,776,890 SQ KM **OFFICIAL LANGUAGE** SPANISH

The eighth largest country on earth has experienced phenomenal recent

growth in its annual tourist figures, with another keen rise forecast for 2009 and 2010. Currently overseen by its second female president, Cristina Fernández de Kirchner – who took over the position from her husband – Argentina may still be in economic recovery, but it has plans to cash in on its ever-burgeoning tourism potential. Aside from spectacular festivals, including the January Buenos Aires Tango Festival and the incredible Gualeguaychú Carnaval in February, it has a keen eye on ecotourism. The tourism sector is fast developing throughout its extensive national parks network, its eight World Heritage sites and into bleak, unpeopled Patagonia tipped by Tierra del Fuego, the fabled 'land of fire'.

ARMENIA

CAPITAL YEREVAN **POPULATION** 3 MILLION **AREA** 29,800 SQ KM **OFFICIAL LANGUAGE** ARMENIAN

Yerevan celebrated its 2790th birthday in 2008 (making it older than Rome), which gives you an idea of the history harboured in this almost-Asian outpost of rocky highlands and ancient forests. Tourist numbers rose 34% in 2007, with most visitors heading to must-sees such as ethereal Lake Sevan and the 12th-century monastery of Noravank (though canyon-poised Tatev Monastery is possibly more spectacular). Less encouraging is the country's ongoing quarrel with Azerbaijan over Nagorno-Karabakh. Early 2008 saw an escalation of violence over the disputed region, which has an Armenian majority but is stranded inside Azeri borders; a resolution does not appear to be in sight.

ARUBA, BONAIRE & CURACAO

CAPITALS ORANJESTAD (A), KRALENDIJK (B), WILLEMSTAD (C) **POPULATION** 100,018 (A), 14,006 (B), 138,000 (C) **AREA** 181 SQ KM (A), 285 SQ KM (B), 471 SQ KM (C) **OFFICIAL LANGUAGES** DUTCH (A, B & C), PAPIAMENTO (A)

The flat, arid ABCs, just off Venezuela's coast, officially lie outside the hurricane belt, though all got a little rain-lashed by 2007's Hurricane Felix. Aruba is a luxury-holiday hit, sprinkled with sporting events: check out its annual Hi-Winds windsurfing contest in April, or the

catamaran regatta in November. Though development aid from the Netherlands will be winding up in 2009, steadily growing tourism suggests it will retain its place as one of the wealthiest of the Caribbean isles. Bonaire, meanwhile, is the place if you're a diver, a donkey or a flamingo, with the world's most idyllic sanctuaries for our four-legged and disco-pink friends. Curacao, the largest of the trio, offers sensational scuba diving, though fears have recently been raised about the impact of tourism on its reefs. Porto Marie's replacement artificial reefs, however, are proving a success, with shoals of tropical fish arriving to inhabit them.

AUSTRALIA

 CAPITAL CANBERRA **POPULATION** 20.4 MILLION **AREA** 7,617,930 SQ KM **OFFICIAL LANGUAGE** ENGLISH

Even the 'Where the bloody hell are you?' TV campaign couldn't stop Australia's tourism, with modest increases in visitor numbers despite the fact the ads were met with confusion in the UK and Japan. British travellers still comprise the most arrivals, with most unable to pry themselves away from the east coast, which offers Sydney's big icons and snorkelling on the Great Barrier Reef. There's a growing trend, however, for authentic Australian experiences: catching the *Ghan* train through Australia's red centre or learning bushcraft from Aboriginal elders in the Flinders Ranges. The atmosphere of reconciliation and optimism of Kevin Rudd's new Labour government has headlines heralding the country 'Kevin Heaven'.

AUSTRIA

CAPITAL VIENNA **POPULATION** 8.2 MILLION **AREA** 83,870 SQ KM **OFFICIAL LANGUAGE** GERMAN

Austria does 'old' well – travellers adore its Habsburg grandeur and musical pedigree (it's all about Haydn in 2009, with concerts commemorating the bicentennial of his death). But Austria's not stuck in the past; a fresh-look cuisine

is challenging schnitzel-serving Beisls. Its cities are modernising: Linz's derelict industrial quarters are bustling with arty invention given the city's been crowned 2009 Capital of Culture. Outside the cities, Austria is mostly alpine splendour. This eco-before-eco-was-hip nation loves its great outdoors, and has managed to keep some parts quiet – cycle the rolling South Styrian wine route or hike in the back-to-nature Bregenzerwald (stopping off at dairy farms for pungent mountain cheese) where it's almost locals-only.

AZERBAIJAN

CAPITAL BAKU **POPULATION** 8.1 MILLION **AREA** 86,600 SQ KM **OFFICIAL LANGUAGE** AZERBAIJANI

Tourism isn't big business on this fringe of Europe – but the country doesn't much care, with plenty of oil money to keep it going. That said, while Caspian Sea–side Baku is basking in black-gold good times, much of the country – from the Caucasus Mountains to the tea plantations of the south – is like a step back in time. In the far north you're in untouched old-world countryside, where villages clack with carpet-weavers' looms, and horses and carts rule the roads. If you only go to one place here, make it Saki – explore the recently renovated Khan's Palace before bedding down in a restored caravanserai like a true nomad.

BAHAMAS

CAPITAL NASSAU **POPULATION** 305,655 **AREA** 13,940 SQ KM **OFFICIAL LANGUAGE** ENGLISH

The Bahamas archipelago of some 700 islands; ranging from bankers' paradise to West Indies backwater and floating in crystal-clear waters; is a top destination for US holidaymakers. Tourism has seen a slight decline though since 2006, perhaps due to a few years of bad hurricanes; 2007's Hurricane Noel dropped nearly 400m of rain in 15 hours. While it's a year-round destination, the most thrilling time to head here is during Christmas,

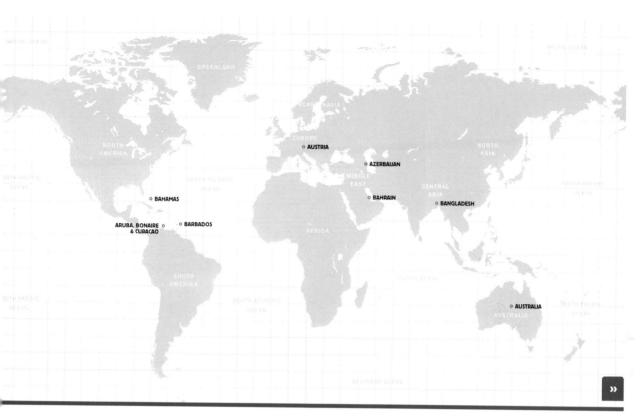

when the carnivalesque Boxing Day Junkanoo festival swings into action well before sunrise. To escape the melee, head to Bahamas' largest but least-visited island of Andros, a wild and spooky mangrove-fringed domain perfect for birdwatchers, beachcombers and divers keen to explore its 140 miles of offshore coral reef.

BAHRAIN

CAPITAL MANAMA **POPULATION** 718,306 **AREA** 665 SQ KM **OFFICIAL LANGUAGE** ARABIC

Liberal, friendly Bahrain, already a firm favourite with Middle East–bound travellers, is fast becoming a guaranteed-sunshine, long-weekend destination from Europe à la Dubai. Visitors head to Manama for top-notch sleeping and dining options (with, unusually for the region, readily available alcohol), and shopping at its fabulous souqs (markets). For something a little more culturally stimulating, head to the Unesco-rated Qala'at al Bahrain fort at Dilmun, where archaeological treasures await. April 2009 meanwhile, sees the sixth annual Bahrain Formula One Grand Prix drawing crowds from across the world, with new hotels springing up all the time to cope with an annually increasing influx. For something a little less noisy, the International Cycling Cup hits the same Formula One Grand Prix circuit in November.

BANGLADESH

CAPITAL DHAKA **POPULATION** 153.5 MILLION **AREA** 144,000 SQ KM **OFFICIAL LANGUAGE** BENGALI

Though the country frequently suffers from one or more of a host of woes, including floods, political instability, cyclones and extreme poverty, more and more visitors are slowly beginning to discover the Bangladesh behind the often tragic headlines. Safaris through the mangrove-filled Sundarbans, with its elusive tiger population and gypsy fisherfolk, are becoming popular with travellers. There are also archaeological sites aplenty, as well as some mellow getaways, such as the little and laid-back St Martin's coral island. Since the country is predominantly Muslim, you might want to avoid travelling during the fasting month of Ramadan, which falls in 2009 between 21 August and 19 September (approximately); opening hours become irregular and food is difficult to find during daylight hours.

BARBADOS

CAPITAL BRIDGETOWN **POPULATION** 280,946 **AREA** 431 SQ KM **OFFICIAL LANGUAGE** ENGLISH

The easternmost Caribbean island, with no neighbours for a good 160km, Barbados is tightly packed, highly developed, a perennial tourist favourite, and enjoys a superior standard of both literacy and living. Its Bajan population may have never quite lost the penchant for all things British, but the local specialities of flying-fish-fry and a good glass of Mount Gay rum are decidedly on the menu. Look out for cricket matches, a Bajan obsession, and for the Crop Over festival – an old-time celebration of the sugar-cane harvest which gets going at the end of July and culminates in a lavish costumed parade on the first Monday in August, Kadooment Day.

BELARUS

 **CAPITAL** MINSK **POPULATION** 9.7 MILLION **AREA** 207,600 SQ KM **OFFICIAL LANGUAGE** BELARUSIAN

Belarus has something of an image problem. Presided over by a virtual dictator who's conveniently dismissed the in-for-two-terms-only rule, it's the last Stalinist state in Europe – a grim flashback to a 1980s Soviet Union. Can tourism ever flourish here? Yes, according to the incumbent minister of tourism, who's convinced Belarus has the ecology and culture to attract many more visitors. It does have four World Heritage sites, one of which – Belavezhskaja Pushcha National Park, a vast tract of ancient woodland roamed by deer, wolf and bison – celebrates its 600th anniversary as a protected area in 2009.

BELGIUM

CAPITAL BRUSSELS **POPULATION** 10.3 MILLION **AREA** 30,528 SQ KM **OFFICIAL LANGUAGES** DUTCH, FRENCH

It's ironic that this EU stalwart can't unify its own population. Tensions between Dutch-speaking Flanders and francophone Wallonia recently bubbled to the point that the country went without goverment for months – 45% of Flems in favour of becoming a separate nation left the government unable to form a ruling coalition. You don't think of Belgium as a hotbed of revolution – more a safe-as-houses domain of sumptuous chocolate, great beer and frites (evidenced by the new Frietmuseum, medieval Bruges' homage to the fried potato). However, one thing that does unite the country is its increasingly well-connected rail network, which will help you access cosy auberges amid the dense Ardennes forest or the medieval castles of the Gueule Valley.

BELIZE

CAPITAL BELMOPAN **POPULATION** 294,385 **AREA** 22,966 SQ KM **OFFICIAL LANGUAGE** ENGLISH

Belize is living the good life with clear Caribbean cayes, a laid-back attitude to life and a multitude of spectacular Mayan sites like Altun Ha. Commune with baboons at the Community Baboon Sanctuary or kick back in a hidden jungle eco-lodge, as canny Belize tourist operators hone in on the current fad for all things eco. With one of the lowest population densities in the world, there is plenty of room for all, and you'll have no problem being understood since English remains the official language. However, unemployment and poverty are both high and violent crime has recently been on the increase – this is something travellers should watch out for, especially in Belize City.

BENIN

CAPITAL PORTO NOVO **POPULATION** 8 MILLION **AREA** 110,620 SQ KM **OFFICIAL LANGUAGE** FRENCH

Diminutive Benin seems keen to start cashing in on its tourism potential, much of which lies in a heady mixture of slave-trade relics and live-and-kicking voodoo culture. With the arrival of George W Bush in 2008 for a fleeting visit – the first of any major national head to a country that was, until 30 years ago, known as Dahomey – there are hopes that people will start to visit, or at least know that Benin exists. Head to seaside Cotonou's Grand Marché du Dantokpa to buy your own DIY voodoo kit, or to the Royal Palaces of Abomey, Benin's sole but impressive Unesco World Heritage site, where three centuries of Abomey kings left their indelible mark.

BERMUDA

CAPITAL HAMILTON **POPULATION** 66,163 **AREA** 53.3 SQ KM **OFFICIAL LANGUAGE** ENGLISH

Bermuda is about far more than shorts, triangles and keeping up with the Douglas-Zeta-Joneses. Though the majority of visitors to this destination land and leave on cruise ships (there are more than half a million each year), a good few stay on to manage its thriving offshore economy – allowing Bermuda to sustain a per capita GDP that is about 50% higher than that of the USA. For independent travellers, away from the gloss put on for the cruise passengers there's pink-sand beach aplenty in this conglomerate of around 138 islands, which are well-served by bus and passenger ferry and conveniently connected by road bridge. Swing by in March and April 2009 for the islands' acclaimed independent film festival.

BHUTAN

CAPITAL THIMPHU **POPULATION** 2.3 MILLION **AREA** 47,000 SQ KM **OFFICIAL LANGUAGE** DZONGKHA

Travel doesn't get much more boutique than a visit to Bhutan. To minimise the impact on this Buddhist culture the only way to see the country is to take a tour conducted by the government. The tours focus on activities such as visiting Himalayan communities, trekking the Snowman trail or taking meditation retreats in working monasteries. Recently built resorts and luxury hotels plus the development of better roads will make it easier to visit, though many fear a negative impact on the country's 'Gross National Happiness' – which Bhutan treats as seriously as any hard-nosed economic indicator.

BOLIVIA

CAPITALS LA PAZ (ADMINISTRATIVE), SUCRE (JUDICIAL) **POPULATION** 9.1 MILLION **AREA** 1,098,580 SQ KM **OFFICIAL LANGUAGES** SPANISH, QUECHUA, AYMARA

Things are not well at present in this beautiful, remote and landlocked country, with a state of emergency having been declared following severe flooding in February 2008. The floods left tens of thousands homeless, and it'll be quite some time before Bolivia's infrastructure is completely repaired and it's back on its feet. There have been violent clashes of late, brought on partly by President Evo Morales' promise to begin penning a new constitution, and exacerbated by poverty and local political wrangling. Still, with the allure of volcanoes, pristine wilderness comprising both the Andes and the Amazon, vast and magical Lake Titicaca, the world's largest salt flats at Salar de Uyuni, and such culinary delights as guinea pig and llama jerky to feast on, it's a place worth adding to any travel wishlist.

BOSNIA & HERCEGOVINA

CAPITAL SARAJEVO **POPULATION** 4.6 MILLION AREA 51,129 SQ KM **OFFICIAL LANGUAGE** BOSNIAN

As beguiling images of Bosnia – which is 52% forest and mountain – circulate in greater numbers than dismal news stories, memories of the country as a war-ravaged nation are being replaced by a growing curiosity. It has been over 10 years since the war ended and Bosnia is more than ready to move forward – EU membership beckons and Mine Action hopes to get rid of the country's remaining unexploded ordnance by 2009. It's a good job too – the countryside is simply begging to be explored: Rakitnica Canyon (which is great for hiking) and the primeval forest of Perućica remain untouched, while a trip to the well-run ecovillage of Umoljani will give visitors a glimpse of traditional life – and an idea of the country's tourism potential.

BOTSWANA

CAPITAL GABORONE **POPULATION** 1.8 MILLION **AREA** 600,370 SQ KM **OFFICIAL LANGUAGE** ENGLISH

With the TV version of the smash hit *No 1 Ladies Detective Agency* having hit the screens in 2008, it is not hard to see why Botswana's tourism potential has surged skyward, and will in all likelihood continue that way. However, while tourism figures continue to climb, the average life expectancy has plummeted shockingly and now stands at just 50.55 years for men. Dismally, one in three Batswana are infected with HIV, though the country is striving to tackle this with a laudably comprehensive treatment programme. Tourism here is not yet designed for the budget traveller. The government's policy has been decidedly low-volume, high-end, in order to conserve the country's precious natural resources. This means that if you can afford to travel in this land, you'll find that you'll have Botswana's spectacular parks and reserves pretty much to yourself.

BRAZIL

CAPITAL BRASÍLIA **POPULATION** 190 MILLION **AREA** 8,511,965 SQ KM **OFFICIAL LANGUAGE** PORTUGUESE

It's impossible to be bored in Brazil – as an annual tourism growth of 7.2% (according to the Brazilian government's tourist board) will attest. As well as an awful lot of coffee, numerous sustainable-tourism opportunities are springing up everywhere: venture out to Fernando de Noronha national park archipelago or the stunning Reserva de Desenvolvimento Sustentável Mamirauá for ecotravel at its best. There are also lots of chances for fitness tourism, with visitors, impressed by the sleek bodies on the Copacabana, signing up for *capoeira* (martial arts–style dancing) holidays to hone their skills and tone their midriffs. Rio's Carnaval is held from 21 to 24 February in 2009, and 13 to 16 February in 2010. Whether you head to Brazil for the soccer, the *caipirinhas*, for Brasília's strange brand of retro-futurism, to drink, samba, shop or trek, the message is clear: head there soon.

BRUNEI

CAPITAL BANDAR SERI BEGAWAN **POPULATION** 381,371 **AREA** 5770 SQ KM **OFFICIAL LANGUAGE** MALAY

Fabulously wealthy Brunei is especially welcoming to well-heeled tourists. Budget traveller numbers are relatively low, and expats benefiting from Brunei's oil-fuelled economy are the most commonly spotted foreigners on Bandar Seri Begawan's peaceful streets. Head to the Temburong district (unconnected to the rest of Brunei, since a swathe of Sarawak soil sits solidly in-between) where ecotours are rapidly developing to entice more travellers. In the Belalong and vast Ulu Temburong National Parks you can take in views of steamy rainforest from the seat of a longboat or whitewater raft, or from a suspension bridge high above the forest canopy. If the slow pace of Ramadan (the fasting month) isn't your thing, avoid a visit in August and September 2009.

BULGARIA

CAPITAL SOFIA **POPULATION** 7.3 MILLION **AREA** 110,910 SQ KM **OFFICIAL LANGUAGE** BULGARIAN

What's not to love about a country where beer costs an average of just US$0.95? Eurozone entry is slated for 2010, but for now Bulgaria is the cheapie of Europe – and bargain-hunters are taking full advantage, flocking to the Rila Mountains ski resorts, Black Sea coast and, er, dentists. There are plenty of un-flocked pockets though – try Ahtopol, the last refuge of traditional charm on the increasingly developed Black Sea, and the wild Strandzha Mountain region which harbours unexplored ruins and eco-adventure. Sofia is worth a look, too – the city is undergoing a spring clean (better paths, more trees, a new museum) in preparation for the 130th anniversary of its capital status in 2009.

BURKINA FASO

CAPITAL OUAGADOUGOU **POPULATION** 14.3 MILLION **AREA** 274,200 SQ KM **OFFICIAL LANGUAGE** FRENCH

Sandwiched largely between Mali, Ghana and the Côte d'Ivoire, landlocked Burkina Faso sees few tourists or travellers. It's one of the poorest countries in the world despite its considerable gold reserves, with around 90% of the population deriving its income from agriculture. For all that, though, the relaxed and friendly capital, Ouagadougou, is remarkably culturally vibrant. The capital also prides itself as one of the top film production centres in West Africa – February and March 2009 will see the fabulous Pan-African Film Festival, Africa's largest – hitting town. Outside the city, visit Karfiguéla's cascading waterfalls or venture further afield to the remote sandstone towers of the Pics de Sindou.

BURUNDI

CAPITAL BUJUMBURA **POPULATION** 8.4 MILLION **AREA** 27,834 SQ KM **OFFICIAL LANGUAGES** KIRUNDI, FRENCH

In 2005 and 2006, two ceasefires were signed, intended to bring an end to the violence that had plagued Burundi – one of the poorest countries on earth – since its independence in 1962. However, it remains a volatile and unpredictable spot, with frequent bursts of violence and subsequent curfews. Foreign offices currently advise against all travel to the country. If and when things do eventually cool down, travellers will finally be able to trek out to Burundi's several beautiful national parks, as well as visit the spot where HM Stanley allegedly had his famous 'Dr Livingstone, I presume?' moment way back in 1871.

CAMBODIA

CAPITAL PHNOM PENH **POPULATION** 13.9 MILLION **AREA** 176,520 SQ KM **OFFICIAL LANGUAGE** KHMER

Emerging from a history of Khmer Rouge tyranny, Cambodia is one of Southeast Asia's more popular destinations. The obvious highlight is Angkor Wat, the ancient citadel of temples that has created a tourist bubble around Siem Reap and which has direct flights from Thailand and Singapore. But these flights miss the postcolonial grandeur of Phnom Penh and the beaches of Sihanoukville

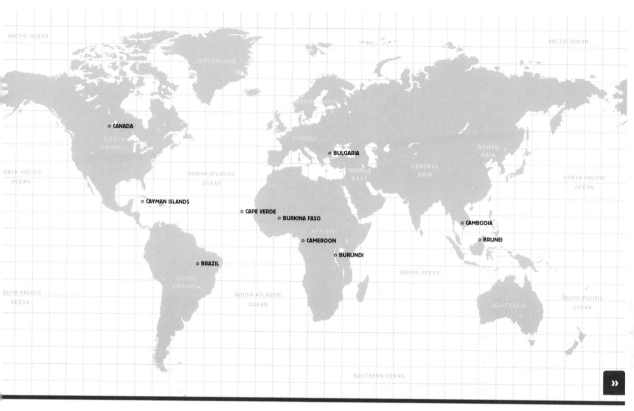

that some backpackers have dubbed the 'new Thailand'. Sadly the legacy of war remains, with unexploded landmines and ingrained government corruption that could swipe the nation's oil profits rather than invest in continued growth.

CAMEROON

CAPITAL YAOUNDÉ **POPULATION** 18 MILLION **AREA** 475,440 SQ KM **OFFICIAL LANGUAGES** FRENCH, ENGLISH

Cameroon has a few troublesome neighbours and its border regions (particularly with Chad and the Central African Republic) should be avoided due to the threat of banditry. But the country rewards the relatively few travellers who make it here to discover its charms. Mt Cameroon, West Africa's highest peak, makes for challenging trekking, while Cameroon's beaches are a delight for lazing with a book and an ice-cold beer. Ecotourism, too, is increasingly becoming a draw here, with a number of new Cameroon-based companies offering specialised tours of the country's natural highlights. The Unesco World Heritage–rated

Dja Faunal Reserve is one such treasure: one of Africa's largest and best-preserved rainforests, where numerous endangered species reside in safety.

CANADA

CAPITAL OTTAWA **POPULATION** 33.2 MILLION **AREA** 9,093,507 SQ KM **OFFICIAL LANGUAGES** ENGLISH, FRENCH

Land of vast open spaces, Rocky Mountains, moose and Mounties, Canada's consistently a magnet for tourists and travellers of all ages, types and wallet-capacities. The country is currently gearing up for a tourism leap with the February 2010 Winter Olympics in Vancouver – if you're into watching people whiz, glide and spin. The city itself offers many charms aside from its snowcapped peaks: chow down in Chinatown, wander through huge Stanley Park – home to friendly raccoons – just west of high-rise downtown, and pick produce at the cute Granville Island farmer's market. Consistently voted one of the world's 'most livable' cities despite all that rain, it's not hard to see why.

CAPE VERDE

CAPITAL PRAIA **POPULATION** 423,613 **AREA** 4033 SQ KM **OFFICIAL LANGUAGES** PORTUGUESE, CRIOULO

Since package-holiday flights started jetting out regularly to the sunny climes of Cape Verde, set just off the coast of Senegal, things have been changing here fast. Once little more than the bleak and barren volcanic islands of Cesaria Evora's haunting *morna* folk refrains (a type of blues), the islands are increasingly known for the resort hubs of Boa Vista and Sal. With 10 main islands and still more islets, it isn't all resort and time-share wintersun madness. One of the best ways to escape the masses is to take a hike up Mt Fogo, a still-active volcano that hasn't erupted in the last decade or so, to peek from the peak at incredible views out over the islands.

CAYMAN ISLANDS

CAPITAL GEORGE TOWN **POPULATION** 46,600 **AREA** 262 SQ KM **OFFICIAL LANGUAGE** ENGLISH

This trio of pretty islands, set in suitably turquoise seas, boasts two

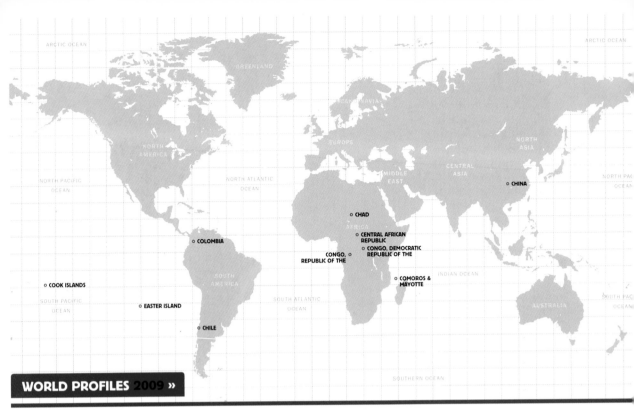

'mosts': the most lavish standard of living of any Caribbean destination (aided by its offshore business boom); and, less happily, the most hurricane strikes of anywhere in the Atlantic basin. Luckily for the Caymans, the last few years have seen more CEOs than sea storms, the last big hit being Hurricane Ivan in 2004. Having bounced right back, the Caymans ranks as one of the world's topmost scuba destinations, while its Georgetown port can experience tourist swells of over 20,000 visitors per day when the cruise ships come pouring in. To escape the cruising crowds, your best bet is to head down beneath the crystalline waves to explore one of the Caymans' long-lost shipwrecks or to duck and dive with friendly manta rays.

CENTRAL AFRICAN REPUBLIC

CAPITAL BANGUI **POPULATION** 4.4 MILLION **AREA** 622,984 SQ KM **OFFICIAL LANGUAGE** FRENCH

Sadly, this warm and welcoming country is one to which travellers are currently strongly advised not to venture. Civil unrest plagues the capital, Bangui, which has been experiencing such disturbances since independence from France, and particularly since 2003's military coup, which caused violence to break out. Nevertheless, the Central African Republic, circumstances willing, might one day become one of Africa's bright new centres for ecotourism. With healthy stocks of gorillas and forest elephants, and a Unesco-rated national park teeming with wildlife at Manovo-Gounda St Floris, the natural resources are in place to attract the tourist dollar that will lift the country's economy. Now all it needs is governmental will.

CHAD

CAPITAL N'DJAMÉNA **POPULATION** 9.8 MILLION **AREA** 1,284,000 SQ KM **OFFICIAL LANGUAGES** FRENCH, ARABIC

Chad ranks sorrowfully high on a hot-list of places to avoid. In February 2008, rebel forces attacked N'Djaména in another attempt to overthrow the president, prompting a state of emergency in several regions. And this is only the latest in a long, long history of violence and forcible domination. But when things do finally cool down, there's plenty to bring the adventurous, nature-loving traveller to Chad. Perhaps the highlight of the country is the glorious Zakouma National Park which, despite tragic elephant slaughters at the hands of poachers, is one bright point of success in Chad's recent, frequently tragic history.

CHILE & EASTER ISLAND

CAPITAL SANTIAGO **POPULATION** 16.2 MILLION **AREA** 756,950 SQ KM **OFFICIAL LANGUAGE** SPANISH

Long and thin like its fiery namesake, Chile's flaming hot reputation doesn't stop at its shape. It is a country that reminds the traveller of the tremendous and various power of Mother Nature. On New Year's Day 2008, Volcán Llaima in the Conguillo National Park in the south of the country erupted, resulting in plenty of smoke and hundreds of home evacuations. And if boiling, bubbling geysers are your thing, there are plenty to be found – along with more volcanoes – at the incredible El Tatio geyser park. For something decidedly chillier, Chile sports glaciers galore and ski fields, increasingly popular with international visitors, at El Colorado. Alternatively, prepare for a cool total solar eclipse on 11 July 2010, which will be viewable in the south of the country and on Easter Island.

CHINA

 CAPITAL BEIJING **POPULATION** 1.3 BILLION **AREA** 9,326,410 SQ KM **OFFICIAL LANGUAGE** MANDARIN

Everything is on a grand scale in China: the Great Wall, the Yangzi River, the 2008 Olympics and, of course, controversy. China's position on Tibet has made it a big target for the international media, but travellers remain intrigued by the Middle Kingdom. After the celebrations of 2008, Beijing is a truly international city with more English spoken and modern transport links. Beyond the capital, Shanghai's World Expo 2010 will draw millions to the southern city known for economic success, flamboyant arts and spacey architecture. Another southern star is Sichuan's Chengdu, which is repairing itself after devastating earthquakes in 2008 – a popular spot for spicy cuisine and panda watching.

COLOMBIA

CAPITAL BOGOTÁ **POPULATION** 44.4 MILLION **AREA** 1,138,910 SQ KM **OFFICIAL LANGUAGE** SPANISH

You'll still hear of the long-prevalent kidnappings, muggings and guerrilla wars, but Colombia's rates of violent crime and paramilitary membership continue to drop. With basic vigilance the country remains one of the best 'new' destinations for tourism in South America. In March 2010 one of the world's largest theatre festivals, the biennual Iberoamerican Festival, will once again be hitting Bogotá, while the annual Rock in the Park concert shakes things up in October 2009. To escape city smog take to the trails of the beautiful Rio Claro reserve or hike the stunning cloud forest routes of the Parque Nacional de Los Nevados, watched over by the still-smouldering Nevado del Ruiz volcano.

COMOROS & MAYOTTE

CAPITALS MORONI (C), MAMOUTZOU (M) **POPULATION** 690,950 (C), 201,230 (M) **AREA** 2170 SQ KM (C), 374 SQ KM (M) **OFFICIAL LANGUAGES** ARABIC (C), FRENCH (C & M)

Floating between northern Madagascar and northern Mozambique, this little collection of islands may currently be troubled but it has the allure, in its history, vistas and culture, of a place many times its size. Since 1975 Comoros has sat through almost two dozen coups. The most recent of these was in 2008 when an invasion of Anjouan, one of the three main islands, sent its president Mohammed Bacar fleeing to Mayotte – unlike Comoros, still a French dependency – for safety. When it all calms down, however, travellers can expect to be back to exploring the islands' volcanoes, rainforests, beaches and intriguing little towns, much like Zanzibar only without the milling honeymooners.

CONGO, DEMOCRATIC REPUBLIC OF THE

CAPITAL KINSHASA **POPULATION** 65.8 MILLION **AREA** 2,345,410 SQ KM **OFFICIAL LANGUAGE** FRENCH

The possibility of travel to the Democratic Republic of the Congo (DR Congo; formerly Zaïre) any time soon seems like the stuff of fantasy. This mammoth country, with its suitably mammoth troubles, has a history of bloody violence from which it simply can't seem to shake free, despite a January 2008 peace deal intended to end the civil skirmishes. If the country does ever find itself welcoming back travellers, there's lots it can offer, including no fewer than five Unesco World Heritage–rated parks and reserves, home to vast stocks of wildlife, from okapi to lowland gorillas.

CONGO, REPUBLIC OF THE

 **CAPITAL** BRAZZAVILLE **POPULATION** 3.8 MILLION **AREA** 342,000 SQ KM **OFFICIAL LANGUAGE** FRENCH

Though the security situation should be closely monitored before and during a trip to the Republic of the Congo, there's plenty to draw

adventurous travellers prepared for a visit that might not be easy but is bound to be rewarding. The capital Brazzaville and Pointe Noir are considered fairly secure, though travel elsewhere should be done by air rather than by road or rail. Luckily, the ecomagnet Odzala National Park, which abounds with gorillas, buffalo, elephants and monkeys, is reachable by plane. Check whether it's safe before attempting a trip here – a visit to the park will not only be a photographer's delight, the entrance fee will go towards preserving the park's peaceable populations.

COOK ISLANDS

CAPITAL AVARUA **POPULATION** 21,750 **AREA** 236.7 SQ KM **OFFICIAL LANGUAGE** ENGLISH

Handy flights from New Zealand and Australia mean that you will be more than likely to run into honeymooners from Auckland or a family from Sydney in Rarotonga. The main island's resorts will be booked out for the 2009 Pacific Island Mini Games when around 20 islander nations compete and rub noses. Explore the further-flung islands with a dip in the caves of Mitiaro, which hold refreshing subterranean pools, or by making your way to Suwarrow, where the famous hermit Tom Neale pitched camp for several years while he penned his book *An Island to Oneself*.

COSTA RICA

CAPITAL SAN JOSÉ **POPULATION** 4.1 MILLION **AREA** 51,100 SQ KM **OFFICIAL LANGUAGE** SPANISH

More than one million tourists end up in Costa Rica every year, ensuring this country is definitely no longer considered an undiscovered emerald. And the number of visitors is steadily on the rise. Ecotourism is very much the happening buzz phrase here, and many travellers opt for stints onboard one of Costa Rica's worthy conservation bandwagons. These include projects ranging from organic farms to jaguars, turtles and quetzals (did you even know that quetzals needed conserving?). One of the most romantically named concerns is Bosque Eternos de los Niños (the Children's Eternal Rainforest) where you can take to the stunning rainforest trails, or simply help maintain them. Otherwise, the expanses of the Parque Nacional Los Quetzales, only inaugurated in 2005, is a stunningly good bet for escaping those trying equally hard to escape the escapees.

CÔTE D'IVOIRE

CAPITAL YAMOUSSOUKRO **POPULATION** 18.37 MILLION **AREA** 318,000 SQ KM **OFFICIAL LANGUAGE** FRENCH

Once a French protectorate (so its name is rarely translated to the Ivory Coast), this West African nation is emerging from a troubled past to become one of Africa's jewels. Tai National Park was geared towards ecotourism long before the concept became fashionable. The park has lodges which use solar power and also practises responsible waste management. The Grand Bassam beachfront has a faded colonial glory that is a magnet for visitors keen to explore the old town, or who are looking to simply chill on the sand. In stark contrast, toxic waste spilled in Abidjan has marred the former capital, so it is falling off visitors' itineraries despite being the commercial and banking centre of the country.

CROATIA

CAPITAL ZAGREB **POPULATION** 4.5 MILLION **AREA** 56,542 SQ KM **OFFICIAL LANGUAGE** CROATIAN

Picture this. Salty fishing villages, sparkly seas, a riddle of lakes and waterfalls – Croatia is selling itself well. Proclaimed the rising star of tourism, big things are predicted in the next five years. Hit Dubrovnik in summer and it seems that its time is now: with the Homeland War a distant memory, its well-restored streets heave with travellers. Head inland and you'll leave behind most of the tourists. Far eastern Slavonia and Baranja are the places for off-beaters – for traditional spa soaking and the swampy bird haven of Kopacki Rit – while the griffon vulture project on the island of Cres is leading the way in Croatian conservation.

CUBA

CAPITAL HAVANA **POPULATION** 11.4 MILLION **AREA** 110,860 SQ KM **OFFICIAL LANGUAGE** SPANISH

The world's most controversial octogenarian may be floundering (care of Cuba having officially passed to Castro's 76-year-old spring chicken of a brother, Raul, in February 2008), but Cuba's tourist industry is not. Two million visitors make it here annually. In early 2008, Cuban citizens were finally granted permission to stay at their own hotels and resorts. Given these restrictions were imposed at the fall of the Soviet Union, a new generation of Cubans can now sip a mojito at the Hotel Nacional or sun themselves by the pool at the Capri for the very first time. Maybe it won't be too long before their American neighbours join them at the bar.

CYPRUS

CAPITAL NICOSIA/LEFKOSA **POPULATION** 788,457 **AREA** 9,250 SQ KM (OF WHICH 3355 SQ KM ARE IN NORTH CYPRUS) **OFFICIAL LANGUAGES** GREEK, TURKISH

Something's afoot in Cyprus. Acrimoniously severed into Greek and Turkish chunks, there have been reunification rumblings in the wall-divided capital (though sceptics argue it's just bluster). Meanwhile, tourism development continues apace, particularly in the villa-infested Greek south – though the northern Turks are catching on. But the wilds are still wild. In the south, take to the Troodos Mountains, where a long-distance walking trail is currently being waymarked. In the north, the Karpas Peninsula beckons – virtually resort-free, its beaches (seasonal home to hatching turtles) are some of the Med's best, and the island's first ecovillage – Buyukkonuk – is the place to make squeaky haloumi, like a true Cypriot.

CZECH REPUBLIC

CAPITAL PRAGUE **POPULATION** 10.2 MILLION **AREA** 78,866 SQ KM **OFFICIAL LANGUAGE** CZECH

Prague, Prague, Prague – the Czech Republic's tourism industry still relies

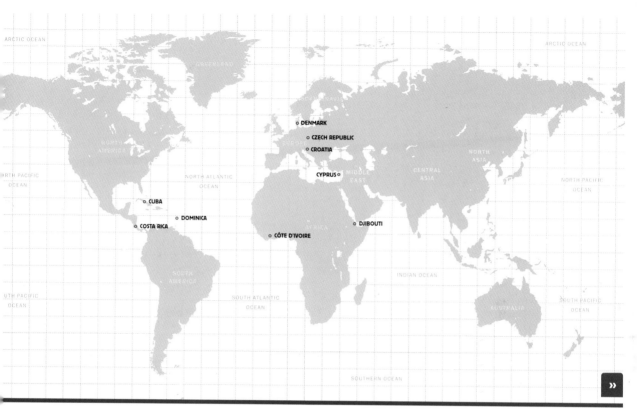

heavily on the medieval city, beloved of sightseers and stag parties, and 60% of all visitors to the country focus on the capital. But there's much more. Hitting the travel radar following a silver screen debut in Disney's *Narnia* films, the Bohemian Switzerland National Park, designated in 2000, is home to Europe's biggest sandstone canyon and a web of walking trails. Don't dismiss Prague though – May 2008 saw its inaugural Czech Beer Festival, heavy on folk dancing and fine local brews. Could this be the Oktoberfest of the future?

DENMARK

CAPITAL COPENHAGEN **POPULATION** 5.5 MILLION **AREA** 43,094 SQ KM **OFFICIAL LANGUAGE** DANISH

Low-lying, liberal Denmark has always boasted better ecocredentials than most, not least for its 10,000km of cycle routes (and look out for more pedal-friendly paths being created in Copenhagen). But the country is making an even bigger grasp for the green dollar: 2008 saw the designation of Jutland's Thy – a coastal haven of dunes, lakes and migrating birds –

as a national park. Four more new protected areas are set to open by the end of 2009. The pink dollar is being courted, too, with the capital staging the second World Outgames next July, a 38-sport Olympic alternative open to competitors of all skill levels and sexual persuasions.

DJIBOUTI

CAPITAL DJIBOUTI CITY **POPULATION** 496,374 **AREA** 23,000 SQ KM **OFFICIAL LANGUAGES** ARABIC, FRENCH

Little Djibouti, a lesser-known East African coastal country tucked between Eritrea, Ethiopia and Somalia, doesn't see too many tourists. Most who make it here either come for a rest after a gruelling trip through Eritrea or Ethiopia (Djibouti boasts both a world-class Sheraton and a Kempinski to splash out on), or to journey to Lac Assal, the lowest point in Africa. The other drawcard is Lac Abbé, a weirdly desolate area covered in bizarre steam-emitting limestone chimneys, where the only dashes of colour are flocks of flamingos and the robes of the local Bedouins. Though travel in Djibouti

doesn't come cheap, you'll currently have the place, in all its strange and barren glory, largely to yourself.

DOMINICA

CAPITAL ROSEAU **POPULATION** 72,386 **AREA** 754 SQ KM **OFFICIAL LANGUAGE** ENGLISH

Heading to Boiling Lake via the Valley of Desolation might sound like the stuff of Conan Doyle, but Dominica's rugged natural charms do have that *Boys' Own*–adventure air. It's a far cry from the lazy beaches of its Caribbean island neighbours. Still largely the preserve of intrepid tourists seeking nature-filled exhilaration, Dominica sees a mere 70,000 or so tourists a year, which has helped preserve its green and glistening state. For a taste of what to expect (though sadly minus Johnny Depp) watch *Pirates of the Caribbean* which was filmed here and, while in residence in Roseau, don't miss a game of cricket (the island's obsession) at Dominica's spanking new 8000-seat Windsor Stadium. Visit soon, while the island's airports are still too small to take commercial-sized airliners.

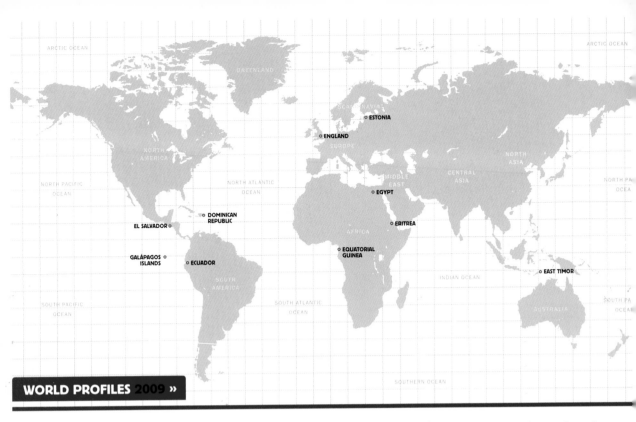

Map labels: ARCTIC OCEAN, GREENLAND, ESTONIA, ENGLAND, EUROPE, NORTH AMERICA, NORTH ASIA, ARCTIC OCEAN, NORTH PACIFIC OCEAN, NORTH ATLANTIC OCEAN, CENTRAL ASIA, NORTH PA OCEA, MIDDLE EAST, EGYPT, DOMINICAN REPUBLIC, EL SALVADOR, ERITREA, AFRICA, EQUATORIAL GUINEA, GALÁPAGOS ISLANDS, ECUADOR, SOUTH AMERICA, INDIAN OCEAN, EAST TIMOR, SOUTH PACIFIC OCEAN, SOUTH ATLANTIC OCEAN, AUSTRALIA, SOUTH PA OCEA, SOUTHERN OCEAN

WORLD PROFILES 2009 »

DOMINICAN REPUBLIC

CAPITAL SANTO DOMINGO **POPULATION** 9.2 MILLION **AREA** 48,730 SQ KM **OFFICIAL LANGUAGE** SPANISH

One of the Caribbean's most visited destinations, the Dominican Republic is an all-singing, all-dancing tourist magnet with beautiful beaches and fully inclusive resorts galore. The republic comprises two-thirds of the large island of Hispaniola; the other third is taken up by Haiti, with whom the Republic keeps cordial, though not especially friendly, relations. Despite fantastic natural resources, diving, whale-watching and beachside lounging, friendly locals and a phenomenal annual tourism growth rate doing wonders for the economy, the nation does have its its darker side. In 2006, Bajos de Haina, located just 19km from the capital, was named one of the world's 10 most polluted places (dubbed the 'Dominican Chernobyl'), due to severe lead poisoning, which has affected almost all of the town's population. This is a problem that this Caribbean gem has yet to completely fix.

EAST TIMOR

CAPITAL DILI **POPULATION** 1.08 MILLION **AREA** 15,007 SQ KM **OFFICIAL LANGUAGES** TETUM, PORTUGUESE

Southeast Asia's youngest nation holds such promise, with its Portuguese colonial heritage, lush mountain interiors and beaches. The journey to democracy, however, is far from smooth: a presidential assassination attempt in 2008 saw UN peacekeepers extend their role early into 2009. Its proximity to Australia should make it accessible, but flights are still limited. Most visitors don't get much further than Dili, but a visit to the fishing village of Com, or a paddle to Atauro to stay in an eco-lodge make excellent trips. Avoid the wet-season extremes (December to March) when Dili swims in downpours.

ECUADOR & THE GALÁPAGOS ISLANDS

CAPITAL QUITO **POPULATION** 13.8 MILLION **AREA** 283,560 SQ KM **OFFICIAL LANGUAGE** SPANISH

Though diminutive for an Andean nation, the biodiversity of Ecuador (with 6000 types of butterfly and 15% of the world's entire species of birds represented) is astonishing. Add active volcanoes, stunning beaches, land-lost-in-time cloud forests and the World Heritage–listed Galápagos Islands, and you've got a place well worth visiting...and preserving. Tragically, the delicate Galápagos ecosystem is being rapidly damaged by a number of human factors, including tourism. Several organisations, including the Galápagos Conservancy, are working to reverse the flow. Visitors are encouraged to make their environmental impact a positive one, with the islands' current US$100 entrance fee being put to use for this very purpose.

EGYPT

CAPITAL CAIRO **POPULATION** 81.7 MILLION **AREA** 1,001,450 SQ KM **OFFICIAL LANGUAGE** ARABIC

As popular with visitors now as it was two millennia ago, Egypt remains a perennial favourite on travellers' lists, despite intermittent security threats and attacks that have sometimes targeted tourists. Ecotourism is increasingly gaining ground here: journey to the western oases for responsible dune adventures around and about the Great Sand Sea, basing yourself at one of several eco-lodges in beehive-like Siwa (nowadays very much on the backpacker trail) or at one of the smaller, lesser-known oases that pepper the vast Saharan sands. Nile cruises, meanwhile, have recently taken a step up with the inauguration of the luxury cruiser *Oberoi Zahra*, with its fully equipped spa and lavishness that not even a Pharaoh could have dreamed up.

EL SALVADOR

 **CAPITAL** SAN SALVADOR **POPULATION** 6.9 MILLION **AREA** 21,040 SQ KM **OFFICIAL LANGUAGE** SPANISH

El Salvador is fast emerging as one of the planet's hottest surf spots. Though wide-scale tourism remains very much in its infancy, canny travellers are hitting the waves at La Libertad, El Este and elsewhere with aplomb. Now is without doubt the time to go before others hone in on its manifold charms, which include volcanoes, national parks and gorgeous, near-deserted islands. Ecotourism, too, is beginning to take hold, with spots such as Chaguantique (a protected tropical forest) and Bosque El Imposible (a beautiful and barely visited national park) perfect for observing wildlife without another visitor about for miles.

ENGLAND

CAPITAL LONDON **POPULATION** 50.8 MILLION **AREA** 130,281 SQ KM **OFFICIAL LANGUAGE** ENGLISH

They do like to be beside the seaside in England, despite the weather. And no more so than in 2009, when once-fashionable but now-faded resorts (Blackpool, Dover, Torbay) are receiving regeneration grants, and perennially popular spots such as Brighton are getting even trendier, with burgeoning festivals and boutique hotels. Campaigners are attempting to secure public access to every inch of the English coastline, which will eventually enable one of the planet's best long-distance rambles. Of course, you can't ignore the impending London 2012 Olympics, which will do more for deprived areas of the capital than the 2008 Capital of Culture crown has done for regenerating newly spruced-up Liverpool.

EQUATORIAL GUINEA

CAPITAL MALABO **POPULATION** 551,201 **AREA** 28,051 SQ KM **OFFICIAL LANGUAGES** SPANISH, FRENCH

Not many travellers get as far as Equatorial Guinea, though the country's new-found abundance of oil on offshore Bioko Island does bring plenty of expatriates looking to grow rich on the pickings. Despite its name, no part of Equatorial Guinea actually lies on the equator, though the mainland portion of the country can get pretty hot and steamy, especially in the lush and gorgeously rainforested Monte Alen National Park. Head here if you're keen to see chimpanzees, gorillas and an abundance of other fauna in pristine conditions. Far off, in 2012, the country will be co-hosting the Africa Cup, of Nations which will doubtless bring the country to the world's attention and a few more tourists, finally, to its shores.

ERITREA

CAPITAL ASMARA **POPULATION** 4.9 MILLION **AREA** 121,320 SQ KM **OFFICIAL LANGUAGE** TIGRINYA

Though it's a decidedly difficult country to travel in at present – with government permits required for all travel outside Asmara, and landmines peppering border regions – those intrepid enough to give it a whirl will find a number of interesting and all-but-abandoned sights. Probably the greatest draw is the Dankalia region, which has recently gained some publicity in the international press as one of the world's most inhospitable places. Travel here is bleak, hot and tiring and, with the least to see of any travel destination, there is no particular reason to do it but for travel's sake alone. Still, if journeying through great empty spaces soothes and empties the mind, this is without question the place to clear out the cobwebs.

ESTONIA

CAPITAL TALLINN **POPULATION** 1.3 MILLION **AREA** 45,226 SQ KM **OFFICIAL LANGUAGE** ESTONIAN

Post-independence, Estonia got a run on its Baltic neighbours thanks to thirsty Finns nipping over for Tallinn's bargain booze and funding a fledgling tourism industry. Consequently, the medieval capital has always been the star of the show (even if the booze has become more expensive). But things are changing. Travellers now venture out to the spas at Haapsalu (bathing is a serious business around the Baltic), to the historic university town of Tartu and to the wild islands of Saarema and Muhu. Eyes will return to Tallinn in July, however: the All-Estonian Song Festival, which explodes with traditional folk tunes every five years, is scheduled for 2009.

feel right at home. Blazing fires, morning teas and sheepdog trials can be followed by a pub lunch and spot of horse racing in tiny, colourful Stanley on Boxing Day. Though a trip here doesn't tick any of your usual South American travel boxes, about 30,000 visitors (mostly cruise-shippers) descend each year. There are certainly plenty of natural wonders to observe, particularly if you're fond of noisy elephant seals, sleek orcas or penguins, after which the weekly Falklands newspaper is named, and of which there are many more than there are human residents.

FEDERATED STATES OF MICRONESIA

CAPITAL PALIKIR **POPULATION** 107,665 **AREA** 702 SQ KM **OFFICIAL LANGUAGE** ENGLISH

There's plenty of action above and below the water in FSM. The justly famous underwater museum of Chuuk Lagoon has enough WWII wrecks to allow for several days of diving and that's even before you explore the atolls surrounding Yap. On Yap, observe the monumental traditional stone money that's large enough to break any bank, or the pair of well-preserved Japanese Zero aircraft. FSM's must-see ruin is Pohnpei's Non Mandol, a series of connected artificial islands strewn with ruins that date back to AD 1500. The relatively youthful 14th-century ruins on Lelu Island offer archaeological exploration with massive burial grounds and hexagonal basalt walls shrouded by thick rainforest.

FIJI

CAPITAL SUVA **POPULATION** 918,675 **AREA** 8,270 SQ KM **OFFICIAL LANGUAGES** ENGLISH, FIJIAN

When it comes to Fiji, memory seems to be short. As soon as the 2006 coup (the fourth since 1987) installed Commodore Frank Bainimarama as the country's leader, the country launched new tourism campaigns targeting 'flashpackers', to promote its new low-cost resorts.

With elections set for 2009 there could be hiccups, though politics hasn't stopped Australians and New Zealanders hopping over to Fiji for mini-breaks or honeymoons. Despite stunning beaches and world-class snorkelling, the highlights are cultural: drinking kava with village elders or watching a *meke* (dance). Perhaps it's because they know how important tourism is to the island nation, but Fijian friendliness survives any political upheaval.

FINLAND

CAPITAL HELSINKI **POPULATION** 5.2 MILLION **AREA** 338,145 SQ KM **OFFICIAL LANGUAGE** FINNISH

Happy 200th birthday Finland! 2009 marks the bicentenary of the country becoming an autonomous region, and celebrations are planned. But it's the land rather than the history that's the real draw. The number of visitors to sparkling, sleigh-crossed Lapland alone has tripled in less than a decade – motivating the creation in 2008 of an Elf Academy (syllabus: storytelling, cookie making) to speedily train up extra helpers for famous resident Santa. Lesser known (but no less magical) wilderness abounds for non-believers: hit the 20,000 islands of the Turku archipelago, or the Hiidenportti National Park, a wonderland of ancient forests stalked by bears and wolves.

FRANCE

CAPITAL PARIS **POPULATION** 60.9 MILLION **AREA** 547,030 SQ KM **OFFICIAL LANGUAGE** FRENCH

As the world embraces slow travel, France – typically contrary – gets faster. High-speed rail links snaked across the country in 2007 and 2008, opening up new routes from perpetual fave Paris. The Champagne houses of Reims are now only 45 minutes from the capital, the winstubs and fondues of pretty-pink Strasbourg just two hours (down from four). By 2011 Lyon will join the network, sadly too late to be useful for 2009's World Ski Championships in February in nearish Val d'Isère. One place where slow is guaranteed is Corsica: France's

WORLD PROFILES 2009 »

ETHIOPIA

CAPITAL ADDIS ABABA **POPULATION** 76.5 MILLION **AREA** 1,127,127 SQ KM **OFFICIAL LANGUAGE** AMHARIC

It seems that Ethiopia's finally shaken off its beleaguered image of the '80s and '90s, and is reinventing itself as one of Africa's best new traveller destinations. Charity bike rides are a big thing, as is a growing ecotourism options, with some impressive eco-lodges on offer in the Rift Valley. It suffered a setback in 2005 due to election-related riots and tensions with neighbouring Eritrea (tensions that should be monitored while on a visit here), but it's back on the itinerary for 2009 and 2010 for those keen to trek its wastelands, experience its hospitality, and go looking for the Ark of the Covenant at unassuming Aksum.

FALKLAND ISLANDS (ISLAS MALVINAS)

CAPITAL STANLEY **POPULATION** 3105 **AREA** 12,173 SQ KM **OFFICIAL LANGUAGE** ENGLISH

If you're a Brit happening upon the Falklands at Christmas, you'll likely

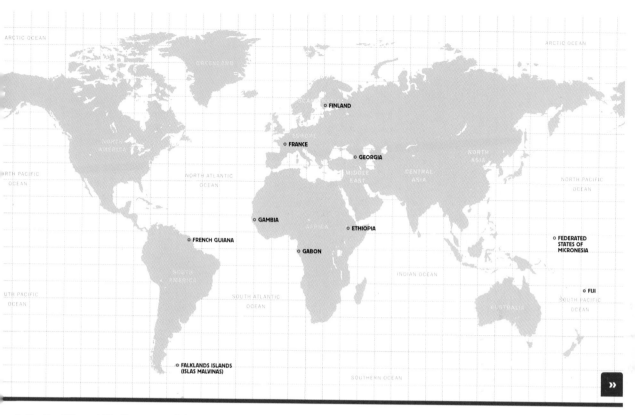

distinctly different Mediterranean isle is a mountain-ruptured land of evil-eye curses, megalithic stones and the continent's best treks.

FRENCH GUIANA

CAPITAL CAYENNE **POPULATION** 199,510 **AREA** 91,000 SQ KM **OFFICIAL LANGUAGE** FRENCH

It's likely that most people couldn't pinpoint French Guiana – not to be confused with Guyana to its north – on a map. This small and distinctly Francophone nation, tucked between Suriname and Brazil, is a curiosity in the region: it belongs to the EU and you can settle your bill in euros. With a beautiful, rugged coastline, and ecotourism to its lush rainforested interior in its infancy, it's a challenging though highly rewarding destination to trek and travel across. If exploration slightly further afield is your thing, head to the Centre Spacial Guyanais, from which around two-thirds of the world's satellites have set out for the final frontier. Check its website (www.cnes.fr) to see if something might be hurtling skyward while you're in town.

GABON

CAPITAL LIBREVILLE **POPULATION** 1.5 MILLION **AREA** 257,667 SQ KM **OFFICIAL LANGUAGE** FRENCH

A tiny population, considering the country's geographical size, and a high GDP due to rich oil and mineral reserves have helped keep Gabon in sterling condition for the moderate numbers of travellers who have made it here so far. Perhaps the main reason that it's not more frequently visited is that it's simply quite hard to get to, with few European carriers (except Air France) jetting down to remarkably cosmopolitan Libreville. This, however, makes it all the more worth the effort. Lie low on dreamy Mayumba beaches, hike the Cirque de Léconi canyon, and enjoy the feeling of being just one of the few to savour this stunning African secret.

GAMBIA

CAPITAL BANJUL **POPULATION** 1.7 MILLION **AREA** 11,300 SQ KM **OFFICIAL LANGUAGE** ENGLISH

The winter-sun destination for frost-weary Europeans in search of some-

thing a little bit exotic, tiny Gambia is firmly on the charter plane flight-path. But there's still something left to see outside the plush resorts and five-star hotels, which seem to make an almost unbroken line along Gambia's 80km of Atlantic coast. Head inland and you'll find a good few eco-lodges and a number of small but diverse national parks such as the exceedingly well-run Abuko Nature Reserve. If you're here during the summer, don't miss 2009's 10th International Roots Festival, a celebration of the country's culture and heritage, held between June and July.

GEORGIA

CAPITAL TBILISI **POPULATION** 4.6 MILLION **AREA** 69,700 SQ KM **OFFICIAL LANGUAGE** GEORGIAN

Stability issues prevent this nation, once part of the former USSR, assuming its rightful place as a travel great. With bandit-controlled hinterlands and almost nightly power cuts, Georgia doesn't have the infrastructure for large-scale tourism. But it's getting better – funds have been earmarked for restoration

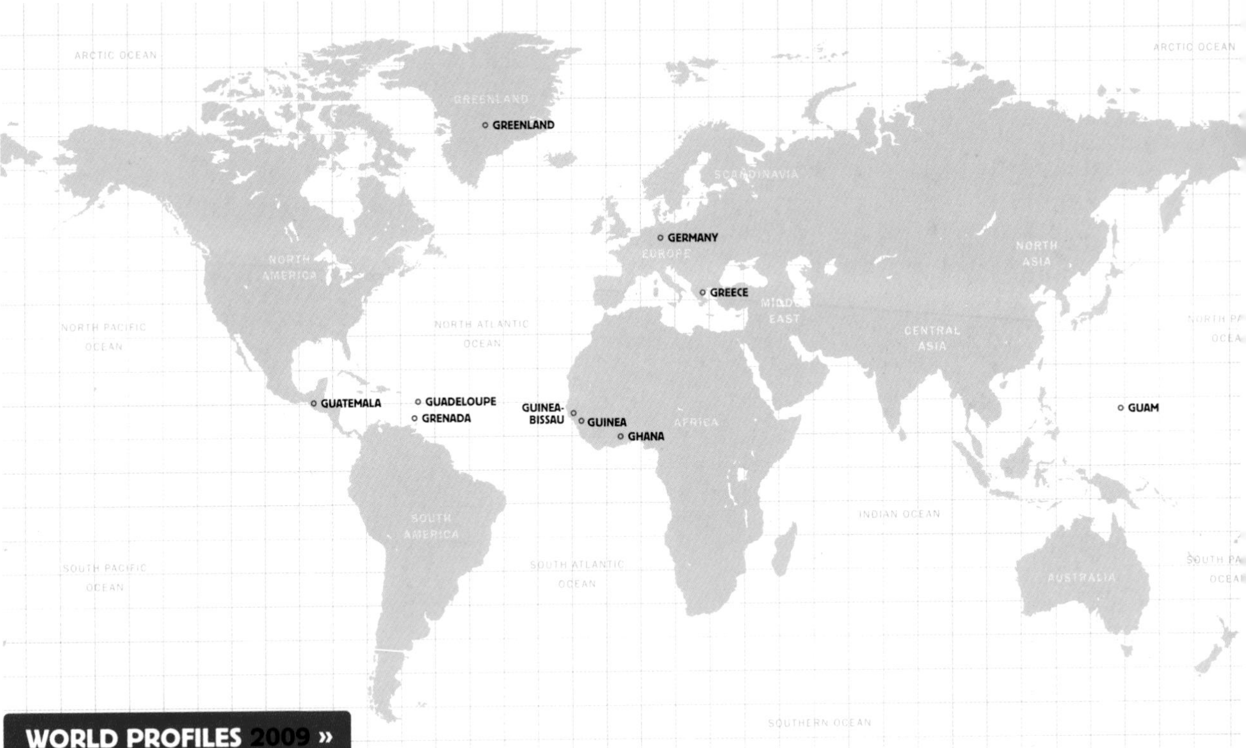
ARCTIC OCEAN
ARCTIC OCEAN
GREENLAND
GREENLAND
SCANDINAVIA
GERMANY
EUROPE
NORTH AMERICA
GREECE
MIDDLE EAST
NORTH ASIA
CENTRAL ASIA
NORTH PACIFIC OCEAN
NORTH ATLANTIC OCEAN
GUATEMALA
GUADELOUPE
GRENADA
GUINEA-BISSAU
GUINEA
GHANA
AFRICA
GUAM
INDIAN OCEAN
SOUTH AMERICA
SOUTH PACIFIC OCEAN
SOUTH ATLANTIC OCEAN
AUSTRALIA
SOUTHERN OCEAN

WORLD PROFILES 2009 »

projects and visa requirements for many nationalities have been waived. Five-star hotels are cropping up in capital Tbilisi, a city with a reputation for song, dance and a never-ending flow of *ghvino* (wine). Flights aren't cheap but increasing inclusion on Central Asian overland itineraries will help travellers reach areas such as the snow-crested High Caucasus and ancient capital Mtskheta, which for now remain woefully under visited.

GERMANY

CAPITAL BERLIN **POPULATION** 82.4 MILLION **AREA** 357,021 SQ KM **OFFICIAL LANGUAGE** GERMAN

November 2009 marks 20 years since the fall of the Berlin Wall, and the now effortlessly cool capital (many of its coolest bits are in the former East) will celebrate the occasion in style. The city's Brandenburg Gate will also feature in the 2009 Athletics World Championships, held from 15 to 23 August – the marathon finishes beneath its iconic columns. It is not all about elite athletes though – activities adventures are on the up and up in Germany, which boasts a world-class network of walking and cycling trails. Some are well trodden, but head to the North Sea and Baltic coasts to get away from the crowds, or to western Pomerania's Mecklenburgische Seenplatte, an absolute delight of sleepy villages and more than 1000 lakes.

GHANA

CAPITAL ACCRA **POPULATION** 22.9 MILLION **AREA** 239,460 SQ KM **OFFICIAL LANGUAGE** ENGLISH

The numerous expats who live in fun-loving Accra can't be prevented from raving about its friendly people, beautiful beaches, reggae beat and numerous other charms. With the opening of the long-awaited and heavily invested-in five star Mövenpick Ambassador Hotel in late 2008, plans are afoot to rival Gambia for the West African tourist dollar. Tourists aren't pouring in yet though, making it an alluring destination for the independent traveller. For fun in the woodland canopy, head to Kakum National Park, which boasts a 30m-high walkway suspended between the trees, for aerial wildlife viewing.

GREECE

CAPITAL ATHENS **POPULATION** 10.7 MILLION **AREA** 131,940 SQ KM **OFFICIAL LANGUAGE** GREEK

Put some effort into your Greek Islands trip and you'll reap rewards. Try Ikaria and Ithaki: both require longish boat trips but compensate with gorgeous walks and a locals-only feel. 2009 is all about the mainland, often neglected but home to 90% of historic sites. In the north, money's improving roads and converting farmhouses into boutique hotels, while in the fairytale villages of the Pindos Mountains you won't find anything so fancy – and so much the better. Athens' New Acropolis Museum opened in 2008, with a room specially constructed for the Elgin Marbles – an unsubtle hint to the British Museum, where the Parthenon friezes currently (and controversially) reside.

GREENLAND

CAPITAL NUUK **POPULATION** 56,344 **AREA** 2,166,086 SQ KM **OFFICIAL LANGUAGES** GREENLANDIC (EAST INUIT), DANISH

Who'd have thought global warming would create a tourist attraction?

Visitor numbers to this vast Arctic island are on the up, as many are eager to witness the front line of climate change – drastically receding glaciers and endangered whales and polar bears. Still, 'on the up' equates to only 50,000 people a year – fewer than the numbers visiting a single London Tube station daily – so Greenland remains very much undiscovered. Cruising has become more popular, the advantage being that it doesn't require onshore hotels or infrastructure and so leaves the environment relatively unblemished. And what an environment, from the spectacular east coast (try hiking around Tasiilaq) to the glaciers near Maniitsoq and Sisimiut, perfect for summer skiing.

GRENADA

 **CAPITAL** ST GEORGE'S **POPULATION** 89,971 **AREA** 344 SQ KM **OFFICIAL LANGUAGE** ENGLISH

Just like buses, there are no hurricanes for ages and then two come along at once. This is how it was with the storms in 2004 and 2005 that battered beautiful little Grenada. Now, though, the Spice Isle famed for its cloves, cocoa and nutmeg has bounced back. St George's is once again the most picturesque Caribbean capital and the place is gearing itself up for ecotourism by promoting its many national parks and natural wonders. And, of course, its stunning beaches. Catch a cricket game at the capital's new and impressive 17,000-seater stadium or head to town for the annual Carriacou Regatta, an impressive sailing race and swinging accompanying festival, in July and August.

GUADELOUPE

 **CAPITAL** BASSE-TERRE **POPULATION** 408,000 **AREA** 1628 SQ KM **OFFICIAL LANGUAGE** FRENCH

You may now be able to enter with your EU passport and pay your way in euros, but the atmosphere in this small and mountainous archipelago of five islands, a French colony for the last four centuries, is still decidedly Creole. Guadeloupe sees the majority of its tourists arrive on cruise ships, but with a little effort independent travellers can easily escape the day-trippers and experience isolated jungle waterfalls, black-sand beaches, and pristine tropical diving waters at the Réserve Cousteau – all washed down by a plethora of sturdy local rums and a big slice of the laid-back good life.

GUAM

 **CAPITAL** AGANA **POPULATION** 175,877 **AREA** 549 SQ KM **OFFICIAL LANGUAGE** ENGLISH

Operating as an air hub for the Pacific Islands, Guam is always busy. Ironically it's a destination that could never be mistaken for a 'Pacific paradise'. Many visitors are drawn to the duty-free shopping, which has earned the island the tag of 'America in Asia' with visiting northeast-Asian bargain hunters. Other visitors are more of a captive audience, doing their duty serving as part of a major US military presence which pre-dates WWII and acted as a crucial strategic link in that conflict. With the US beginning a major transfer of marines in from Okinawa in 2010, Guam's future will definitely feature more khaki.

GUATEMALA

CAPITAL GUATEMALA CITY **POPULATION** 12.7 MILLION **AREA** 108,890 SQ KM **OFFICIAL LANGUAGE** SPANISH

Though Guatemala is ripe for the ecopicking, with a wealth of volcanoes, isolated Mayan remains and tracts of stunning cloud-forest, the country is currently experiencing a rising violent crime rate. Many of the attacks have been aimed against travellers and tourists which is discouraging visitors from discovering the country's tremendous and endearing charms. With basic safety precautions, including avoiding night-time and solo travel, visiting Guatemala can still be an extremely rewarding experience. Head here for the colourful countrywide Semana Santa celebrations with feasts and processions in abundance the week before Easter, but leave your expensive digital camera or nice new Breitling watch safely behind at home.

GUINEA

CAPITAL CONAKRY **POPULATION** 9.9 MILLION **AREA** 245,857 SQ KM **OFFICIAL LANGUAGE** FRENCH

A few social and political hiccups have brought the threat of instability to what's long been considered a dependably steady country in a restive region. Travellers heading to Guinea should monitor the situation carefully but not call off plans to visit. Like many of its neighbours, tourism isn't yet a major concern for this country. Its principal hope is that a major oil discovery in the next few years will skyrocket its economy. Until the black stuff emerges, Guinea remains a laid-back destination, roughly the size of the UK, where you can trek through wilderness, climb Mt Nimba's peak or soothe yourself on Cape Verga's mellow sands.

GUINEA-BISSAU

CAPITAL BISSAU **POPULATION** 1.5 MILLION **AREA** 36,120 SQ KM **OFFICIAL LANGUAGE** PORTUGUESE

Despite fighting along its borders with Senegal, which has left this part

with laudable programmes for involving and aiding local indigenous Amerindian populations. Guyana is currently angling for recognition in the form of a Unesco World Heritage rating, and it certainly won't be long before the crowds start to arrive – despite the current poor infrastructure and relatively high levels of crime in its capital and in coastal New Amsterdam. Be vigilant, but don't let this discourage your own personal voyage of discovery.

HAITI

 **CAPITAL** PORT-AU-PRINCE **POPULATION** 8.7 MILLION **AREA** 27,750 SQ KM **OFFICIAL LANGUAGES** FRENCH, CREOLE

Visiting poor old Haiti is, at present, a sadly risky business for travellers. Though a UN stabilisation force is in place in this historically war-torn country to try to aid its long-term security, kidnappings of foreigners aren't at all unknown and street gang violence remains rife. Add to this endemic poverty and environmental degradation resulting in just 2% of its original forest cover still remaining, and a far from pretty picture emerges. That said, however, Haiti retains a good few charms, including an incredibly friendly population, a swath of beautiful cloud forest, and a joyful and riotous Easter-time Mardi Gras, when the country's woes are forgotten and partying becomes the only order of the day.

HONDURAS

CAPITAL TEGUCIGALPA **POPULATION** 7.5 MILLION **AREA** 112,090 SQ KM **OFFICIAL LANGUAGE** SPANISH

Like a number of its Central American neighbours, Honduras offers that compelling combination of lush wilderness, exceptional wildlife, poor infrastructure and a violent past, so enticing to the adventurous traveller. Though tourism is steadily increasing, especially around the diver-friendly Caribbean Bay Islands, it's still a great location to trek without seeing another soul, wander around eerily empty ruins, and discover the Mosquito Coast (though it's worth

taking along your insect repellent since it lives up to its name). Perhaps the biggest draw is the immense Reserva de la Biósfero del Rio Plátano, Central America's largest tropical rainforest and a Unesco World Heritage site for almost three decades. Visit in February or March to see a multitude of migrating birds.

HONG KONG

POPULATION 6.9 MILLION **AREA** 1042 SQ KM **OFFICIAL LANGUAGE** CANTONESE

One of the world's great shopping destinations, this former British colony enjoys a 'one country, two systems' form of socialistic government, with China allowing plenty of autonomy, especially when visitors want to spend big bucks. A large expat community makes this an accessible destination for non-Cantonese speakers (though Cantopop may get on your nerves), and many mainland Chinese are exploring Hong Kong's freedom with budget flights from Beijing and Shanghai. The 2009 East Asian Games will bring in even more neighbouring nations as athletes, swimmers and…er, ballroom dancers brave the famously smoggy city in December.

HUNGARY

CAPITAL BUDAPEST **POPULATION** 9.9 MILLION **AREA** 93,030 SQ KM **OFFICIAL LANGUAGE** HUNGARIAN

2009 marks the 20th anniversary of the fall of communism in Hungary, and it shows. Budapest particularly has a youthful, forward-thinking verve, its art nouveau charm boosted almost daily by funky new eateries – come 2010, the dilapidated warehouses of Kozraktar Street will become a trendy hub of bars and restaurants serving goulash-fusion and Tokaj cocktails. Even better, high-speed trains will soon power in, increasing the viability of getting here by rail. Beyond Budapest, historic Pécs takes on the Capital of Culture mantle in 2010, low-cost airlines are opening up the shores of Lake Balaton, and galloping across the great plains of Hortobágy National Park is the must-do experience.

of the country inaccessible to visitors, Guinea-Bissau has begun to stretch its tourism wings since peaceful elections in 2005 brought stability to the country. However, it's not exactly a bastion of tourism, making it ripe for exploration as an emerging 'hot' destination. Though travel isn't smooth and prices are relatively high, there's a lot of natural splendour, and now's the time to see it. Head for lazy Ilha de Bolama or the gorgeous Arquipélago dos Bijagós, a Unesco World Heritage–rated biosphere reserve of sandy beaches, hippos and sea turtles, and succumb to the country's charms.

GUYANA

CAPITAL GEORGETOWN **POPULATION** 769,095 **AREA** 214,970 SQ KM **OFFICIAL LANGUAGE** ENGLISH

With around 80% of the country still thick with forest and a startlingly diverse and exciting ecosystem, Guyana is the new place for ecotourism. An absolutely unmissable highlight of the country is the Iwokrama Rainforest, almost a million acres of virgin rainforest

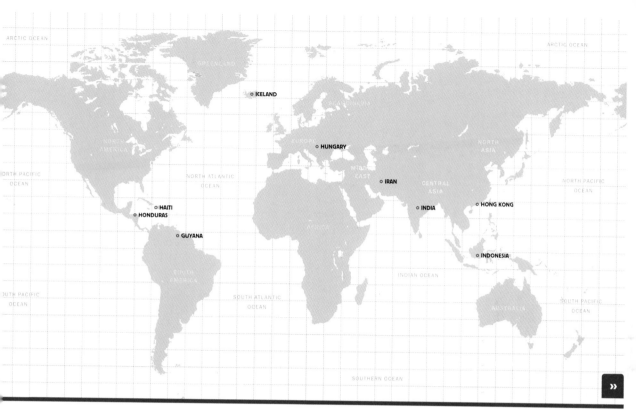

ICELAND

CAPITAL REYKJAVÍK **POPULATION** 301,931 **AREA** 103,000 SQ KM **OFFICIAL LANGUAGE** ICELANDIC

Life's good in Iceland – officially. The UN has decreed it the world's most desirable country in which to live, but visiting is pretty good too. In 2008, glacier-full Vatnajökull National Park became Europe's largest protected area, great for watching geysers spew and icefields shimmer. Conservation is key countrywide: with car hire companies offering hydrogen-fuelled vehicles and businesses powered by geothermal power, tourists can be almost carbon neutral. This is a great excuse to head beyond ice-cool Reykjavík into the remote but dramatic West Fjords and maybe hike around Mjóifjörur in overlooked east Iceland.

INDIA

CAPITAL NEW DELHI **POPULATION** 1148 MILLION **AREA** 2,973,190 SQ KM **OFFICIAL LANGUAGES** 22; ENGLISH FOR NATIONAL, POLITICAL AND COMMERCIAL COMMUNICATION

With the Commonwealth Games scheduled for New Delhi in 2010, plans are afoot to improve the city's facilities and infrastructure ahead of the expected massive influx of visitors. Improvements seem well on the way, with an impressively modern metro system and renovations beginning on existing sporting venues. Meanwhile India remains as popular a destination as ever, with ever-increasing numbers of tourists jetting in to experience its eternal and bountiful charms. In some areas, however, this is putting considerable strain on natural resources, with many of Goa's once pristine beaches, in particular, having fallen prey to the tourism boom. Increasing interest in ecotourism is to some extent balancing this out but, as with all things in India, the effects will take time to be seen.

INDONESIA

CAPITAL JAKARTA **POPULATION** 237.5 MILLION **AREA** 1,919,440 SQ KM **OFFICIAL LANGUAGE** BAHASA INDONESIA

Indonesia looks set to continue as a travellers' favourite in 2009 and beyond. Though fears of terrorism and natural disasters linger, its enormous charms overshadow the unease. With over 18,000 islands to choose from, there's something to fit every visitor's agenda. If Bali's beaches are the place for you, try to time your visit between March 18 and 28, when its spectacular Galungan and Kuningan festivals see the gods descending to earth to join the island-wide revelry. The Maluku 'spice' islands, meanwhile, are currently experiencing an upsurge in tourism following 10 years of civil disturbance, making them a sure hit this year for divers and beachcombers alike. For something rather more gruesome, head to Tana Toraja in Sulawesi, to see its famed, but often bizarre, summertime funeral rituals.

IRAN

CAPITAL TEHRAN **POPULATION** 65.9 MILLION **AREA** 1,648,000 SQ KM **OFFICIAL LANGUAGE** PERSIAN

With all the bad press it's been getting lately and the rampant rumours concerning its budding nuclear programme, it's hardly surprising that Iran isn't topping any current tourism

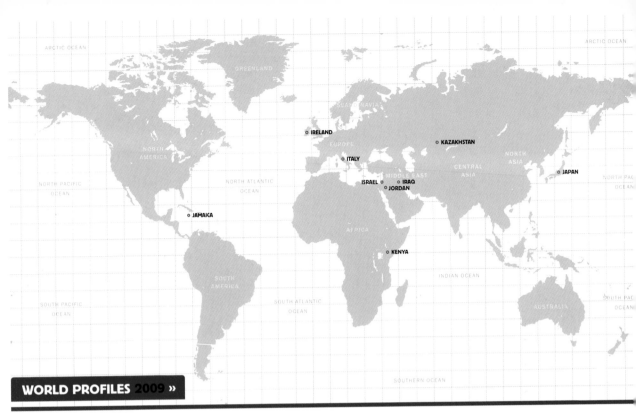

lists. But for those still making their way here – and there are plenty of independent travellers still doing so – the welcome is as warm as ever. You'll find plenty of space to explore its ruins, such as the impressive ziggurat at Choqa Zanbil, or even ski its slopes at Shemshak or Dizin where you'll encounter a surprisingly lively (though alcohol-free) après-ski scene. Try to avoid travel during Ramadan (September in 2009), when almost everything shuts up shop during daylight for a month or so, but do look out for the more ebullient Magnificent Victory of the Islamic Revolution of Iran Day on 11 February.

IRAQ

CAPITAL BAGHDAD **POPULATION** 28.2 MILLION **AREA** 437,072 SQ KM **OFFICIAL LANGUAGES** ARABIC, KURDISH

Unless you're a journalist, NGO-worker or persistent businessperson, chances are you're not planning a trip to Iraq soon. Ongoing strife, including suicide bombings, continues to hamper any chances of the country's post-Saddam recovery. If, by some miracle, 2009 or 2010 do see peace,

intrepid adventurers will find that Iraq still hosts a wealth of fascinating sights, despite some major looting by unscrupulous treasure hunters during the ousting of Saddam. Amongst its thousands of archaeological sites are the alleged birthplace of Abraham and the remains of Babylon: brush up on your Bible stories before you explore the sorrowfully violence-blighted 'cradle of civilisation'.

IRELAND

CAPITALS DUBLIN, BELFAST **POPULATION** 5.9 MILLION (EIRE: 4.1 MILLION; NORTHERN IRELAND (NI): 1.7 MILLION) **AREA** 83,856 SQ KM (EIRE: 70,280 SQ KM; NI: 13,576 SQ KM) **OFFICIAL LANGUAGES** ENGLISH, GAELIC

Raise a pint of Guinness to Ireland in 2009 – the black stuff turns 250 and the craic will be cranked up at the stout's Dublin-based brewery. But can the Emerald Isle escape its clichés? No problem. Eire's west is becoming better known for surf breaks than boozers, and the newly opened North West Trail, a 326km circular cycle that passes through Donegal, Tyrone and Sligo, is great for pedalling off the hangover through tiny villages and past the

crashing Atlantic. Now-peaceful Northern Ireland is seeing the real change – Belfast is buzzing, and wild pockets such as the Mourne Mountains are beckoning with hiking trails and solitude.

ISRAEL

CAPITAL JERUSALEM **POPULATION** 7.1 MILLION **AREA** 20,770 SQ KM **OFFICIAL LANGUAGE** HEBREW

Though best known for its continuing security problems, Israel is increasingly making travellers' long-weekend lists, with the last intifada seeming to finally be behind it. Budget airlines are targeting Tel Aviv as prime territory for all-night partying, shopping and winter rays, and its newly redeveloped port is filled with bars and top-end shops. To escape the city, head north to the Golan Heights – disputed territory with Syria – for wilderness trekking in its numerous national parks. Alternatively, float it out in the Dead Sea while you still can: it's diminishing at an alarming rate and it may not be possible to get that perfect shot of you toes-up and reading *The Times* for very much longer.

ITALY

CAPITAL ROME **POPULATION** 58.1 MILLION **AREA** 301,230 SQ KM **OFFICIAL LANGUAGE** ITALIAN

You'd think it would be difficult to discover anything new in Italy, perennial travel favourite that it is. But the past year has seen some significant historical finds – the House of the Surgeon in Rimini and the Palazzo Valentini Mosaics in Rome, for instance. New regions of the country are peeping from the economically challenged south to tempt visitors away from Tuscany or Venice: the subterranean towns of Basilicata (film set for Mel Gibson's *The Passion of the Christ*) are goodies. Most intriguingly, the latterly closed isle of Montecristo, made famous by Dumas's novel, is allowing 3000 visitors a year onto its mysterious, wildlife-rich shores for the first time in decades.

JAMAICA

CAPITAL KINGSTON **POPULATION** 2.8 MILLION **AREA** 10,991 SQ KM **OFFICIAL LANGUAGE** ENGLISH

For the last 70 years or so Jamaica has been firmly on the tourist agenda, drawing package-holiday crowds, honeymooners and independent travellers in equal measure. Nothing, not even the constant crime in Kingston Town, seems to keep them away. With new resorts springing up all the time, it's increasingly hard to find space to yourself on the island, though the Blue Mountains are still a serene alternative to chaotic beach life. Keep your eyes peeled in 2009 for news on the improbable Jamaican dog-sled team, which is set to compete in Canada's winter 1000-mile Yukon Quest, the most gruelling contest of its kind in the world and a definite canine *Cool Runnings* in the making.

JAPAN

CAPITAL TOKYO **POPULATION** 127.4 MILLION **AREA** 374,744 SQ KM **OFFICIAL LANGUAGE** JAPANESE

Japan has cornered the market on kooky, from anime to Zen, but many travellers put off visiting because they perceive it as being too pricey. True, you'll pay plenty for a plush room in Tokyo or ringside seats at a sumo bout, but the undervaluing of the yen means there are bargains to be had off the beaten track by hopping a budget flight to Osaka, staying in Kyoto's traditional machiya houses or hiking the alps of Hokkaido. Recent changes to Japan's immigration system that include the fingerprinting and photographing of all foreigners have had an impact on visitor numbers.

JORDAN

CAPITAL AMMAN **POPULATION** 6.2 MILLION **AREA** 92,300 SQ KM **OFFICIAL LANGUAGE** ARABIC

Even with neighbours like Israel and Iraq, Jordan has enjoyed a relatively stable lifestyle under King Abdullah II (r 1999–), which has made it an attractive pocket of the Middle East for travellers. Bombings in Amman in 2005 saw the king call for a 'war on extremism' to keep his country peaceful. Most visitors head for Petra, the magnificent ancient city rendered in rose-coloured stone, though even without leaving Amman you can see a Roman theatre and fragments of the Dead Sea Scrolls. Pilgrimages are still made to the river Jordan where John the Baptist performed the holy rites on Jesus, though pollution of the waterway has stopped this practice.

KAZAKHSTAN

CAPITAL ASTANA **POPULATION** 15.3 MILLION **AREA** 2,717,300 SQ KM **OFFICIAL LANGUAGES** KAZAKH, RUSSIAN

Until Borat's recent arrival on the big screen not many people knew where Kazakhstan was, let alone contemplated going there. But though the country itself was unhappy with its portrayal, it's undoubtedly worked wonders for its visibility, and visitor numbers are growing rapidly. Bleak and oil-filled, Kazakhstan's tourism offerings might be fairly few and far between, but for those with a penchant for desolate open spaces, they're enchanting. Climb soaring Mt Talgar in the Almatinsky nature reserve or spend 77 hours train-bound from Moscow across the

empty steppe. Vegetarians who shun plov rice and manty dumplings might relish a quick trip to Govinda's in Almaty for what must count as one of the world's most unusual locations for a Hare Krishna feed-up.

KENYA

CAPITAL NAIROBI **POPULATION** 38 MILLION **AREA** 569,250 SQ KM **OFFICIAL LANGUAGES** ENGLISH, KISWAHILI

While Kenya may not be the poster child of progressive Africa it once used to be before the civil unrest that surrounded the 2007 elections, it remains one of the continent's most impressive natural wonderlands. Even as the world's media tagged the country with labels like 'unrest' and 'civil conflict', the Swahili word 'safari' remained a powerful reason for visiting this nation. Kenya's array of national parks offers grand spectacles like the mass migration of wildebeests in the Masai Mara and the dramatic peaks of Mt Kenya. And then there are the charms of Swahili cities and stretches of beach that continue to attract tourists despite the troubles.

you book yourself on an expensive organised tour, since independent tourism is absolutely not allowed. If you are lucky enough to make it to this strange and reclusive country – usually only heard about when its leader, Kim Jong-Il, has said something odd or provocative – time your tour for the opening days of the Arirang Festival, held in 2009 from April 15 onwards to commemorate the death of the late Communist leader Kim il-Sung. Here you'll find one of the world's only mass games, in which tens of thousands of Korean schoolchildren hold up placards, flip-book style, to form colourful mosaics in favour of the country's regime.

KOREA, SOUTH

CAPITAL SEOUL **POPULATION** 49.2 MILLION **AREA** 98,480 SQ KM **OFFICIAL LANGUAGE** KOREAN

South Korea has begun to appeal to travellers who've pretty much done the rest of the Asian continent and are looking for something new. Increasing tourism isn't South Korea's only economy-booster. In 2008, new president Lee Myung-bak (also known as The Bulldozer for his forceful determination) took up office with the promise 'Economy First', planning to boost the economy, cut unemployment, and become a major world player in the face of competition from China and Japan. Visitors, though, will probably spend more time in the great outdoors than experiencing Seoul's economic growth, with skiing, ice festivals, mineral springs and national parks all on the South Korean cards.

KOSOVO

CAPITAL PRISHTINA **POPULATION** 2.1 MILLION **AREA** 10,887 SQ KM **OFFICIAL LANGUAGES** ALBANIAN, SERBIAN

Welcome to the world's newest country – declared amid protests and controversy. Serbia is not happy about relinquishing this breakaway republic and things could be fractious in parts for a while. But the UN has recognised Kosovo, so consider it to be on the travel map. And it deserves

it: you wouldn't believe that this café-culture–loving nation was embroiled in a bloody war just 10 years ago. Infrastructure has come on apace and sights are plentiful. From the monasteries of Decani and Pec to the Ottoman town of Prizen and the ski-friendly Rugova Mountains, it's more than just a novel stamp in the passport.

KUWAIT

CAPITAL KUWAIT CITY **POPULATION** 2.6 MILLION **AREA** 17,820 SQ KM **OFFICIAL LANGUAGE** ARABIC

Finally, Kuwait is freeing itself from its association with its deeply troubled neighbour Iraq, and projecting a high-tech modern image that's enticing visitors to take a look. Kuwait City's vast new mall, The Avenues, should be open for business in 2009 to become one of the Middle East's biggest indoor shopping experiences. When you're all shopped out, head to the seashore to indulge in the Kuwaiti passion for power boating, then dine with a view at Kuwait Towers' revolving restaurant. You'll have to forgo that sunset glass of wine though since, despite its increasingly Western veneer, Kuwait remains a staunchly alcohol-free zone.

KYRGYZSTAN

CAPITAL BISHKEK **POPULATION** 5.4 MILLION **AREA** 198,500 SQ KM **OFFICIAL LANGUAGES** KYRGYZ, RUSSIAN

With a small population inhabiting a vast space that borders China to the east, Kyrgyzstan has long been considered one of Central Asia's most accessible countries for travellers. This has never been truer than now. Despite ongoing political tensions, tourist facilities are beginning to develop wholeheartedly across the country. Head to Kyrgyzstan before the masses do, to ride horseback across the plains, ski the glaciers of the Ala-Archa canyon, and hike the incredible trails around Karakol. Unless you've a strong stomach, though, you might want to avoid being guest of honour when the national dish Besh Barmak is served, since you'll likely be presented with bits of horse head and eyeballs, along with encouraging smiles.

KIRIBATI

 CAPITAL TARAWA **POPULATION** 110,356 **AREA** 811 SQ KM **OFFICIAL LANGUAGES** ENGLISH, I-KIRIBATI

Tourism provides one-fifth of the GDP for residents of the Gilbert, Line and Phoenix Islands: 33 Pacific Ocean atolls sprinkled across the equator and on either side of the international date line. Hard to get to, largely poor and with only basic accommodation on offer, this is only a place to go if you like your diving deserted and your travel largely back-to-basics. Explore the wreckage of the fierce WWII fighting that took place off Kiribati's shore, visit Abemama where Robert Louis Stevenson once set foot, or head to more touristed Kiritimati (Christmas Island), the first place in the world to see the dawn of the new millennium. It may be rough, but it's worthwhile.

KOREA, NORTH

CAPITAL PYONGYANG **POPULATION** 23.5 MILLION **AREA** 120,540 SQ KM **OFFICIAL LANGUAGE** KOREAN

Unfortunately, you won't be heading to North Korea any time soon unless

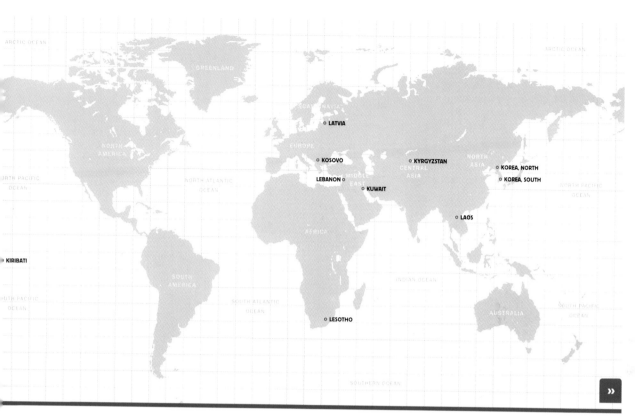

LAOS

 CAPITAL VIENTIANE **POPULATION** 6.5 MILLION **AREA** 230,800 SQ KM **OFFICIAL LANGUAGE** LAO

Though it was once a crucial corner of the Golden Triangle, opium crops in this tiny country have declined in recent years as Laos gears itself up for tourism. For the first time Vientiane will host the Southeast Asian Games in 2009, bringing together 11 countries from across the region to admire the country's economic progress. To the north, new freedom of travel for Chinese citizens is bringing in a new crowd to mingle with backpackers. These backpackers have already discovered the majestic former capital, Luang Prabang, and Mekong cruises, opting for ecotours and participating in volunteering for even more memorable travel experiences.

LATVIA

CAPITAL RIGA **POPULATION** 2.3 MILLION **AREA** 64,589 SQ KM **OFFICIAL LANGUAGE** LATVIAN

Now that low-cost airlines have landed in Riga, the country is welcoming tourists as never before. New foreigner-friendly signage, roads and cycle paths are appearing and the railways are getting a revamp, the aim being to improve the whole of the Baltic region's tracks by 2013. Visitors are exploring beyond the art nouveau capital too, from taking the medicinal waters at seaside Jurmala (where the painstakingly restored 1930s sanatorium is due to open as a plush spa by 2009) to hitting the ecotrails in bog- and bird-full Kemeri National Park. Don't miss Kuldiga, recent recipient of a European Destinations of Excellence award: this Latvian Venice is touted as one of the continent's best emerging rural tourism spots.

LEBANON

CAPITAL BEIRUT **POPULATION** 4 MILLION **AREA** 10,400 SQ KM **OFFICIAL LANGUAGE** ARABIC

A tiny country with a big history and even bigger problems, Lebanon's shaky security situation will govern whether or not visitors continue to trickle back in 2009. Though most of its infrastructure has been repaired since the 2006 summer Hezbollah-Israeli war, occasional bomb blasts aimed largely at anti-Syrian politicians and occasionally at UN interim forces, continue to cause physical and political damage. Nevertheless, Lebanon remains an extremely welcoming country to visit, with incredible archaeological remains, a wild Beirut nightlife and stunning mountain hiking amongst its charms. Sure, check the news before you go, but don't be deterred from seeing its sights while you can do so minus the crowds.

LESOTHO

CAPITAL MASERU **POPULATION** 2.1 MILLION **AREA** 30,355 SQ KM **OFFICIAL LANGUAGES** SESOTHO, ENGLISH

A country landlocked by South Africa and ravaged by AIDS (average life expectancy now teeters at 40 and the HIV infection rate is over 28%), Lesotho has not had an easy time of it in recent decades. But tourists still come steadily to this welcoming and high-altitude country, where the lowest point is a good 1400m above sea level. Since the opening

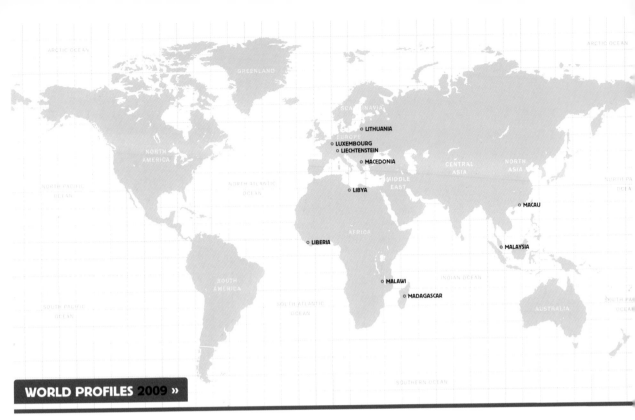

of Afri-Ski in 2005 in the northern Maluti Mountains, thousands of South African visitors have started to arrive for a ski season that extends between roughly May and September. But if skiing's not your thing, trek the isolated outreaches of the Sehlabathebe National Park, or join the substantial numbers of volunteers working on the country's numerous and worthy concerns.

LIBERIA

 **CAPITAL** MONROVIA **POPULATION** 3.2 MILLION **AREA** 111,370 SQ KM **OFFICIAL LANGUAGE** ENGLISH

Liberia's destructive civil wars (1989–96 and 1999–2003), estimated to have killed around 200,000 Liberians seem to be behind it, but the scars remain. Relative calm has been imposed since 2006's elections but few foreign offices would suggest that travel to this West African coastal country is risk-free. Increasingly, violent crime is plaguing Monrovia (sometimes targeting visitors) and travel outside the capital is also not advised. If things do change, though, there's a good deal to experience, including the rainforested Sapo National Park and, even more compellingly, top-notch (and completely unexploited) surfing at Robertsport, along with long stretches of beautiful, more leisurely beaches, at Silver Beach and around.

LIBYA

CAPITAL TRIPOLI **POPULATION** 6.2 MILLION **AREA** 1,759,540 SQ KM **OFFICIAL LANGUAGE** ARABIC

Libya, with its stunning desert landscapes and some of the best ruins in the region, has been grabbing travel magazine headlines in recent years and will likely continue to do so in 2009. Comprised largely of desert and ruled for decades by charismatic if controversial Muammar Qaddafi, even US citizens are now coming here to delight in its beautiful beaches, shop at chaotic Tripolitanian markets, and explore one of the greatest wonders of the ancient world at Leptis Magna. To escape the slowly increasing visitor numbers, venture out to Jebel Acacus, an eerie basalt landscape filled with pre-historic cave paintings, or to the stunning Ancient Greek remains at Cyrene.

LIECHTENSTEIN

CAPITAL VADUZ **POPULATION** 34,247 **AREA** 160 SQ KM **OFFICIAL LANGUAGE** GERMAN

While the Euro 2008 football championships played out around it, Austria and Switzerland–sandwiched Liechtenstein attempted to assert itself on the tourist scene. No mean feat for this small, little-known and oft-forgotten tax haven, which has no cities and no airport. It doesn't even show off what it's got – its impressive art collection (belonging to the ruling prince) is on display in the Liechtenstein Museum…in Vienna. So what is there to entice travellers beyond a novelty stamp in their passport? Well, the skiing is good at Malbun, the Alpine countryside pretty, and the wine, supped in the prince's own cellar, delicious.

LITHUANIA

CAPITAL VILNIUS **POPULATION** 3.6 MILLION **AREA** 65,200 SQ KM **OFFICIAL LANGUAGE** LITHUANIAN

It's an important year for Lithuania, with the European Capital of Culture baton being passed to Vilnius in 2009.

It means the city will be dripping in festivities (including Street Musician Day in May and an Art in Unusual Places project) but it also means the rest of the country's tourism industry – transport links, hotels – has been beefing up for the occasion. It's hoped visitor numbers will grow by 20%. The Baltic coast is tipped to be the next big thing: Palanga is where locals like to spend their summers, but head further south to the wooden-house villages of the Curonian Spit, a skinny finger of shifting sand and the highest drifting dunes in Europe.

LUXEMBOURG

CAPITAL LUXEMBOURG **POPULATION** 480,222 **AREA** 2586 SQ KM **OFFICIAL LANGUAGES** LUXEMBOURGISH, GERMAN, FRENCH

Just 980,000 people visit this diminutive grand duchy each year. Perhaps they're the ones who know it has more Michelin stars per square kilometre than any other country. Or perhaps they've twigged that Luxembourg is the first city to have been named European Capital of Culture twice (1995 and 2007). The capital of culture tag spurred a legacy of ecothinking, new hiking trails and a spaghetti tangle of cycle tracks that's still being extended and should cover 900km by the time work's completed. Cyclists be warned: it's hilly but the pretty trail along the Mosel River is flatter and allows for wine-tasting along the way.

MACAU

POPULATION 456,000 **AREA** 28.2 SQ KM **OFFICIAL LANGUAGE** CANTONESE

Overtaking Hong Kong as the hotspot for mainlanders' mini-breaks, development of this former Portuguese island has been faster than the spin of a roulette wheel. Casinos and big-ticket hotels, and an attempt to win over families, have earned it the title of China's Las Vegas. Since Portugal relinquished control in 1999, violence and crime have disappeared faster than savings in a slot machine, and the emergence of budget airlines and snappy ferry links to Hong Kong have encouraged international visitors. New developments like the Playboy Mansion casino will rival Sands Macau for the title of the largest casino on the planet.

MACEDONIA

CAPITAL SKOPJE **POPULATION** 2.1 MILLION **AREA** 25,333 SQ KM **OFFICIAL LANGUAGE** MACEDONIAN

Macedonia may have a new name by the time you read this. The country, vying for EU-inclusion, is being blocked by Greece, who insist the word 'Macedonia' belongs to them. But whatever this chunk of ex-Yugoslavia is called, it's a fascinating addition to the travel map. Alexander the Great's homeland is dotted with exquisite Byzantine monasteries and frescoed churches (explore those around lovely Lake Orhid), a new set of archaeological projects is unearthing unknown treasures – including the Roman city of Stobi – and the raucous Strumitsa Carnival just before Lent is growing into one of the best street shindigs in Europe.

MADAGASCAR

CAPITAL ANTANANARIVO **POPULATION** 19.4 MILLION **AREA** 581,540 SQ KM **OFFICIAL LANGUAGES** ENGLISH, FRENCH, MALAGASY

Add Madagascar to your travel wish list and you'll have something in common with legions of under-10 year olds frantic to visit since Sacha Baron Cohen's tuneful lemur hit the big screens. Madagascar's appeal as a mainstream tourist destination has certainly widened in recent years, but this vast island with its line in prehistoric species, glittering beaches, and gorgeous rainforests still has enough room to support them all, and leave plenty spare for escape artists. Visit the Ifaty region for diving, beach-bumming and whale-watching during July and August, or stroll through the Parc National de Ranomanfana, prime territory for 12 species of our ring-tailed friends. Meanwhile the strenuous trails of the more remote Parc National de l'Isalo are perfect for strong-legged souls who like to move it, move it.

MALAWI

CAPITAL LILONGWE **POPULATION** 13.6 MILLION **AREA** 118,480 SQ KM **OFFICIAL LANGUAGES** ENGLISH, CHICHEWA

Malawi has been an African travel favourite for some years now and continues to draw a steady stream of visitors each year (though not too many to spoil the experience). It's popular because it has a little bit of all the things you're looking for in an African sojourn: there are the beaches at Nkhata Bay and Cape Maclear, the hiking around Mt Mulanje, national parks like the huge Nyika National Park and quiet Vwaza Marsh Wildlife Reserve and, of course, a friendly, welcoming population. If you're visiting in October 2009, don't miss the fantastic world music festival, Lake of Stars.

MALAYSIA

CAPITAL KUALA LUMPUR **POPULATION** 25.3 MILLION **AREA** 329,750 SQ KM **OFFICIAL LANGUAGE** BAHASA MALAYSIA

Tourism to Malaysia has never been so healthy, as it's one country in the region that has remained largely

free from natural disasters, terrorism and political turmoil. Travellers flock here year-round to experience the country's beaches, lush interiors and numerous festivals. If diving's your thing, bear in mind that the reefs of the gorgeous Perhentian Islands are being rapidly damaged by insensitive over-tourism, so it might be wise to take to the waters elsewhere. New ecotourism possibilities are springing up all the time, including tours within the dense and spectacular Taman Negara national park. Or, for a spot of good old-fashioned afternoon tea, nothing beats the England-that-time-forgot atmosphere of the Cameron Highlands, in all its chintzy glory.

MALDIVES

CAPITAL MALE **POPULATION** 370,000 **AREA** 300 SQ KM **OFFICIAL LANGUAGE** MALDIVIAN DHIVEHI

Once considered the ultimate destination for getting away from it all, the Maldives has struggled to come to democracy with bombings in 2007 and troubled elections in 2008. Still, there are over 1100 coral islands in this group so glamping (roughing it without the rough) on your own island is possible with a yacht or custom cruise. Definitely not a budget destination, the celebrated reefs and pure-white beaches are the big drawcards. Divers still flock to Banana Reef for its mix of caves, cliffs and stunning sea life, including manta rays gliding by cleaning stations scattered amid the coral.

MALI

CAPITAL BAMAKO **POPULATION** 12 MILLION **AREA** 1,240,140 SQ KM **OFFICIAL LANGUAGE** FRENCH

If you've ever wanted to go to fabled Timbuktu, now's your chance, as Mali creeps further onto the tourist map. The country is one of the few in this part of Africa that travellers don't come to seeking safari: here, it's the weird and wonderful lunar landscapes that draw visitors to its empty, empty spaces. Visitors to Mali in 2009 can look out for competitors in the mammoth Budapest-to-Bamako Great African Run car rally, an alternative to the good old Paris–Dakar. The race concludes in poverty-stricken but generally smiling Bamako, where parties to celebrate those who make it this far are the order of the day.

MALTA

CAPITAL VALLETTA **POPULATION** 401,880 **AREA** 316 SQ KM **OFFICIAL LANGUAGES** MALTESE, ENGLISH

Malta was in the tourism doldrums until it finally welcomed low-cost airlines in 2007. Things picked up as a new type of traveller was transported to the south Med and a hip crowd flocked to the Isle of MTV music-fest, so popular it's set to rock Valletta every June until 2010. But is it all about to go Pete Tong? The adoption of the euro in 2008 could mean off-putting price hikes, though early indicators show costs haven't rocketed – good news for those keen to stroll fortified Mdina, nip over to little-developed sister island Gozo for a farmhouse stay, or down a rum in The Pub, where *Gladiator*-filming Oliver Reed drank his last.

MARSHALL ISLANDS

CAPITAL MAJURO **POPULATION** 63,174 **AREA** 181 SQ KM **OFFICIAL LANGUAGES** ENGLISH, MARSHALLESE

Although the Marshalls have a history as a business destination, they are moving towards a new future. In 2007 they became members of the International Labor Organization, which means that dodgy treatment of workers won't be an option anymore. Secondly, Majuro bagged the host spot for the Micronesian Games, which may be scaled down due to the limited facilities of the tiny island. Still, it's a better reason to visit than the Reagan Missile Test Site on Kwajalein Atoll, which brings in hundreds of US army visitors every year. To avoid the booms, dunk your head and look at Bikini's underwater wrecks or Rongelap's marine fauna.

MARTINIQUE

CAPITAL FORT-DE-FRANCE **POPULATION** 436,130 **AREA** 1100 SQ KM **OFFICIAL LANGUAGE** FRENCH

A sweet slice of *pain au chocolat* in the middle of the Caribbean Sea, Martinique is largely the domain of French tourists (comprising 80% of each year's visitors). Most flock to the southern beaches, leaving plenty of room on the black-sand stretches of the northern coast and the lush mountainous interior for others to escape to. Though French culture is inevitably dominant in this sleepy overseas department of France, there's a heady dose of Creole mixed in, evident in the food, the music and the annual carnival, which will take place in February 2009. Don't miss the transgender 'weddings' on the Monday before Ash Wednesday, when men across the island dress up in their wives' wedding attire, and vice versa.

MAURITANIA

CAPITAL NOUAKCHOTT **POPULATION** 3.3 MILLION **AREA** 1,030,700 SQ KM **OFFICIAL LANGUAGE** ARABIC

A small population and a whole lot of space continue to make Mauritania a popular destination for thousands of

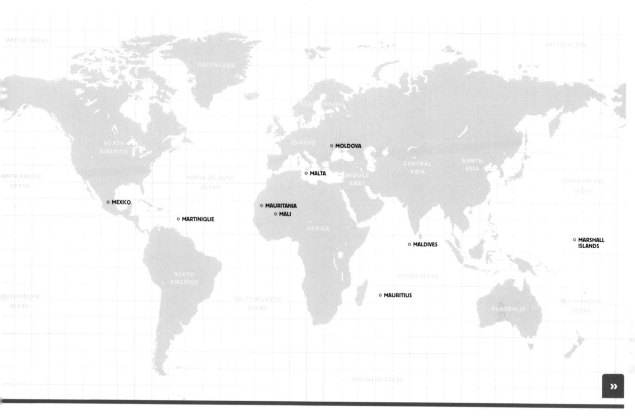

visitors each year, who come seeking the solitude of the desert. Like most West African countries, much of its population is on the poverty line and the country has numerous problems. In December 2007, four French tourists were killed during a robbery in the Aleg region; the French authorities subsequently cancelled the 2008 Paris–Dakar rally due to security concerns. It therefore pays to monitor the news carefully, and take local advice while on the road. If conditions permit, don't miss a trip out to the Unesco World Heritage Site at Oualâta, an ancient and evocative semi-ghost town that will one day become a firm favourite on any self-respecting traveller's itinerary.

MAURITIUS

CAPITAL PORT LOUIS **POPULATION** 1.3 MILLION **AREA** 2040 SQ KM **OFFICIAL LANGUAGE** ENGLISH

Mark Twain had a point when he suggested that heaven was modelled after Mauritius. With its winning combination of tropical beaches, happy locals and hotpot of Creole, Indian and Chinese cultures, many

visitors feel compelled to come back again and again. It's unlikely that you'll be able to visit the Indian Ocean island gem of Mauritius in 2009 without stumbling across a festival or two. From Chinese New Year to Holi, the island's mélange of cultures celebrates every possible occasion with colour and intensity. The only thing you won't find here is the dodo (except on the republic's coat of arms), which was done away with for eternity around 1861.

MEXICO

CAPITAL MEXICO CITY **POPULATION** 108.7 MILLION **AREA** 1,923,040 SQ KM **OFFICIAL LANGUAGE** SPANISH

There are big bucks going into promoting 'south of the border' to the USA, and Mexico's tourism board is spending US$3 million targeting Chinese visitors. New budget carriers in 2006 began price wars that saw even more North Americans vacationing here, around four in 10 of whom ended up in Cancun. Sure, Cancun has the Spring Break partying and easy all-inclusive hotels (many of which were refurbished after

Hurricane Wilma) but there's more to explore. Try snorkelling around Cozumel or plunging into another liquid in Guadalajara, the birthplace of tequila. Personal security should feature in your plans, though, as Mexico has violent drug-related crime.

MOLDOVA

CAPITAL CHISINAU **POPULATION** 4.3 MILLION **AREA** 33,843 SQ KM **OFFICIAL LANGUAGE** MOLDOVAN

Visitor numbers are definitely on the up in this tiny former fragment of the Soviet Union – but from such a low base it's unlikely you'll see much evidence of it as you wander around leafy Chisinau. And you will wander the capital, as there's barely a hotel outside it. Day trips will take you to the surrounding (and excellent) wineries and underground monasteries – Orheiul Vechi comes with a feisty resident monk – but also to the weird world of Transdniestr. Expect a chilly reception in this breakaway republic that shows no sign of giving up its battle for independence from Moldova, but also expect a glimpse of a truly secret Europe.

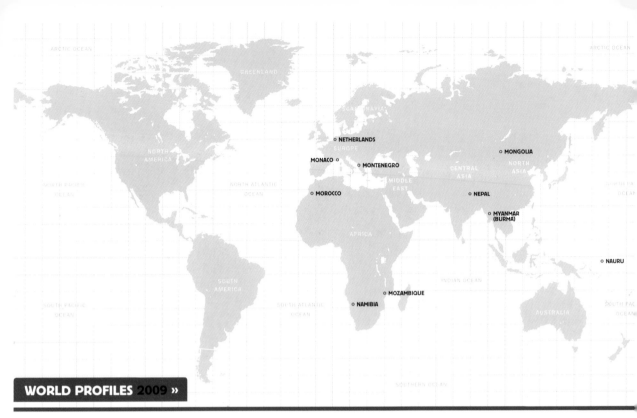

MONACO

CAPITAL MONACO **POPULATION** 32,671 **AREA** 1.95 SQ KM **OFFICIAL LANGUAGE** FRENCH

Monaco hardly needs your travel dollars – as millionaires gamble the GDP of small African nations at the 130-year-old casino it seems there's already enough cash in this principality. But more visitors than ever will flock here in 2009, and not just for the annual Grand Prix in May. Come July cyclists usurp cars as the Tour de France makes its grand start amid Monte Carlo's surrounds. But the main emphasis is still on entertainment, and the new live-music venues and eclectic restaurants will ensure that high-rollers – and intrigued travellers – won't get bored or hungry between bets.

MONGOLIA

CAPITAL ULAAN BATAR **POPULATION** 2.95 MILLION **AREA** 1,564,116 SQ KM **OFFICIAL LANGUAGE** KHALKHA MONGOL

Quietly sitting to the north of China, Mongolia has seen its tourist numbers steadily build over the last few years. Its secret? They've built up winter activities outside of the busiest season (June to September), which include extreme trekking in Gun-Galuut Nature Reserve and nomad sleigh-racing at the Ice Festival on Lake Hovsgol. The Ice Festival has come to rival the Naadam festival, which showcases traditional Mongolian sports like archery, horseback riding, and wrestling that's on par with sumo for toughness. The other secret of success has been improved air access with new facilities at Niksal and Wamol, along with more frequent flights to the capital.

MONTENEGRO

CAPITAL PODGORICA **POPULATION** 684,736 **AREA** 14,026 SQ KM **OFFICIAL LANGUAGE** MONTENEGRIN

Brand new Montenegro – only declared a country in 2006 – is touted the 'brand new Croatia'. The latter is perhaps loved too much, while new-kid Montenegro has a less-developed Adriatic coastline and unexplored interior. It suffers air accessibility issues – it's the most poorly connected of the Balkans – but there's much to come for. Historic towns such as Ulcinj, with a long stretch of sand, and bayside Kotor are already popular, while rafting in Durmitor National Park is a must. Rugged and remote Proketije (some say it's the most beautiful massif in Europe) is as yet undiscovered, and is lined up all set to become the country's fifth national park.

MOROCCO

CAPITAL RABAT **POPULATION** 34.3 MILLION **AREA** 446,300 SQ KM **OFFICIAL LANGUAGE** ARABIC

You'd expect the country that gave the world *Casablanca* to have a hearty film history and Morocco also has leading roles in *Lawrence of Arabia*, *The Last Temptation of Christ* and *Gladiator*. With a major expansion of studios in Ouarzazate, you'll be seeing more Moroccan vistas in Hollywood movies. Away from the silver screen the world is getting a taste for Moroccan cuisine, with couscous and tajines now common on menus. Travellers who want the real deal are stocking up in the markets of Djemaa el-Fna, which are fragrant with mint, saffron and preserved lemon.

MOZAMBIQUE

CAPITAL MAPUTO **POPULATION** 20.9 MILLION **AREA** 801,590 SQ KM **OFFICIAL LANGUAGE** PORTUGUESE

Mozambique is, without doubt, the next big African destination. Those in the know already swear by its beaches, high-end ecotourism offerings, and slow and steady pace of life. Despite its dark history and fairly regular violent crime in Maputo, Mozambique's offerings seem to know no bounds. If your budget will allow it, head to the Bazaruto Archipelago for sea and sands from a dream, now largely designated a marine reserve to protect its stunning coral reefs. If you're in a volunteering frame of mind, there are plenty of projects throughout the country looking for willing participants, such as the sanitisation charity Estamos, which won the 2008 Goldman Environmental Prize. Whatever you do, get there soon, before everyone else does.

MYANMAR (BURMA)

CAPITAL NAY PYI TAW **POPULATION** 47.4 MILLION **AREA** 657,740 SQ KM **OFFICIAL LANGUAGE** BURMESE

Moving the capital to the newly created Nay Pyi Taw in 2005 may have been a strategic move to quell trouble in the central Shan, China and Karen states, but it backfired with protests by monks against the military junta and international condemnation in 2008. Later the same year Cyclone Nargis struck, creating a relief worker's nightmare as the junta attempted to pick and choose between various aid providers. The long-term problem of the government not recognising the democratically elected leader Aung San Suu Kyi and her house arrest that has lasted almost 20 years continues. Suu Kyi recommends not visiting her country, though some in the travel industry believe that travelling can put pressure on the junta and expose human rights abuses. If you decide to visit Myanmar, avoid giving the government your tourist dollars by seeking out grassroots businesses wherever possible.

NAMIBIA

CAPITAL WINDHOEK **POPULATION** 2.1 MILLION **AREA** 825,418 SQ KM **OFFICIAL LANGUAGE** ENGLISH

Since Brangelina produced Shilo here in 2006, Namibia has hit the world stage as a traveller destination par excellence. With the country's growing interest in ecotourism, and the vast Kalahari on offer to the intrepid adventurer, there's no end of reasons to make a beeline for Namibia in 2009 before the crowds start to descend in earnest. If bird-watching's your thing, absolutely don't miss Etosha National Park, where flamingos and pelicans congregate in their thousands, whilst the treacherous shores of the evocative Skeleton Coast are ripe for exploration. Recent price hikes at many parks and reserves have made visiting Namibia a more costly affair than in years past, but no less worthwhile for that.

NAURU

CAPITAL YAREN **POPULATION** 13,770 **AREA** 21 SQ KM **OFFICIAL LANGUAGE** NAURUAN

This phosphate-rich rock has been stripped of much of its mineral wealth, leaving behind an eerie moonscape. With the mining interests gone, the economic future is similarly bleak for Nauru. Until 2007 the nation was part of the Pacific Solution, holding asylum seekers for Australia in a custom-built camp, but a change in policy saw 100 Nauruans become unemployed and the island's major industry lost. The resulting political instability saw snap elections in the country in 2008. Most visitors to Nauru use the country as a stepping stone to Kiribati or the Solomon Islands when they fly with Our Airline (the re-branded Air Nauru).

NEPAL

CAPITAL KATHMANDU **POPULATION** 29.5 MILLION **AREA** 140,800 SQ KM **OFFICIAL LANGUAGE** NEPALI

Nepal certainly hasn't had an easy run of it in recent years, what with

Maoist insurgencies, strikes and spiralling tensions surrounding governmental elections. But, all being well, 2009 will see enchanting, unforgettable Nepal back on more travellers' itineraries. With eight of the world's 10 highest peaks, its mountains offer plenty for lovers of mountaineering or scenery-gazing, and there's much more besides, including lovable, bustling Kathmandu. Trek mountain pathways for weeks on end, spot rhinos at the gorgeous Royal Chitwan National Park, get spiritual at the Bodhnath stupa, or live it up with the locals at one of dozens of colourful religious festivals. Nepal's tourism comeback is without a doubt a welcome phenomenon for everyone.

NETHERLANDS

CAPITAL AMSTERDAM **POPULATION** 16.6 MILLION **AREA** 41,526 SQ KM **OFFICIAL LANGUAGE** DUTCH

Is Amsterdam losing its edge? Recent legislation has closed a third of the infamous Red Light District's brothels and the 2008 smoking ban has hit the city's 'coffee shops' (though you

travellers' lists, with stunning scenery and resorts blessed with French-style service. Ecotourism in the Loyalty Islands is slowly developing, but the big activity is diving the world's largest coral lagoon – home to the rare dugong and the nautilus, a mollusc that serves as New Caledonia's emblem.

NEW ZEALAND

CAPITAL WELLINGTON **POPULATION** 4.17 MILLION **AREA** 268,021 SQ KM **OFFICIAL LANGUAGES** ENGLISH, MAORI

The Land of the Long White Cloud (Aotearoa) has been topping travellers' must-see lists since well before the *Lord of the Rings*, for its variety: whale-watching, wineries, hiking and, not forgetting, bungee jumping. It's a natural destination for sustainable tourism, with ecotours and low-impact hiking, and there's a renewed interest in experiencing Maori culture beyond a staged performance. Taking an indigenous-led cycling tour, visiting a marae with elders or getting the inside word with a local-history walk are just some of the ways tourists are getting a deeper look at Kiwi culture.

NICARAGUA

CAPITAL MANAGUA **POPULATION** 5.7 MILLION **AREA** 129,494 SQ KM **OFFICIAL LANGUAGE** SPANISH

One of the region's best emerging travel destinations, with its troublesome days of war and strife long gone, Nicaragua is welcoming travellers keen to experience its manifold delights. Whether it's well-preserved colonial cities you're after or vast tracts of untouched wilderness, you'll find them here – all served up with a touch of the Caribbean coastline (the only area currently drawing significant numbers of tourists). But whatever brings you to this cheap, cheerful and undeniably beautiful destination, Nicaragua is certainly up there with El Salvador and Honduras as one of the places to get to soon before it becomes a footprint on the travellers' trail.

NIGER

CAPITAL NIAMEY **POPULATION** 12.9 MILLION **AREA** 1,267,000 SQ KM **OFFICIAL LANGUAGE** FRENCH

Though Niger possesses more than its fair share of bandits, guerrillas, militias and landmines, travel in this dramatic, desert-dusted country is still possible, though visitors should keep a careful eye on the news and listen out for local advice. The main accessible drawcard remains Agadez, the great Saharan entrance point to the Aïr Mountains and Ténéré Desert, a town with a millennium of history on the ancient caravan route toward Algeria and Libya. Sadly, at present, the areas to the north and south of Agadez are considered unsafe, keeping all but a handful of hardy travellers away and its deserts emptier than ever.

NIGERIA

CAPITAL ABUJA **POPULATION** 135 MILLION **AREA** 923,768 SQ KM **OFFICIAL LANGUAGE** ENGLISH

With recent kidnappings of foreign oil workers throwing visitors' security into question, Nigeria's reputation for bad deeds is, sadly, extending beyond the realms of internet con artists. Add to this a rise in violent crime in Lagos, and it doesn't exactly seem to be welcoming tourists with open arms. If you're planning on visiting anyway, keep a close watch on the news, especially since religious tensions are always seething under the surface. And allow plenty of time to obtain a visa – in late 2007 Bill Gates was initially denied a tourist visa on the grounds that he might stay and prove a strain on the welfare system.

NORTHERN MARIANA ISLANDS

CAPITAL SAIPAN **POPULATION** 82,460 **AREA** 477 SQ KM **OFFICIAL LANGUAGE** ENGLISH

A world away from the bustle of Guam, these 15 islands promise a contrary mix of tranquillity and package tours. Recently added air services from Korea and charter flights from Russia have taken up the slack caused by the withdrawal

can still toke in designated rooms). But the capital is as vibrant as ever, its cultural side – as well as that of nearby Rotterdam, Utrecht and The Hague – surging to the fore as part of the Holland Art Cities initiative, which will showcase Dutch art throughout 2009. There's plenty of outdoors fun too – despite the Netherlands' compact proportions hidden corners remain. Try canoeing around Wieringen, an island-turned-mainland with Viking intrigue, or waddling (messing about on mudflats) off the West Frisian Islands.

NEW CALEDONIA

CAPITAL NOUMEA **POPULATION** 224,824 **AREA** 19,060 SQ KM **OFFICIAL LANGUAGE** FRENCH

Still an overseas territory of France, this collection of islands is moving closer to autonomy. France has granted more power to the local congress in the lead-up to the 2013 referendum, which will decide if New Caledonia will be an independent state. The unique bouillabaisse of French and indigenous Kanak culture has put New Caledonia high on many

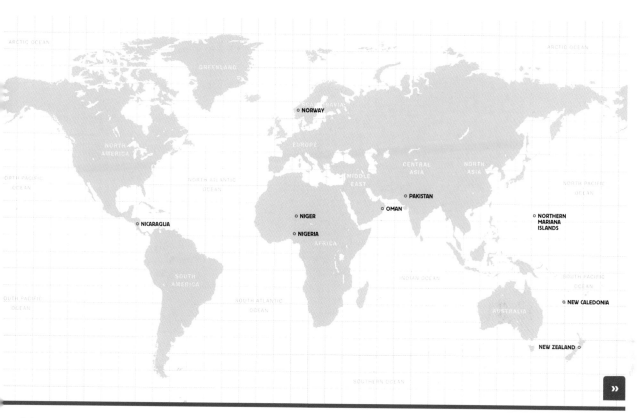

of Japanese airlines, though new providers are now taking up the routes to what's been called 'Japan's Hawaii'. Golf and diving are popular activities, and independent travel can get you close (but not too close) to the active volcanoes of Anatahan, Pagan and Agrihan. Rota offers excellent twitching excursions to Sagua'gaga Seabird Sanctuary and the chance to cool your boots in lovely swimming holes.

NORWAY

 **CAPITAL** OSLO **POPULATION** 4.6 MILLION **AREA** 323,802 SQ KM **OFFICIAL LANGUAGE** NORWEGIAN

Polar bears, twinkling aurora and sledding across snowfields behind a pack of pooping huskies – not a scene from movie *The Golden Compass* but a reality in Arctic Norway and the Svalbard archipelago. Perhaps the increasing numbers of travellers heading that way are attracted by the food: the Red Polar Bear, Svalbard's new eatery, is causing a stir...for being the world's most northerly kebab van. For the more refined, 2009 is Norway's Year of Cultural Heritage, offering up 52 weeks' worth of exhibitions and festivities – not least of which is the centenary of the Oslo–Bergen Railway, which slices its way between snow-coated mountains to be one of the planet's most 'wow' commutes.

OMAN

CAPITAL MUSCAT **POPULATION** 3.3 MILLION **AREA** 212,460 SQ KM **OFFICIAL LANGUAGE** ARABIC

Oman continues to develop as a tourist destination in 2009, with its emphasis divided between top-end luxury and a growing trend in ecotourism. To sample a bit of both, spend a few days soaking up the sun at the incredibly popular new Shangri-La Barr al Jisr spa hotel, then head to stunning Wadi Shab for its serene aquamarine pools and waterfalls. Travel the frankincense-producing Dhafar highlands, roam Muscat's heady souqs, palaces and walled city, touch Oman's heritage at the newly opened Frankincense Land Museum, and explore its 2000km of largely unpopulated coastline: there's really never been a better time to visit. Hit town in January 2009 for the colourful Muscat Festival, or head here for the Khareef Festival in July and August.

PAKISTAN

CAPITAL ISLAMABAD **POPULATION** 167.8 MILLION **AREA** 803,940 SQ KM **OFFICIAL LANGUAGE** URDU

If events of 2009 follow those of previous years, Pakistan won't be a viable destination for most travellers for a while. The assassination of Benazir Bhutto in late 2007 shook the country, while waves of terrorist attacks, especially in the northwest, rocked its cities. It's a great shame that the massive country won't be hosting more visitors soon since there's unquestionably so much on offer. History buffs will have a field day exploring the Mughal treasures of Lahore, the mountain trekking is simply sublime and the long-fabled Karakoram Highway, part of the ancient Silk Road to China, passes the breathtaking Hunza Valley in the north. If you do decide to travel here, monitor the news carefully and heed local warnings.

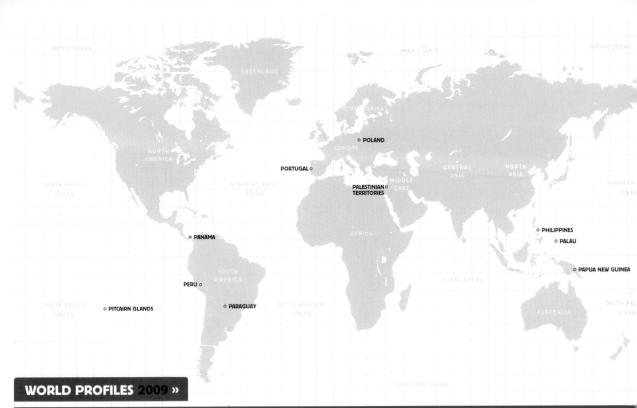

PALAU

CAPITAL KOROR **POPULATION** 21,093 **AREA** 458 SQ KM **OFFICIAL LANGUAGES** ENGLISH, PALAUAN

In the scuba-diving world, Palau is revered as a sacred site promising coral-inlaid temples and bountiful marine life. The pick of the bunch is Blue Corner, popular for its schooling sharks and huge barracuda, but local charters can get divers out to secret spots and secluded gardens of hard and soft corals. The legendary Peleliu Wall offers more submarine fauna, including hawksbill turtles gliding through black coral forests. More than two-thirds of the tiny nation's GDP comes from tourism, so ever-friendly islanders offer tours and plenty of alternatives to big resorts.

PALESTINIAN TERRITORIES

POPULATION 4,149,173 **AREA** 7378 SQ KM **OFFICIAL LANGUAGE** ARABIC

With Gaza having descended into bloody chaos of late, this seaside strip is definitely off travellers' itineraries for the foreseeable future. But so long as things remain relatively stable in the West Bank, there's little – except for dozens of checkpoints, roadblocks and the occasional curfew – to stop the intrepid visitor from venturing in to catch a slice of life behind Israel's controversial security wall. The obvious tourist attractions of Bethlehem's Manger Square aren't the only draw; there's also Ramallah's remarkably urbane café culture, the ancient town of Jericho, and the only microbrewery in the Middle East (producing a mighty tasty beverage) at the tiny hilltop town of Taybeh. Monitor the security situation before you go, but don't be deterred from experiencing the reality behind the grim headlines.

PANAMA

CAPITAL PANAMA CITY **POPULATION** 3.2 MILLION **AREA** 78,200 SQ KM **OFFICIAL LANGUAGE** SPANISH

Yet another of Central America's grand combinations of culture, beaches and abundant wildlife, Panama has as yet nowhere near the tourist traffic of its neighbour Costa Rica. Twenty-five thousand expats – brought here by Panama's multitude of international banks – are pleased to call the country home, lending an global flavour to Panama City's own brand of 'wildlife' found in its red-hot bars and nightclubs. To discover hidden treasure, head out to the inaptly named Isla Grande, a tiny island hideaway with a community of just a few hundred, and which, with no dive-shacks to lure the underwater brigade, is the perfect place to laze on a beach without a flipper or oxygen tank in sight.

PAPUA NEW GUINEA

CAPITAL PORT MORESBY **POPULATION** 5.8 MILLION **AREA** 452,860 SQ KM **OFFICIAL LANGUAGE** PIDGIN

The word you hear most about PNG is 'potential'. Whether it's ecotouring to find tree kangaroos and the huge Queen Alexandra butterfly or discovering WWII wrecks while diving at Rabaul, the country promises a variety of outdoor experiences. Then there's the diversity of people who speak more than 850 languages and predominantly lead traditional lives in rural areas. Yet only 2% of the Pacific's holidaymakers visit PNG. Many are dissuaded by security issues such as violent crime in Port Moresby and Mt Hagen, plus the volatile no-go zone around Panguna mine in Bouganville. You be the judge.

PARAGUAY

CAPITAL ASUNCIÓN **POPULATION** 6.7 MILLION **AREA** 406,750 SQ KM **OFFICIAL LANGUAGES** SPANISH, GUARANI

Though Paraguay has developed lately into a great place for an off-the-beaten-track adventure, 2007 saw outbreaks of both dengue fever and yellow fever marring its reputation as another 'new' destination for the intrepid traveller. Since there's no vaccination against dengue fever, it may well be that Paraguay's aspirations to become a new tourist hotspot are, for the moment at least, dampened, and potential tourists are being advised by their foreign offices back home to stay away. When the epidemics do blow over, there's much to recommend a trip to Paraguay – its arboreal highlights ranging from serene subtropical rainforests to the dense and forbidding thorn forests of Defensores del Chaco.

PERU

CAPITAL LIMA **POPULATION** 28.7 MILLION **AREA** 1,285,220 SQ KM **OFFICIAL LANGUAGES** SPANISH, QUECHUA

Though these days it seems even your parents are off in their finest North Face boots to hike the trail to Machu Picchu or do the rounds from Cuzco to Puno, the lure of the immense and magnificent Andes means there's plenty of airspace for hikers who prefer desolate mountain tracks to tourist comforts. Peru has long been one of South America's top attractions, and is well set up for the hundreds of thousands of annual visitors keen to experience its cultural and natural highlights. Tips for getting away from it all include trekking Cañon del Cotahuasi, the world's deepest canyon (which makes the Grand Canyon look positively shallow) and observing the ornithological splendour of the Reserva Ecológica Chaparrí.

PHILIPPINES

CAPITAL MANILA **POPULATION** 92.7 MILLION **AREA** 300,000 SQ KM **OFFICIAL LANGUAGES** FILIPINO, ENGLISH

You never know – Terminal 3 of Manila's international airport, on which work began in 1997, might finally be open by 2009. If this is the case, more flights than in recent years should start bringing visitors to this string of 7000 islands which, though they might not rank as highly on travellers' wishlists as Malaysia or Indonesia, have a lot to offer. Kayak the waters of the Hundred Islands National Park, hike in the sweet Chocolate Hills, or get away from it all amid the high rice-terraces of the Cordillera Mountains. At some point the crowds will come, but for now, the Philippines is still a cheap and welcoming departure from south Asia's backpacker circuit.

PITCAIRN ISLANDS

CAPITAL ADAMSTOWN **POPULATION** 48 **AREA** 47 SQ KM **OFFICIAL LANGUAGE** ENGLISH

It was easier to get to the Pitcairns in 1790, when Fletcher Christian and the crew of the *Bounty* decided to turn on their captain and find their own piece of the Pacific. Today, there are no direct international flights and leaving can be a matter of hitching a ride on a passing yacht. It redefines remote. Visitors still track down relics from the original settlers such as the cannon at Bounty Bay and the original Bible of Fletcher Christian, but most kick back to enjoy the slow pace of island life.

POLAND

CAPITAL WARSAW **POPULATION** 38.5 MILLION **AREA** 312,685 SQ KM **OFFICIAL LANGUAGE** POLISH

Bydgoszcz, Szczecin, Rzeszów…just three of the unpronounceable places now on the inquisitive traveller's map, thanks to the explosion of low-cost airlines servicing the country. But while Poland lacks vowels, it doesn't lack sights – most in the process of becoming better linked ahead of that big deal, football's

»

Euro 2012. For now, Warsaw's still the place for trendy bar-hopping (though getting pricier) while stunner Kraków is seeing a rise in Jewish tourism (klezmer music and kosher cafés) despite its negligible Jewish population. Weirder wonders beckon: plunge into the Baltic (whatever the weather) with Gdansk's fearless Walrus Club or strike out into Slowinski National Park, one of Europe's only deserts.

PORTUGAL

CAPITAL LISBON **POPULATION** 10.6 MILLION **AREA** 92,391 SQ KM **OFFICIAL LANGUAGE** PORTUGUESE

It's not all about the Algarve's beaches. While half of Portugal's annual 12 million tourists head south, the unspoilt rural interior – once partly responsible for branding the country 'Spain's backward sibling' – is now a desirable asset. The Xisto villages of central Portugal, with their olive groves and chestnut *talasnico* cakes, are the place to taste real Portugal. Likewise the vast Alentjo, where specialist groups are exploring its archaeology and cycling to its

QATAR

CAPITAL DOHA **POPULATION** 928,635 **AREA** 11,437 SQ KM **OFFICIAL LANGUAGE** ARABIC

Rich in gas and oil, and served by one of the world's very best airlines, 2009 marks the 20th anniversary of tourist visas being issued for Qatar. Those who come here, either to experience Qatar or as part of a stopover en route to elsewhere, won't be short of entertainment. Kiteboarding along the country's plentiful coastline is a current favourite, while exploring the dunes around the vast saltwater inlet at Khor al-Adaid is one of Qatar's premier attractions. Sporting types should look out for the Qatar Masters golf championships in January 2009, the Emir GCC Camel Race finals in April, and Doha's Powerboat Races in November. More cerebral urges can be satisfied by the citywide Doha Cultural Festival in February and March.

RÉUNION

CAPITAL ST-DENIS **POPULATION** 787,580 **AREA** 2517 SQ KM **OFFICIAL LANGUAGE** FRENCH

Though it's undoubtedly a pricey destination for travellers – most of whom, unsurprisingly, arrive here direct from France – tourism is alive and well in Indian Ocean jewel Réunion after a couple of years' run-in with the mosquito-borne chikungunya virus. Hiking or biking its three cirques, along with a host of adventure activities such as canyoning and kayaking, are increasingly popular; there are several dozen canyons that make good venues for these high-adrenaline pastimes. For something far more sedate, visit in October 2009 for the idiosyncratic Lentil Festival, or sample the sweet annual Honey Festival in January.

ROMANIA

CAPITAL BUCHAREST **POPULATION** 22.3 MILLION **AREA** 237,500 SQ KM **OFFICIAL LANGUAGE** ROMANIAN

As Dracula, the country's unlikely poster boy, might say: Romanian tourism is looking bloody good. It's the planet's fourth fastest–growing tourism economy, with visitor numbers predicted to rocket between now and 2016. Low-cost airlines are making Bucharest accessible, but it's the countryside that's best, offering one of the last true wildernesses in Europe. Retezat National Park, recently declared one of Europe's Protected Area Network of Parks (PAN Parks), is a great example – an ancient woodland home to wolf, lynx and bear and scarcely any tourists. Having to negotiate boat hire from a Romanian fisherman in the watery fingers of the Danube Delta will prove tourism hasn't yet taken off all over the country.

RUSSIAN FEDERATION

CAPITAL MOSCOW **POPULATION** 141,377,752 **AREA** 17,075,200 SQ KM **OFFICIAL LANGUAGE** RUSSIAN

Vast Russia – a land of opportunities. Yet the government has ignored the tourist rouble, content to grow fat off oil and gas, leaving swathes of steppe unvisited. A reputation for extortionate hotel rates doesn't help: Moscow is the world's most expensive city to bed down in. The upcoming 2014 Sochi Winter Olympics from 7 to 23 February offers hope – though distant, the games are triggering infrastructure improvements, possibly opening up areas beyond the western cities. And what areas: the scarcely visited Altai Mountains, dotted with archaeological sites; offbeat Kamchatka, the far east peninsula where bears and volcanoes vie to be the most dangerous; and the badlands of north Siberia, somehow populated by reindeer-herding nomads little known to the West.

RWANDA

CAPITAL KIGALI **POPULATION** 9.9 MILLION **AREA** 26,338 SQ KM **OFFICIAL LANGUAGES** KINYARWANDA, FRENCH, ENGLISH

Emerald-green Rwanda still bears memories for many of the attempted massacre of the Tutsi tribe in 1994, which left hundreds of thousands

wine cellars. Improved air links are doing wonders for Portugal's offshore interests too, with tiddly Porto Santo and the remote, whale-frequented Azores now better served than ever.

PUERTO RICO

CAPITAL SAN JUAN **POPULATION** 3.9 MILLION **AREA** 9104 SQ KM **OFFICIAL LANGUAGE** SPANISH

Puerto Rico's a funny old fruit, caught between its relationship with the US, of which it's an unincorporated territory, and its Spanish Caribbean heritage. Add to this the fact that the majority of its tourists are American, many coming in on cruise ships, and you get a strange combination of US big city conveniences – skyscrapers, strip malls – and traditional Spanish Caribbean culture. For fun that's not beneath the sun, head out under a new moon to the bioluminescent bays in Vieques and near Fajardo, which light up magically at night courtesy of billions of microscopic organisms. For another sort of beauty, Puerto Rico's set to host the 2009 Miss Universe pageant, courtesy of a certain Mr Trump.

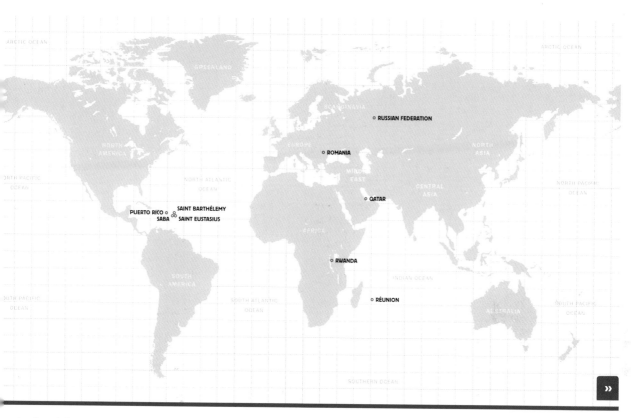

dead and the country in ruins. Nevertheless, some tourists are finally being lured back with the promise of spotting those famous silverback mountain gorillas at the Parc National des Volcans for which Rwanda, before the horrors of a decade ago, was renowned. And deservedly so. These days, visitors can expect a warm welcome from a beautiful and relatively serene country, with only the sometimes-volatile border regions to steer well clear of. 2009 is expected to see an answer to Rwanda's application to join the Commonwealth of Nations, so if all goes well its athletes will be bringing Rwanda to the world's attention before too much longer.

SABA

 CAPITAL THE BOTTOM **POPULATION** 1600 **AREA** 13 SQ KM **OFFICIAL LANGUAGE** DUTCH

How can you possibly go wrong with a place whose capital is named The Bottom, whose only road is named The Road, and whose highest peak is called Mt Scenery? With just 20,000 or so visitors per year, this Netherlands Antilles island is the least visited of all Caribbean islands. This makes it a particularly great destination for the keen diver, as there's plenty of underwater treasure to explore. Unsurprisingly, there's not much overground action on Saba: with no beaches of the usual Caribbean kind, those not diving come here to hike or simply bask in its air of remoteness. Even for thrill-seekers, the plane journey here on a windy day will be enough to warrant a few days' rest and recuperation.

SAINT BARTHÉLEMY

CAPITAL GUSTAVIA **POPULATION** 6852 **AREA** 21 SQ KM **OFFICIAL LANGUAGE** FRENCH

On 20 February 2007 St Barthélemy's status changed from being a commune of neighbouring Guadeloupe to an overseas collectivity of France. Not that this changes much about this diminutive island, best known to jet-setters who arrive by private plane or yacht to populate its sleek villas and ultra-pricey hotels. If you happen to be packing your Prada and heading here in March or April, catch the St Barths Bucket, an annual yacht regatta around the island or, in January, the St Barths Music Festival. Be prepared to rub shoulders with people straight out of the pages of *Hello*, and watch out for those pesky paparazzi hiding in the bushes (you can spot them by their T-shirt-covered telescopic lenses).

SAINT EUSTATIUS

CAPITAL ORANJESTAD **POPULATION** 2800 **AREA** 30.5 SQ KM **OFFICIAL LANGUAGE** DUTCH

Commonly known as Statia, this tiny island sees only a few thousand visitors per year, most of whom come for the top-notch diving around suitably atmospheric sunken shipwrecks. At its 18th-century peak, this place was known as the Golden Rock, gladly sold arms to anyone with purchasing power, and had a population that ran to 10 times that of today. Now it's distinctly unhurried, with a breezy colonial-backwater vibe, and doesn't attract too many tourists due to its lack of golden Caribbean beaches found in innumerable holiday brochures. For most visitors who do make it out here, this is exactly the reason for its charm.

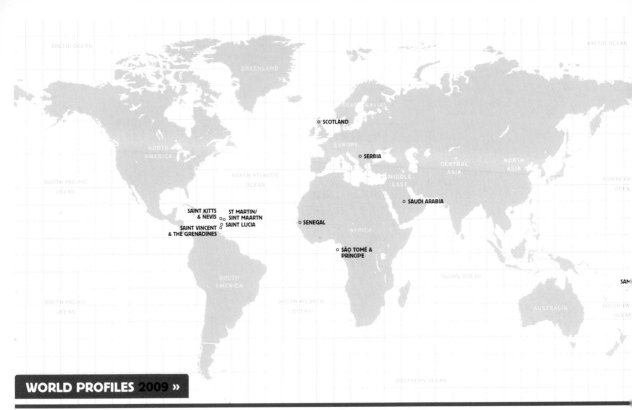

SAINT KITTS & NEVIS

CAPITAL BASSETERRE **POPULATION** 39,349 **AREA** 261 SQ KM **OFFICIAL LANGUAGE** ENGLISH

Saint Kitts & Nevis are the chalk and cheese of the Caribbean, Saint Kitts being as much about partying and casinos as Nevis is about respite. Both are highly visited, with beach weddings a lucrative source of tourist dollars. Around 400,000 cruise ship visitors arrived in 2007, with cruise lines expanding services for 2009 and beyond. Nevis isn't quite as quiet as it once was, with a huge Four Seasons resort now gracing its shores, but it remains a good option for those looking for a slower pace of spending. One day the pair may part company, with Nevis trying to separate from its lively sibling. For now they remain close-knit, mismatched in everything but their Caribbean beauty.

SAINT LUCIA

CAPITAL CASTRIES **POPULATION** 170,649 **AREA** 616 SQ KM **OFFICIAL LANGUAGE** ENGLISH

Once, Saint Lucia was famous for nothing more than a whole lot of bananas, but nowadays tourism is the undisputed watchword. With the Caribbean's largest tourism conference hosted here in January 2009, and the country regularly topping polls as the UK's favourite overseas wedding destination, things are not as calm and sedentary as in days past. Nevertheless, its beaches haven't suffered much under the tourist invasion, despite the planeloads of package holidaymakers who descend on a fortnightly basis, and the island still hosts a wealth of serene natural treasures. Bathe in the mineral waters of the Malgretout Waterfall or trek up to the Qualibou volcano for an idyllic taste of the good old quiet life.

SAINT MARTIN & SINT MAARTEN

CAPITALS MARIGOT (ST MARTIN), PHILIPSBURG (SINT MAARTEN) **POPULATION** 35,000 (ST MARTIN), 34,000 (SINT MAARTEN) **AREA** 54.4 SQ KM (ST MARTIN), 41.44 SQ KM (SINT MAARTEN) **OFFICIAL LANGUAGES** FRENCH (ST MARTIN), DUTCH (SINT MAARTEN)

No, St Martin and Sint Maarten aren't just alternative spellings of the same place name, but two neighbouring dependencies on a tiny land mass shared by France and the Netherlands. Unlike many of the smaller Caribbean isles, Sint Maarten is neither sleepy nor exclusive: charter planes fly in with enthusiasm, bringing in thousands to populate its casinos, clubs and duty-free extravaganzas, whilst condo development seems to know no bounds. St Martin, the island's second face, is casino-less (for the moment, at least) with finer dining and more space on the sands, including, if you're in the mood for nude, one of the Caribbean's only naturist resorts, near Orient Beach.

SAINT VINCENT & THE GRENADINES

CAPITAL KINGSTOWN **POPULATION** 118,149 **AREA** 389 SQ KM **OFFICIAL LANGUAGE** ENGLISH

With a reputation for exclusivity, and both David Bowie and Mick Jagger calling parts of its 32 islands home, this nation (whose name is suited to a groovy gospel choir) is far from a budget destination. Agriculture, principally banana production, still tops tourism as its main source of income, and with unemployment at 22% (not counting the idle aristocrats in residence) there's a definite gap between the haves and the have-nots. The filming here of *Pirates of the Caribbean: Dead Man's Chest* in 2006 helped expose the area to a wider tourist market, but for now it remains a low-key, laid-back destination, reserved for those able to spend an average of US$250 per day (or more!) on its glittering charms.

SAMOA

CAPITAL APIA **POPULATION** 176,910 **AREA** 2944 SQ KM **OFFICIAL LANGUAGE** ENGLISH

Verdant rainforests, thundering waves and blindingly white beaches – is it any wonder Robert Louis Stevenson said goodbye to dreary Scotland to move to Samoa? The advent of the 2007 South Pacific Games allowed Samoa to clean up its act (including a wild-dog cull), though the loss of King Malietoa Tanumafili II in the same year brought great sadness. The new king, Tuiatua Tupua Tamasese Efi, was elected for a five-year term and has begun ushering in a new era. As much as for the stunning beaches and dive sites, visitors come to be a part of Fa'a Samoa ('the Samoan way'), which observes a serene Sunday and celebrates cheerful community.

SÃO TOMÉ & PRÍNCIPE

CAPITAL SÃO TOMÉ **POPULATION** 199,579 **AREA** 1001 SQ KM **OFFICIAL LANGUAGE** PORTUGUESE

Though it might sound contradictory, the main draw for tourists to these tiny, peaceable West African volcanic islands is that there are no tourists. Hard to get to, and equally hard to leave, these green specks in the ocean offer all that an island getaway should: miles of empty beaches, diving to die for, and rainforest trails to explore amid twittering birdlife. All's not entirely at ease in this floating utopia though: vast and unexploited reserves of oil lying just beneath its shimmering waters have inevitably started to cause arguments. How should the cash be spent when the black stuff comes up? Let's hope it's not on a 747-size landing strip, a casino, or a slew of luxury hotels.

SAUDI ARABIA

CAPITAL RIYADH **POPULATION** 28.2 MILLION **AREA** 1,960,582 SQ KM **OFFICIAL LANGUAGE** ARABIC

Whether tourists will be arriving in Saudi in 2009 depends very much on whether it remains on many foreign offices' no-go lists. Tourist visas might remain elusive but are not as impossible to obtain as they once were, and those who make the effort to get here never fail to be impressed by the wealth of activities. Don't miss Habalah, a deserted village with incredible views from its cable car, gasp at the wonders of ancient Petra-like Nabatean city Madain Saleh, and dive the crystal-clear waters of the Red Sea. While non-Muslims will have to skip Mecca and Medina, a visit in February will ensure access to the colourful two-week Al Jenadriyah culture and heritage festival near Riyadh.

SCOTLAND

CAPITAL EDINBURGH **POPULATION** 5.1 MILLION **AREA** 77,925 SQ KM **OFFICIAL LANGUAGE** ENGLISH

Auld Lang Syne will be sung with extra gusto this Hogmanay, heralding the 250th anniversary of the birth of national poet Robert Burns. Whether it'll be accompanied by bagpipes is unsure, after recent revelations that the love-hate instrument – alleged soundtrack to ancient skirmishes – was invented just 200 years ago by middle-class Londoners. But pipes of some kind should salute Scotland's good intentions to become the world's first carbon-neutral destination. Help out by visiting its green spaces: the North West Highlands Geopark is one of the most sparsely populated (and geologically magnificent) areas in Europe, while at the Alladale Estate an unconventional landowner is using African game-park practices to reintroduce moose and, possibly, wolves to their natural home.

SENEGAL

CAPITAL DAKAR **POPULATION** 12.5 MILLION **AREA** 196,190 SQ KM **OFFICIAL LANGUAGE** FRENCH

Suave and sophisticated Senegal bursts with reasons to visit, not least its prolific arts scene and world-class festivals: the vast Festival Mondial Des Artes Negres will hit breezy Dakar in December 2009 and the wonderful biannual Dak'Art Biennale is in 2010. This West African beauty sees a solid amount of annual tourism (mostly from France and Spain), largely in its beach destinations around the Petite Côte. Tourist itineraries will one day include the beaches around Cap Skiring in the southwestern Casamance region, often off-limits due to occasional outbreaks of fighting and lawlessness. If you're planning on making it down here, heed local advice before heading out.

SERBIA

CAPITAL BELGRADE **POPULATION** 8 MILLION **AREA** 77,474 SQ KM **OFFICIAL LANGUAGE** SERBIAN

They're singing in Serbia – not only are foreign visitor numbers on the up

can afford to set foot here. Because budget traveller territory they still ain't. If you're one of the lucky ones heading for a spot of luxuriant basking in 2009, time your visit for the end of October, when you'll be able to glimpse the islands' Creole culture at the week-long Festival Kreol.

SIERRA LEONE

CAPITAL FREETOWN **POPULATION** 6.1 MILLION **AREA** 71,740 SQ KM **OFFICIAL LANGUAGE** ENGLISH

The civil war is slowly becoming a distant memory and, though care should still be taken on roads outside the capital due to a certain amount of crime and banditry, Sierra Leone now offers an enticing combination of beach life and national park wildlife. Dive amongst Portuguese shipwrecks off the shores of the Banana Islands, or soak up the rays at one of the growing number of luxury hotels springing up on the Freetown Peninsula. Linger with chimps at the Outamba-Kilimi National Park, or clamber to the top of Mt Bintumani for stunning views of the dense rainforest surroundings. If peace continues, you'll be hearing great things from Sierra Leone in years to come – so see it now, if you possibly can.

SINGAPORE

CAPITAL SINGAPORE **POPULATION** 4.6 MILLION **AREA** 682.7 SQ KM **OFFICIAL LANGUAGES** MALAY, TAMIL, MANDARIN, ENGLISH

The squeaky clean (no drugs, no spitting) Asian city-state is the ideal venue for the first Youth Olympic Games in August 2010. Some might say it's so safe it's dull, but with mega-developments in Clarke Quay and the plastic fantastic-theme park, Sentosa, there's plenty to keep the under-18s out of trouble. Singapore has been preparing for international events by giving over its streets to its first Grand Prix in 2008 and by upscaling Changi Airport to rival Bangkok as the hub of Southeast Asian travel. It's an ever-popular stopover between Europe and Australia, with a compact city centre that can be sampled in a day.

SLOVAKIA

CAPITAL BRATISLAVA **POPULATION** 5.4 MILLION **AREA** 48,845 SQ KM **OFFICIAL LANGUAGE** SLOVAK

Ahoj euro! will be the cry ringing round Bratislava in January 2009 as Slovakia adopts the European currency. But euros tend to mean higher prices, off-putting to those considering visiting a country in which tourism development thus far has been 'chaotic and fragmented' – the words of its own Ministry of Economy. However, there is a growing desire to ensure that as prices rise here, so does the quality of the experience – and in Slovakia there are (little-known) experiences in spades, from rural retreats in the High Tatras, to rafting along the wild Dunajec River to the exploration of cave networks that are still being discovered – start with the crystalline formations hidden inside Ochtinska Aragonit.

SLOVENIA

CAPITAL LJUBLJANA **POPULATION** 2 MILLION **AREA** 20,273 SQ KM **OFFICIAL LANGUAGE** SLOVENIAN

You don't hear bad things about Slovenia – pretty, compact, stable in the face of its more volatile neighbours, it's where Austrians go to get away from it all. And now it's garnering a following among others wanting a dose of lakes, mountains and authentic hospitality. The country's hotspots have been a little isolated, but plans are afoot to improve transport and map out cycle trails to help you get to Slovenia's best bits. Highlights include grassroots wine tours in Posavje and Podravje (which see thirsty punters sleeping in homestay cottages) and the floral spectacle around Lake Bohinj, celebrated annually since May 2007, during the International Wild Flower Festival.

SOLOMON ISLANDS

CAPITAL HONIARA **POPULATION** 581,318 **AREA** 28,450 SQ KM **OFFICIAL LANGUAGE** ENGLISH

The Solomons remain famous for three things: diving, diving and

but it seems to be the place for music. Following an, er, melodic Eurovision in 2008, the plaudit-heaped EXIT festival in Novi Sad (July) and the raucous battle of Balkan brass that is the Guca Trumpet Festival (August) have proved to be two of the continent's best knees-ups. This is a country that, Kosovan independence issues aside, is emerging from its bomb-blasted past as a place to party, especially as these days you don't have to be a dissident to delve into one of Belgrade's (many) secret cellar bars.

SEYCHELLES

CAPITAL VICTORIA **POPULATION** 81,895 **AREA** 455 SQ KM **OFFICIAL LANGUAGES** ENGLISH, FRENCH, CREOLE

What can we say about these specks in the Indian Ocean that a holiday brochure hasn't already said? Yes, they're beautiful. Yes, they're romantic. And yes, they're the preferred slice of paradise for the barefoot-wedding brigade. But with 115 islands dotted over a mind-boggling million square kilometres of sea, there's plenty of space for as many canoodling couples as

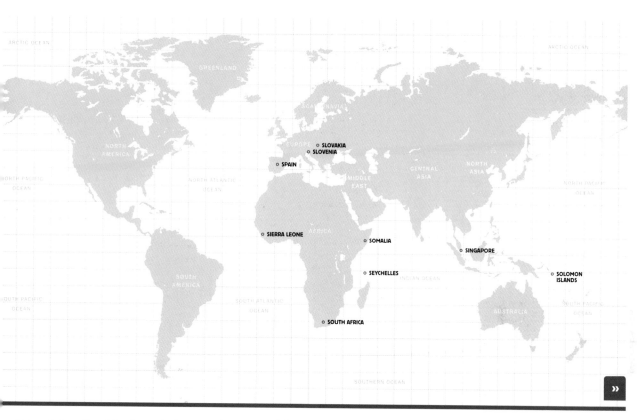

more diving. Consistently ranked one of the world's best places to get on down beneath the waves, diving's the lure that brings a steady stream of visitors to its beautiful shores – though surfers, too, are increasingly heading here to skim the surface. Though it's had a fair share of strife, with political unrest plaguing its recent history, things are looking pretty calm of late for the nation; it pays to monitor the news just in case. If you can tear yourself away from the underwater world, head out to remote Lake Te'Nggano, the South Pacific's largest body of fresh water, to while away the hours observing its diverse birdlife.

SOMALIA

CAPITAL MOGADISHU **POPULATION** 9.1 MILLION **AREA** 637,657 SQ KM **OFFICIAL LANGUAGE** SOMALI

Chances are that unless you're a reckless, devil-may-care sort of traveller with a particular penchant for armed conflict, you won't be heading to Somalia any time soon. One of the world's most dangerous destinations, it is, in theory, possible to venture

into parts of the self-proclaimed northern Republic of Somaliland – and indeed a tiny trickle of travellers do so. Except for that, few foreigners fill plane seats on the limited number of flights into Mogadishu, unless they're brought here under the mantle of international aid agencies. Somalia remains a place to watch in the news headlines, rather than from the seat of a bus.

SOUTH AFRICA

CAPITAL PRETORIA **POPULATION** 43.8 MILLION **AREA** 1,219,912 SQ KM **OFFICIAL LANGUAGES** AFRIKAANS, ENGLISH, ISINDEBELE, ISIXHOSA, ISIZULU, SEPEDI, SESOTHO, SETSWANA, SISWATI, TSHIVENDA, XITSONGA

Struggling with a history that includes the Boer Wars and apartheid, South Africa is stepping onto the world stage. Wildlife and wine (best not mixed) are strong drawcards for the Cape, but in 2009 the clash of the codes will bring international attention. The FIFA Confederations Cup kicks off with thousands of international soccer fans taking over the country, and before anyone can catch their breath the touring

British Lions will bring the grunt of world-class rugby. Luckily it's still possible to escape to the vineyards of Stellenbosch or Franschoek or to wildlife reserves like Kruger National Park, which will seem tame after all that testosterone.

SPAIN

CAPITAL MADRID **POPULATION** 40.4 MILLION **AREA** 504,782 SQ KM **OFFICIAL LANGUAGE** SPANISH

Good old Spain. Despite a robust euro it's still great value – and more aware than ever that we don't all want to bake on beaches. Themed itineraries are booming, such as Rioja wine-and-truffle trips, concerts galore at Palau de la Música (celebrating its 100th year in 2008–2009), and nature tours in an Ibiza keen to shed its hedonistic reputation. Ecotravellers will be happy, too. High-speed trains now link Madrid and Barcelona in 2½ hours (down from six), while walking is the new black – 200,000 pilgrims follow the long-distance Camino de Santiago across the country's in-vogue north. New hotels en route are planned to house them in greater comfort.

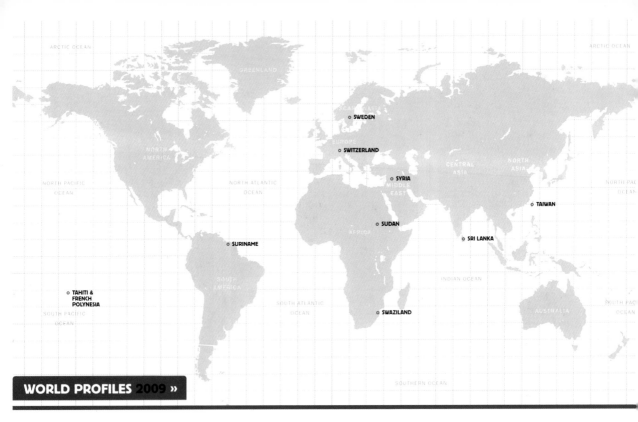

SRI LANKA

 **CAPITAL** COLOMBO **POPULATION** 21.1 MILLION **AREA** 65,640 SQ KM **OFFICIAL LANGUAGES** SINHALA, TAMIL

Life's been hard to Sri Lanka of late. The fight between the Tamils and the majority Sinhalese, which has plagued the island for three decades, continues to surface, most recently in bombings that left dozens of civilians dead. For a long time, fighting was confined to the north and east coasts – but if attacks escalate in Colombo, travellers will start to stay away from the hot spots of the south coast too. Should things quieten down, 2009 will be a terrific year to visit, with its uncrowded beaches and ancient sites in which to wander in peace. Don't miss the Kandy Esala Perahera if you're here during July, 10 days of the country's biggest and most colourful festival.

SUDAN

CAPITAL KHARTOUM **POPULATION** 39.4 MILLION **AREA** 2,505,810 SQ KM **OFFICIAL LANGUAGE** ARABIC

Though the largest country in Africa encompasses an area around the size of Western Europe, little of it is currently on travellers' itineraries. With the humanitarian crisis in Darfur having reached epic proportions, civilian strife in western Sudan and instability in its border regions, it seems there's little of Sudan that would make travel here rewarding. Should its crises be resolved, Sudan might finally emerge from the dark shadows that have left an estimated 1.5 million dead and even more displaced in the last half-century. With rich natural resources – including untapped oil reserves – and an evocatively named capital city that's home to sprawling souqs, whirling dervishes, a well-stocked national museum and the confluence of the Blue and White Niles, there could well be hope for Sudan.

SURINAME

CAPITAL PARAMARIBO **POPULATION** 470,784 **AREA** 163,270 SQ KM **OFFICIAL LANGUAGE** DUTCH

Unless you are Dutch you may be forgiven for thinking – like many seasoned travellers have before you – that Suriname is situated somewhere not too far from Vietnam. Few people know that this country on the eastern South American seaboard has the most ethnically diverse population on the continent, and few travellers make it here to find out. But this fascinating place, filled with Dutch colonial architecture, natural wonders and wildlife galore, is slowly creeping onto ecotourists' and adventure-travellers' itineraries, and with good reason. Trek its 1.6 million hectares of gorgeous rainforest at the World Heritage–listed Central Suriname Nature Reserve, then party along to Christian, Hindu or Islamic festivals, of which there are an abundance.

SWAZILAND

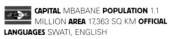 **CAPITAL** MBABANE **POPULATION** 1.1 MILLION **AREA** 17,363 SQ KM **OFFICIAL LANGUAGES** SWATI, ENGLISH

A poor and landlocked kingdom with the highest rate of HIV/AIDS infection in the world (38% of its population are estimated to be infected) leading to an average life expectancy of just 31 to 32 years, Swaziland is quite surprisingly one of Africa's most

stable and easy-going countries. Unless you're here to volunteer for one of its highly necessary charity programmes, the main reason to visit is to trek through one of Swaziland's absolutely stellar national parks. Birds are the main attraction at Malolotja; horseback trips to spot giraffe and zebra are the order of the day (and overnight) at Milwane. But if it's the highly endangered black rhino you're after, head to Mkhaya, which offers the best chance of a sighting in the whole of Africa.

SWEDEN

 **CAPITAL** STOCKHOLM **POPULATION** 9 MILLION **AREA** 449,964 SQ KM **OFFICIAL LANGUAGE** SWEDISH

Sweden is heading to new heights: as well as being voted best destination in one UK survey, its Arctic Esrange Space Station will be Virgin Galactic's second launch pad, with flights into the northern lights mooted from 2012. Back at ground level, Stockholm is welcoming two firsts: December 2008 welcomes the Jumbo Hostel, where travellers can bed down in a grounded Boeing; while dancing queens rejoice in June 2009 at the opening of ABBA the Museum. West Sweden is less kitsch, more kitchen, its cuisine tempting gourmets worldwide – here you'll find Michelin star–grabbing Göteburg, lobster safaris off the Bohuslän coast and more farm shops than you can shake a pickled herring at.

SWITZERLAND

CAPITAL BERN **POPULATION** 7.6 MILLION **AREA** 41,290 SQ KM **OFFICIAL LANGUAGES** GERMAN, FRENCH, ITALIAN, ROMANSCH

To call Switzerland bland does it a gross injustice. And yet…this proudly independent nation, a peaceful mix of cultures arranged around mountains so grand you'll choke on your fondue, has somehow become the butt of an incomprehensible joke. It's got the looks. It's got the infrastructure (at a price). Perhaps it's the fact it lacks edge? Or that it used to:

efforts have been made to entice a younger crowd with cities that are becoming increasingly more vibrant, and Zürich and Basel now buzz with short-breakers. There's adrenaline action too: *vie ferrate* (fixed cable climbs) score the slopes, and the world's highest rollercoaster (3000m) opened in 2007. Cross a swaying suspension bridge between the hostile peaks of undiscovered Haslital and then tell us it's bland…

SYRIA

CAPITAL DAMASCUS **POPULATION** 19.7 MILLION **AREA** 185,180 SQ KM **OFFICIAL LANGUAGE** ARABIC

Although the USA recently issued a warning against travel to Syria, this misunderstood country on the 'axis of evil' continues to have a healthy independent traveller turnout. With a reputation for having some of the friendliest locals in the Middle East, Syria's appeal is beginning to translate into an upturn in tourism services, with boutique hotels popping up in Damascus and Aleppo, and ecotourism starting to emerge around the country. By no stretch of the imagination though is the country overrun with backpackers, making now a perfect time to explore. Travel to Qala'at Samaan, Syria's most atmospheric archaeological site, and then onward to explore the spooky ancient Dead Cities ghost towns, before returning to civilisation for a gourmet meal and a soak in a luxury-hotel tub.

TAHITI & FRENCH POLYNESIA

CAPITAL PAPE'ETE **POPULATION** 283,019 **AREA** 4167 SQ KM **OFFICIAL LANGUAGES** TAHITIAN, FRENCH

Ever since the paintings of Paul Gauguin brought the laid-back life of French Polynesia to Europeans, there has been constant traffic to the islands. Witnessing the total solar eclipse in July 2010 is the latest reason to visit, with astronomers and hippies agreeing that the eclipse will be best viewed in French Polynesia, ideally on board a yacht with a cocktail in hand. Several

»

specialist tours are focusing on the phenomenon that will last no more than five minutes. On land, Pape'ete is swamped with traffic and grim urban architecture, but has indoor spectacles like the Pacific International Documentary Film Festival in 2009.

TAIWAN

CAPITAL TAIPEI **POPULATION** 23 MILLION **AREA** 32,260 SQ KM **OFFICIAL LANGUAGE** MANDARIN

China's big publicity push on Taiwan is starting to pay off. Budget carriers are bringing in more international visitors, and independent travel is even easier with the Taiwan High Speed Railway bullet train that traverses the island from Taipei to Kaohsiung City. It's arrived just in time for the 2009 World Games in Kaohsiung, an alternative Olympics that includes parachuting, canoe polo and roller skating. Add to this the 2009 Deaflympics in Taipei and the nation's dance card is looking full. There's still plenty of room to escape into the wilds of Ilha Formosa (Beautiful Island) or the nation's network of hiking and cycling routes.

TAJIKISTAN

CAPITAL DUSHANBE **POPULATION** 7.2 MILLION **AREA** 143,100 SQ KM **OFFICIAL LANGUAGE** TAJIK

Mountainous Tajikistan, host to the ancient Silk Road, has been an inviting destination for travellers for quite some time. More tour companies are cottoning on to the country's potential, particularly in the realm of ecotourism. A Hyatt Regency is scheduled to open in Dushanbe some time in 2008, meaning that after a spot of strenuous mountain hiking there'll be a more luxurious place to lay your head than has existed up till now. Become a fan of the Fan Mountains, explore the Zoroastrian ruins of the Wakhan Corridor and revel in the satisfaction of arriving before the crowds catch wind of what's on offer.

TANZANIA

CAPITAL DODOMA **POPULATION** 39.4 MILLION **AREA** 945,087 SQ KM **OFFICIAL LANGUAGES** SWAHILI, ENGLISH

With the winning trio of Kilimanjaro, the Serengeti and Zanzibar on offer, it's unlikely that Tanzania's popularity with tourists will ebb any time soon. Safari-hungry flocks head here to see more big game gathered than anywhere else on the planet, and although Kilimanjaro's snowcap is shrinking fast, it's still a hit with hikers and climbers. Visit in April, when the migration starts and herds are at their most impressive. To escape the khaki-clad crowds in 2009, hide away on the Mafia Island archipelago, heavy with marine life and whose white-sand beaches are less busy than Zanzibar's; or track Tanzania's last wild chimpanzees in the remote Mahale Mountains.

THAILAND

CAPITAL BANGKOK **POPULATION** 65 MILLION **AREA** 511,770 SQ KM **OFFICIAL LANGUAGE** THAI

Just as Thailand was rebuilding its tourism industry after the tsunami tragedy, it began making headlines for all the wrong reasons: terrorism in the south and post-election coups in a country known as a bastion of serenity in the region. But tourism in Thailand is so firmly established that the impact of these events has not been major. Budget airlines have made short stays possible and an emphasis on wellness tourism, such as massage classes or Buddhist retreats, have created good reasons to rediscover the ancient kingdom. And there's still the checklist that made Thailand the pick of the 1990s: Buddha, beaches and Bangkok.

TIBET

CAPITAL LHASA **POPULATION** 2.7 MILLION **AREA** 1,221,601 SQ KM **OFFICIAL LANGUAGE** MANDARIN

In the news for its troubled relationship with China, Tibet seized upon the 2008 Olympics as a chance to take its struggle for independence to the world. Tourism became easier with a new rail line from Golmud in China, though many observed that trains can transport troops as easily as tourists. Should you go to Tibet? With regular media and tourist lock-outs, it's more a case of whether you can. Maintaining international attention on the Central Asian region and witnessing the unique culture and spectacular landscapes of the country will certainly do much to make the independence cause more widely known.

TOGO

CAPITAL LOMÉ **POPULATION** 5.7 MILLION **AREA** 56,785 SQ KM **OFFICIAL LANGUAGE** FRENCH

Following its free and, by Togo's standards, democratic legislative elections in late 2007, it seems that calm has been officially sanctioned in tiny Togo. Already back on the more innovative traveller's circuit, those in the know favour Anejo Beach for a spot of seaside relaxation on the Bight of Benin, not far from the balmy coastal capital Lomé and its bustling markets that sell everything. Upcountry, the Tamberma Valley is a unique sight, with its fortified *tata* homes (castle-like compounds), founded in the 17th century by those escaping slavery in Benin. If there's a sign of things to come in Togo, this is it: tour guides are already congregating in droves, ready to pounce on the unwitting traveller. Visit soon, before the tour-guide culture takes over nationwide.

TONGA

 CAPITAL NUKU'ALOFA **POPULATION** 119,009 **AREA** 748 SQ KM **OFFICIAL LANGUAGES** TONGAN, ENGLISH

This collection of almost 170 islands has been impressing tourists with its laid-back charm ever since Captain Cook dubbed them the 'Friendly Isles' after his visit. The death of King Tupou IV in 2006 saw rioting, with many Tongans wanting to move away from traditional monarchy to democracy. Much of rioting took place in the downtown area of Nuku'alofa. King Siaosi Tupou V has done much to restore stability and tourism, and beyond the capital most of the country was untroubled – the outlying islands are still an ideal location to get away from it all.

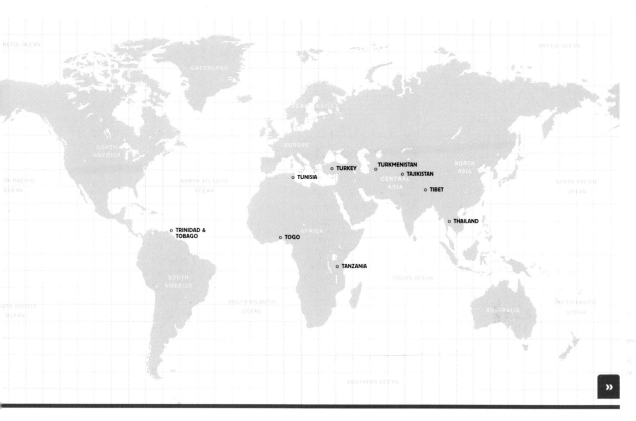

TRINIDAD & TOBAGO

 CAPITAL PORT-OF-SPAIN **POPULATION** 1.1 MILLION **AREA** 5128 SQ KM **OFFICIAL LANGUAGE** ENGLISH

Heading to this Caribbean odd-couple in 2009? The time to hit Trinidad's capital is just before Ash Wednesday, when the Carnival bursts into town in all its calypso glory. Tourism provides a steady (but not yet explosive) income to these little and large islands, which rely heavily on international business, steel and liquefied natural gas exports. Here you'll likely experience a far more local vibe than at many other Caribbean destinations. But there are fears for Tobago's icing-sugar beaches, which are suffering from the tourist onslaught. To give something back, check out SOS Tobago, which is helping to preserve Tobago's leatherback turtles.

TUNISIA

CAPITAL TUNIS **POPULATION** 10.4 MILLION **AREA** 163,610 SQ KM **OFFICIAL LANGUAGE** ARABIC

Long an option in package-holiday brochures, bewitching Tunisia has recently taken an upmarket twist. To make the most of a stay in its new slew of boutique hotels, especially in Tunis's medina area and in atmospheric Carthage, visit in summer 2009 and catch a host of international festivals. Along with the El-Jem International Symphonic Music Festival in July, there's the Carthage International Festival (July and August), whose dance, theatre and music performances take place within the Roman theatre itself. Later in the year, look out for the biennial Carthage International Film Festival in October, with its emphasis on African and Middle Eastern film fare. To escape the crowds on Tunisia's many glorious beaches, head up to the quiet north coast or to delicious El-Mansourah, near Kélibia on Cap Bon.

TURKEY

CAPITAL ANKARA **POPULATION** 71.9 MILLION **AREA** 770,760 SQ KM **OFFICIAL LANGUAGE** TURKISH

A gateway to two continents, Turkey's shore is lapped by no less than three seas – the Mediterranean, Black and Aegean – making it a getaway for Europe and the Middle East. It boasts treasures like the archaeological ruins of ancient Troy and Aya Sofya, one of the world's greatest religious monuments – but also attracts a basketball crowd with events like the 2010 FIBA World Championships (from 23 August to 5 September). Safety concerns after bombings in Izmir and Ankara will make some rethink their visit, and the border with Iraq will continue to be a no-go zone for some time – but a country that has seen empires rise and fall will survive the latest upheavals.

TURKMENISTAN

CAPITAL ASHKHABAD **POPULATION** 5.2 MILLION **AREA** 488,100 SQ KM **OFFICIAL LANGUAGE** TURKMEN

Bleak and barren, with vast un-explored potential oilfields and 80% of its land the dusty Karakum Desert, Turkmenistan remains a destination for travellers who thrill to the allure of massive tracts of nothingness. But that doesn't mean there's nothing to see amid all that sand. Traditional Turkmen Bedouin villages inhabit the plains, whilst the blazing flames from

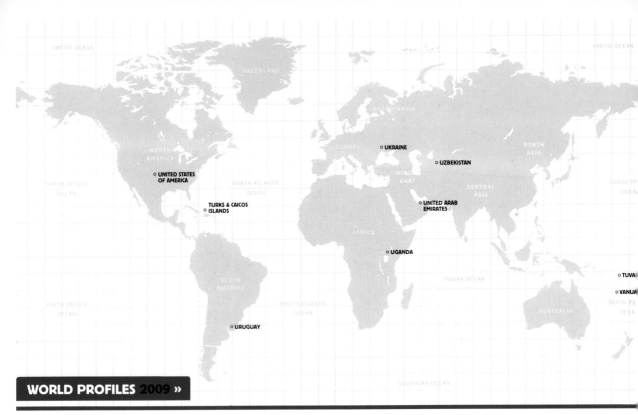

the Darvaza Gas Craters rank among the world's weirdest sights. Get even closer to the sense of the prehistoric by visiting Dinosaur Plateau, where dinosaur footprints are preserved in lava, then pick up a carpet for the hall back home at the mammoth Tolkuchka Bazaar. You won't find many tourists here yet, so 2009's a great year to go.

TURKS & CAICOS ISLANDS

CAPITAL COCKBURN TOWN **POPULATION** 21,746 **AREA** 430 SQ KM **OFFICIAL LANGUAGE** ENGLISH

Tourism and offshore investment services continue to boost the islands' economy, prospering due to increasing numbers of US visitors and cruise-ship traffic. The main reason to come here remains the top-notch dive sites, filled with enticing shipwrecks, marine life and unparalleled reef action. The beaches, too, are highly acclaimed: in 2007 Grace Bay Beach on Providenciales won the World's Leading Beach award at the World Travel Awards. Of its 40 islands and cays, only eight are inhabited, meaning there's plenty of room to explore without seeing another soul.

TUVALU

CAPITAL FUNAFUTI **POPULATION** 12,177 **AREA** 26 SQ KM **OFFICIAL LANGUAGE** TUVALUAN

This tiny collection of six atolls and three islands has been making headlines for its environmental stance ever since it changed its name from Ellice Islands in the 1970s. The country's extremely low altitude means that the islands are sinking due to global warming, so Tuvalu was a strong campaigner for the Kyoto Protocol. Shrinking land mass means responsible tourism is crucial. Just under three hours' flight from Fiji, Tuvalu's remoteness means that few visitors experience this vulnerable destination, despite appealing beaches and the small friendly community.

UGANDA

CAPITAL KAMPALA **POPULATION** 30.3 MILLION **AREA** 237,040 SQ KM **OFFICIAL LANGUAGE** ENGLISH

Following the success of *The Last King of Scotland*, Uganda is back in the public's imagination, although hopes that the rebel Lord's Resistance Army (LRA) would finally call a halt to its two-decade-long war, have not yet materialised. However, with the exception of the LRA-heavy Murchison Falls area, many of Uganda's treasures are absolutely within the traveller's reach, including some unforgettable mountain gorilla–tracking at Bwindi Impenetrable National Park. With its rapidly growing economy and sharp decline in HIV/AIDS infection rate (from over 30% down to 4.1%), Uganda can be termed a success story. Outside Kampala, visit the 19th-century Tombs of Buganda Kings; for more thrilling activity, head to Jinja at the source of the Nile, for whitewater rafting or whizzing on a zip-wire across the great river itself.

UKRAINE

CAPITAL KIEV **POPULATION** 46.3 MILLION **AREA** 603,700 SQ KM **OFFICIAL LANGUAGE** UKRAINIAN

Good old Eurovision – following Kiev's staging of the 2005 camp croon-athon, visa requirements for EU members were scrapped and visitors poured in (at least by previous standards). 2008 looked like a record year for short breaks to Kiev and trips by train between cities such as Old Habsburg Lviv and Black Sea-hugging Odessa. But for 2009 the intrepid should delve into the Carpathian Mountains, where the scenery is spectacular and the land is dotted with Hutsul communities – isolated farmers whose embroidered dresses, hand-painted *pysanky* (wooden eggs) and folk tales add vibrancy and humanity to the wild landscape.

UNITED ARAB EMIRATES

CAPITAL ABU DHABI **POPULATION** 4.6 MILLION **AREA** 82,880 SQ KM **OFFICIAL LANGUAGE** ARABIC

Though for the vast majority of visitors the UAE begins and ends with Dubai, capital Abu Dhabi – along with other parts of the UAE's seven separate sheikhdoms – is currently cornering a chunk of the long-weekend tourism market that's taken the region by storm. International visitors are now heading out from Abu Dhabi on adventure trips to Liwa Oasis, to visit dunes and tiny villages on the edge of Saudi Arabia's Empty Quarter, proving there's more to a visit than duty-free shopping. Recently, the UAE has gained notoriety for its fierce drug laws, apprehending some tourists bringing cold medicines – or even poppy seeds – into the country. Check regulations and your pockets thoroughly to avoid ending up in a spot of bother.

UNITED STATES OF AMERICA

CAPITAL WASHINGTON DC **POPULATION** 303.8 MILLION **AREA** 9,161,923 SQ KM **OFFICIAL LANGUAGE** ENGLISH

Whether you're a sybarite longing for lounge-lizarding in New York City or a rugged get-away-from-it-aller hoping to hit the Rocky Mountain Trails, the USA has it in spades. And with the country's president-elect set to be inaugurated on 20 January 2009, these are exciting times for the grand ole US of A. When the votes are finally counted and the new president is warming the seat of the White House, the world will be looking on carefully to see how the beleaguered countries of Afghanistan and Iraq will fare from US foreign policy, and the new government's approach towards the Middle East and global terrorism. However, this doesn't look set to affect the country's appeal to tourists from across the globe, arriving in droves to find their own piece of the American Dream.

URUGUAY

CAPITAL MONTEVIDEO **POPULATION** 3.4 MILLION **AREA** 176,220 SQ KM **OFFICIAL LANGUAGE** SPANISH

Uruguay's not the in-the-know-traveller's-secret it once was, but that's because this compact place – the second-smallest country in South America – offers so many tempting reasons to visit. Nowadays far less crumbling, Montevideo is slowly on the up, with new, cool boutique hotels springing up alongside bustling bars. Inland you'll find colonial small-town gems and cattle ranches raising prime beef for dinner, while the sparkling beaches are a hit particularly with Argentinean and Brazilian tourists. Come here too for the dazzling Easter Carnaval. Uruguay is, by local standards, a particularly progressive place: late 2007 saw it become the first Latin American country to legally recognise same-sex civil unions, a sign of even better things to come.

UZBEKISTAN

CAPITAL TASHKENT **POPULATION** 28.3 MILLION **AREA** 447,400 SQ KM **OFFICIAL LANGUAGE** UZBEK

There are few names as evocative as Samarkand, Bukhara and Tashkent, and Uzbekistan possesses all three. Over the last few years, Uzbekistan has seen a good flow of both independent travellers and tour groups arriving to view its ancient Silk Road sites, though they remain far from crowded even at the height of summer. In 2009, if you really want to escape the road

most travelled, head out to what little remains of the Aral Sea – and Moynaq, the eerie near-ghost-town that once made its living from fishing the Aral. Now a tragic, desolate area of grounded ships and poisonous dust storms, it's a sobering reminder of man's sometimes shocking effect on the environment.

VANUATU

CAPITAL PORT VILA **POPULATION** 215,446 **AREA** 12,200 SQ KM **OFFICIAL LANGUAGE** BISLAMA

Budget flights to Port Vila in this Pacific paradise have seen an increase in visitors seeking an ideal short break. The country, a mix of French, British, Melanesian and Polynesian heritage, also pulls its fair share of suits and sailors given it operates as a tax haven, and flagging a ship here is more affordable than most of the world's ports. With over 80 islands in the group, travellers are seeking out their own undiscovered pockets and unexplored beaches. The destination is marred only by infrequent earthquakes (in 2002 and 2007) and appearances on TV show *Survivor*.

by 1.5 million between 2000 and 2006 and most pundits believe this will only continue, with the World Travel & Tourism Council predicting it will be one of the top 10 tourist spots by 2016. While Europeans and even Northern Americans (don't mention the war!) are discovering Vietnam, the big numbers are from locals like China, Japan and Korea. With the November 2009 Indoor Asian Games – which includes events such as dragon dancing, electronic sports and BMX events – coming to Hanoi, there'll be even more visiting neighbours and development in the capital.

VIRGIN ISLANDS

CAPITALS ROAD TOWN (BVI), CHARLOTTE AMALIE (USVI) **POPULATION** 23,100 (BVI), 124,778 (USVI) **AREA** 153 SQ KM (BVI), 352 SQ KM (USVI) **OFFICIAL LANGUAGE** ENGLISH

Popular as ever among holidaymakers from the USA, it might seem there's nowhere much for the Virgin Islands to go except to continue on the tourism road it's been travelling for quite some time. Still, this duty-free haven of crystalline seas and tourist-brochure beaches – in parts British (BVI), in others US-governed (USVI) – has pockets still ripe for discovery. Head to St John for the Virgin Islands National Park, a vast tract of unpopulated parkland, or to the parks and ecological reserves on St Croix, which despite possessing an international airport is less touristed simply because it's slightly further from the other islands. Otherwise there's not much to do except bask on beautiful beaches like Loblolly Bay, along with the cruise-ship crowds.

WALES

CAPITAL CARDIFF **POPULATION** 2.9 MILLION **AREA** 20,732 SQ KM **OFFICIAL LANGUAGE** ENGLISH

Wales is embracing its Welshness more than ever. Its government has greater autonomy and the Welsh language is enjoying a resurgence – one survey says 50% of locals believe the country will be increasingly bilingual by the mid-21st century. 2008's two films about national poet Dylan Thomas will only further boost patriotism and increase traffic to his old haunts – Tenby, Laugharne and Swansea, home to November's Thomas Festival. However, the most fuss is being made in the mountains – come 2009 the volunteer-constructed Snowdonia Railway, a 60km chug through the Welsh uplands, will puff once more (despite some local opposition), creating one of Europe's most scenic steam-train trips.

YEMEN

CAPITAL SAN'A **POPULATION** 23 MILLION **AREA** 527,970 SQ KM **OFFICIAL LANGUAGE** ARABIC

In 2007 and 2008 Yemen remained quite a risky destination for tourists, with terrorist attacks rattling San'a and resulting in the deaths of several foreigners. It looks likely that 2009 will continue in the same vein, with foreign offices warning against all but essential travel. In case this does change you'll find a country ripe for exploration, with historic sights and souqs galore. It's also becoming quite a target for adventure-hungry surfers, who are hitting its shores between May and September, though not without the attendant tour operator and fistful of permits. If you weren't born a water baby, the World Heritage–listed Old City of San'a is well worth dipping into.

ZAMBIA

CAPITAL LUSAKA **POPULATION** 11.7 MILLION **AREA** 752,614 SQ KM **OFFICIAL LANGUAGE** ENGLISH

With Victoria Falls high on any traveller's to-do list, Zambia is busy attracting visitors who can't currently get to the falls' other side from troubled neighbour Zimbabwe. Zambia's recent tourism gains, in light of Zimbabwe's misfortune, has brought a much-needed boost to its impoverished economy, and seems set to continue to do so in 2009. Livingstone, at the edge of the falls, is booming, with rafting and bungee jumping on offer once you've edged out to the Knife Edge precipice to see the falls from above. Travellers are also slowly starting to spread out across the country: more than ever

WORLD PROFILES 2009 »

VENEZUELA

CAPITAL CARACAS **POPULATION** 26 MILLION **AREA** 912,050 SQ KM **OFFICIAL LANGUAGE** SPANISH

It's surprising that more travellers don't find their way to Venezuela which, for a start, boasts a longer Caribbean coastline than any other country. The nation is still probably best known, however, for outspoken president Hugo Chávez who, at the time of writing, was contemplating a 2010 referendum to allow him to extend his term in office for as many years as he continues winning elections (seemingly undaunted by having lost a similar referendum in 2007). Whatever happens, it's clear that tourism isn't yet approaching its full potential, so visit now while two of the world's 'biggest' and 'longest' (waterfalls and cable cars) are still without the associated hordes of camera-clicking tourists.

VIETNAM

CAPITAL HANOI **POPULATION** 85.2 MILLION **AREA** 325,360 SQ KM **OFFICIAL LANGUAGE** VIETNAMESE

In case you haven't noticed, Vietnam is booming. Visitor numbers jumped

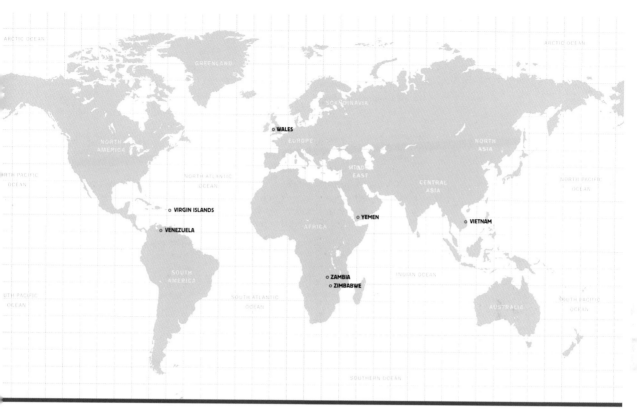

are making it to Kafue National Park, one of the largest tracts of national park wilderness in the world.

ZIMBABWE

 **CAPITAL** HARARE **POPULATION** 12.4 MILLION **AREA** 390,580 SQ KM **OFFICIAL LANGUAGE** ENGLISH

Beautiful, nature-rich Zimbabwe is sadly not the tourism hub it once was. Its recent years have seen a severe humanitarian and economic crisis (annual inflation at one point surpassing an incredible one million per cent), with legions of Zimbabweans upping and leaving home. In March 2008 elections sent the country spiralling out of control, with demonstrations being violently suppressed by the police and fears of further chaos to come. Though a few travellers do still brave Zimbabwe's uncertain times, most foreign offices are advising visitors to stay away. When it is safe to return, tourists will find a wealth of natural wonders in addition to the glorious Victoria Falls, including the Nyanga and Hwange National Parks, the latter a particularly good place for elephant spotting.

INDEX

ACKNOWLEDGEMENTS

ASSOCIATE PUBLISHER Ben Handicott

COMMISSIONING EDITOR Ellie Cobb

IMAGE RESEARCHER Craig Newell

DESIGNER Mark Adams

LAYOUT DESIGNER Jim Hsu

COORDINATING EDITOR Maryanne Netto

ASSISTING EDITORS Gennifer Ciavarra, Rowan McKinnon, Kirsten Rawlings, Dianne Schallmeiner

MANAGING EDITOR Geoff Howard

PRE-PRESS PRODUCTION Ryan Evans

PRINT PRODUCTION MANAGER Graham Imeson

TOP TRAVEL LISTS written by Bridget Blair, Belinda Dixon, Ethan Gelber, Ben Handicott, Abigail Hole, Nana Luckham, David Lukas, Kathryn Lukas, Brandon Presser, Kalya Ryan, Sam Trafford, Kerry Walker, Nigel Wallis, Clifton Wilkinson, Rachel Williams.

WORLD PROFILES written by Sarah Baxter, George Dunford, Amelia Thomas.

LONELY PLANET'S BEST IN TRAVEL 2009
November 2008

PUBLISHED BY
Lonely Planet Publications Pty Ltd
ABN 36 005 607 983
90 Maribyrnong St, Footscray,
Victoria, 3011, Australia
lonelyplanet.com

Printed by Colorcraft Ltd, Hong Kong
Printed in China

PHOTOGRAPHS
Many of the images in this book are available for licensing from Lonely Planet Images.
lonelyplanetimages.com

ISBN 978-1-74179-243-0

LONELY PLANET OFFICES
AUSTRALIA – Locked Bag 1, Footscray, Victoria, 3011
Phone 03 8379 8000 Fax 03 8379 8111
Contact us on www.lonelyplanet.com/contact/
USA – 150 Linden St, Oakland, CA 94607
Phone 510 893 8555 Toll free 800 275 8555
Fax 510 893 8572 Email info@lonelyplanet.com
UK – 2nd fl, 186 City Rd, London EC1V 2NT
Phone 020 7106 2100, Fax 020 7106 2101
Email go@lonelyplanet.co.uk

FRONT COVER IMAGE Lorne Resnick // Getty Images, **TITLE PAGE IMAGE** David Madison // Corbis, **CONTENTS PAGE IMAGE** Trip // Alamy, **P7** Ben Heys, **P8** Ed George // Getty Images, **P9** Stockbyte // Corbis, **P239** Martin Harvey // Getty Images, **INSIDE BACK COVER IMAGE** Tara Moore // Getty Images

LONELY PLANET'S

BEST IN TRAVEL
PLANNER

2009

JANUARY

THREE KINGS PARADE » SPAIN
Kick-start the New Year in Barcelona, where fireworks and a right royal welcome greet the biblical three kings at the harbour, before a confetti-strewn parade and fiesta; see p159.

TOUR D'AFRIQUE » AFRICA
Spend four months on two wheels with one goal: pedalling from Cairo to Cape Town. It's all for charity and it's all downhill – on the map, at least; see p178.

ICE & SNOW FESTIVAL » CHINA
Head to Harbin in China's northeast, where lasers and lanterns illuminate some impressive ice and snow sculptures. Be sure to pack the winter woollies; see p104.

JOURNÉE DE LA TRUFFE » FRANCE
Follow the fungi fiends to the south of France, where Uzès honours the truffle by making it the essential ingredient in a day of food and festivities; see p44.

FEBRUARY

REINDEER RACE » NORWAY
Cheer with the crowds as reindeer fly through the snowy streets of Tromsø and the skiers in tow hang on for dear life at speeds approaching 60km/h; see p158.

SÃO PAULO'S CARNAVAL » BRAZIL
Leave the tourists in Rio and kick up your heels with the locals at Carnaval in São Paulo – the parade gets bigger and the parties bolder every year; see p68.

LA FERIA DE BIODIVERSIDAD » CHILE
Step off the mainland and onto Chiloé – the archipelago where old ways are still a part of everyday life – for this event showcasing local agriculture and culture; see p38.

WORLD SKI CHAMPIONSHIPS » FRANCE
Ascend the Alps at Val d'Isère, which the world's best descend at death-defying speeds during the World Ski Championships – a purist's delight with not a snowboard in sight; see p202.

MARCH

ARCTIC CIRCLE RACE » GREENLAND
Forget Aspen and St Moritz: this is real skiing. Arctic-style. Go cross-country for days through stunning barren landscapes, and for après ski bed down in a tent; see p20.

OMIZUTORI » JAPAN
Wind back the clock at Todai-ji in Nara. Once a year, the reputedly anti-ageing waters are drawn from a well at 2am; see p118.

CHICAGO'S ST PATRICK'S DAY PARADE » USA
Celebrate all things Irish on St Patrick's Day in Chicago, where parades, parties and green beer aren't enough – for a few hours even the river flows green; see p60.

SUNFEST » NORWAY
Join the planet's northernmost locals in celebrating the return of the sun to the sky – after three months of darkness. Naturally, the party lasts a week; see p50.